THE QUEST FOR A M

Kenan Malik is ... lecturer and broadcaster. He combines academic research with ... broadcasting, ... played a prominent role in ... nature, the social ... -lar-ism and the limits ... n, Europe and Australia. He is a presenter ... a panelist on *The Moral Maze*, also on BBC Radio 4, and a columnist for the *International New York Times*, *Göteborgs-Posten* and *Bergens Tidende*. His books include *Man, Beast and Zombie*, *Strange Fruit* and *From Fatwa to Jihad*, which was shortlisted for the 2010 Orwell Prize.

'This is an extraordinarily rewarding investigation of the most striking, and contested, aspect of our humanity . . . To read it is not only to be better informed but also to be more alert to the assumptions that have guided human beings in the past, and to our capacity for goodness and wickedness.' Raymond Tallis

'What I love about Kenan Malik's book is its unashamed, unabashed ambition: he wants to write the history of moral thought, not just in the Western tradition, but of all the traditions that make up the global argument about the direction that the human moral compass should point. The result is a tour de force of lucidity and narrative skill.' Michael Ignatieff

'*The Quest for a Moral Compass* is a remarkable achievement . . . While demonstrating genuine command of the subtleties of the hundreds of topics covered, he consistently chooses the accessible, the concise, the precise, and the broad-ranging over the technical, theoretical, and trivial. I learned more than I can say and will no doubt be consulting this book often in the future.' Austin Dacey

'Lucid and engaging . . . Fascinating' *Literary Review*

'This thrilling and all-encompassing history of moral thought is not to be missed' *Good Book Guide*

'Malik is admirably evenhanded in considering the history of ethical thought. An excellent survey for intermediate students of philosophy and a fine course in self-education for general readers.' *Kirkus Reviews*

Also by Kenan Malik

From Fatwa to Jihad
Strange Fruit: Why Both Sides are Wrong in the Race Debate
Man, Beast and Zombie
The Meaning of Race

THE QUEST FOR A MORAL COMPASS

A Global History of Ethics

Kenan Malik

ATLANTIC BOOKS
London

First published in hardback in Great Britain in 2014 by Atlantic Books Ltd.

First published in paperback in Great Britain in 2015 by Atlantic Books.

The author and publisher would like to thank the following for permission to reproduce copyright material: Extract from 'Little Gidding' from *Four Quartets* by T. S. Eliot © Estate of T. S. Eliot and reprinted by permission of Faber and Faber Ltd; Extract from 'Translation' by Roy Fuller from *Selected Poems* (2012) used by permission of Carcanet Press Limited.

10 9 8 7 6 5

A CIP catalogue record for this book is available from the British Library.

E-book ISBN: 978-1-78239-0-305
Paperback ISBN: 978-1-84887-481-7

Printed in Great Britain.

Atlantic Books Ltd
An imprint of Atlantic Books Ltd
Ormond House
26–27 Boswell Street
London
WC1N 3JZ

www.atlantic-books.co.uk

For Maya,
the most moral person I know
(though who will, no doubt, disagree with most of this),
and for Carmen,
whose moral sense already puts mine to shame

Contents

CHAPTER ONE

On the capriciousness of gods and the tragedy of Man

1

> Sing, goddess, of the anger of Achilleus, son of Peleus, the accursed anger which brought uncounted anguish on the Achaians and hurled down to Hades many mighty souls of heroes, making their bodies the prey to dogs and the birds' feasting; and this was the working of Zeus' will. Sing from the time of the first quarrel which divided Atreus' son, the lord of men, and godlike Achilleus.[1]

So opens the most celebrated work of Greek poetry, the earliest expression of European literature, and, to some, its greatest too. Homer's *Iliad* tells the story of the Trojan War, the ten-year struggle by Achaean Greeks to avenge the abduction of Helen, wife of Menelaus, the king of Sparta, by Paris, son of the Trojan king Priam. (The Achaeans were the first Greek-speaking inhabitants of what we now call Greece.) The *Iliad* forms one half of a poetic diptych with the *Odyssey*, in which Homer recounts the tale of Odysseus' struggle to return home after the fall of Troy, a struggle that was to last as long as the war itself.

Written in the eighth century BCE, the *Iliad* and the *Odyssey* are distilled from a long and rich tradition of oral poetry, the work of generations of illiterate singers in an illiterate age who composed and passed on their epics of men and gods, love and death, adventures and conquests, without the aid of writing. Over centuries these tales melded together into a stock of myths that gave the audience that listened to the itinerant poets a sense of time and place. The

Homeric poems were both the culmination of this tradition and its transformation, works that drew upon the oral lore but whose depth of vision, breadth of imagination, and sheer ambition gave voice to a new kind of literature and to a new kind of myth. The *Iliad* and the *Odyssey* gave ancient Greeks a sense of their history, turned a fable about their origins into the foundation stone of their culture, nourished generations of poets and sculptors and artists and established a framework for their moral lives. It is a good place from which to embark on our journey of exploration through the history of moral thought.

The *Iliad* is a poem about the Trojan War. And yet it is not a poem about the Trojan War. The beginnings of the conflict and the sacking of Troy both lie offpage. The whole story of the *Iliad* is contained within a span of fifty-two days in the tenth and final year of the war. The main action, running through twenty-two of the poem's twenty-four books, occupies just four days.

The quarrel of which Homer speaks in the opening line of the *Iliad* is not the quarrel between the Greeks and the Trojans, but that between Agamemnon, the leader of the Greek forces, and Achilles, son of the goddess Thetis and the most famous of the Greek warriors. Homer begins his tale by telling of how Chryses, priest to the god Apollo, asks Agamemnon to allow him to ransom his daughter Chryseis whom the Achaean king had captured as a war trophy and claimed as a slave. When Agamemnon rudely rejects him, Chryses prays to Apollo for help. Apollo sends a plague upon the Greeks. To pacify the god, an assembly of Greek warriors demands that Agamemnon return his slave girl to Chryses. Agamemnon agrees, but only if he be given, in exchange, Achilles' concubine, Briseis, another prize captured in war. Humiliated and dishonoured, Achilles withdraws himself and his warriors from the conflict.

Agamemnon's 'wicked arrogance' and the 'ruinous wrath' of Achilles provide the raw material for Homer. His theme is not the war but the tragedy of the human condition, the unintended consequences of human sentiment and the nature of fate in governing human life. All the major dramatic moments of the poem spring fatefully and inevitably from the quarrel between Achilles and Agamemnon. With Achilles out of the battle, Hector, brother of Paris, successfully breaches the Greek camp, with backing from the gods. Achilles' closest friend, Patroclus, who had also withdrawn from the war, re-enters the fray, dressed in Achilles' armour. He manages to repel the Trojans but is killed in battle by Hector. In revenge, a distraught Achilles defeats Hector in single combat, then defiles his corpse for days, until King Priam persuades him to give up the body. The *Iliad* ends with Hector's funeral. The death of Achilles and the fall of Troy lie outside the narrative of the poem. But we know that both will happen, for they are as inevitable as were the deaths of Patroclus and Hector, two more moments in the unbroken sequence that had sprung from Achilles' anger.

'And so the plan of Zeus was fulfilled,' Homer writes of the consequences of Achilles' wrath. Achilles' 'accursed anger' had set forth a train of events that had 'brought uncounted anguish on the Achaeans and hurled down to Hades many mighty souls of heroes'. But both that anger and that train of events were also part of a divine plan. Throughout the *Iliad*, divine and human causation are inextricably linked. Achilles and Agamemnon are responsible for their actions. They – and not just they – have to pay the price for their pride, arrogance and folly. And yet their actions are shaped by the gods, and their fates decided by Zeus' scales.

The drama on the battlefield is shadowed by the drama on Mount Olympus. We see the gods holding council, quarrelling and sulking, laughing and partying and making love, and descending from their Olympian heights to change the course of human affairs. When Achilles is dishonoured by Agamemnon, his distraught mother, the goddess Thetis, appeals to Zeus, who promises her major Trojan success so as to 'bring honour to Achilles'. As Paris is about to be defeated by Menelaus in a duel he has foolishly called, Aphrodite 'snatched him away with the ease of a god, wrapped him in thick mist, and set him down in his sweetly-scented bedroom'. When Hera, the wife of Zeus, who has championed the Achaeans, protests about her husband's support for the Trojans, he accepts that she can have her way and see Troy sacked but also issues a warning: 'Whenever I in my turn am eager to destroy a city peopled by men who are dear to you, do not try to thwart my anger, but let me have my way.'[2]

Homer's gods are not wise and judicious like the later gods of Judaism, Christianity and Islam. Rather, they are capricious, vain, vicious and deceitful. But however savage and immoral the gods may be, they are also all-powerful, or seemingly so to humans. It is in part a reflection of the world as the Ancients saw it: messy, chaotic, largely unpredictable, barely controllable, and yet inescapable. Not only have human choices to be made against the background of divinely ordered fate, but the gods often force humans to act against their wishes. Perhaps no figure better expresses the conundrum of human choice than Helen, whose abduction launched the Trojan War. Trojans hold Helen responsible for the war and for the suffering that it has brought. Helen herself accepts responsibility for the tragedy. And yet she, and Homer, recognize that she has been manipulated by divine forces, and in particular by Aphrodite, who had engineered Helen's initial seduction by Paris.

In one poignant passage, Aphrodite tries to force Helen into Paris' bed against her will, to comfort the Trojan prince. 'Go sit by him yourself,' Helen retorts, 'abandon the paths of the gods, never again turn your feet back to Olympus; no, stay with him, for ever whimpering around him and watching over him, until he makes you his wife – or else his slave.' 'I will not go to him,' Helen insists, for 'that would bring shame on me' and 'I have misery enough in my heart'.[3] Yet, however much she detests the goddess's imperatives, Helen knows that she is powerless to resist them. She follows Aphrodite to Paris' bedroom.

This, for Homer, is the tragedy of being human: to desire freedom, and be tortured by a sense of autonomy, and yet be imprisoned by forces beyond our control. Fate, to Homer, is a social reality, and neither will nor cunning can evade it. Indeed, a man who does what he ought to moves steadily towards his fate and his death. Achilles and Hector go into battle knowing they are fated to die, but knowing, too, that without surrendering to their fate they would also surrender their honour.

With tragedy, however, comes dignity. Gods act according to whim; only humans are truly accountable for their actions. Human life is framed by the gods and yet humans cannot rely upon them. They must depend upon their own wit and resources. It is human reason that imposes order upon an unpredictable world, and discovers dignity and honour within it.

The fraught relationship between Man and God lies at the heart not just of Homer's work, nor even just of Greek philosophy, but also at the heart of all moral thought. In part, the history of moral thought is the history of attempts to address the problem of reconciling fate and free will. It is a dilemma with which not just believers but atheists, too, have been forced to wrestle. When 'we feel ourselves to be in control of an action', the contemporary neuroscientist Colin Blakemore has suggested, 'that feeling itself is the product of our brain, whose machinery has been designed, on the basis of its functional utility, by means of natural selection.' According to Blakemore, 'To choose a spouse, a job, a religious creed – or even to choose to rob a bank – is the peak of a causal chain that runs back to the origin of life and down to the nature of atoms and molecules.'[4]

For Blakemore, unlike for Homer, fate lies not in the hands of gods but in the nature of atoms and molecules. But the same questions are raised about human actions. If all action is predestined, what could free will mean? Or ethics? From the beginnings of the philosophical tradition to the latest thoughts on neuroscience, the questions of fate and free will have been inextricably bound together in an ethical knot. Part of the story of the quest for a moral compass is the story of the attempts to untie that knot, to understand it, to live with it.

2

As Agamemnon and Achilles quarrel over the slave girl Briseis at the council of warriors, the ageing King Nestor intervenes. 'You, *agathos* though you are,' he tells Agamemnon, 'do not take the girl from him, but let her be, as the sons of the Achaians gave her to him in the beginning as his prize.' Then turning to Achilles, Nestor warns, 'Do not seek open quarrel with the king, since there is no equality with the honour granted to a sceptred king, whom Zeus has glorified. You may be a man of strength, with a goddess for your mother, but he is more powerful because his rule is wider.'[5]

The *Iliad* provided the ancient Greeks with a framework within which to understand the hopes and sorrows that shaped their lives. It told of the desires of Man, the capriciousness of gods and the implacability of fate, and of how all three knitted together. Homer's epic was not, however, just a way of making sense of the tragedy of the human condition. It was also a way of understanding how to meet the challenge of being human. Nestor's speech gives us a glimpse of the moral rules by which Homer's heroes lived.

The Greek word αγαθος (*agathos*), which Nestor uses to describe Agamemnon, is often translated as 'good', in the sense of an action or a trait that is morally admirable. It is also, in Homer, a description of a person's standing. Indeed, in Nestor's speech, *agathos* is often rendered in English as 'great man'. In Agamemnon's world, a man's social status and his moral worth are almost indistinguishable.

In premodern societies, and especially in 'heroic' societies at the edge of historical records such as that which Homer describes, the structure of society is a given, as is the role that each individual occupies and the privileges and duties that derive from that role. A person knows who he is by knowing his role within society, and in knowing this he knows also what he owes and what is owed to him by every other individual.

Being king gives Agamemnon his *agathos*. Yet possessing *agathos* does not stop him taking Briseis. Nor does his taking of Briseis undermine his *agathos*. Agamemnon is to be judged – and defined – solely by his ability to be kingly. To be kingly one had to possess not just kingly virtues such as courage, cunning, military skill and the ability to command men, but also the wealth and leisure necessary for the development of such character and skill. To be good one must be born into a good family. The greater one's nobility, the greater one's goodness. Achilles may have been dishonoured by Agamemnon's action, but his honour, as Nestor points out, could never be equal to that of Agamemnon because he is not king, and nor could his goodness equal Agamemnon's.

Ordinary folk cannot, it seems, be good at all. The duties of a swineherd or a miller, as much as those of Agamemnon or Achilles, derive from the roles they occupy within the given structure of a community. Unlike for Agamemnon and Achilles, the rules that assign their roles and define their duties also determine that in lacking nobility they also lack *agathos*.

The *Iliad* is clearly a moral tale. But it describes an alien moral world, not simply because its moral rules are so different from those of our world but also because its very notion of what constitutes a moral rule is alien to us. When, as modern readers, we enter Homer's world, it is almost inevitable that we pass judgements upon his characters that are different from those of Homer himself. Paris is a kidnapper, a shirker, a man whom we would probably describe as morally dissolute. Homer would not portray him as such. Even though Paris fails to perform the actions of a good man, he remains good in Homer's eyes because his hereditary gifts, social background and material advantages embody such an important part of his *agathos*.

Agamemnon's pride and arrogance led to the tragedy of the Trojan War. To a modern reader, this places upon him a moral responsibility for the conflict. To Homer, Agamemnon's pride and arrogance are a matter not of morality but of fate. 'I am not to blame,' Agamemnon insists, the gods 'put a cruel blindness in my mind at the assembly on that day when by my own act I took away his prize from Achilleus.'[6]

In the modern world, morality is inseparable from choice. Homer's warriors cannot choose to be moral or not. Each is simply good or bad at performing the duties of his role. Human choice adds texture to the cloth already woven on the loom of fate, but cannot unpick the threads. There is in the *Iliad* and the *Odyssey* only the faintest glimmer of what we would recognize as free will or choice. Indeed, it is not clear that any of Homer's characters possess a 'mind' as we understand it, nor an interior life. In Homer's epics, the psychologist David Olson observes, 'there is an absence of such terms as "decided", "thought", "believed", "doubted" or "equivocated".'[7] Homer's characters do all of these things, but not in the self-conscious way that we do them. Agamemnon's wrath and Achilles' pride describe not emotions inside their selves, but their actions and the actions of the gods that determine their fate.

Lacking a concept of an interior life, Homer turns that life into a spectacle of gods in battle over the human world. He cannot access the drama inside the human head, because he possesses no language through which to understand it. So the drama takes place outside human life through the gods' quarrels, loves, obsessions and desires. Hence the humanness of Homer's gods. So beautifully wrought is that divine drama that in the modern world we continually plunder it for metaphors through which to understand our own desires and motivations – think of the importance to modern psychoanalysis of Oedipus and Narcissus, Prometheus and Antigone.

Homer was wrestling with no mere metaphor. The inner world was opaque to him, but the divine world was a reality. Homeric gods form the cosmic intelligence that drives the universe. They form also the inner intelligence that drives every human being. The gods inhabit our heads as well as heaven.

Over time, the inner world became more transparent, but the divine world more opaque. The drama played out in myth was both an attempt to make sense of a disorderly world and an acceptance that such a world is too disorderly to make sense of. Increasingly philosophers discovered order in the world, and the rules by which nature was organized and that made natural events predictable. As the cosmos appeared more ordered and predictable, so the plurality of gods acting on whim and caprice came to be replaced with a single Creator who governed with reason and judgement. In time that single Creator was Himself dethroned and replaced by a mechanical universe. Just like the outer world, the inner world, too, came to be seen as ordered and, to a degree, predictable. At the same time, humans came increasingly to be seen as *agents* – wilful beings with minds of their own.

The moral world bound by myth is different to that embodied in religion or that which makes sense in a world that entrusts to science. Moral thought does not inhabit a sealed-off universe. It cannot but be closely related to the social structure of a community and to the perceptions within it of what it is to be human. Homeric values emerged from the structure of heroic society, shaped by its needs and constrained by its particular conception of human nature. As society changed, and as new languages developed through which to understand the human soul, the human mind and humanity's place in the cosmos, so inevitably moral ideas also evolved.

3

Aeschylus' magnificent *Oresteian* trilogy begins where the *Iliad* ends. Troy has fallen. Greek warriors are returning home. The first play, *Agamemnon*, opens with Clytemnestra, wife of the Greek king and sister of Helen, awaiting her husband's homecoming in the city of Argos. She is brimming with fury and rage. Ten years previously, on the eve of the war, Agamemnon had sacrificed their daughter Iphigenia to placate the gods and ensure favourable winds. Now Clytemnestra wants revenge. The play climaxes with the brutal murder of Agamemnon, his wife hacking him down with an axe, as if she were ritually sacrificing an animal.

In *The Choephoroi*, the second of the *Oresteian* plays, Agamemnon's son Orestes, who has lived his life in exile, returns to Argos at Apollo's command to avenge his father. He is faced with a terrible dilemma: murder his mother or leave his father unavenged. He kills both Clytemnestra and her lover.

In the final part of the trilogy, *The Eumenides*, Orestes is pursued by the Furies, ancient pre-Olympian deities, more hag-like than god-like, whose role was to exact vengeance for major sins: blasphemy, treachery and the shedding of kindred blood. Orestes finds refuge in Athens where, on the Acropolis, Athena convenes a jury of twelve to try him.

Apollo acts as attorney for Orestes, while the Furies become advocates for the dead Clytemnestra. The jury is split. Athena casts her vote in favour of acquittal, a verdict that enrages the Furies, who accuse her, Apollo and the other 'young gods' of usurping the power of the older divinities whom they represent. Athena eventually wins them over, renaming them *Eumenides* (the Kindly Ones), and assuring them that they will now be honoured by the citizens of Athens.

Aeschylus wrote the *Oresteia* in the middle decades of the fifth century BCE. This was the dawn of the era of 'classical Greece', an era which saw an extraordinary flourishing of art, architecture and philosophy, and at the heart of which stood the city of Athens. In the 800 years between the fall of Troy and the rise of Athens there had been a great transformation in Greek life. Not long after the sacking of Troy, the Mycenaean civilization, to which Homer's Achaean warriors belonged, itself collapsed, through a combination of economic decline, internal strife and invasion. The invaders were Dorians, like the Achaeans a Greek-speaking people from the north; their arrival ushered in what is often called the Greek Dark Ages. The kingdoms of Mycenaean Greece gave way to a more fragmented landscape of small, independent regions based around kinship groups. Famine led to the abandonment of cities. Art and culture became denuded. Written language seems to have disappeared.

Not for another three centuries, until the beginning of the eighth century BCE, is there evidence of economic recovery. With a rise in population, a new form of social organization, the city state, or polis, begins to develop out of the kinship-based communities. Cultural life re-emerges. A new alphabet is adopted from the Phoenicians. One of its first exponents is Homer.

'Polis' meant to the ancient Greeks much more than 'city state' means to us. It carried a spiritual sense and embodied a sense of 'home' and belonging. It embodied also the sense that only through membership of the polis was humanity raised above the level of barbarism. Most of the new city states began as monarchies. Through the eighth century many overthrew their kings and evolved into oligarchies, ruled largely by their wealthiest citizens. A few – most notably Athens – took the oligarchic experiment further, turning themselves into democracies. These were not democracies in a modern sense – women, foreigners and slaves were, for instance, all disbarred from governance. Athenian democracy nevertheless expressed the impulse that 'rule by the many' was better than 'rule by the few', an impulse that was to shape all progressive thought in the centuries that followed.

Athens had, by the beginning of the fifth century BCE, displaced Sparta as the dominant Greek city state, in large part because of its role in thwarting the ambitions of the Persian Empire. Twice, in 490 BCE and again ten years later, Persian forces attempted to invade the Greek mainland. Twice they were beaten back, thanks in great measure to Athenian naval prowess. Success in the Persian Wars brought with it not just prestige but wealth and power too. This wealth and power, together with the city's democratic reforms, attracted to Athens artists and philosophers from all over Greece. It also created a leisure class able to afford them patronage. The result was an extraordinary explosion of intellectual energy. Socrates and Plato, Aristotle and Euripides, Aeschylus and Sophocles, Herodotus and Xenophon, Thucydides and Aristophanes, Phidias and Praxiteles – some of the greatest philosophers, playwrights, poets and sculptors lived in the city in the two centuries that followed Athens' triumph.

Presiding over this intellectual pantheon was still the ghost of Homer. The virtues that made for a good citizen in a city in which all 21,000 free men of the right age could sit in the decision-making Assembly were necessarily different to those that had driven aristocratic warriors to submit to heroic fate. For Homer, honour was bound with nobility. In democratic Athens, the power of the nobility was constrained by the Assembly, and there existed a moral equality between commoners and nobles previously unknown. How could a moral code crafted in an age of warriors and heroes translate into an age of philosophers and democrats? Why should there be a moral equality between commoners and nobles? And what could justice mean when it was no longer linked to a warrior's search for honour? These were the questions that Aeschylus addressed in his *Oresteian* trilogy.

The Furies, in the *Oresteia*, represent the old virtues of Homer, rooted in honour, blood and revenge. Athena embodies the new civic virtues of Athens, the determination to apply reason and the democratic spirit, rather than arbitrary divine fiat, to the application of justice. For Aeschylus, the Furies are arbitrary in their moral judgement – they condemn Orestes for the murder of Clytemnestra but not Clytemnestra for the murder of Agamemnon. They refuse to acknowledge the moral dilemma in which Orestes was placed, and they fail to recognize that justice cannot always be dispensed by following a set law. Athena's judgement is righteous because she recognizes both the fallibilities of humans and the dilemmas that they face.

Like Homer, Aeschylus understands the human condition as tragic, caught as humans are between a yearning for freedom and the necessity of fate. The citizens of fifth-century Athens are, however, freer than the inhabitants of twelfth-century Troy. Their yearning for freedom has been given concrete expression in the political structures of democratic Athens. The moral code has, therefore, to reflect these new ideas of human sovereignty. Aeschylus does not want, though, to detach himself entirely from either Homer's world or the ancient deities. He views human life as lived in the shadow of the gods and accepts fate as a fact of life. Not only are some questions too difficult for humans to resolve – Athena herself, after all, has finally to decide Orestes' fate – but the Furies must not be discarded; rather they must be given an honourable, though different, role in the new moral cosmos. In democratic Athens, Greeks were freer than they had been in heroic Troy. But greater freedom only made even sharper the tragic condition in which humans find themselves.

4

The 800 years between the fall of Troy and the rise of Athens did not just see a transformation in what Greeks considered were virtues or in how they imagined the good life. Those eight centuries saw also a transformation in the very way that people came to reflect upon morality.

The *Iliad* and the *Odyssey* provided a means by which ancient Greeks made sense of their moral lives. They were, however, works of poetry, not of philosophy. Homer articulated no comprehensive philosophical framework, but imagined a story within which his readers, and listeners, found both an explicit history and an implicit morality. The history and the morality made sense because Homer shared with his audience an understanding about gods, fate and how they worked. As Achilles battles with Hector, Odysseus speaks with the dead in the Underworld, or Hera seduces Zeus while Poseidon rouses the Achaean army, so the *Iliad* and the *Odyssey* extend that common story and infuse it with new meaning. Myth gave moral texture to people's lives, made manifest their sense of wonderment and fear and helped link their particular lives with the eternal.

From the sixth century BCE, a new kind of moral account began to develop in which ideas about what constituted a virtuous act or a good life were not implicitly crafted, and intuitively grasped, through the narrative of myth, but explicitly established through rational argument. These new accounts did not so much tell stories as ask questions. What is a virtue? Why should I behave virtuously? Why is justice good? And they answered such questions not by turning to their foundational myths but by attempting to reason from first principles. This was the emergence of philosophy as distinct from poetry and mythology.

The first of the new breed of thinkers who, in Aristotle's words, 'spoke by demonstration' rather than 'invent clever mythologies' came to be called the 'Presocratics', because they had the misfortune, as Anthony Gottlieb has put it, 'of being born before Socrates'.[8] Both the Ancients and modern philosophers came to see Socrates as the man with whom philosophy, and in particular moral philosophy, began. Socrates was, as we shall see, a key turning point in the history of moral thought. The Presocratics were, however, far more than the *amuse bouche* to set before the Socratic feast. They were little interested in questions of morality, being captivated more by 'numbers and movements, with the problem whence all things came, or whither they returned', as Cicero was later to put it.[9] But in investigating 'the problem whence all things came, or whither they returned', the Presocratics began to develop a way of thinking about the universe, and of humanity's place in it, that was to have a profound impact on moral thought.

The earliest of the Presocratics was Thales, born in Miletus, on the Anatolian coast of what is now Turkey, around 580 BCE; the last was Democritus who survived Socrates by some twenty years. As they left only fragments of original work, almost all we know of them and their ideas comes through the comments of later philosophers, especially Aristotle, Plato and Theophrastus. They were not a homogeneous group. Some, like Anaximander and Heracletes, saw the world as a manifestation of divine justice. Others, such as Leucippus and Democritus, saw no place for a divine presence in the cosmos. What connected them all was a commitment to explain the world in terms of its own inherent principles. Unlike Homer, who viewed the world as fundamentally disorderly, the Presocratics saw order everywhere. The apparent chaos of the world concealed a permanent and intelligible organization, which could be accounted for by universal causes operating within nature itself. The best tool to discern such order was the human mind.

The Presocratic thinkers set out to explain the stuff of which the world was made and the principles by which that stuff interacted. This has led some to describe them as the 'first scientists'. They were not. The Presocratics did not observe nature and draw conclusions from their observational data in the manner of a modern scientist. They speculated largely about the unobservable – the origin and destruction of the world, the nature of the heavenly bodies, the causes of motion and change. Their arguments can often seem as wild, visionary and mystical as those of Homer. Anaximenes defined the primary substance from which all is made as air which through 'rarefaction and condensation . . . manifests in different forms in different things'. Anaximander thought the earth was 'cylindrical in shape, and three times as wide as it is deep'. Anaxagoras believed that 'Mind ordered all the things that were to be.'[10]

Such tales about the origins and functioning of the universe may seem to have more in common with creation myths than with rational cosmology. They were, in fact, a dramatic breakthrough; not because of what they told us about the cosmos, but because of what they told us about ourselves as human beings. To understand the world, the Presocratics argued, we need to go beyond the observable and comprehend the underlying principles at work. These underlying principles could not be explained through divine action that, by definition, was not regular and ordered, but capricious and unpredictable. Such principles had, the Presocratics insisted, to be both naturalistic and reductionist. Naturalistic because phenomena had to be explained without recourse to divine intervention but only by reference to natural causes and events; reductionist because complex phenomena could be understood in terms of simpler processes, and explanations of the world should rely on as few principles as possible. In a sense, the Presocratics depended as much on faith as did Homer, but it was a different kind of faith: faith that the world was ordered in such a way that it could be intelligible to reason; and faith in the capacity of reason to make sense of the ordered world. They did not know that the world was so ordered, or that reason was so capable. They simply believed it. And in believing it, they helped transform the way in which humans came to think about the world and their place in it.

Not just the natural world but human affairs, too, were, for the Presocratics, ordered by laws and regularities. Few concerned themselves with questions of human behaviour. However, their belief that human life could be studied like the stars and the stones influenced others, most notably Herodotus. Born around 485 BCE in the colony of Helicarnassus, near Bodrum in present-day Turkey, not far from Troy, he lived in the disputed borderland between Greece and Persia. It was to be the wars between the two, which began in 499 BCE and lasted for almost half a century, that formed the heart of his *Histories*, often seen as the first true historical work. Like Almásy's notebook in Michael Ondaatje's *The English Patient*, the *Histories* is cut and pasted from stories, observations, anecdotes and thoughts. It is, however, unlike any previous histories. Herodotus did not merely rely on myth to recreate the past; he attempted systematically to collect historical data and, to a degree, test their accuracy.

The language of Herodotus, and the manner of his tales, are rooted in the

Homeric tradition. The *Histories* is an epic poem rendered in prose. 'I see him', Almásy tells Hana in *The English Patient*, 'as one of those spare men of the desert who travel from oasis to oasis, trading legends as if it is the exchange of seeds, consuming everything without suspicion, piecing together a mirage.'[11] Yet the *Histories* also belongs to a different world to that of the *Iliad* and the *Odyssey*. It is an *historia*, a word that until then had been used to describe an investigation of natural phenomena (a sense that was later to be preserved in the English phrase 'natural history'). In appropriating that word, Herodotus reveals both his indebtedness to the Presocratics and his intention to march further.

Herodotus examines the customs, beliefs and institutions not just of the Greeks but also of Persians, Egyptians, Libyans, Scythians and Arabs. Differences, he insists, are neither accidental nor the result of divine intervention but derive from material, earthly causes. The Egyptians have unusual customs because of their need to deal with their unusual climate. The natural poverty of Greece encouraged its inhabitants to develop appropriate laws and institutions to overcome it. The success of the Athenians was rooted not simply in the endeavours of great individuals but also in a democratic system that had nurtured a sense of common responsibility.

Herodotus attempted to use rational explanations to understand the social and cultural differences between cities and nations, peoples and ages; he also believed that such differences helped in turn to explain the movement of history. The Trojan War, the rise of Athenian democracy, the Persian invasion of Greece, the conflict between Athens and Sparta – none could be explained by appealing simply to individual decisions or whims, whether human or divine. Each was also the result of the way in which people in a given society with particular customs could be expected to act in certain circumstances.

The early Presocratics had tried to account for natural phenomena by borrowing concepts used to describe human interactions. Anaximander, for instance, suggested that all things came in opposites, such as hot and cold, wet and dry. These opposites were kept in balance because they were in a state of war and had to 'give justice and reparation to one another for their injustice in accordance with the ordinance of Time'.[12] Naturalists they may have been, but the only language the early Presocratics possessed through which to understand the workings of the cosmos was the language of human action and agency. By seeing human history as the product not simply of individual agency but also of the environment, social, physical, cultural and historical, that the agents inhabited, Herodotus turned on its head this relationship between humans and nature. Human society was not a model for the understanding of nature. Nature provided a template for the understanding of human society. In this, the classicist David Sansone suggests, 'Herodotus invented not only history, but the social sciences as well.'[13] He also opened the way for a new way of understanding both human nature and human morality.

CHAPTER TWO

Gods of reason

1

He was poor, wrote nothing, claimed he knew nothing and acknowledged that he was 'full of defects and always getting things wrong in some way or other'.[1] Yet he is, in the eyes of most philosophers, the founding father of Western philosophy. Its first saint. And its first martyr. In 399 BCE a jury of Athenian citizens found Socrates, then aged seventy, guilty of impiety and of corrupting the minds of the youth of Athens. It condemned him to death by hemlock.

Few philosophers were held in greater esteem in the ancient world than Socrates. He was, wrote Cicero, 'the first who brought down philosophy from the heavens, placed it in cities, introduced it into families, and obliged it to examine life and morals, and good and evil'.[2] Why, then, did Athens put its most famous son to death? The trial of Socrates, and his execution, took place against the background of the Peloponnesian War. The twenty-seven-year conflict between Athens and Sparta had ended with Athenian defeat in 404 BCE, five years before the trial. Athens was reduced to a state of subjection, never regaining its pre-war influence or prosperity, while Sparta established itself as the leading power of Greece. Athenian democracy was overthrown and replaced by a Spartan-imposed oligarchy, a group of men who came to be known as the Thirty Tyrants.

'Tyranny' in ancient Greece meant not a cruel despotism but the concentration of political power in an individual other than a hereditary monarch.

The Thirty were, however, tyrannical in a modern sense. They crushed the rights of Athenian citizens, restricting the franchise to the wealthiest, purged many of the democratic leaders, executed hundreds and forced thousands more into exile. The Tyrants were overthrown after a year of bloody mayhem; democracy was finally restored in 401 BCE. Sparta had not relinquished its influence, though. In 403 an amnesty was declared for all supporters of the Thirty, ostensibly to unify the city. Embittered democrats were left without a target for vengeance.

Socrates had close links to the Thirty. Critias, the leader, and a particularly bloodthirsty man, was a former disciple, as was Charmides, one of his deputies. It is unclear the degree to which Socrates supported the Thirty, but he openly espoused anti-democratic views, often praising the laws of Sparta.

It was not just Socrates' politics, but his philosophy, too, that aroused suspicion. Many saw his teachings as undermining Athens by questioning traditional values. The 'Socratic method' sought to establish moral truth not directly by explaining what it was to be pious, courageous or virtuous but indirectly through questioning others' beliefs about piety, courage or virtue, and showing them to be confused, contradictory or false. The relentless questioning seemed to many not to unearth the truth but to turn the world upside down.

Socrates could not be indicted on political charges because of the amnesty. He was arraigned instead for religious and moral transgressions that were, to many Athenians, as disturbing as the political crimes and physical savagery of the Thirty. Socrates was accused of rejecting the city's recognized gods, of introducing new divinities and of corrupting the young men of Athens by 'making the inferior argument superior'. Certainly, these were trumped-up charges. But they also gave a sense of the anxieties many Athenians felt about the dislocation of their lives during the course of the fifth century.

2

Socrates wrote nothing. His very philosophical method precluded him from doing so. Philosophy, for him, was an active, collaborative process, not one that could be captured forever on a page. Truth emerged through discussion and debate, and could be kept alive only through dialogue. When others wanted to explain Socrates' thoughts they often did so in the form of a dialogue. Plato's in particular have come to be a monument to his philosophical master, though he so hero-worshipped his teacher that we need to treat with caution the saintly figure that emerges through his dialogues.

Philosophical thought in fifth-century Athens was dominated by the Sophists. Thanks largely to Plato's criticism, 'sophistry' has come to mean that which is dishonest, deceptive or disingenuous. At that time, however, the word carried no negative connotations. A sophist was a teacher (the word comes from *sophia*, meaning wisdom).

The Sophists were the products of two key developments in fifth-century Athens, the one political, the other intellectual. The first was the rise of Athenian democracy, the second, the reverberations felt from the arguments of the Presocratics. Democracy had placed a premium on a new set of social skills, in particular the ability to speak, hold an argument and convince an audience. The Sophists sold themselves as the teachers of such talents. To their critics Sophists seemed less philosophers than flimflam artists, seeking not to uncover truth but to entangle, entrap and confuse their opponents, and to teach their students a stock of arguments to prove any position. The Sophists were not, however, mere rhetoricians. Many taught literature, politics, history, physics and mathematics. Some, such as Protagoras and Gorgias, were genuine philosophers. Their ideas were shaped not just by the needs of democracy but also by the paradoxes and dilemmas thrown up by the Presocratics. Some Sophists embraced the sceptical consequences of the arguments of thinkers such as the atomist Democritus, who insisted that humans could not rely on their 'bastard senses' to provide truths about the world, but could trust only to reason. Many, such as the Sceptics, became distrustful of reason, too, believing it impossible to resolve differences among contrary opinions and arguments. Others, such as Protagoras, challenged scepticism but in so doing seemed to undermine the very possibility of objective truth. For Democritus, if the same water appears cold to you and warm to me it was because our senses are unreliable. For Protagoras, it is because the water really is both cold and warm. Reality, and truth, are self-created and subjective, not independent and objective. In an age in which the alternatives seemed to be the scepticism unleashed by Democritus or the relativism of Protagoras' rebuttal of such scepticism, there was plenty of space for the idea that the ability to argue and persuade was more important than the content of one's argument.

Many saw Socrates' arguments in the same light. His method of relentlessly questioning his students or opponents until there appeared no substance left in their argument, and yet seemingly having no answer of his own as replacement, appeared to his critics to be pure 'sophistry'. Socrates was in fact unabashedly hostile to the Sophists. He was obsessed with the need for righteous living, and the Sophists had, he maintained, little understanding of righteousness. 'After all', Socrates says in Plato's *Cratylus*, 'if what each person believes is true for him, no one can truly be wiser than anyone else.'[3] Socrates was dismissive of the Sophists' relativism, while also having little time for the kind of speculation about the natural world in which the Presocratics had indulged. The only important question, he insisted, was about how one ought to live, and in particular about how people could care for their souls by acquiring the virtues.

But what is a virtue? Traditionally there were five: courage, moderation, piety, wisdom and justice. In a world made uncertain by Democritus and Protagoras, the meaning of such qualities no longer appeared certain. Socrates' response to the moral cul-de-sac created by scepticism and relativism was to insist that morality had to be rethought from scratch. Moral inquiry, for Socrates, was philosophical, not rhetorical, because it was concerned with truth, not persuasion. It appealed to rational argument, not custom, tradition or authority. Neither was it naturalistic in a Presocratic way. Socratic moral thought relied on principles derived not from natural speculation but from a rational study of the human condition.

3

Socrates meets Euthyphro in the agora, the central marketplace of Athens, outside the offices of the magistrate who investigates charges of religious impropriety. Socrates has just been charged with impiety and corruption, charges that would lead eventually to his trial and execution. Euthyphro, a friend who believes himself to be a religious expert, is about to prosecute his father for the murder of one of his servants. The victim was himself a murderer, who had killed a fellow slave 'in drunken anger'. Euthyphro's father had tied him up, thrown him into a ditch and sent a messenger to ask a priest what he should do next. The messenger was delayed in returning, so much so that the neglected prisoner had in the meantime died.

Socrates is shocked by Euthyphro's action, which appears to disregard both convention and his obligations to kin. Euthyphro replies haughtily that he 'would not be superior to the majority of men, if I did not have accurate knowledge of all such things'. 'It is indeed most important', Socrates responds, 'that I should become your pupil', for this is the very knowledge he needs to escape the charge of impiety brought against him. 'Tell me then', he demands of Euthyphro, 'what is the pious and what the impious?'[4]

So begins Plato's *Euthyphro*, one of his earliest Socratic dialogues, and one of the most significant in philosophical history. It lays bare the Socratic method, gets to the heart of Socrates' moral concerns and sets up one of the great dilemmas of moral thought.

Euthyphro's first answer to Socrates' question is to suggest that to be pious 'is to do what I am doing now, to prosecute the wrongdoer'. But, Socrates protests, this is just an *example* of what it is to be pious. He wants a universal definition – 'that form itself that makes all pious actions pious' – so that he can use it as a model to say 'that any action of yours or another's that is of that kind is pious, and if it is not that it is not'. This was an argument to which Socrates returned again and again in his moral dialogues: that to know what piety or justice or goodness meant was to know what each meant in every circumstance.

So Euthyphro proposes a definition: 'What is dear to the gods is pious, what is not is impious.' This cannot be, Socrates responds, because both men agree that 'the gods are in a state of discord' and that some gods see certain actions as pious while others look to different actions. Euthyphro modifies his definition, suggesting that 'the pious is what all the gods love, and the opposite, what all the gods hate, is the impious'.

Socrates now asks his most important question, one that two millennia later still causes consternation. 'Is the pious', he wonders, 'being loved by the gods because it is pious, or is it pious because it is being loved by the gods?' Unless the gods love something for no good reason, then they must love something as pious because it inherently possesses value. But if it inherently possesses value, then it does so independently of the gods. It cannot be pious, as Euthyphro supposes, simply because the gods love it.

The so-called 'Euthyphro dilemma' was to become of increasing importance in theology and philosophy, especially as the great monotheistic religions – Judaism, Christianity and Islam – developed over the next millennium. In these faiths, the plethora of gods of Greek and other pantheistic religions gave way to a single omnipotent Creator. This Creator was the source of goodness and value in the world. But, as the German philosopher Leibniz asked at the beginning of the eighteenth century, if it is the case that whatever God thinks, wants or does is good by definition, then 'what cause could one have to praise him for what he does if in doing something quite different he would have done equally well?'[5] If, on the other hand, God recognizes what is good and promotes it because of its inherent goodness, then goodness must exist independently of God. It might now make sense to revere God's goodness but God is no longer the source of that goodness, nor do we need to look to God to discover that which is good.

We will return to this dilemma later. Socrates did not possess the vocabulary to pursue this theological argument. Nevertheless, in making the distinction between the idea of goodness as something loved by the gods and that of gods as loving that which is good, Socrates hints at the idea that morality had to possess its own measure of value, not one that could be alienated to heaven.

Euthyphro cannot answer Socrates' question (indeed, he does not understand it) but suggests eventually that piety is a form of justice. Socrates responds that 'where there is piety there is also justice, but where there is justice there is not always piety'. What is it, he asks, that makes piety different from all those other actions that we call just? And so it goes on.

Eventually, the perplexed Euthyphro falls back on the argument that honour, reverence and sacrifice must 'please' the gods. But this, as Socrates points out, is to take the argument full circle, for they have already agreed that piety cannot be that which the gods love. 'So we must investigate again from the beginning what piety is,' Socrates insists. At which point Euthyphro makes his excuses. 'Some other time, Socrates,' he says, 'for I am in a hurry now and it is time for me to go.'

Euthyphro takes us to the heart of the Socratic method. Socrates strikes an ironic pose: he claims to know nothing of piety and is eager to be a student of the knowledgeable Euthyphro. The student relentlessly questions the arguments of the supposed master, until every one of the master's arguments is shown to be untenable. Socrates (and the reader) seemingly comes away empty handed. Euthyphro leaves without being able to establish the meaning of piety; and while Socrates has mown down all his definitions, he has not replaced them with one of his own. And yet, Socrates has established something important, not just about piety, or goodness, but about morality itself, by suggesting that goodness, and hence morality, should have an objective existence independent of either gods or humans. This raises, however, a host of new questions. What does it mean for morality to have an objective existence? If moral laws come neither from gods nor from humans, whence do they derive? Socrates never answered such questions. It is not clear that he even thought them important. Nevertheless, they became central issues for philosophers who followed, beginning with Socrates' pupil Plato.

4

Plato's birth is shrouded in mystery. He may have been born in Athens, and was probably born sometime between 429 and 423 BCE. What is certain is that he was born into royalty, both literally and metaphorically. Plato could trace his descent from Codrus, the last of the legendary kings of Athens, killed during the Dorian invasion in the eleventh century, and Melanthus, king of Messenia. His mother was a descendant of Solon, the sixth-century poet and statesman whose political and economic reforms laid the foundations for Athenian democracy. It was a family saturated with power, prestige and influence.

From such a background, Plato might have been expected to enter politics.

He was, however, temperamentally unsuited to such a life, not to mention cynical about it. In 'all states now existing', he concluded, 'without exception their system of government is bad'.[6]

What troubled Plato was not simply politics in general, but the particular political form championed in Athens – democracy. The single event that more than any fired both Plato's cynicism of politics and his scepticism of democracy was the execution of his moral god Socrates.

Philosophy, not politics, was for Plato the guide to a better world. Around 387 BCE he founded his Academy. The Academy was actually a walled public park about a mile to the north of Athens, named after the mythical hero Academus who had supposedly created it. Inside was a sacred olive grove dedicated to Athena, goddess both of the city and of wisdom. Inside, too, was a small house and garden that Plato had inherited and in which he opened a school for philosophical debate and instruction that could train politicians in philosophy and philosophers in politics.

The key work in which the many threads of Plato's argument about the relationship between politics, philosophy and the conception of the good life come together is *The Republic*. Written in 360 BCE, at the heart of the masterpiece is the question 'What is justice?' The Greek word δικαιοσύνη – *dikaiosune* – which is usually translated as 'justice', had a wider meaning to Plato, more akin to the modern idea of morality itself.

The Republic, like most of Plato's works, is written in the form of a dialogue, with Socrates acting as Plato's mouthpiece. It opens with Socrates' companions Cephalus and Polemarchus attempting to define what they believe to be justice. The Sophist Thrasymachus enters the fray. 'Coiled like a wild animal about to spring,' Socrates recalls, 'he hurled himself at us as if to tear us to pieces.' Rejecting the very idea of morality, Thrasymachus insists that 'Justice is nothing other than the advantage of the stronger'. There were, Thrasymachus observes, many kinds of cities in Greece – democracies, oligarchies, military dictatorships, tyrannies. Each had a different conception of justice, but all benefited the ruling class. 'Democracy makes democratic laws, tyranny makes tyrannical laws', Thrasymachus argues, and all 'declare what they have made – what is to their advantage – to be just for their subjects, and they punish anyone who goes against this as lawless and unjust'. What is called justice is, for Thrasymachus, simply injustice writ large. Those who commit small crimes 'are called temple-robbers, kidnappers, housebreakers, robbers and thieves'. But if someone 'kidnaps and enslaves the citizens', then 'instead of these shameful names he is called happy and blessed'.[7]

Conventional morality, in other words, is a scam, a set of rules invented by the ruling class to promote its own interests and to keep everyone else in check. Reject the scam, is Thrasymachus' advice, pursue your interests rather than the interests of others, and disregard justice whenever you can get away with it.

In picking up Thrasymachus' challenge, Plato responds at two levels. First, he sets out plans for a social Utopia to show how naked self-interest is harmful to both the individual and the collective soul. Second, he gives a metaphysical account of what it is to be good, challenging the claim that justice is relative to particular cities. In so doing he not only takes on the Sophists but also attempts to get to grips with two questions raised by Socrates. How can one define terms such as piety or goodness rather than simply illustrate instances of such ideas? And how can we find objective moral truths?

5

All humans divide naturally, in Plato's eyes, into three classes, each suited for one of the three indispensable social roles. Labourers produce the material needs of society. Soldiers guard the state. And rulers rule.

The tripartite division of the population mirrors the tripartite division of the soul into appetitive, spirited and rational parts. The appetitive part of the soul is linked to bodily desires, such as the yearning for food or pleasure. The spirited is concerned with honour, and with anger and indignation. The rational is driven by a desire for knowledge and truth. This division, especially between the appetites, or bodily desires, and reason, or the mind, was to exert enormous pressure upon subsequent ethical thinking. For Plato, and for many of those who followed in his footsteps, reason and desire, the body and the mind, the ego and the id, were locked in mortal combat.

Humans, according to Plato, fall into one of three categories depending on which part of their soul is dominant, three categories that correspond, of course, to the three social roles necessary for the healthy functioning of the state. The common people are driven by base desires, soldiers by a yearning for honour, while rulers look to reason. Upbringing may help an individual regulate his soul and thereby change the group to which he should belong. Mostly, though, it is a matter of birth – we are born to be blacksmiths or soldiers or philosopher kings.

A healthy soul is one in which there is a balance between its three parts; a soul in which reason rules, spirit assists by providing the necessary emotional qualities of courage, self-control and strength of will, and appetite is kept in check, inhibited from doing more than satisfying essential physical needs. As with the soul, so with the state. In a healthy state, the labourers, the soldiers and the rulers live in harmony; and they do so because such a state is ruled by those whose souls are most guided by reason. Justice is expressed in the maintenance of balance, in the soul, and in the city. A city is 'thought to be just when each of the natural classes within it did its own work'.[8]

Plato described five different types of societies, and ranked them according to how rational, successful and just each was. Four were kinds of city states that already existed in Greece – timocracy, oligarchy, democracy and tyranny. The fifth was his own Republic, a society ruled by philosopher kings, and which Plato called an aristocracy. This was the best of societies, one in which 'the desires of the inferior many are controlled by the wisdom and desires of the superior few'.[9]

Next on Plato's scale of the good society came timocracy, or military dictatorship. Sparta was the model (as indeed it was for the Republic itself). It was a bleak, austere society built upon military conquest and mass enslavement in which slavery allowed not for a life of luxury but for one of unremitting asceticism. Sparta demanded obedience and sacrifice from its citizens to sublimate their interests to those of the community. All manual work in Sparta was the lot of slaves and of helots – Greeks captured in battle and enchained as bonded labour – because all male Spartans were trained almost from birth to become professional soldiers. To us, Sparta may seem anything but an ideal society, but the discipline, selflessness and attachment to the ideals of the polis won Spartans the admiration not just of Plato but of most ancient Greeks.

Timocrats, Plato believed, are ruled by the desire for honour, a passion more worthy than that of bodily desire, but less so than that of reason. If neither aristocracy nor timocracy were possible, then Plato considered oligarchy as the next best society. The souls of oligarchs are dominated by an ignoble passion, the desire for material goods. They nevertheless have to show a degree of self-control to accumulate wealth. Then comes democracy, a society ruled by people dominated by lowly appetites for food, drink, sex and pleasure. It is a society without order or discipline. A democrat puts all 'his pleasures on an equal footing', 'always surrendering rule over himself to which ever desire comes along, as if it were chosen by lot'. Political equality inevitably leads to a coarseness of culture and an anything-goes morality, a claim that finds an echo among modern conservatives.

The only society worse than a democracy is a tyranny. This is not the opposite of democracy but is rather democracy fully played out, a society in which every form of behaviour, including murder and disrespect for law, becomes acceptable. The moral of the story is that 'extreme freedom can't be expected to lead to anything but a change to extreme slavery, whether for a private individual or for a city'. Tyranny enslaves not just the population but the tyrant too. A tyrant's soul, Plato observes, must be 'full of slavery and unfreedom, with the most decent parts enslaved and with a small part, the maddest and the most vicious, as their master'. He is 'like the city he rules', full of 'fear, convulsions and pains throughout his life'.[10]

This is Plato's response to Thrasymachus. Pure self-interest cannot be in the interest of the self, because it makes one unhappy and enslaved. To live well is to have an ordered soul, one that is in harmony with itself. 'How can it profit anyone to acquire gold unjustly', he asks, 'if, by doing so, he enslaves the best part of himself to the worst?'[11]

6

Why should the rulers of Plato's Republic be so much better than other rulers at maintaining the balance of the soul and the harmony of the city? Because they are philosopher kings. Rulers are born to rule. But the 'superior few' in

Plato's Utopia are especially wise and rational. They are not merely special by birth, but their specialness has been honed to a pitch by singular training.

From birth to cradle, members of the potential ruling class are subject to a regime that would make North Korea seem like a playboy's paradise and leave English public schoolboys yearning for the days of fagging and cold showers. But it is not one at which any Spartan would cavil, for it is from Spartan life itself that Plato draws inspiration. A special breeding programme ensures that 'the best men . . . have sex with the best women as frequently as possible', while the 'opposite' is the case with 'the most inferior men and women'. Newborn children are culled, with the finest taken to a 'rearing pen' while low-grade specimens are whisked off to 'a secret and unknown place' and killed. (In Sparta, according to Plutarch, 'puny and deformed' infants were thrown into a chasm on Mount Taygetos known as the *Apothetae*, Greek for 'deposits'; many classicists now think this is a myth.) The lucky survivors 'are to be possessed in common', as are women. The children are put through a strict programme of education, indoctrination and discipline. They are forbidden from eating fish or confectionery. Homer is banned, as are all dramatists, not to mention music from Lydia, which, apparently, is too sorrowful.

The reward for such a regimen of breeding, indoctrination and discipline is the creation of a class of citizens, not just upstanding and virtuous, but one whose souls are so well ordered, and so able to sublimate their animal desires to the dictates of reason, that they can see beyond this world and into a realm of transcendence. And so Plato introduces us to his theory of the Forms.

Ordinary people, Plato believed, 'are living in a dream'. What they take to be real objects or feelings or qualities are mere shadows, fleeting phantoms of authentic existence. Shadows of what? Of the Forms, the true reality, that exist in a transcendent realm separate from the physical world and independent of our senses. Sensible things – things that we understand through our senses – come to be, change and perish. They are in constant flux. That is why our senses deceive us. True reality is not the physical world revealed to our senses but the ideal world accessible only by reason.

A non-philosopher, Plato believed, 'likes beautiful sounds, colours, shapes and everything fashioned out of them'. But he is 'unable to see and embrace the nature of the beautiful itself'. A philosopher, on the other hand, is enamoured not just of beautiful things, or of truthful things, but of Beauty and Truth themselves. When Socrates searched for definitions, he was, Plato suggests, looking for the Form of that which he was trying to define. The Form provides the objective definition of terms such as justice or piety. The highest of the Forms is that of goodness. To most Greek philosophers, to be 'good' was to fulfil one's proper role in the order of things. The Form of the Good established the purpose and goal of all things in the cosmos. Apart from the gods, only a philosopher could comprehend the Form of the Good.

To illustrate the contrast between the opinion of ordinary people and the knowledge of true philosophers, Plato gives us the famous allegory of the Prisoners in the Cave. Most humans are like prisoners chained in a deep subterranean cave, manacled in a line and able only to look at the rock face in front. 'Far above and behind them' is a fire, the only source of light in the cave. Between the fire and the prisoners, people are moving, carrying various objects that cast flickering shadows on the rock face. The prisoners have only ever seen these shadows. They have never cast eyes on the real objects creating them. They have no idea that such objects exist. The prisoners, Plato observes, 'would in every way believe that the truth is nothing other than the shadows of those artefacts'.[12] And that is how humans exist too. The unseen real things correspond to the Forms, the sensuous objects and qualities we take to be real are the shadows on the wall.

Now, suppose one of these prisoners had been freed from his chains and taken outside. He would be 'pained and dazzled' by the light and 'unable to see the things whose shadows he had seen before'. But once his eyes had adjusted, he could view things afresh and he would discover a new world. If now he returned to the cave, he would find it difficult to see the shadows. He would 'invite ridicule' from the other prisoners who would say of him that 'he'd returned from his upward journey with his eyesight ruined and it isn't worthwhile even to try to travel upwards'. If he tried to free the prisoners and lead them up to the real world, 'if they could somehow get their hands on him, wouldn't they kill him?'[13]

This was not, for Plato, a rhetorical question. Socrates, after all, had been put to death by the democratic cave-dwellers of Athens. Only in Plato's

Republic would Socrates have been given his true due, for only there would society have been ruled by those who knew the Forms.

7

In *The Republic*, Plato links a political argument about the best form of society to an ethical argument about what constitutes the good and how to discover it, and binds the two together with a psychological claim about how best to achieve happiness. Goodness and happiness are, for Plato, the offspring of harmony, both of the soul and of the city.

The psychological, the political and the metaphysical arguments have all proved influential, from Christian theology's appropriation of the transcendental Forms to Sigmund Freud's tripartite distinction between the ego, id and superego. There is, however, to the modern mind at least, something dissatisfying about Plato's theory. It is not so much an ethical as a psychological refutation of Thrasymachus. Plato dismisses naked self-interest not as ethically unsound but as mentally unhealthy. To be unjust is to suffer from an unbalanced mind.

In large part Plato's failure to make a properly ethical case against the pure pursuit of self-interest rests on his inability to recognize the force of Thrasymachus' moral argument. The idea of self-interest is, perhaps surprisingly, not self-evident. At different times, in different societies, 'self-interest' has possessed different meanings. Compare, for instance, Thrasymachus and Achilles. Achilles was obsessed by his personal desires. He did not wish to lose his war prize Briseis. He was more consumed by preserving his honour than by defending the interests of the Greeks. That, at least, is how a modern reader would view it. For Achilles, though, his withdrawal of his men from battle in outrage at Agamemnon's action was not a case of selfishness, nor even of self-interest, but a matter of following the code laid down by his community. That code was often not in the interests of the individual. The highest honour, after all, was death in battle, a fate that was to befall Achilles himself. But, in prizing individual honour above wider needs, nor was it often in the interests of the community either. This was one reason that such honour codes slowly evolved into other forms of moral life.

Thrasymachus possessed a different concept of self-interest. Self-interest to him was unrelated to the interests of the community; individuals should not take into account needs other than their own. Philosophers, ancient and modern, have shown why such an egoistical view makes little sense. Humans are not solitary creatures but exist only within a community. It is only through a community of others that an individual can assert his or her own interests. Nevertheless, in time, Thrasymachus' claim that justice is a scam, that it is merely an expression of power, and that the most rational behaviour is to disregard justice where possible and pursue one's self-interest was to prove almost as influential as Plato's own arguments. Hobbes, Nietzsche, Marx: all in their own ways were to echo Thrasymachus. They are three disparate thinkers. What connects them is that they are philosophers of the modern era, attempting to make sense of the meaning of political power, individual agency and social need at a time when traditional moral concepts were in disarray. To be able to draw on the idea of 'self-interest' at the heart of Thrasymachus' argument, they also had to draw upon a notion of the 'self' that neither Homer nor Plato possessed. It was not that Hobbes, Nietzsche or Marx would necessarily have agreed with Thrasymachus. It is more that the social and intellectual changes that marked the coming of modernity made an argument rooted in individual self-interest that much more plausible. Even those who disagreed with such ethical claims had nevertheless to take them more seriously.

In Plato's world, notions of the inner self were barely articulated, an individual's identity and interest were bound up entirely with the community in which he lived, the very notion of the individual was far more constrained than it is today, and ethics was a means of regulating the social roles and relationships within a community. The importance of the community was expressed in the almost spiritual quality that the polis possessed in ancient Greek life. It was through the polis that the individual citizen discovered his identity and through which he became part of a history and a heritage. Even today there is a fraught debate about how to balance individual rights and social needs. Two millennia ago the idea of naked egoism as expressed by Thrasymachus may, indeed, have seemed a form of mental illness.

CHAPTER THREE

On human flourishing

1

In *The Name of the Rose*, Umberto Eco's beguiling philosophical whodunnit, the Franciscan friar William of Baskerville and his novice, Adso of Melk, investigate a series of murders at a Benedictine monastery in northern Italy to which they have travelled to participate in a theological debate. William's investigation leads him to uncover a plot to keep hidden a single book in the abbey's library, the greatest in Christendom. In the novel's denouement, amidst the ruins of a burning library, William asks the blind librarian, Jorge of Burgos, why he has devoted his life to protecting the world from any knowledge of this single work. 'Because it was by the Philosopher,' replies Jorge. 'Every book by that man has destroyed a part of the learning that Christianity had accumulated over the centuries.'

The Philosopher was Aristotle, the man whose work until modern times shaped the way that most European thinkers – and many non-European ones too – viewed the physical world and understood the nature of the divine. Despite the Book of Genesis revealing 'what has to be known about the composition of the cosmos', Jorge bemoans, 'it sufficed to rediscover the *Physics* of the Philosopher to have the universe reconceived in terms of dull and slimy matter'.

Aristotle was born in 384 BCE in Stagira in northern Greece. His father was court physician to the king of Macedonia. At seventeen Aristotle went to Athens to attend Plato's Academy, which became his home for the next twenty years. He was the Academy's star pupil, but also fiercely independent. That may be why, when Plato died in 347 BCE, Plato's nephew Speusippus was chosen to head the Academy. Aristotle went back to Macedonia, becoming court tutor to the young Alexander, later to be Great.

Twelve years later, Aristotle returned to Athens where he set up his own Academy, the Lyceum. By this time most of the Greek city states had come under Macedonian rule, generating much resentment. When Alexander died in 323 BCE, there was an anti-Macedonian revolt in Athens. Aristotle was indicted on fabricated charges of impiety. Not wishing to suffer the same fate as Socrates, he went into exile, where he died the following year.

Aristotle wrote all his major works in the twelve years after his return to Athens. All have been lost. Nothing remains but his notes. But what notes! There are almost two million words whose range is phenomenal. Aristotle made major advances in logic, mathematics, biology, physiology, astronomy, philosophy, literature and rhetoric. He was, as Dante put it in *The Inferno*, 'the master of those who know'.

Aristotle was a different kind of philosopher to those that had gone before. One of Raphael's most famous paintings, *Scuola di Atene* or *The School of Athens*, is a fresco on the walls of the Apostolic Palace in the Vatican, depicting most of the great Greek philosophers. At the centre stand Plato and Aristotle, holding copies of their books in one hand, and pointing with the other, Plato upwards to the heavens, Aristotle down to the Earth. The two gestures express their two philosophies. There was in Aristotle none of the poetical, speculative or mystical. He was, rather, methodical, balanced, even plodding and staid, one who thought, and wrote, like a professor not a prophet. His attention to detail, close observation and slow, reasoned argument were perfectly suited to the study of the physical world. But applied to ethics, Aristotle's method often lends his arguments a 'bleeding obvious' quality that can make them appear both profoundly sensible and insufferably trite.

'Every art and every investigation, and similarly every action and pursuit, is considered to aim at some good. Hence the good has been rightly defined as "that at which all things aim"'.[1] So begins *The Nicomachean Ethics*, Aristotle's key moral work. Like all his surviving texts, it was a collection of notes to aid him with his lectures at the Lyceum. It was dedicated to his son Nicomachus, who probably edited it too – hence the modern title. Its starting point, the claim that the good is that which we desire, was a typical Aristotelian formulation, both profound and trite.

There are, Aristotle observed, many things we desire, and different people desire different things. There exist, therefore, many goods. However, if 'our activities have some end which we want for its own sake, and for the sake of which we want all the other ends', then 'this must be . . . the supreme good'. The knowledge of this supreme good 'is of great importance to us in the conduct of our lives'.[2]

This supreme good is εὐδαιμονία – *eudaimonia*. It is a concept that in Greek moral thought goes back at least as far as Socrates, but which is most associated with Aristotle. The word is usually translated as 'happiness'. To the Greeks *eudaimonia* meant much more. It was not a matter of the satisfaction of immediate desires, nor even of a sense of wellbeing, but described more broadly a state of human flourishing, or a state of being that is worth seeking, that which Aristotle calls 'living well and doing well'.[3] It is at one and the same time an objective measure of human wellbeing and a value-laden concept of flourishing.

Eudaimonia, Aristotle argues, cannot simply be pleasure, as some Sophists believed. One who possesses *eudaimonia* will necessarily find pleasure in his way of life. But finding pleasure is not the same as possessing *eudaimonia*. A torturer might take pleasure in his perverse and corrupt activities. But we would not say of him that he lived a flourishing life.

Cultured people often associate *eudaimonia* with honour, while a businessman might prize wealth. Honour and wealth are, however, means to an end, not ends in themselves. Not even virtue is the same as *eudaimonia*. The state of happiness was not for Aristotle a passive state but one achieved through practical activity. 'The possession of goodness', on the other hand, Aristotle points out, may be compatible 'with leading a life of inactivity'. It may also be compatible 'with the most atrocious suffering or misfortune'.[4] Socrates suggests in *Gorgias* that 'doing what's unjust [is] worse than suffering it, and not paying what is due worse than paying it'. A man committing evil can never be as happy as a man suffering evil, while a man who has acted unjustly but has been punished for it is happier than a man who has got away with acting unjustly, even if such punishment involves being 'put on the rack, castrated' and having one's 'eyes put out'.[5] At which point Polus, one of Socrates' interlocutors and a student of Gorgias, simply laughs. Aristotle is unlikely to have laughed at Socrates, but he certainly dismissed the idea that a virtuous person living a life of abject poverty or being torn to pieces on a rack could be considered happy in any sense of the word. Virtue for him was a means to an end, not an end in itself.

Goodness could not be defined in transcendental terms, either, as Plato had attempted. The good, Aristotle observes, exists in many forms; so 'there cannot be a single universal common to all cases'.[6] Knowledge of the Forms was knowledge of something unchanging and eternal. Ethical knowledge, on the other hand, was the kind of knowledge necessary to guide our actions. It would therefore have to be knowledge of things that changed. Knowledge of the Forms would be knowledge of universals, whereas ethics required knowledge that took into account the specific context of any action. The good, Aristotle insists, must be a description of something that exists, and is desired for, in this world, not in a transcendental realm.

2

Aristotle had established that which *eudaimonia* could not be. To understand what it *was*, he suggests, we have to appreciate the function of a human being, to comprehend what it is that makes humans distinctive.

The concept of an object's function was central to Aristotle's philosopy. Every object, he believed, had a natural place it inhabited and an essence that made it behave in its customary fashion. Each had a purpose; every change in the natural world was the result of objects attempting to fulfil their purpose or to return to their natural place in the order of things. Why does an acorn become an oak? Because that is its purpose. The acorn is potentially, but not actually, an oak. In becoming an oak it becomes what it already was potentially, fulfilling its purpose and confirming its nature.

An object could only be understood in relation to its purpose or function. This was as true for humans as for every other species. There are many characteristic features of human life – humans breathe, sleep, act, think. Most of these characteristics are shared with other creatures. What truly distinguishes humans, Aristotle argues, is the possession of reason. Hence the exercise of reason is the proper function of a human being. Happiness consists in acting in accordance with reason. Or, to be more precise, it means acting virtuously in accordance with reason.

There were, for Aristotle, two kinds of virtues: moral and intellectual. Moral virtues are character traits, of which Aristotle mentions twelve: courage, temperance, generosity, magnificence, magnanimity, pride, patience, honesty, wittiness, friendliness, modesty and righteous indignation. Intellectual virtues consist of abilities such as intelligence or foresight that help formulate plans and calculate consequences.

The two kinds of virtues are related to two distinct parts of the soul, the rational and irrational. Intellectual virtues, rooted in the rational soul, are embodiments of reason. The moral virtues are housed in the irrational part of the soul; they are, nevertheless, able to 'listen' to reason and in so doing to incline one to act in certain ways. Those who do not act in a virtuous fashion often fail to do so because they find it difficult to make their desires 'obedient' to reason.

Aristotle's division of the soul is clearly indebted to Plato. But where Plato looked to reason to repress physical desires, for Aristotle the role of reason was to guide desire, and allow it to express itself to the right degree. Feelings themselves could be an embodiment of reason, but only if both reason and feelings were properly cultivated.

Not all humans can control their feelings because not all humans possess intellectual virtue. Women have less control than men. Slaves cannot rein in their desires at all, which is why they have to be controlled by their masters. Yet, while Aristotle saw women and slaves as naturally incapable of being as virtuous as freeborn men, he did not view virtues as naturally given. Intellectual and moral virtues have to be nurtured, each in their own way. Intellectual virtues can be taught, though not necessarily in the classroom. There are, in fact, two kinds of intellectual virtues. *Theoria* is the ability to think about the nature of the world; it is akin to science and is used to contemplate universal laws. *Phronesis*, or practical wisdom, helps us 'contemplate things that are variable'. It is the knowledge of how to act in particular situations. It cannot be learnt like biology or physics or even philosophy but understood only through concrete experiences.

Moral virtues cannot be taught at all, at least formally. They are dispositions to behave in certain ways that are acquired in childhood almost unconsciously through good upbringing and reinforced through repeated use. One becomes honest by being brought up to be honest. Every time one is faced with a situation in which one could be dishonest, but chooses not to, the stronger becomes one's disposition to be honest. To be virtuous is to possess the disposition to act virtuously, and the practical wisdom to know how and when to do so.

The Greek word for virtue is ἀρετή, or *arete*. An arête is also, for mountaineers, a sharp ridge, with steep cliffs falling away on either side. It is a good metaphor for Aristotle's vision of *arete* as moral virtue. An Aristotelian virtue is like a narrow path with a chasm of vice to right and left. Courage is the virtuous path between rashness and cowardice, righteous indignation the path between envy and spitefulness. To act virtuously in accordance with reason is for Aristotle to observe a balance between excess and deficiency in all things, to thread a path along the arête between the vices on either side. This takes us to the famous 'doctrine of the mean'. 'It is in the nature of moral qualities', Aristotle wrote, 'that they are destroyed by deficiency and excess'. Take courage. 'The man who shuns and fears everything and stands up to nothing becomes a coward,' Aristotle observes; 'the man who is afraid of nothing at all, but marches up to every danger, becomes foolhardy.' Similarly with temperance: 'The man who indulges in every pleasure and refrains from none becomes licentious; but if a man behaves like a boor and turns his back on every pleasure, he is a case of insensibility.'[7] It is *phronesis*, the wisdom acquired through thinking about one's experiences, that enables the virtuous man to find the mean and keep on the mountain ridge.

Aristotle's ethics, Bertrand Russell famously suggested, may be 'useful to comfortable men of weak passions; but he has nothing to say to those who are possessed by a god or a devil'. To anyone 'with any depth of feeling it is likely to be repulsive'.[8] There is an element of truth in this. Don't be too angry, nor too emollient either. Walk a line between prodigality and meanness. Neither obsequious nor cantankerous be. Aristotle's moral voice can often seem like that of the school matron at assembly. But Russell's is also a misreading of Aristotle. For his is not simply a counsel of moderation. Discovering the mean, in Aristotle's ethics, is not necessarily the same as choosing a mid-point. Aristotle makes a distinction between what he calls the 'mean in relation to the thing' and the 'mean in relation to us'. The former is that which is 'equidistant from the extremes, which is one and the same for everybody'. The latter is 'that which is neither excessive nor deficient, and this is *not* one and the same for all'.[9]

Finding the 'mean in relation to the thing' is about locating the absolute centre between deficiency and excess, the spot where you will find the school matron and Russell's 'comfortable man of weak passions'. Observing the 'mean in relation to us', on the other hand, means not necessarily being moderate but doing the right thing at the right time. It may sometimes be rational to be furiously angry, or to show a degree of courage that at other times may seem rash. Such anger or courage is not moderate but, insofar as it is rational, constitutes in Aristotle's eyes the mean. The trouble is, this is a classic 'bleeding obvious' argument. The idea of the 'mean in relation to us' may not be the tepid counsel of moderation that Russell feared. But to suggest that 'one should do the right thing' to 'the right person to the right extent at the right time for the right reason in the right way'[10] is to replace the tepid with the vacuous. No one could disagree with the advice, but one would hardly need to be Aristotle to give it.

3

A virtuous man had, in Aristotle's eyes, obviously to possess a virtuous character and be able to apply practical wisdom to moral questions. But, like Plato and many before him all the way back to Homer, Aristotle believed that he had to possess something more too: wealth, power and leisure. Wealth was not an end in itself. Nor was it virtuous to be greedy. Nevertheless, 'a poor man cannot be magnificent because he has not the means to meet heavy expenses suitably'. Workers, traders and husbandmen should not be citizens because a working life 'is not noble, and it militates against virtue'.[11]

For Aristotle, as for Plato, ethics was subordinate to politics. The primary good was the good of the community rather than the good of the individual. Moral rules grew out of the structure of the community, and ensured the maintenance of that structure. A polis was, for Aristotle, a natural phenomenon. Just as it was in the nature of humans to be happy, so it was in the nature of humans to come together in groups capable of supporting and sustaining happiness. No citizen, he argues, 'should think that he belongs just to himself'. Rather, 'he must regard all citizens as belonging to the state, for each is a part of the state; and the responsibility for each part naturally has regard to the responsibility for the whole'. Hence, 'while it is desirable to secure what is good in the case of an individual, to do so in the case of a people or a state is something finer and more sublime'.[12] There is more than an echo here of Plato's argument in *The Republic*.

The polis was necessary not simply for survival, but also for flourishing, for *eudaimonia*. This was particularly so, Aristotle suggested, because the masses 'living under the sway of their feelings . . . pursue their own pleasures and the means of obtaining them, and shun the pains that are their opposite'. Unlike the prosperous and well-heeled readers of Aristotle, the uneducated masses do not respond to rational 'argument and fine ideals' or even to 'shame' or 'disgrace' but primarily to 'fear' and to 'compulsion and punishment'. What every polis required, therefore, was 'a proper system of public supervision' to ensure that those who could not be virtuous nevertheless behaved in an appropriate manner.[13]

For Aristotle, the law is not simply a means by which the state regulates relations with citizens and between citizens. It is a much more creative, formative agent, through the use of which a community can instruct its members in their moral and social duties and help craft the ideal citizen. 'The student of ethics', Aristotle writes on the very last page of *The Nicomachean Ethics*, 'must therefore apply himself to politics'. That is just what Aristotle does in *The Politics*, the work that in a sense completes the investigation begun in the *Ethics* by revealing the laws, regulations and institutions that best allow human flourishing. It is 'legislators [who] make citizens good by habituation'.[14]

The most important task for the politician is to frame the appropriate constitution for the polis – the laws, customs, institutions and system of moral education for the citizen. Aristotle distinguishes between just constitutions that aim 'at the common good' and are 'in accord with absolute justice', and unjust constitutions that 'aim only at the good of the rulers'. There are three right types of just constitutions: monarchy, aristocracy ('so called because the *best* men rule') and polity, in which 'political control is exercised by the mass of the populace in the common interest'. Each just constitution has a corresponding 'deviation': tyranny, oligarchy and democracy. 'Tyranny', Aristotle writes, 'is monarchy for the benefit of the monarch, oligarchy for the benefit of the men of means, democracy for the benefit of the men without means'.[15]

A constitution is just if it distributes political power in proportion to individuals' merit or desert. Democrats believe that free birth constitutes merit, oligarchs that wealth or good family does. Both are wrong. Since the ultimate end of the polis is neither as a business to maximize wealth nor as a union to assure equality, but rather as a community to promote the good life, the correct conception of justice is the aristocratic belief that the true criterion for the distribution of power is 'excellence'.

The best society is one ruled by an absolute monarch who is also absolutely virtuous. Aristotle is pragmatic enough to recognize that such individuals are as rare as good-mannered gods, and that most societies, like most humans, are more corrupt, more tainted, more mixed. Of existing constitutions, the best is a mixture of oligarchy and democracy. In such societies, the poor and the rich balance out each other's immoral tendencies. Aristotle applies the principle of the mean, not simply to character, but to the constitution too. The best society is one with a large 'middle class' – those who are neither too rich nor too poor, but 'have a middling, adequate amount of property', those who are a bit like an Athenian philosopher.[16]

4

'Excessive striving for unification is a bad thing in a state'.[17] So wrote Aristotle about Plato's Utopia. Plato, he argued, overvalued political unity in *The Republic*, failed to recognize that his system of shared ownership was antagonistic to human nature and neglected the happiness of individual citizens.

Yet, the themes that unite Aristotle and Plato are at least as significant as the differences. Like Plato, Aristotle saw ethics and politics as inextricable. Like Plato, Aristotle saw the needs of the individual as subordinate to those of the collective. Like Plato, Aristotle believed that laws were necessary to make us good. Like Plato, Aristotle lauded aristocratic society as the rule of the best. Most strikingly, perhaps, Plato and Aristotle agreed on the polis that best embodied their ideals. Plato modelled his Republic on Sparta. For all his criticisms of *The Republic*, Aristotle, too, saw the Spartan constitution as the best existing example of the 'well-mixed democracy and oligarchy'. Athens was for Aristotle, as it was for Plato, the worst form of democracy, because it allowed the basest feelings of the masses to become manifest.

Today we see Sparta as a repulsive society, a military dictatorship on a permanent war footing, the majority of whose population was enchained, 'a model, in miniature', in Bertrand Russell's view, 'of the State the Nazis would establish if victorious'.[18] To ancient Greeks it appeared differently. Plutarch tells the story of an old man coming late to an Olympiad and looking in vain for a seat. Most of the crowd mocks him for his age and infirmity. Then he enters the section where the Spartans are seated. Every man among them rises to his feet and offers him his seat. Somewhat abashed, but nevertheless admiringly, the other Greeks applaud the Spartans. 'Ah,' the old man observes with a sigh, 'all Greeks know what is right, but only the Spartans do it.' Even Greeks who were critical of the Spartan constitution admired their attachment to traditional ideals.

It is in Athens that we see the spirit of ancient Greece, and in whose magnificence we recognize how much we owe the Ancients. But it is in Sparta that we find its ethical heart, and in whose virtues we understand how different is the modern world. Or, to put it less crudely, in the modern world we have come to see Athens alone as evocative of the spirit of ancient Greece, and to dismiss Sparta as an aberration, whereas ancient Greeks looked upon both cities as giving concrete expression to their values, traditions and accomplishments, though in different ways. The Spartan constitution seemed to express best the almost sacred commitment of ancient societies to the sanctity of the community as the source of value, the insistence on social harmony, the attachment to tradition, and the subordination of the needs of the individual to that of the state. That is why philosophers forged in the furnace of Athens, the crucible of ideas and free thought in ancient Greece, should seek to idealize Sparta, a city that despised the freedoms granted by Athens.

In the journey from Homer to Aristotle, the Greeks crafted what we now call 'virtue theory', establishing the importance of character, community, flourishing and practical wisdom as the central themes of a virtuous life. This became the dominant ethical view over the next two millennia. Not till the eighteenth century did competing ethical frameworks develop in Kantianism and utilitarianism, the first stressing the importance of duty and conscience, the second the significance of the consequences of one's actions. On that journey from Homer to Aristotle were developed the ideas of virtue as a disposition to act according to reason; of practical wisdom as a skill that inclines one to do the right thing at the right time and to the right degree; of morality as requiring one to think not of single acts but of one's life as a whole; and of the virtuous person as someone who can be judged only according to the needs of the community of which he is a part and to which he is subordinate.

In creating this knot of beliefs to bind together their ethics, the Greeks found themselves grappling with two basic instincts about what constitutes the good life. On the one hand there was Socrates' conviction that 'the unexamined life is not worth living', the belief that what made humans human was their capacity for reason and for critical self-examination. On the other was Aristotle's insistence that one should 'regard all citizens as belonging to the state', the almost visceral attachment to the common good and to the sublimation of individual interests to those of the community. These two instincts were not always easy to reconcile. The desire for rational scrutiny often cut against the demand for the preservation of the community and of the common good. One way to understand the relationship between Athens and Sparta is as different attempts to reconcile these two impulses.

Two millennia later, the spirits of Athens and Sparta remain at war in ethical thought. Indeed, the conflict between individual conscience and rational scrutiny, on the one hand, and the needs of the community, on the other, has become sharper in the modern world. From the global controversy over the

Danish cartoons to that surrounding Guantanamo Bay, from the debate about whether the Catholic Church should be allowed to discriminate against gays to that over whether prospective British citizens should have to pass a citizenship test, the clash between the rights of the individual and the needs of the collective has shaped much of our moral landscape. Two thousand years on from Socrates, Plato and Aristotle, it remains a landscape we still have not learnt how to negotiate.

5

Aristotle died in 322 BCE. A year earlier his patron Alexander had died. The deaths drew the curtain on classical Greece. Historians talk of the period between the death of Alexander and the Roman annexation of Egypt three centuries later as the 'Hellenistic period'. It was an age in which Greek influence was at its greatest, but one also in which Greek ideas were diluted and its passion largely spent.

It was Philip II who first established Macedonian rule over the Greek city states, after a crushing victory over the combined armies of Thebes and Athens at Chaeronaea in 338 BCE. His son Alexander transformed Philip's kingdom into a vast dominion, overpowering Egypt, conquering the Persian Empire and shaking the borders of India. Hellenistic kingdoms were established throughout South-west Asia, the Middle East and North Africa. These new realms came under the influence of Greek culture, language and philosophy, not to mention the influence of Greek colonists themselves. Athens gave way in cultural importance to cities such as Alexandria and Antioch.

It was a period of great social change and dislocation. Alexander had defined himself through conquest and, as he dictated on the battlefield, so he governed in society. He was a brutal ruler for whom ruthless intimidation, rather than civil administration, was the means to bind together an empire. His death unleashed decades of repressed tension and plunged his realm into chaos and civil war. Four new dynasties eventually emerged, each established by one of Alexander's generals. The Ptolemies ruled in Egypt, the Seleucids took possession of the eastern part of Alexander's old domain, the Antigonids triumphed in Macedonia and Greece, and the Attalids carved out a kingdom in Asia Minor. The new rulers possessed no legitimacy but upon the battlefield, and so it was upon the battlefield that they continually had to assert their authority. Challenge came not just from each other, but from internal revolts and external foes too – the Mauryan Empire in India, marauding tribes in Europe, the ominous menace of Rome.

As the settled and stable life of the polis disintegrated, so it became much harder than in the time of Socrates or Plato or Aristotle to define what should be the moral goals of life or the rules one should observe to achieve moral ends. Philosophy came to reflect these anxieties. 'Empty are the words of that philosopher who offers no therapy for human suffering,' wrote Epicurus. 'For just as there is no use in medical expertise if it does not give therapy for bodily diseases, so too there is no use in philosophy if he does not expel the suffering of the soul.'[19]

Epicureanism was one of two schools of moral thought that sought in the wake of Aristotle and Plato to offer 'therapy for human suffering'. The other was Stoicism. The two embodied contrasting temperaments – the one celebrating pleasure, the other promoting asceticism. Both, however, sought out tranquillity as the aim of life. Both called on the spirit of Socrates, insisting that the point of philosophy was to lead people to the good life. But whereas Socrates, like most Greek philosophers, was outward-looking, and saw philosophy as a way of engaging with society, the new philosophies counselled people, in the words of the Stoic Roman Emperor Marcus Aurelius, to 'retire into yourself'.[20]

Epicurus was born around 342 BCE into a family of Athenian expatriates on the Aegean island of Samos. In 306 he took up residence in a house just outside the walls of Plato's Academy in Athens, which became a kind of philosophical commune. Though he apparently wrote more than three hundred books, all that survive of his writings are three letters and two sets of maxims. Much of what we know of Epicurus, we know from the sketch provided by Diogenes Laertius, the famous third-century biographer, in his *Lives of the Eminent Philosophers*.

The starting point of Epicurus' philosophy was the attainment of pleasure, which he described as 'the beginning and end of the blessed life'.[21] He was not, however, a hedonist in the way that we might understand it. He and his commune lived more like Mahatma Gandhi than Mick Jagger; they abstained from sex, partied little, and survived mainly on a diet of bread and water. A Saturday night knees-up at Epicurus' commune was clearly an occasion to lift the spirit. 'I spit on luxurious pleasures', Epicurus wrote, 'because of the inconveniences that follow them.' The wise man would not only abstain from sex but would 'not fall in love' or 'marry and rear a family'. Nor would he partake in any form of public life. It was best to avoid both fame and power, Epicurus thought, for these created enemies. And 'Since the attainment of great wealth can scarcely be accomplished without slavery to crowds or to politicians', so 'a free life cannot obtain much wealth'. Pleasure was not about self-gratification but about the elimination of pain, by which Epicurus meant not just physical pain but also fear, worry, passion and envy. Pain was everywhere, in every desire, every temptation, every act of consumption. It was a notion of pleasure that could only make sense in a stormy, turbulent era when the idea of withdrawal to a safe harbour might have seemed the most precious of luxuries. 'Our one need', as Epicurus put it, 'is untroubled existence.'[22]

6

The philosopher Zeno was once flogging a slave who had stolen some goods. 'But I was fated to steal,' the slave protested. 'Yes, and to be beaten too,' Zeno responded.[23] Zeno (334–262 BCE) was the founder of Stoicism. For Stoics, neither pleasure nor the elimination of pain but the acceptance of one's fate was the road to tranquillity.

Zeno was a Phoenician born in Citium in Cyprus. He studied under Crates who, as a Cynic, preached a philosophy rooted in contempt for wealth and propriety. 'Cynic' means 'dog-like' and the Cynics were so named because their founder, Diogenes, took to living like a dog, sleeping in a tub in the marketplace and begging for a living. Zeno never took to the life of a dog but he nevertheless remained influenced by the Cynics' outlook, not least their devotion to Socrates. Socrates' indifference to bodily comforts, his plainness in matters of food and clothing, his refusal to flee Athens when charged with a capital crime and his calmness in the face of death all shaped Stoic thinking. Zeno took also from the Cynics their insistence that nothing mattered aside from virtue.

Zeno gave lectures from the *Stoa Poikile*, or Painted Porch, in the agora in Athens. In that porch the Stoics found their name. Unlike Epicureanism, the tenets of which barely changed after the death of its founder, Stoicism was a school of thought that evolved and was refined across five centuries. Over time, the hub of Stoicism moved from Athens to Rome. Much of what we now know of the philosophy comes from the work of later Roman Stoics, especially Epictetus and Seneca.

At the heart of Stoicism was the belief that serenity came from learning to live with the inevitable. 'Seek not that the things which happen should happen as you wish,' Epictetus counselled, 'but wish the things which happen to be as they are, and you will have a tranquil flow of life.'[24] Driven by a deep-set materialism drawn from the Presocratics, the Stoics saw the universe as governed by a set of inviolable laws. These laws constituted fate, for they admitted of no exception. They also constituted Providence, for they were laid down by a beneficent God for the profit of humanity. The Stoics saw no contradiction between their commitment to materialism and their belief in a providential Creator. Unlike the Epicureans, who denied any purpose or goal in the universe, the Stoics held that God had imbued the universe with meaning. God was not separate from the universe; God *was* the cosmos, its 'soul', materially expressed in the *pneuma*, or cosmic breath, that is dispersed throughout all the individual bodies and organisms, maintaining each in its proper state and in its proper relation to its environment.

From the Stoic point of view, that which will be will be, and no amount of rage or desire will suffer to change it. The rational response to fate is to accept it and, in Epictetus' words, to 'wish the things which happen to be as they are'. You may be suffering from a debilitating illness, but it would be irrational to whine about it, as it would make no difference to your health. You may be falsely imprisoned, but no amount of anger and resentment will break down the door, so you might as well accept your fate, however undeserved, with equanimity.

Humans, Epictetus wrote, have no control over their bodies, property or reputation. What do lie within our powers are our opinions, desires and fears.

Don't worry, be happy and you will live a contented, virtuous life. Rage against fate, try to change the unchangeable, and your life will be neither happy nor virtuous. Virtue, for the Stoics, was the sole good. For Aristotle, virtue was a means to an end, not an end in itself. Happiness was not compatible with suffering or misfortune. Material, physical and social wellbeing was a necessary condition of *eudaimonia*. Stoics disagreed. You could be facing penury, your body ravaged by disease, your name reviled in your community. And yet you could still be ecstatically happy. Happiness was all in your mind. There was a social element to this disagreement too. Aristotle denied that the poor could be as virtuous as those better endowed with wealth. The Stoics opened up virtue to everyone. The poor could be virtuous – but only if they resigned themselves to their poverty and sought not to combat it.

As a philosophy of personal endurance rather than of social transformation, Stoicism was appealing to ruling elites. 'Nearly all the successors of Alexander – we may say all the principal kings in existence in the generation following Zeno – professed themselves Stoics,' suggested the nineteenth-century classicist Gilbert Murray.[25]

It became more or less the official philosophy of the upper classes in the Roman Empire, especially after Emperor Marcus Aurelius championed it. Beyond Rome, the Stoic acceptance of the world as it is found an echo in Christianity, and through Christianity in many Western philosophical traditions.

7

The Stoic belief in fate led to the insistence that one should be resigned to the inevitability of life as it is given. Their belief in Providence suggested that one should be resigned with a happy heart. Fate is not a chain around our necks by which a malevolent master pulls us hither and thither. It is, rather, a well paved road to a virtuous world along which humans are guided by a beneficent Creator. But if the universe is guided by a Providential God who has the best interests of humans at heart, how come there is so much pain and suffering in the world?

We only imagine that evil exists, or that the good suffer, the Stoics responded, because we do not have insight into God's greater plan. Despite this, Stoics did attempt to find rational explanations for suffering. Even the most minor inconvenience, Chrysippus suggested, had been carefully designed by God for our benefit. God had created bedbugs to 'awaken us out of our sleep' and mice to encourage humans to be tidy. Chrysippus argued, too, that it would have been impossible for good to exist without evil, for humans would not know the meaning of justice without perceiving injustice, or courage without cowardice, or wisdom without foolishness. Seneca suggested that those who seem to suffer unjustly should say to themselves: 'God has deemed us worthy instruments of his purpose to discover how much human nature can endure.'[26] Such justifications of suffering and evil came to be known as 'theodicy' and was influential in shaping Christian moral thought. There may appear to be something callous in such validation of torment and misery. For Stoics, however, accepting the inevitable was not about rationalizing wretchedness and injustice, but of asserting human control over a world that appeared out of control. Despite the insistence that one should be resigned to one's fate, and despite Marcus Aurelius' counsel to 'retire into yourself', the Stoics, unlike the Epicureans, set great store by public service. They believed in setting an example, in not just behaving virtuously but encouraging others to do so, in acting, in modern terminology, as role models.

The Stoic acceptance of fate fused with the sense of public duty and a fearless view of death to create a startlingly sanguine, seemingly celebratory, view of suicide. There was, to Stoics, an almost redemptive quality to taking one's life. The difference between life and death, they claimed, was insignificant when compared to the difference between virtue and vice. Faced with a situation in which it is impossible to live up to one's ideals, noble suicide is better than dishonourable acquiescence to injustice.

The Roman statesman Cato, famed for his moral integrity, distaste for corruption and immunity to bribes, and an implacable opponent of Julius Caesar, committed suicide after the latter seized power, rather than submit to his unjust rule. According to Plutarch, Cato had supper with friends, engaged in a philosophical discussion, and then retired to his room to read Plato's *Phaedo*, in which Socrates argues that a true philosopher regards all of life as a preparation for death. He called for a sword so that he could be 'master of the course which I decide to take'. He then disembowelled himself. When his 'physician went to him and tried to replace his bowels, which remained uninjured, and to sew up the wound', Cato pushed him away, 'tore his bowels with his hands, rent the wound still more, and so died'.[27]

Cato's distressing death raises a perplexing question. How could Cato be 'master of the course which I decide to take' if fate rules all? If fate does rule all, what is the point in setting an example to others, or in suffering to remain honourable? And since, for the Stoics, the mind, like all of the cosmos, is rigidly determined by inviolable laws, how can our thoughts and feelings (including the decision we take whether or not to be virtuous) be our own, rather than predestined? Caesar was fated to act disreputably, Cato to take his life to defend his honour. In what way, then, could one be said to be better than the other, or either be held responsible for his actions?

These questions return us to the debate about free will and fate that runs back to Homer and beyond and forward to our own age. The Stoic answer was that our actions might be fated, but we still have to assent to our fate. How any individual acts, Chrysippus suggested, is the result not simply of external forces but of his or her internal character too. Suppose you push a cylinder down a hill. It rolls partly because you pushed it, but partly also because of its cylindrical shape. A cube would not have rolled so easily or so far. The nature of an object determines at least partly the actions it is fated to take. So it is with humans. Cato behaved honourably and Caesar disreputably because of their respective natures.

The argument is an important step in the attempt to understand the relationship between fate and free will. The trouble is, there is a hole at the heart of it because it conflates the ideas of responsibility and of agency. Cato and Caesar were responsible for their actions because each responded to circumstances according to their different natures. But those natures were themselves imposed upon them by fate. Through the workings of fate, each was born with particular dispositions, each exposed to particular experiences, and each developed particular personalities. Chrysippus might have explained why even those who lack freedom of will should be held responsible for their actions. But he did not explain what free will meant in a determined world (though for many modern philosophers, as we shall see, to explain why someone should be held responsible for their actions is to explain free will).

Despite this conundrum, Chrysippus' distinction between the two kinds of causes was important for it helped establish better the idea of fate not simply as something external to agents, a force that operates *upon* them, but also as a force that operates *through* agents. When, almost two thousand years later, Marx was to write that 'Men make their own history', but not 'under circumstances of their own choosing, but under circumstances existing already given and transmitted from the past',[28] he was expressing that distinction first drawn by Chrysippus. In Marx's time, the idea of humans 'making history' seemed far more credible than it did in the time of Chrysippus, and so the idea of human agency seemed also more meaningful. For Chrysippus, free will was about accepting with good heart what fate has thrown at you. For Marx it was about challenging such fate. It is, as we shall see, in that historical transformation in human possibilities that free will acquired new meaning.

Perhaps the most important Stoic legacy to the history of moral thought was the concept of universal humanity. In his famous *Elements of Ethics*, the second-century Stoic philosopher Hierocles imagines every individual as standing at the centre of a series of concentric circles. The first circle is the individual, next comes the immediate family, followed by the extended family, the local community, the country, and finally the entire human race. To be virtuous, Hierocles suggested, is to draw these circles together, constantly to transfer people from the outer circles to the inner circles, to treat strangers as cousins and cousins as brothers and sisters, making all human beings part of our concern. The Stoics called this process of drawing the circles together *oikeiosis*, a word that is almost untranslatable but means something like the process by which everything is made into your home.

There were limits, of course, to the Stoics' benevolence. Epictetus might have been a freed slave, but Stoics had little to say about slavery. Stoics certainly thought that slaves should be treated decently, but they did not believe it possible to challenge the actual institution. The slavery that mattered to Stoics was the slavery not of the body but of the soul. Physical slaves, they believed, could transcend their brute bondage, indeed could only do so, by exercising their freedom of spirit.

Nevertheless, in an age in which rights and duties were defined solely in relation to the polis or the state, in which barbarians were regarded as fit for enslavement, and in which Aristotle defended slavery on the grounds that some people were naturally created to be enslaved, there is something hugely impressive about the Stoics' pursuit of *oikeiosis*. 'Never in reply to the question, to what country you belong, say that you are an Athenian or a Corinthian,' Epictetus wrote, 'but that you are a citizen of the world. For why do you say that you are an Athenian, and why do you not say that you belong to the small nook only into which your poor body was cast at birth?' From God, Epictetus continued, 'have descended the seeds not only to my father and grandfather, but to all beings which are generated on the earth'. So why should not every human being 'call himself a citizen of the world?'[29] It is a cosmopolitan vision that would be startling today, let alone two thousand years ago.

CHAPTER FOUR

Heaven and hell

1

Moses is tending his flock on the slopes of Mount Horeb. Suddenly, 'in a flame of fire out of the midst of a bush' appears 'the angel of the Lord'. As Moses turns to see this great sight, God thunders a warning: 'Draw not nigh hither.' Moses 'hid his face; for he was afraid to look upon God'.[1]

I have 'heard the cry of the children of Israel', God tells Moses. The Israelites had been forced by famine to flee to Egypt, where they had been enslaved. Now God has chosen Moses to 'bring forth my people . . . out of Egypt'. 'When I come unto the children of Israel', Moses asks, 'and shall say unto them, The God of your fathers has sent me unto you; and they shall say unto me, What is his name? what shall I say unto them?' And God roars, 'I AM THAT I AM,' adding, 'Thus shalt thou say unto the children of Israel, I AM hath sent me unto you.'[2]

So begins the Biblical story of the Exodus, the tale of how the Children of Israel escaped their enslavement in Egypt and returned home. It is the key story in the Tanakh, or Hebrew Bible, better known to Christians as the Old Testament. It is also a key moment in the transformation of God in the human imagination. Ancient gods, whether Greek or Babylonian or Hindu, were very human. There existed no great chasm between the human realm and the divine realm, nor even between human nature and divine nature. The God of Moses is not remotely human, He insists on humans keeping their distance, quite literally: 'Draw not nigh hither'. Ancient gods were often gruesome and dreadful, but there is a terrifying majesty about the Mosaic God never seen before.

I am 'the God of thy father, the God of Abraham, the God of Isaac, the God of Jacob,' God tells Moses. Abraham (or Abram as he still was) had been an old man of seventy living in Haran, in what is now Turkey, when Yahweh – the Hebrew God whose name translates as 'He Brings Into Existence Whatever Exists' – came to him and told him to travel to Canaan, that strip of land in the Eastern Mediterranean that became the ancient home of the Jews and embraces what is today the state of Israel, the Palestinian Territories and parts of Syria and Jordan. From his grandson Jacob's twelve children descended the twelve tribes of Israel. For all three monotheistic religions – Judaism, Christianity and Islam – Abraham is a crucial figure.

The God of Abraham often appears different to the later God of Moses. Abraham's God appears as a friend, sometimes assuming human form and sharing his food. 'I will make of thee a great nation,' God tells Abraham, 'and I will bless thee'; He will also bless 'them that bless thee, and curse him that curseth thee: and in thee shall all families of the earth be blessed'.[3] This is the covenant that God makes with Abraham. To Moses, too, He makes a promise. He also delivers a warning.

Moses does God's bidding, leading the Israelites out of Egypt and taking them back to Mount Horeb (which we now call Mount Sinai) for a meeting with Yahweh. 'If ye will obey my voice indeed,' God tells the Israelites, 'and keep my covenant, then ye shall be a peculiar treasure unto me above all people.' The Israelites are God's Chosen People. But if they disobey God's commandments, or fail to honour him, they will be punished with ferocious severity for He is 'a *jealous* God, visiting the iniquity of the father upon the children unto the third and fourth *generation* of them that hate me'.[4] Three days after making the covenant, God summons the Israelites back to Mount Sinai, which is covered in fire and smoke. Moses alone is permitted to walk to the summit. There, God bestows His Ten Commandments, which He later inscribes on two tablets of stone that he presents to Moses.

For the Greeks, order and harmony were experienced in the very nature of the universe (*kosmos* meant to the Greeks both the physical universe and a sense of order and harmony). The rules by which humans should live were to be discovered in the order of nature or to be crafted through the activities of Man. They were not so much fixed commands as ways of inculcating wisdom and nurturing good habits. Even Plato, the most rule-bound of the Ancients, viewed morality more as a means of educating the mind than of observing a law. The God of Moses saw it differently. He handed down from on high the laws inscribed in tablets of stone for all to obey. There was no discovery here, nor crafting, simply the Revelation of God's will, the disclosing of truth to, and through, a prophet. With the God of Moses comes both rule-bound morality and the idea of the good as revealed truth.

With the coming of revelatory faith came also the prophetic tradition. Prophets were not new in the ancient world. What was distinctive was the idea of a prophet as an authentic representative of God, an individual whose ethical specialness had led Yahweh to choose him or her to speak on His behalf and to convey His message. Prophecy, the Polish American philosopher Abraham Joshua Heschel has written, 'is the voice that God has lent to the silent agony, a voice to the plundered poor, to the profane riches of the world'. In a prophet lies the 'crossing point of God and man'.[5]

The Talmud suggests that there may have been more than a million prophets through history. Just fifty-five are named in Jewish scriptures, including Abraham, Aaron, Elijah, Isaiah, Sarah and Esther. The greatest of all was Moses. All subsequent prophecy, it was said, was merely an expression of what Moses had already seen. Prophets are a necessity for this world only. In the world to come, all people will be spiritually and ethically perfect, and all will have the gift of prophecy.

2

The 'Children of Israel' who first arrived in Canaan were probably marginalized and dispossessed nomads who had roamed the Fertile Crescent. Each group would have had its own story of where it came from, whom its gods were and what were the rules upon which they insisted. Over time this patchwork of tales became stitched together into a single narrative of common history and shared gods. Central to that common history was the story of Abraham and Moses and their covenants with Yahweh.

What made the new settlers of Canaan different from other nomads was that their stitched-together story came to seal a new kind of relationship with God, with each other and with their past, a relationship that helped them forge a unique identity able to endure a history of invasion, exile and trauma that previously would have erased their existence as a community. The history of the Children of Israel helped forge their identity. That identity helped them survive their history.

The original settlers had arrived in Canaan sometime in the first half of the second millennium BCE. According to traditional myth, the various tribes of Israel were united into a single kingdom by Saul, a charismatic military commander. His successors, David and Solomon, extended the borders of the kingdom and captured for the first time Jerusalem, a city whose very foundations resonate with the myths of so many faiths. Here Solomon built a Temple to house the Ark of the Covenant, the sacred wooden chest that contained the tablets given to Moses by God.

After Solomon's death, the kingdom split into two, with Judah in the south, retaining Jerusalem as its capital, and Israel in the north. Israel was destroyed by the Assyrians in 722 BCE and many of its people killed, assimilated or driven into exile. A century and a half later, in 587 BCE, Judah, too, was overrun, this time by the Babylonians. Solomon's Temple was sacked and many Jews exiled to Babylon, a traumatic event recalled in the haunting Psalm 137:

> By the rivers of Babylon, there we sat down, yea, we wept,
> when we remembered Zion.

The period around the invasion of Judah and the exile to Babylon, a period of great dislocation and uncertainty, was also an age of great intellectual creativity. It was now that the Torah, or Law, was consolidated into scriptures and committed to writing as the Pentateuch, the first part of the Tanakh. The most important fruit of this creativity was Deuteronomy, the fifth of the five books of the Torah. It was a major step in the transformation of Judaism into a religion of the book. Myth transmitted by word of mouth is allusive and elusive. Faith committed to paper is less oblique and ambiguous. In entrusting religious truth to the written word, Deuteronomy helped transform the very character of faith. Mythos gave way to logos, poetry to theology, allegory to orthodoxy.

Half a century after the Babylonians overran Judah, Babylon itself was sacked by the Persians. The Golah, the exiled Jews who now returned home, carried with them nine sacred scrolls. Among these were revisions and rewritings of Genesis, Exodus and Deuteronomy. There were also two new books – Leviticus and Numbers – that came to be incorporated into the Torah. The earliest parts of the Torah were committed to writing at around the same time as the *Iliad* and the *Odyssey*. Like Homer's epics, the Torah came to define the origins, history and identity of a people.

3

Judaism began as a faith like any other in the ancient world. Over the space of a millennium it transformed itself and its God in a way previously unseen. The plurality of gods that inhabited most ancient faiths was erased and replaced with the one God, who demanded absolute obedience on pain of punishment. Other gods were not simply to be foresworn, but to be ferociously suppressed, as were the people who still clung to them. Deuteronomy commands the Israelites to 'utterly destroy' the other nations that inhabit the Promised Land, forbidding them from making a covenant with other tribes or from showing 'mercy unto them'.[6] Such purity of faith was without precedent in the ancient world. The crowded, noisy, disorderly house of gods pictured by the Greeks, the Babylonians, the early Canaanites and most ancient peoples was an essential way of acknowledging the complexity of divinity and of nature. Every god in the pantheon expressed an authentic aspect of reality; and every god in the pantheon gave necessary succour to particular human needs and tasks. In dispensing with all gods but one, the Israelites were placing extraordinary trust in that one God. They were also placing new emphasis on moral activity, for in binding themselves to one God alone, the norms and laws that He laid down now became uniquely important. In return for making the Israelites His

Chosen People, Yahweh demanded total obedience. This again was a new idea to the Ancients, but one that was to influence much modern ethical thinking.

The new God was a transcendental deity, inhabiting a realm distinct and distant from humanity. Ancient gods had always been immanent in nature, and companions in everyday life. Not so Yahweh, who was separate and other. 'For my thoughts are not your thoughts,' the Lord tells the prophet Isaiah, 'neither are your ways my ways.'[7] Judaism provided a template for a new kind of faith, a template from which both Christianity and Islam were later to be constructed. For believers, the new faiths also provided a template for a new kind of ethics. Every Jew, Christian and Muslim believed – and still believes – that the nature of God and of the relationship between Man and God defines the moral rules by which we live. What is striking about the monotheistic religions, though, is that they combine an unyielding attachment to God's word with an immensely flexible understanding of what those words mean.

Deuteronomy is an angry work that insists on the worship of Yahweh, and Yahweh alone, the brutal suppression of those who worship other gods and, indeed, the slaughter of other ethnic groups. The Yahweh that inhabits Leviticus, a book written down during exile in Babylon and in the century that followed the return to Jerusalem, is a more inclusive and compassionate figure. True, many of the rules laid down in Leviticus echo the temper of those of Deuteronomy. If a 'man committeth adultery', it warns, then both 'the adulterer and the adulteress shall surely be put to death'. It threatens that 'if ye walk contrary unto me and will not harken unto me; I will bring seven times more plagues upon you according to your sins'. Yet it expresses also a different moral tone, commanding Israelites that 'thou shalt not avenge, nor bear any grudge against the children of thy people, but thou shalt love thy neighbour as thyself', and beseeching them that 'The stranger that dwelleth with you shall be unto you as one born among you, and thou shalt love him as thyself.'[8]

Deuteronomy and Leviticus both became key works not just of the Jewish scriptures but of the Christian Bible too. The anger and the savagery, and the compassion and the inclusivity, were all woven into Biblical law. At different times, and in the service of different needs, believers listened to different moral imperatives. Christians and Jews have looked to the Bible both to justify slavery and to deem it evil, both to slaughter their enemies and to turn the other cheek, both to condemn gays to death and to ordain them as priests.

The flexibility of religious moral law should not surprise us. Moral codes, whether religious or secular, grow out of social structures and needs. As communities evolve, so do the duties and obligations of their members to each other, and the possibilities, social and moral, that are open to them. The difference between the moral tone of Deuteronomy and that of Leviticus is, in part at least, the difference between the needs of Israelite communities in the eighth century BCE and of those in the sixth century. In the eighth century, there was an intense sense of loss and dislocation, as Israel was destroyed, its people killed, deported or assimilated, and Judah left precariously to stand alone. The stormy, savage feel of Deuteronomy, and its harsh view of other groups and religions, was the consequence. In the sixth century, the experience of exile and return allowed for a calmer view.

There is, in other words, nothing special about religious conceptions of morality. The real innovation of monotheistic religions was to establish not a new set of moral rules but a new reason for abiding by those rules: God tells you. Why should one do as God demands? Not simply because God was all-powerful and all-knowing, but also because God had rescued the Israelites, and made them His Chosen People. The idea of God as an unquestionable moral authority because only through Him could humans be rescued from their own wickedness and weakness marked the distinctiveness of monotheism. God was to be obeyed not simply because of His all-encompassing power but also because of His all-encompassing love for human beings and because of humans' fundamental moral frailty.

All moral codes possess two elements: a set of values to pursue and a reason for pursuing those values; or, to put it another way, they both elucidate the means of being good and demonstrate the end to which the means take us. In ancient Greece, the virtuous life was the means. The end – the reason for submitting to such a life – changed over time. For Homer the prize was honour, for Plato justice, for Aristotle happiness. These shifts, as we have seen, reflected social changes. But however the end was conceived, what made the moral rules acceptable was that most people perceived a relationship between means and end, and embraced the end as a prize worth striving for.

In the Hellenistic period, the relationship between means and ends frayed. As social life became more fragmented, so it became much harder than in the time of Homer or Socrates or Plato or Aristotle to define what should be the moral goals of life and what should be the conduct one must observe to achieve such ends. Stoicism and Epicureanism were attempts to answer this dilemma. Both expressed a kind of escapism from the tribulations of the world, a shift away from the Homeric idea of heroic accomplishments or the Aristotelian emphasis on the excellence of action.

The most enduring answer to the question of morality in an age of social dislocation came, however, through the new monotheistic religions. These drew upon Greek moral ideas, but they developed a novel way of thinking about the relationship between means and ends. The end was God. God also made the rules that one followed to reach the end. Why follow the rules? Because God tells us to and only by following God's commands could humans be rescued. In collapsing moral rules and moral ends, the new faiths provided a reason to be moral at a time of great social trauma, when the disruption of social life often made it difficult to understand the link between rules and ends.

4

In 66 CE Jews took up arms against the Roman occupation of Palestine, a revolt orchestrated by a small sect, the Zealots. For four years the rebels held off the might of Rome. Fearing that the rebellion would spread through the Jewish diaspora, the Roman authorities decided to crush it with the utmost ferocity. In 70 Titus, son of Emperor Vespasian, finally recaptured Jerusalem. At the heart of the battle was a struggle for the great Temple that had been built over the ruins of Solomon's Temple, razed to the ground by the Babylonians. The new Temple, too, was destroyed in the Roman assault and most of the 6,000 Zealots who had barricaded themselves into its inner courtyards perished in the flames. It was never restored.

The destruction of the Temple was not simply a physical loss. It was also a catastrophe that came fundamentally to shape the very character of Judaism. It also helped create the identity of a new faith – Christianity.

The Second Temple, like Solomon's first, had become the physical embodiment of God's covenant with His people. Not just pillars and altars but teaching and scholarship, too, had perished in the embers. The new spiritual leadership of the community produced hundreds of commentaries on the Tanakh, established new regulations rooted in Mosaic law, stiffened the canon of authentic Judaic works, redrew the boundaries of everyday spiritual life and created a far more circumscribed sense of what it was to be Jewish.

In helping define Judaism in a more exclusive way, the destruction of the Temple also helped define Christianity. Until then, the so-called 'Jesus movement' had simply been another Jewish sect that had observed the Torah, regarded itself as the guardian of the true Israel, and whose aim was not to establish a new faith but to guide Judaism back to its destined path. It was in the sorrow that followed the destruction of the Temple that Christian ideas were first formally set down. Matthew, Luke, Mark and John wrote their Gospels in the last four decades of the first century. The letters of St Paul, written earlier in the '50s, an attempt to explain to followers traumatized by the crucifixion the meaning of Jesus' ministry and of his divinity, found new resonance after the destruction of the Temple. In these works, which form the heart of the New Testament, the first Christian thinkers grapple with the question of how people should live, and why they should so live. Christian ethics were drawn from Judaism and from pagan sources, especially Stoicism. But those ethics became embedded in a new theology, a distinct explanation of why Jesus taught what he taught and why his followers should live as he commanded.

5

He was born in Bethlehem, to Joseph, a carpenter, and Mary, both of whom lived in Nazareth but had travelled to the city of their ancestors to take part in a Roman census. He grew up a highly charismatic, deeply devout man, whose teaching was grounded in the belief that the Kingdom of God was imminent. He chose twelve special companions as his disciples, all Jews from Galilee, who shared their lives, their possessions and a burning desire to spread the word of God. His highly moral teaching, rooted in the Jewish scriptures, and the miracles he performed, attracted a passionate band of followers.

His death came in Jerusalem. He and his followers had travelled there to celebrate Passover. Inflamed by his claim to be the Son of God, and by the adoration of the crowds that acclaimed him as the Messiah, Jewish leaders had him arrested. He was betrayed to the Temple guards by one of his own Apostles, Judas. He was put on trial, accused of blasphemy and sedition, handed over to the Roman prefect of Judea, Pontius Pilate, and eventually sentenced to be crucified, the standard Roman way of executing common criminals. He was stripped, flogged, mocked, crowned with thorns, and crucified between two thieves, executed, it said on his cross, for aspiring to be the King of the Jews. 'My God, my God, why hast thou forsaken me?' he cried, reciting Psalm 22. Three days after his agonizing death, he rose again, leaving an open and empty tomb, and ascended to heaven.

Or so the story goes. The trouble is that Jesus, like Socrates, wrote nothing. Most of his followers were illiterate and there exists no eyewitness account of his life or ministry.[9] Virtually all that we know about him and his beliefs comes from the Gospels and the letters of St Paul. How many of the stories in these accounts are true has been a matter of debate for two millennia. Modern scholars dispute even whether Jesus was born in Bethlehem, and there is no certainty as to what charges were levelled against him at his trial and who was responsible for sentencing him to death.

There were originally around twenty Gospels, accounts of the life and ministry of Jesus designed to transmit both his memory and his teaching. Four eventually became part of the official Christian canon. Matthew, Luke, Mark and John were all educated Greek-speaking Hellenized Jews, outsiders to Judea.

Mark's was the earliest of the canonical Gospels, written perhaps during the years of the Jewish rebellion. It is Matthew, however, who opens the New Testament. Thought to have come from a community in the Hellenic city of Antioch, Matthew is much more wedded to Jewish tradition and scripture. His is an account of the life of Jesus that acts as a bridge from the Jewish Old to the Christian New Testament.

Matthew's Gospel is also the one that most makes the ethical case for Jesus' divinity. Here we find the celebrated Sermon on the Mount, in which many of Jesus' sayings are pulled together into a single address to create perhaps the most powerful expression of Christian ethics. The Sermon opens with the Beatitudes, blessings that Jesus confers on the poor, the meek and the righteous. The Beatitudes describe the moral qualities required of Christian believers to enter the Kingdom of God. Jesus insists it was not sufficient simply to observe the letter of the Torah. One had to be guided by the spirit of God's law. 'Ye have heard that it was said by them of old time, Thou shalt not kill,' Jesus tells his flock, 'But I say unto you, That whosoever is angry with his brother without a cause shall be in danger of the judgment'. While Exodus, Leviticus and Deuteronomy all talk of 'an eye for an eye, and a tooth for a tooth', Jesus is adamant that 'ye resist not evil: but whoever shall smite thee on thy right cheek, turn to him the other also'.[10] We are witness here to a Christian version of virtue ethics, a belief in the importance not just of performing good acts but of being a good person. It is an ethics that emerges, however, less through reasoning about the good life than by unconditionally embracing God's love.

Virtue, Jesus insisted, is a good in itself. Those who pray, fast or give alms so that they could be seen to do so show no righteousness and will not be rewarded for their ostentatiousness. He warns, too, against coveting material wealth, for 'No man can serve two masters'. All have to choose between 'God and mammon'. He concludes with the famous 'Golden rule': 'whatsoever ye would that men should do to you, do ye even so to them'. Or as we would say these days, 'Do unto others as you would have others do unto you.' This, he insists, is the essence of 'the law and the prophets'.[11]

There is, in truth, little new in the Sermon. The extensions of the Mosaic law upon which Jesus insisted were already part of the Jewish tradition, in the teachings of prophets such as Isaiah and Jeremiah. So was the aversion to the hoarding of wealth. The Golden Rule has a long history, an idea hinted at in Babylonian and Egyptian religious codes, before fully flowering in Greek and Judaic writing, and independently in Buddhism and Confucianism too. The insistence on virtue as a good in itself, the resolve to turn the other cheek, the call to look inwards, the claim that correct belief is at least as important as virtuous action – all were important Stoic themes.

Jesus preached in the belief that the end of the world was nigh and that God's Kingdom was imminent. His morality was a morality to prepare people for this coming transformation. An ethics for the end of the world, the Sermon on the Mount can seem both compliantly passive and defiantly subversive. Nietzsche famously described the idea that the meek shall inherit the earth as expressing the slave mentality of Christianity. For Jesus, however, and for his first followers, what mattered was not striving to transform this world but rather to repent one's sins to ensure entrance to the next. It is this indifference to this-worldly struggles that can often give Jesus' words an air of submissive acquiescence. But that very indifference to worldly needs also allowed the Sermon on the Mount to confront conventional morality, to challenge the claims of the rich and the powerful and to turn upon its head traditional notions of the good and the righteous. Jesus reveals salvation, as the Marxist critic and occasional atheist Terry Eagleton observes, to be a matter not 'of cult, law and ritual', but of 'feeding the hungry, welcoming the immigrants, visiting the sick, and protecting the poor, orphaned and widowed from the violence of the rich'.[12]

Over the past two millennia Christians have read the Sermon on the Mount in both these ways, both as an ethics of conformity and as a challenge to the social order. The early Jesus followers fully expected to see Christ return to Earth in their lifetimes. The decades passed and no Kingdom came. Christians eventually had to take a set of ethics crafted for the end of the world and transform it into one applicable for societies still stuck in history. This only deepened disagreements about how to read Jesus' words. God's word it may have been, but that word had to be read, interpreted and translated into deeds by mere mortals. The moral compass may have, in Christian eyes, derived from God, but it was humans who had to decide which way lay moral North.

6

The 'one thing we must not say', the twentieth-century Christian writer C.S. Lewis insisted, is that 'I'm ready to accept Jesus as a great moral teacher, but I don't accept His claim to be God.' Many non-believers are happy to honour Jesus as an ethical teacher. For most Christians, however, it is simply not possible to accept Jesus' teachings without acknowledging his divinity. 'A man who was merely a man and said the sort of things that Jesus said', Lewis wrote, 'would not be a great moral teacher. He would either be a lunatic . . . or else he would be the Devil.'[13]

Lewis was making here not simply a claim about the nature of Christ. He was making also a claim about human nature. Just as the ability to walk on water makes sense only when set against the laws of physics, so the divinity of Christ makes sense only when set against the moral helplessness of Man. For Aristotle, humans were capable both of establishing what constituted the good and of working their way towards it. For Plato, the Good was defined by a transcendental Form in a different realm. Humans, or at least some humans, were capable of apprehending that Good and of attempting to create the good life on Earth. For Christians, only through the grace of God could humans be moral. 'For by grace are ye saved through faith; and that not of yourselves,' wrote St Paul in his Letter to the Ephesians; 'it is the gift of God.'[14] It is in the letters of Paul that we find the beginnings of Christian theology and the attempt to remake our understanding of ethics.

Born Saul, Paul was a Pharisee, a diasporan Jew from the Cilician city of Tarsus. Originally hostile to Jesus' followers, he had travelled to Jerusalem to witness the stoning to death of Stephen, the first Christian martyr after Christ's crucifixion. On the road from Jerusalem to Damascus, 'suddenly there shined round about him a light from heaven: And he fell to the earth, and heard a voice say unto him, Saul, Saul why persecutest thou me?'[15] The voice was that of Jesus. Struck dumb for three days by his vision, Saul changed his name and transformed his faith and began a lifetime of evangelism for his new Lord, helping plant churches throughout the Hellenistic world. Paul wrote many letters to the Christian communities that he had created, counsel-ling them, cajoling them, answering their doubts and fears, and in the process clarifying the theological meaning of Jesus' life.

As a believer in the imminence of the Second Coming, Paul could never have imagined that those letters would survive. But survive they did, and were eventually collected together in the New Testament as the Epistles (though only seven of the fourteen Epistles are thought definitely to be in Paul's hand). In these letters Paul comforted Christian communities while wrestling with his own considerable demons. One cannot read them without being struck by the sense of sheer terror that Paul must have felt at the thought of not doing right by God. The passionate and often tortured eloquence of these letters has echoed through the ages, so much so that Paul, rather than Jesus, has often been seen as the real founder of Christianity.

Paul had not known Jesus, and there is little mention in his letters of Jesus' teaching or of his earthly life. Paul's Christ has relevance primarily through his death and resurrection. The Jesus movement had felt humiliated by the betrayal, torture and execution of Christ. How could a Messiah whom they believed would deliver the Kingdom of God have been left to die as a common criminal, nailed to a cross and in bestial pain? It was Paul who began to sketch an answer. The very nature of Jesus' death, Paul argued, revealed the essential goodness of God. Jesus had been willing to die in such an unspeakable fashion to atone for human sins, revealing an unconditional love for humankind. In the past, the blood of bulls and calves sacrificed in the Temple had served to 'purify the flesh'. The blood of Christ on the cross was far more powerful, the ultimate sacrifice to 'purge your conscience from dead works to serve the living God' and obtain 'eternal redemption for us'.[16] For Paul, the death and resurrection of Christ had brought forth a new era for humankind in which all who had faith in Jesus would enter God's Kingdom. Faith, a blind trust in God's goodness and in the redemptive power of Christ, trumped both Law and reason.

In reworking the meaning of crucifixion, Paul transformed a scandalous embarrassment into the defining symbol of Christian faith. But the obsession with the battered and bloody body of Christ created also a morbid attachment to the righteousness of pain, and a terror of the flesh and of worldly pleasures. 'I rejoice in my sufferings for you,' Paul told the Colossians, wishing to endure 'the afflictions of Christ in my flesh for his body's sake'. He fulminated against 'vile affections', raging against those who celebrated 'uncleanness through the lusts of their own hearts, to dishonour their own bodies between themselves'.[17] Flesh was for Paul, and for many Christians who followed, a symbol of fundamental human weakness, of the moral imperfection that defined the human condition.

Why are humans so frail? This question perplexed Christians in the centuries after Christ's death and led to widespread debate. Eventually, by the fifth century, the Church settled on an answer that was radically different from that of the Greeks and of the Jews. Christians came to believe that humans were weak and lost souls because of Original Sin. All humans are fallen because of Adam and Eve's transgression in the Garden of Eden in eating of the Tree of Knowledge of Good and Evil, having been forbidden to do so by God. 'The overwhelming misery which oppresses men and their inclination towards evil and death', as the Catechism of the Catholic Church puts it, 'cannot be understood apart from their connection with Adam's sin and the fact that he has transmitted to us a sin with which we are all born afflicted.'[18]

There were hints of the consequences of Adam's disobedience in many early Christian works, including in Paul's letters. It was St Augustine, however, who most developed the concept and ensured its central place in Christian thought. Augustine was perhaps the most important bridge between the classical world and the world of medieval Europe – the last classical philosopher and the first medieval thinker as he has aptly been called – and one whose in-between role has made him a truly contradictory personality. He was a key figure in the fusing of Christianity and Greek philosophy. Yet he learnt Greek only late in life, had slight interest in Greek literature, and read little of Plato or Aristotle in their own words. He was a deeply intellectual man who came to see uninhibited curiosity as a great evil. He was a man of extreme passions, and of acute self-awareness, whose *Confessions*, infused as it is with an almost existentialist sensibility, gave birth to a new form of introspective, self-confrontational, autobiographical writing. But he became highly suspicious of the passions, viewing desire and lust as undermining will and corrupting the soul. He was an intensely moral man, but one who portrayed himself in later life as having been in his youth debauched and immoral, a self-perception that seems shaped more by guilt than by reality, and whose lasting legacy is a view of not just himself but of humanity as being inherently sinful and depraved.

7

Augustine was born in 354 in the North African town of Thagaste, in what is now Tunisia, and which then lay inside the Roman Empire. Augustine's father Patricius was a pagan, his mother Monnica a pious Christian with whom he had an intense and often conflictual relationship that helped shape the way he thought about God. Pursuing a promising intellectual career, Augustine became a teacher of rhetoric, first in Carthage, and then in Rome, before taking up a post as an imperial orator in Milan. Increasingly he felt himself tormented by emotional doubt, a torment driven by a desire to make sense of good and evil, and leading to an ever more desperate search for a safe spiritual harbour.

While still in North Africa, he was drawn towards Manichaeism, a dualistic philosophy first taught by the third-century Persian prophet Mani that saw the world as trapped in an eternal struggle between good and evil. All matter was intrinsically evil, while good was embodied in spirit. The human body, like all matter, was evil, and had been deliberately designed by the forces of darkness as the mechanism for imprisoning the soul. Augustine became unhappy with the idea, implicit in the philosophy, that the forces of good could be defeated by the battalions of evil. What he ached for above all was an unassailable notion of the Good. This yearning led him to Platonism, or rather to Neoplatonism, a spiritualized, mystical form of Plato's cosmology whose most influential proponent was the Egyptian-born, Greek-speaking philosopher Plotinus (204–70). Plotinus taught that there exists a supreme, transcendent 'One' that is above all material being, contains no division or distinction, is self-caused and is absolutely good. The One did not create the cosmos through thought or action (for it is beyond either), but through a series of 'emanations' that originate in the One, but are not actively caused or willed by it. Plotinus uses the analogy of reflections in a mirror that create something new without diminishing or altering the object being reflected. Plotinus crafted also an ethics that, though distinctive, again drew upon important Greek themes. Evil, Plotinus believed, was associated with matter. Human beings, because of their bodily attachment, were open to being evil. Human flourishing required the separation of the soul from its bodily impediment, a separation that is managed through the virtues. Happiness for Plotinus is 'a flight from this world's ways and things'. The 'perfect life' is one in which the disembodied soul lives a life of contemplation.[19]

Augustine found in Plotinus a description of an eternal, unassailable, transcendental reality, the source of creation, of goodness and of happiness, an explanation of evil rooted in a contempt for the material world, and an other-worldly view of morality whose significance could be grasped only by letting go of attachments to sensual pleasures. These were all themes that would resonate down the centuries with Christian theologians, for whom Plato, imagined through the spiritual lens of Plotinus, provided an indispensable intellectual foundation. Augustine also found a void in Plotinus, for his was a transcendental reality to be grasped by reason, not faith. It was faith, not reason, for which Augustine yearned, a faith that could fulfil his need for moral certainties and emotional security.

So it was that Augustine came full circle and discovered those certainties and that security in his mother's faith that he had once rejected as intellectually unappealing. His conversion was sudden and dramatic. He was in a garden in Milan, apparently suffering an emotional breakdown, when he heard the voice of a child from a neighbouring house 'chanting, and oft repeating, "Pick up and read, pick up and read."' Taking this to be a 'divine command', Augustine picked up a copy of Paul's Epistles lying nearby and, opening it at random, found himself confronted by a line from the Letter to the Romans:

> Not in riots and drunken parties, not in eroticism and indecencies, not in strife and rivalry, but put on the Lord Jesus Christ, and make no provision for the flesh in its lusts.

'With the last words of this sentence', Augustine recalls, 'it was as if a light of relief from all anxiety flooded into my heart. All the shadows of doubt were dispelled.'[20]

Augustine's experience of his own conversion to Christianity, his sense of being overwhelmed by an abundance of grace from God that washed away his old sinful, egotistical self, liberated him from his torment and despair, and made anew his soul and his faith, indelibly shaped his sense of Christianity and framed his theology. What he saw as the drama of his own life – that of a weak-souled, morally blind, emotionally wretched man being saved by the unconditional goodness of God – was also the drama that was being played out on the cosmic stage. As with the man, so with mankind. Through Augustine this desolate vision of human nature came to shape Christianity itself.

God's most important gift, Augustine insisted, was His love. That love had a darker side too. The immensity of God's grace had to be set against the wretchedness of human beings. Love of God required humans to deny their love of self and of flesh. But they had only become so besotted with self and flesh because they had rebelled against God. In that rebellion the God of love seems, in Augustine's eyes, to have become transmuted into a brutal, even sadistic, figure. He sees God as full of 'chastisement', always 'mercifully punishing me, touching with a bitter taste all my illicit pleasures'. 'You fashion pain to be a lesson,' Augustine writes, 'you strike to heal, you bring death upon us so that we should not die apart from you.'[21] This was not a Platonic God but the God of the Old Testament.

God, Augustine insisted, endowed humans with self-awareness, understanding and free will. But freedom and will had been fatally compromised by Adam's sinfulness in the Garden of Eden. The only act of true free will had been his decision to eat of the forbidden fruit. Once Adam had taken that first bite, humanity was lost. 'Human nature was certainly originally created blameless and without any fault,' Augustine wrote, 'but the human nature by which each one of us is now born of Adam requires a physician, because it is not healthy.'[22]

Displaying the deep-seated terror of pleasures of the flesh that he had discovered in Manichaeism, and that had already become woven into the Christian tradition, Augustine believed that Original Sin was passed down the generations through the very act of sexual intercourse. Jesus alone is without sin because 'the Virgin conceived without this concupiscence', an

Augustinian word for what he saw as a whirlpool of desire, lust, greed and coveting that was bound to the physical act of sex. Every human who 'comes into being by natural birth is bound by original sin', their soul degraded, their moral faculties befuddled, and their will to do good corrupted, the result of 'lust's darkness'.[23]

Original Sin made it impossible for humans to do good on their own account, because it degraded both their moral capacity and their willpower. Only through God's grace could humans achieve salvation. So enslaved is every human to the service of sin that without God's grace he lacks the will even to choose to accept salvation. There is perhaps no philosopher who has written more joyously of the love of God and of its liberating presence. And there is perhaps no theologian who has portrayed more bleakly his contempt for the human condition and the wretchedness he felt at being human.

Not all Christians were willing to accept this desolate, guilt-ridden view of human nature. A major theological debate erupted in the fifth century when a Welsh monk, Pelagius, challenged Augustine's vision. Pelagius argued that it was possible for humans to achieve salvation independently of God's grace through the power of reason and the exercise of free will, though he accepted that God's grace assisted every good work. The relationship between humanity and God was like the relationship between a mariner and the wind. A sailor can set off on his own accord, but the wind helps him reach his destination. Adam's sin was to set a bad example for his progeny, but that progeny did not inherit an indelible moral stain. What, Pelagius wanted to know, was the point of God giving the Ten Commandments, or of Jesus teaching his Sermon on the Mount, if humans are so full of sin that they could not choose to follow the strictures? It is the responsibility of human beings to follow the Gospels, and to suggest that 'the frailty of our own nature' makes us incapable of doing so is 'to indulge in pointless evasions'.[24]

At the heart of the debate between Pelagius and Augustine was the question of whether humans are to be defined by depravity and sinfulness or by reason and the capacity for good. Are humans moral agents? Or are we so crippled by sin that it is impossible for us to have a clear idea of right and wrong? Pelagius belonged to an ethical tradition that drew upon both Greek and Jewish concepts of morality and human nature. Augustine, too, wanted to draw upon the authority of Greek philosophers, Plato in particular, but he reworked Greek themes for a much darker, more pessimistic view of the human condition.

Augustine won the dispute. Pelagius, and those who supported him, were declared heretics and banished from Rome. In the struggle between Augustine and Pelagius we can see two threads of Christian thought, two contradictory views of God, salvation and human nature that Christianity has never truly resolved. On the one hand an embrace of a loving God, on the other a sense of terror at God's wrath and vengeance; on the one hand an understanding of humans as moral agents possessed of free will and capable of good works, on the other a condemnation of humans as corrupted sinners, incapable without God's grace of telling right from wrong or acting upon it; on the one hand a belief in the Law as God's gift to humankind that called forth the moral responsibility without which believers could not enter the Kingdom of God, on the other an insistence that not through adherence to the Law but only through faith in Jesus Christ could salvation be realized.

Early Christianity found its spiritual energy in the tension between Law and grace, free will and sin. Augustine's victory over Pelagius shifted the balance and transformed the very character of Christian ethical discussion. Pelagius had wondered what was the purpose of the Ten Commandments, or of the Sermon on the Mount, if humans were incapable of exercising their moral will. That question could be asked another way. If humans are made moral solely by God's grace, why talk of ethics at all? As the theologian Stephen Long wryly puts it in the opening sentence of his *Very Short Introduction to Christian Ethics*, 'To bring the terms "Christian" and "ethics" together and treat them as referring to a common subject might strike persons of faith or those without it as odd, perhaps even as a contradiction.'[25]

8

Early Christian circles were small, diverse and isolated. Christians faced great hostility from the communities in which they were embedded. They placed upon themselves immense moral demands and yet in their isolation often lacked the cultural and emotional resources necessary to meet them.

There developed within Christian communities a yearning for a common identity and a hunger for defined spiritual boundaries. Jews, as scattered as Christians, and often as persecuted, found an inner strength in a collective identity bound together by an extraordinary history, a distinctive tradition, a special language, exclusive rituals and a unique book, the Torah. Christians possessed none of these. Over time, a set of symbols, the cross in particular, and a collection of rituals, such as baptism and the Eucharist, emerged. What truly gave the new faith its common voice, however, was the creation of a framework of authority, an authority invested in both a canon of sacred texts and in a powerful institutional structure.

As the dozens of stories about Jesus and the Apostles were sifted down to the handful chosen to define the Christian faith in the New Testament, so in these texts became frozen the essence of Christian truth and out of them emerged the doctrines of Christian faith. The idea of a revealed truth fixed for all time was startlingly different to the ways in which Greeks, and even Israelites, had allowed their myths and stories to emerge, to flex and to change, and the ways in which they had discovered truths within them. A myth was like an improvised score flowing to the rhythms of history, and bar by bar its meaning could change over time. The New Testament spoke to the desire for a more definitive meaning, for a tune that remained the same in every congregation and in every age.

As the canon emerged, so did the structures of institutional authority in which was vested the right absolutely to interpret scriptures and develop doctrines. The Church was built around bishops, religious leaders with wide authority elected for life, a kind of authority for which there had been no precedent in the pagan world. By the second century the Church claimed that the first bishops had been appointed by the Apostles, and it was from the Apostles that all subsequent bishops took their warrant, giving them an awesome power over their congregations.

The combination of fractured communities and a deep desire for scriptural authority gave rise to a characteristic feature of Christianity: the ferocious doctrinal disputes that often rent the faith, and the denunciation of opponents as 'heretics' whose heresy often had to be expunged not simply through excommunication, but sometimes through torture and death. Increasingly, too, there was an insistence on placing faith above reason. 'Let us Christians prefer the simplicity of our faith, which is the stronger, to the demonstrations of human reason,' wrote Basil of Caesarea, an influential fourth-century theologian and monastic. 'For to spend much time on research about the essence of things would not serve the edification of the church.' Theologians did not reject reason as such. Rather, they insisted that reason had to be subordinate to faith. 'Unless you believe, you will not understand', as Augustine put it, borrowing a phrase from Isaiah. Reason was not only subordinate to faith, it was, as in many classical cultures, seen also as exclusive to the elite, who alone could be entrusted with it. For the masses, faith was the cement of obedience. Faith, wrote Origen (185–245), perhaps the first great Christian theologian, is 'useful for the multitude', a means of teaching 'those who cannot abandon everything and pursue a study of rational argument to believe without thinking out their reasons'.[26] Faith, in other words, no longer meant a state of surrender or openness to Revelation but rather an absolute trust in the Church hierarchy, which alone possessed the reason to discern God's meaning. Faith had become the means of enforcing authority.

By the time that Augustine and Pelagius were locked in doctrinal combat over sin and salvation, Christianity had moved from being a fringe, persecuted faith to being one of power and authority, the official religion of the Roman Empire. The key moment was Emperor Constantine's Edict of Milan in 313 legalizing Christian worship. Constantine did more than end persecution. He converted to Christianity and became a patron for the faith, supporting it financially, promoting Christians to high office, and building an extraordinary number of basilicas. When between 324 and 330 Constantine transformed Byzantium, an ancient Greek town on the Bosphorus, into his new imperial capital, Constantinople, he turned it into a Christian city, building churches within the city walls but no pagan temples. The edict of Thessalonica in 380 made Christianity the official state religion of the Roman Empire.

The now-powerful Church had as much need for authority as did the earlier marginalized one, though for different reasons; no longer to gather together the persecuted fragments of the house of God, but to ensure that no one broke the unity of the Church that had been established. As Christians found a new home in the upper reaches of the Roman Empire, so the Church became an instrument for the imposition not just of religious but of temporal power too. Politics, as well as theology, had driven Constantine into Christ's embrace. In a rapidly fragmenting empire, the ability of Christians to hold together, despite the greatest of threats, and create a common identity was an immense political resource that Constantine wished to tap. The great gifts that Christianity offered to the imperium, Constantine recognized, were the symbols and rituals of unity and of common belonging. Constantine recognized, too, that Christianity was for the Roman Empire a double-edged sword. It might help bind together a vast empire comprising peoples of different cultures and religions. But each ecclesiastical struggle within the faith could easily transform itself into a political struggle within the empire, creating the very disorder that Constantine had embraced Christianity in order to dampen. The commingling of Church and State ensured that Christian doctrines became crucially important not just to the religious authorities but to the temporal powers too. It was Constantine who in 325 convoked the famous first ecumenical council in Nicea, at which Jesus was acknowledged as both fully God and fully human and the doctrine of the Trinity – God as Father, the Son and the Holy Spirit – affirmed. Critics of the so-called 'Nicene creed' were denounced as heretics and many were exiled.

The temporal needs of the Roman Empire shaped also the debate between Pelagius and Augustine. Pelagius argued for individual conscience and moral perfection. He insisted that as humans possessed unrestrained free will, so they had an obligation to strive for moral purity. It was, in many ways, an echo of Jesus' argument in the Sermon on the Mount, and like Jesus Pelagius was an ascetic, critical of wealth, corruption and injustice, a man who saw himself as speaking for the poor and the dispossessed, demanding social change and spiritual renewal. Little wonder that the imperial elite was unnerved by Pelagius and his disruptive theology.

Augustine, while also drawn to asceticism, had developed a theology of authority and order. 'It is in the natural order of things', he preached, 'that women should serve men, and children their parents, because this is just in itself, that the weaker reason should serve the stronger.' As with family, so with society. It was given by nature for the lower orders to serve the upper orders, and for all to serve the emperor. Slavery, too, was 'ordained as a punishment by that law which enjoins the preservation of the order of nature, and forbids its disturbance'.[27]

War, repression and the torture even of innocent men[28] were all acceptable to compel obedience and to secure order. But while the rulers of a society could take punitive action to defend social peace, individuals had no such right. In Augustine, the theologian John Rist observes, 'the powers of ordinary citizens are almost non-existent'. Plato and Aristotle, Rist adds, who themselves worried about the mob and feared for social peace, nevertheless 'would have shuddered at such an empty concept of citizenship'.[29]

For Pelagius and Augustine, social views and theological doctrines were closely enmeshed, but in contrasting fashion. In Pelagius' eyes, the existence of free will made social renewal an imperative. Augustine saw free will as crippled by sin, and so insisted that humans had to follow authority, whether that of God, bishops or the emperor. Augustine wrote to Innocent, the Bishop of Rome, demanding that he condemn Pelagius, pointing out that too great a stress on free will would inevitably undermine the authority of the bishops. Emperor Honorius, too, did not take much persuasion that Pelagian ideas did not bode well for imperial stability and his own supremacy. He ordered Pelagius and his followers to leave Rome.

In the space of four centuries, Christianity had transformed itself from a faith for the dispossessed to a 'religion fit for gentlemen', as the historian Diarmaid MacCulloch has aptly described the imperial Church. Jesus insisted that 'it is easier for a camel to go through the eye of a needle than for a rich man to enter into the kingdom of God'. Augustine suggested that 'the poor could act as heavenly porters to the wealthy, using their gratitude to carry spiritual riches for their benefactors into the next life'.[30]

'If God does not exist, everything is permitted.' Dostoevsky never actually wrote that line, though so often is the phrase attributed to him that he may as well have. It has become the almost reflexive response of believers when faced with an argument for a godless world. One of the great selling powers of monotheistic religions throughout their history has been their importance as a bedrock of moral values. Without religious faith, runs the argument, we cannot anchor our moral truths or truly know right from wrong. Without belief in God we will be lost in a miasma of moral nihilism. Yet the transformation in the first four centuries not just in the fortunes of Christianity but also in the ethical ideas that animated it reveals the flexibility of religious precepts. Believers may see religious ethics as absolute. They have to, in order to believe. But God Himself appears to be highly pragmatic. The absoluteness of religious precepts can seem unforgiving, less so the precepts themselves. The success of religious morality derives from its ability to cut its beliefs according to social needs while at the same time insisting that such beliefs are sacred because they are God-given.

CHAPTER FIVE

Nirvana

1

It is an epic struggle, one that transforms history and nearly destroys the world. On one side are the Pandavas, the five sons of King Pandu, on the other, the Kauravas, the hundred sons of Pandu's brother, the blind King Dhritarashtra. The cousins become bitter rivals in the struggle to inherit the ancestral kingdom of Bharata on the Ganga river in northern India.

The rivalry culminates in an apocalyptic battle on the vast field of Kurukshetra. Armies from all over India arrive to do combat, kings and chiefs allying themselves with one side or the other. After eighteen days of fighting, just twelve warriors are left standing. All the Kauravan brothers perish; the five Pandavas survive.

Yudhishtira, the eldest of the Pandavan brothers and their leader, is crowned king. The emptiness of the world that they have won will, however, colour the rest of the brothers' lives. Yudhishtira eventually gives up the throne and, with the other Pandavas, embarks on a spiritual quest. All come to perish on that final journey.

The *Mahabharata*, the story of the Kauravas and the Pandavas and their deadly rivalry, takes its place among the celebrated epics of world literature. It is one of the two great Sanskrit narrative poems of ancient India (the other being the *Ramayana*) and a foundation stone of Hinduism. A monumental work, comprising some 106,000 couplets, the *Mahabharata* weighs in at around eight times the size of the *Iliad* and the *Odyssey* combined, three times that of the Bible. It is not simply a story, but a theology, a philosophy and, for believers, a form of history. Within it is much of the lore of the classical Hindu tradition – myths and legends, the great creation stories and the codes of moral law, including the immensely important *Bhagavad Gita*.[1]

According to myth, and to the *Mahabharata* itself, the epic was written by the sage Vyasa, who also appears in the story as the grandfather of both the Kauravas and the Pandavas. Like all ancient epics the stories within the *Mahabharata* undoubtedly emerged out of oral lore, countless tales told and retold by poets, sages and priests, the earliest layers possibly more ancient than the earliest stories of Abraham and of Moses. It was eventually committed to paper, probably over the space of many centuries on either side of Christ's birth.

On one reading, the *Mahabharata* is the story of the battle between good and evil, and of the vanquishing of the demonic by the divine. The Pandavas were fathered not by Pandu but by gods. Gods assisted the Pandavas throughout the struggle, most importantly the supreme god Vishnu who had descended to Earth in the human form of Krishna to rescue *dharma*, a concept that embodies the notion both of natural law and of those righteous behaviours considered necessary for the maintenance of the natural order of things. The Kauravas, on the other hand, were fathered by demons and had initially won the kingdom through deceit, ensnaring Yudhishtira into a loaded game of dice, during the course of which he loses not just his palaces, lands and servants, but himself, too, and his brothers and Draupadi, the wife shared by all the Pandavas. Yet, in telling this story of good and evil, the *Mahabharata* subverts those very ideas. Victory was necessary to maintain the integrity of the divine order, to protect *dharma*. But the war itself, and the character of the victory, corrupted that order, disrupting the moral code that gave harmony to the cosmos.

The Kauravas' four commanders had once been as fathers and brothers to the Pandavas. Nevertheless all had to be slain, but none could be killed except through immoral means. It was the deceit and treachery of the Kauravas that led to the war. But the war was won largely because of the deceit and treachery of the Pandavas and of Krishna.

After eighteen days of war, the world had irrevocably changed. The apocalypse on the field of Kurukshetra caused a faultline in time. The *Dvapara Yuga* – the age of heroes and of heroic values, an age in which people understood their tasks in life and remained faithful to the principles of their castes – gave way to the *Kali Yuga*, the last age of the world in which values erode, Law fragments and evil gains sway.

If in myth the world had transformed, so too in history. How much of the action described in the *Mahabharata* was based on historical events, and when these events occurred, is still a matter of considerable controversy. Most scholars believe that the dynastic struggle and the great war are based on events that took place between 1200 and 800 BCE. The *Mahabharata* is rooted in a history not too distant in time from the Trojan War or the forging of the kingdom of Israel from the various Hebrew tribes in Canaan. It solidified into a written narrative sometime between the creation of the *Oresteia* and the transformation of the Bible into a canonical text. The Greek tragedies were an attempt to understand human conduct after the breakdown of heroic society and the rise of Athenian democracy. The stories of the Bible, written and rewritten over the space of almost a millennium, attempted similarly to make sense of righteousness and moral order in a time of great social dislocation. The stories of the *Mahabharata* may appear to be intoxicated with the spirit of the heroic age, stories more akin to the epic yarns of the *Iliad* and the *Odyssey*, or to the terrifying tales of El and Baal and other ancient gods, than to the more sceptical, questioning works of Sophocles and Euripides or the more philosophical counsel of the Biblical books of Wisdom. And yet, despite its heroic form, the *Mahabharata* was a product of the breakdown of that age, and the ethical predicaments posed by the erosion of traditional heroic social relations. Indeed, many of the moral quandaries at the heart of the *Mahabharata* echo those to be found in the *Oresteia* or the Book of Job. What is it to be good? Why do the righteous suffer? Is it possible to evade fate?

2

Hinduism is not a single religion, but a term for a variety of different religious traditions native to India. It appears in such a bewildering array of shapes and forms and is understood by its own adherents in such a multitude of ways that defining it is almost impossible. Hindus themselves see their faith not as a faith but as *sanãtana dharma*, or eternal law, universally binding precepts defined by every individual's standing in society. Within the framework of the *sanãtana dharma* flourish a multitude of religious communities, each with its own beliefs, rituals and ways of living.

The oldest of the Hindu scriptures, the *Vedas*, came originally with the Sanskrit-speaking Aryans, a loose-knit network of tribes that lived on the Caucasian steppes. Around the middle of the second millennium BCE, some Aryan tribes migrated south and east, through the mountains of Afghanistan and the Hindu Kush, settling eventually in what is now the Punjab, on the borders of modern India and Pakistan. Here they found the remnants of the ancient Indus Valley civilization, a sophisticated urban culture that once had been larger than either Egypt or Mesopotamia. The Aryans carried with them an ancient sacrificial religion, the myths, the hymns, the rituals and the laws of which were laid down in the *Vedas*, a title that derives from the Sanskrit word for 'wisdom' or 'knowledge'. They comprise a huge body of text that forms the most primeval layer of Sanskrit literature and the most ancient, and sacred, of Hindu scriptures. To call the *Vedas* 'scripture' is a misnomer; Hindus talk of *sruti*: 'that which has been perceived through hearing'. The *Vedas* for most Hindus embody not the word of God but the eternal law that exists beyond the reach of any personal lawgiver.[2]

It is said that Vyasa, the mythical author of the *Mahabharata*, also compiled the *Vedas*, dividing them into four parts. The oldest of these is the *Rigveda*, a collection of sacred mantras necessary for rituals, composed in the second half of the second millennium BCE, in the period when the Aryans first migrated to India. The other three Vedic collections are the *Yajurveda*, basic instructions for performing ceremonies, the *Samveda*, the tunes for reciting hymns, and the *Artharveda*, a collection of spells and incantations.

Vedic religion came of age in the scriptures known as the *Upanishads*, or

Vedānta, the 'end of the Vedas'. Produced between the seventh and second centuries BCE, *upanishad* means 'sitting down near', that is at the feet of a guru to receive instruction. There are more than two hundred *Upanishads*, of which the oldest dozen are regarded as the most important and referred to as the *mukhya* or principal works.[3]

At the heart of the *Vedas*, and of the *Upanishads* in particular, is a discussion of the beliefs and actions necessary for the attainment of *moksha*, or enlightenment. *Moksha* is, in fact, one of four goals that Hinduism recognizes, the others being *artha* (wealth), *kama* (pleasure) and *dharma* (duty). All these are important, but only *moksha* can break through *maya*, the veil of cosmic ignorance thrown up by the material world. The recognition that the world and its contents are an illusion, that material objects inevitably decay, that skills and talents fade, that no relationship lasts for ever, is the first step towards *moksha*. If acknowledgement of the illusory character of the material world is a necessary step towards enlightenment, it is also an insufficient one. Beyond seeing through the veil of *maya* must come the attainment of true self-knowledge. One only comes to *know* the self, the *Upanishads* suggest, by *becoming* the self, and one only becomes the self by recognizing that at some fundamental level the self and the world are one. In Hindu terms this means the fusion of *atman* and *brahman*, which are perhaps best thought of as the 'self' and the 'ground of being', though neither of these definitions properly captures the essence of the original concepts. In the Vedic tradition, the concept of *brahman* helps define both epistemology and ontology – both the meaning of knowledge and the structure of reality. It is the deepest level of reality, the essence of being, of which the sensible world is but a modification. While worldly phenomena are transient, the ground of being is eternal and unchanging. True knowledge derives not from scientific investigation of the universe, which results in the apprehension only of the transient and the ephemeral, but through transcending such knowledge, by leaving behind all understanding based on sense perception and inference.

For Hindus, *atman* and *brahman* are, at the most intimate level, identical. *Atman* is the pure, essential self, that part of the ground of being that is manifested in every individual human being. *Moksha*, enlightenment, is recognition of this identity.

Moksha is important for Hindus not simply in the abstract sense of gaining enlightenment. It is a means also of breaking the cycle of birth, death and rebirth that in Hindu philosophy is the inevitable burden of human life. Everything that humans do creates *karma*, by which is meant both the actions performed and the accumulated moral consequences of such actions. Every thought or action has a consequence in two senses. It causes a change in the world; and the moral impact of such change returns to each actor, good being repaid with good, evil with evil. And not just in this lifetime. Because life is an eternal cycle of birth, death and reincarnation, so everyone experiences birth or rebirth with the *karma* that they have accumulated through previous incarnations. To this is added the *karma* accumulated in this lifetime. This in turn determines the starting conditions for the next cycle of experience. The only way to break out of this cycle is by achieving *moksha*.

3

The concept of *karma* embodies the sense both of free will and of fate. Every person is responsible for her acts and thoughts, and hence for her *karma*. The character of the next incarnation will be shaped by the accumulation of past and current deeds. An individual may be constrained by her actions in past lives, but each can shape her own future through actions in the here and now.

Karma provides an explanation for one of the most troubling questions within monotheistic faiths: why do bad things happen to good people and good things to bad people? It is a question at the heart of the Book of Job, among the Hebrew Bible's most magnificent creations. A narrative of great power, both psychological and spiritual, the Book of Job tells the story of a righteous man whose wealth, health and happiness are ripped away by God (or rather by Satan, then still an archangel in heaven, acting as God's lieutenant), in an attempt to test his faith in Yahweh. Job is tormented, wondering what he has done to deserve such punishment.

Questions such as 'Why does evil exist?', 'Why do those who do not deserve to, suffer?' and 'Why should one obey God?' had little meaning in traditional pantheistic religions. Good and evil were woven into the fabric of the universe. The righteous suffered because gods could be nasty, vindictive, brutal and immoral. One obeyed – or, rather, appeased – gods because one did not wish to make enemies of such powerful, yet often capricious, beings. It was the irrational, unpredictable nature of the gods that led Socrates, Plato and Aristotle to look to secular reasons for piety and righteousness.

The question of evil had an entirely different character within faiths in which God is seen both as omnipotent and as willing good upon the world. The existence of evil suggests either that God is not omnipotent or that He is responsible for such evil. Since neither view was acceptable to believers, a new kind of explanation was required. This was the issue that Job raised. Over time, a host of different answers emerged within Judaism, Christianity and Islam. Notions of heaven, hell and the afterlife developed to undergird the idea that even if the righteous suffer in this world, God would ensure that their piety received reward in the next, while evil-doers would suffer. It was not so much an explanation of immoral suffering as a promissory note of divine recompense. Within Christianity there emerged the idea of Original Sin, the claim that all humans are sinful, all carrying the stain of Adam and Eve's transgression in the Garden of Eden, and hence that no human was undeserving of suffering.

As a faith, Hinduism is pantheistic, but it takes the question of why the righteous suffer as seriously as the monotheistic faiths. The Hindu explanation is tied to *karma* and reincarnation. Everyone gets what they deserve for their actions both in this life and in their past lives. We imagine that the distribution of good and evil is random, even immoral, only because we are ignorant of the deeds an individual may have committed in past lives.

At a metaphysical level the concept of *karma* embodies an argument for free will. At a social level, however, it transforms itself into an argument for fate. Indeed, fate as a social phenomenon is justified by free will as a metaphysical claim. Your life cannot be otherwise because of past *karma*. Free will in the past becomes, in other words, an explanation for fatedness in the present.

This link between the social and the metaphysical is important because the *Vedas* were not simply an exposition of a metaphysical system. They were also a justification of a particular social structure – the caste system. It was this above all that made it important for Hinduism to take seriously the question of why evil befell good people.

The *Vedas* were composed at a time when old clan and tribal structures were giving way to more complex, hierarchical and rigid social forms. They provided the ideological underpinning for this transformation. The significance of the *Vedas* was that they illuminated a way not only of involving the supernatural in defence of caste but also of pinning blame on the individual for the iniquities of the social system. In its own highly distinct way, *karma* is the Hindu version of the Christian notion of the Fall.

The *Vedas* introduce us to four castes: *brahmins* (priests), *kshatriya* (aristocrats and warriors), *vaishya* (merchants and farmers) and *shudra* (labourers). The creation of these castes reflected initially a struggle over the structuring of the ruling classes, in particular between the rajas, or clan leaders, and the priests who, through their rituals, anointed them with greatness. The priests won that struggle, and *brahmins* were deemed the highest and purest classes. The *kshatriya* comprised the most aristocratic of clan leaders, the *vaishya* those of less distinguished descent who had forsaken their warrior past for wealth-making pursuits.

The first three castes, the *brahmin*, the *kshatriya* and the *vaishya*, emerged through the structuring of kin relations within the clan. The inclusion of the fourth category, *shudra*, reflected major social changes, the introduction of non-kin labour, the creation of a social group whose function it was to labour for others. The term *dasa*, which in the *Rigveda* was used to designate a person of a different culture, usually a member of an indigenous group, now came to mean one who laboured for a living, a contemptuous term applied not simply to indigenous peoples but to the *shudra* too. Eventually a fifth caste was constructed: the untouchables, or *Dalits* as they are now known. They were outcasts, so impure that they existed outside the caste system, forced to carry out the most menial tasks in society, but to live effectively outside of it, slaves without being slaves.

The Vedic name for the new social structure was *varna* or 'colour', the different castes being identified with different colours. New stories developed within Vedic mythology to explain and justify caste. In a creation myth at the beginning of the *Rigveda*, Purusha (meaning in Sanskrit 'man', 'self', 'spirit' or 'consciousness'), the supreme, authentic self, is sacrificed (or perhaps sacrifices himself) to create the world and humankind. From his mind is created the moon, from his eyes the sun, and his breath becomes the wind. From his sacrifice, too, the social order is crafted. His mouth becomes the *brahmin*, from his arms are forged the *kshatriya*, out of his thighs spring the *vaishya* and from his feet are produced the *shudra*.

The breakdown of the clan structure that gave rise to the Vedic castes did not end with the creation of those castes. Over time the caste system was restructured, shaped to meet local needs and vastly expanded. No longer were there simply four primal castes; dozens of new castes kept springing up, until eventually Indian society was laced together by some three thousand of them. A new term emerged to describe the caste system: *jati*, from a verb meaning 'to be born'. Where *varna* had placed emphasis on the degree of ritual purity, with *jati* caste was defined by bloodline. A community was identified by the job or profession its members were supposed to follow, a job or profession that was inherited by subsequent generations born into that community, a stricture reinforced by stringent marriage rules and taboos on activities such as commensality (eating with members of another caste). *Jati* did not displace *varna*. The two operated side by side, *varna* providing the ideological framework, *jati* the practical expression. Each *varna* came to contain several *jatis*, each of which had its own customs and practices. The whole system institutionalized in religion a form of social control, bound together by belief in karma and rebirth.

4

The *Mahabharata* has the feel of a valedictory work, an epic that attempts to frame a disappearing world. The *Ramayana*, the other great Indian epic of the middle of the first millennium BCE, has a different texture. If the *Mahabharata* is the swansong of an old order, celebrating a vanishing past, the *Ramayana* looks forward to what is to come. Out of the social ferment unleashed by the erosion of clan structures emerged new ideas of social order. Primary among them was the concept of kingship, and of automatic succession by right of birth, a notion alien to the old Aryan tradition. The *Ramayana* tells the story of Rama, heir to the kingdom of Kosala, who is tricked out of his birthright by his stepmother, and forced into exile for fourteen years. While in exile, wandering through the forests, his wife Sita is abducted by the demon king Ravana. Rama is, in fact, an earthly form of the god Vishnu, who has opted to be born as a human because Ravana can only be destroyed by a mortal. Rama organizes an army with the help of Hanuman, the king of the monkeys, defeats Ravana, rescues Sita and regains his kingdom.

The *Ramayana* is, as the historian Romila Thapar observes, 'an epic legitimizing the monarchical state'.[4] When Rama returns to his capital Ayodhya, it is not to reaffirm Vedic values but to create his own Utopia, bringing order, justice and prosperity through his personal rule. The *Rana-rajya* (or *Ram-raj* in Hindi), as Rama's reign came to be known, is still the Indian political ideal in which countless politicians, secularists as well as Hindu nationalists, find their lodestone. In 1992 hardline Hindu activists destroyed the Babri Mosque in Ayodhya, constructed by Babur, the founder of the Mughal Dynasty in India, claiming it to be the birthplace of Rama and the site of a former Hindu temple, and unleashing a wave of anti-Muslim violence across India that left 2,000 people dead. The following year India's Supreme Court ruled that the site of the mosque was indeed the birthplace of Rama, whom it described as 'both a juristic person and a deity', and insisted that two-thirds of the site must be given up to Hindu groups. The significance of the *Ramayana* to contemporary Indian life, and to notions of right and wrong, could not have been made clearer.

Rana-rajya was not, however, the only answer to the breakdown of the old clan structures. This was an era of urbanization, the first since the cities of the original Indus Valley civilization. There developed a host of different social forms, oligarchies, republics, even proto-democracies. The most important of these new forms was the *gana-sangha*, meaning 'equal assemblies', which bore some similarities to Greek city states. New methods of agricultural production, and the growing need for intensive labour, led to new social demarcations, based not on caste but on class. A *gana-sangha* was broadly divided between the rulers, the *raja-kulas*, and the workers and slaves, the *dasa-karmakaras*. Unlike in the monarchies, all those in the ruling class, who in a large *gana-sangha* may have numbered several thousand, could play a role in governance.

Religious beliefs, too, were in flux. A myriad new philosophies emerged, from mysticism to nihilism to materialism to atheism. This was the *Kali Yuga*, the *Mahabharata*'s age without values. It was actually a time of great intellectual vitality, perhaps as vigorous and wide-ranging as that of Presocratic Greece, but the historical memory has been wiped clean by successive generations of religious mythmakers, who have dominated the writing of ancient history, and by Western myths about the purely irrational character of traditional Indian philosophy.

What is striking about the middle centuries of the first millennium BCE is that a similar kind of social turbulence should beset all the great civilizational centres of the world. Not just in India, but in Greece, Israel, Persia and China, too, the heroic age was giving way to a more structured world at around the same time. In this process, in all these civilizations, new philosophies, faiths and moral ideas were being moulded – from the Socratic tradition in Greece, through the remaking of Judaism in Israel, to Confucianism in China. The German philosopher Karl Jaspers described it as the 'Axial age' in which 'the spiritual foundations of humanity were laid simultaneously and independently in China, India, Persia, Judea, and Greece'.[5]

In India, asceticism and the renunciation of conventional life became an important response to the bewildering changes of the Axial age. People withdrew from society, either as individual hermits or in small groups, to find a way of living away from towns and villages and the social obligations and religious rituals that such communities imposed. The final spiritual journey of the Pandavas and the fourteen years of wandering for Rama both reveal the significance that such quests came to acquire. For some ascetics, social isolation was a means of distancing themselves from Vedic laws and social structures. Others took to the ascetic life in an attempt to acquire new mental or bodily powers through meditation or yoga. In an age in which there was much social ferment but no mechanism for social transformation, renunciation provided a means of challenging conventional rules and ethics and of attempting to establish new ways of living.

The social turbulence gave rise also to the opposite response. A number of materialist schools of thought flourished, such as the Lokāyata and Cārvāka (Lokāyata means 'philosophy of the people', while Cārvāka translates as 'agreeable speech'). The materialists denied the existence of non-perceivable entities such as God or a spiritual realm. They were strongly empiricist in their outlook, rejecting the authority of scripture and testimony. They rejected, too, asceticism and meditation, celebrating instead the pleasures of the body. These schools became marginalized as social and religious order was restored, but elements of materialism continued to influence even religious thought throughout Indian history.

Of the hundreds of challenges to the Vedic tradition posed by philosophers, holy men, ascetics and renouncers, two came to have an enduring legacy. One was Jainism, the roots of which lie way back in ancient Indian history – some suggest as far back as the Indus Valley civilizations. Its ideas were given formal shape by the sixth-century philosopher and ascetic Vardhamana Mahavira. Enlightenment, for Jains, came not through perfection of knowledge but through living the perfect ethical life. They possessed an almost obsessional belief in non-violence, an insistence that not a single living creature should be killed, tormented or harmed. The more orthodox Jains wore a muslin mask over the face to prevent the involuntary inhalation of even the tiniest insect. For a certain time, particularly in the first half of the second millennium CE, Jainism wielded considerable influence in some parts of India. It was, however, the second major movement that developed in the sixth century BCE that was to be truly influential and revolutionary. Buddhism, the faith that grew out of the teachings of Siddharta Gautama, came to be the principal Indian contribution to the Axial age.

5

Siddharta Gautama was born in what is now Nepal around the end of the sixth century or the beginning of the fifth century BCE. His was a prosperous, aristocratic family, part of the powerful Shakya clan. For most of his early life, he was shielded from the reality of the poverty and degradation that surrounded him. In his late twenties he was finally forced to confront sickness, suffering and death, coming face to face with an old man, one who was mortally sick and a corpse. So shocked was he by these encounters that Gautama left his family and comfortable home life, taking to the road to become a wandering ascetic, debating the nature of suffering with yogis and mendicants. Six years of self-denial brought about no change to his sense of dissatisfaction. He turned to meditation. For forty-nine days and nights he sat under a fig tree in Gaya, a small village in north-east India. 'I have obtained nirvana,' Gautama claimed as he rose from his contemplation. He had found an understanding both of the cause of worldly suffering and of the means of transcending it.

That, at least, is the traditional story of the Buddha ('the enlightened one'), as Gautama came to be known, and of his spiritual journey. In fact, we know almost nothing with certainty about a man who lived two centuries before Aristotle. The main sources of his life and teachings are a variety of different, and often conflicting, traditional biographies, the earliest of which, the epic poem *Buddhacarita*, dates from the second century CE. Of the actual words of the Buddha nothing is left. Early in its history, Buddhism divided into innumerable sects, possibly more than thirty, each with its own story of Gautama's life, each with its own canon of scriptures.

Whatever the historical truth, there are certain teachings now accepted as genuine by virtually all Buddhists. By tradition, the Buddha gave his first talk at the Deer Park in Sarnath, on the banks of the Ganges, where he gathered his first five disciples. The so-called 'Discourse on the Turning of the Wheel of Dharma' is to Buddhists as Jesus' Sermon on the Mount is to Christians. Like the Sermon on the Mount, the Buddha's discourse is likely to have been patched together by later followers, shaped to reflect subsequent readings of his thought, and the changing needs of Buddhists, and then projected back to establish a canonical text.[6]

At the heart of the 'Discourse on the Turning of the Wheel of Dharma' are the Four Noble Truths. The first truth is that the world is permeated with suffering, or *duhkha*, a concept that refers not just to pain and sorrow but also to dissatisfaction and unfulfilment. *Duhkha* is one of the Three Marks of Existence (*trilakshana*), or features of earthly life. They stamp our lives so indelibly that those who ignore their reality will find nirvana always to be beyond their reach. The other Marks of Existence are *anitya*, or impermanence, and *anatman*, meaning 'no self' or 'egolessness'. *Anitya* expresses the belief that everything in the phenomenal world is in a state of flux. This includes human beings themselves. Hence *anatman*, or lack of self. All human existence, for the Buddha, is a series of discontinuous moments. The image he presents is of a row of unlit candles. The first candle is lit, used to light the second, but is itself then extinguished; and so on it continues down the row. Human existence, too, consists of a series of moments, lit up and snuffed out. Each moment of consciousness gives birth to the next and then ceases to be, so no person is constant from one moment to the next. For Buddhists, the belief that humans possess a self, that there is an essential 'me', is part of the illusion of permanence that must be discarded if an individual is to achieve enlightenment.[7]

The second of the Buddha's Noble Truths is that the cause of all suffering is human desire, the thirst for that which cannot satisfy, including the desire to be a self. Originally a place of bliss, the world had been reduced to a place of suffering by human capitulation to desire, a sentiment that was, half a millennium later, to be echoed in certain strands of Christian thought, though in Buddhism the cause of degradation is not sin, as in Christianity, but ignorance. Suffering can only be ended through renunciation of all desire, the third of the Noble Truths. Renunciation of desire is the path to nirvana, or liberation from rebirth, the Buddhist version of the Hindu idea of *moksha*. Like Hindus, Buddhists believe in the cycle of birth, death and rebirth in a new form that is the inevitable burden of human life. Only through enlightenment – *moksha* or nirvana – can one break that endless cycle. What rebirth means when one does not possess a self, and when every individual's life lacks continuity from one moment to the next, let alone from one birth to the next, is a conundrum that Buddhists have endlessly debated, and upon which arguments have endlessly foundered.

The fourth Noble Truth upon which Buddha insisted was that desire can only be renounced through following the 'Eightfold Path', eight principles of actions that lead to a balanced, moderate life. These include the acceptance of the Four Noble Truths; the resolve to live according to the Buddhist way; the wisdom to adopt the right kind of livelihood, rejecting, for instance, jobs that involve killing, such as being a butcher, a hunter or a soldier; and the determination to act ethically by avoiding stealing, prohibited sexual activity, unjust speech and intoxicating drinks.

6

There is something Stoic about the Buddha's conception of the good life. There is also something Aristotelian about it (or there would be were it not anachronistic to describe as Aristotelian the ideas of a man who lived two centuries before Aristotle). Reason rather than Revelation is the starting point for his thinking, and ethics rather than metaphysics its endpoint. The Buddha rejected Vedic metaphysics (even though his teachings drew upon certain Hindu metaphysical concepts). He was even more hostile to brahminical ritual, especially the sacrificing of animals. What he demanded was a commitment to ethical behaviour. Buddhist ethics wrenched itself away from Hinduism, neither rooted in the privileges and tyrannies of caste identity, nor seeking to justify the caste system, though it never properly challenged it either. It emerged, rather, out of a concern for the welfare of humanity as a whole. There is a reasonableness, even triteness, about Buddhist prescriptions that again is reminiscent of Aristotle. The Buddha described the Eightfold Path as the 'Middle Way' between the extremes of asceticism and hedonism, of poverty and luxury, an idea that finds an echo in Aristotle's 'doctrine of the mean'.

Yet Buddhism is fundamentally different to an Aristotelian conception of the world and, despite its humanist approach, is in certain ways closer to a theistic vision of the human condition. There has been a tendency, by some of its advocates, especially in the West, to overplay the rational and humanistic quality of Buddhism. At its core Buddhism is a doctrine of salvation. Unlike Aristotle, the Buddha did not view ethics as a means of building the good life on this Earth, but rather as a means of escaping the bad life of this Earth. His teachings embody an intensely pessimistic view of the world as a place of unremitting hurt and disappointment. Suffering without end in a futile round of rebirths after rebirths – that is the fate of most mortals. Escape comes through nirvana.

Buddhism never specifies what is meant by 'nirvana'. It defines what nirvana delivers us from but not what it delivers us to. It is, as the philosopher of religion Edward Conze puts it, 'a transcendental state which is quite beyond the ken of ordinary experience, and of which nothing can be said except that in it all ills have ceased, together with their causes and consequences'.[8] It is paradise without a deity or a theology, a paradise not discovered outside, but realized within.

There is in Buddhism, unlike in monotheistic or pantheistic faiths, no attempt to look to a deity as an explanation for the creation and preservation of the cosmos, or as the source of moral values. The Buddha himself was, however, viewed as God-like, at least in traditional accounts, being possessed of such abilities and characteristics as omniscience, the ability to 'suppress karma', the ability to survive without food or sleep, and having been conceived without intercourse and born without having caused pain. And like most religions, Buddhism divided its adherents into clergy and laity. In most strands of Buddhist thought, only monks can achieve nirvana. Lay Buddhists are deficient in the 'merit' accumulated through past lives. A layperson's key religious act is to increase his or her store of merit by observing the basic ethical precepts and by supporting the work of the monks.

The Buddha's teachings were in large part a response to the social changes that were then convulsing India, in particular the new urbanization, the transformation of class structures and the emergence of the state. In the West, similar developments helped give rise to the monotheistic faiths. Judaism, Christianity and, as we shall see, Islam all arose in times of great social dislocation, when the foundations of traditional ethics no longer appeared sure. God seemed essential to many as a source of moral concrete. The Axial age saw also, of course, the emergence of Greek rationalism. But that Greek tradition itself became a victim of the great upheavals of the Hellenistic period and came to be swallowed up, for a millennium at least, by the monotheistic faiths.

Monotheism, particularly Islam, flourished in parts of Asia primarily through invasion and conversion. The indigenous response to the kinds of social upheavals that helped create monotheism in the West came not in monotheistic but in non-theistic forms of faith, of which Buddhism was the first. There has been a great debate over the centuries about the extent to which we should look upon Buddhism either as a philosophy or as a religion. It is perhaps best understood as a philosophy that historically, and socially, has played the role of faith. It did so not just in the sense of offering a source of spirituality and solace, but in the sense also of defining, as the monotheistic faiths did as well, the meaning of right and wrong, of acceptable and unacceptable behaviour, and of acting as the mortar in the foundation of social order.

There has been a tendency in the West to see Western philosophies as rooted primarily in reason while those of the East as irrational, rooted primarily in mysticism. There are, in fact, many strands of irrationalist philosophy in the West (and, ironically, one of the reasons for the myth of the irrational East is that Western irrationalists have tended to champion Eastern mysticism). At the same time, India, and, as we shall see, China, have been home to a number of rational, humanist outlooks. But these were, in the main, forms of reason and humanism whose social and ethical consequences were strikingly different to that which developed out of the Greek tradition. Christianity and Islam may have talked of souls and of an afterlife, but the monotheistic faiths also possessed a sense of agency and progress that a more overtly humanistic philosophy such as Buddhism lacked, and which was essential to the development of modern humanist ethics.

CHAPTER SIX

The view from the mountains

1

The great plain was surrounded by high mountains, bleak steppes and hostile jungle. Summers were hot, winters icy, and always the north wind blew. Again and again the river burst its banks, devastating the land; every time it did so thousands perished, not just from the floods but from disease and famine too. Time and again the river changed its course, forcing settlements to be uprooted and rebuilt. Not for nothing was it known as the Land of Sorrows.

Yet, there are few places on Earth that bear such witness to the development of human civilization as those plains surrounding the Yellow River in China. *Homo erectus* strode these lands more than a million years ago, leaving behind not just his bones but his stone tools too. When the first modern humans – *Homo sapiens* – appeared here remains a matter of great controversy, some suggesting that it may have been as early as a hundred thousand years ago. The first Neolithic settlements were built about fourteen thousand years ago. Then, around 2000 BCE came the Bronze Age, out of which emerged a culture unrivalled anywhere else in the world for the skill and beauty of its metalwork and jade carvings. By now the Xia, the first of the great Chinese dynasties, though one surrounded by myth as much as by history, had emerged to rule over this land. Even before Homer began reciting the *Iliad* and the *Odyssey*, and half a millennium before those poems were committed to writing, we can glimpse the first strands of Chinese literature. Around this time, a thousand years before the birth of Christ, the Zhou Dynasty overthrew the Shang, which itself had overturned the Xia and ruled for more than six centuries. In the Zhou period, which ran from the eleventh to the third centuries BCE, the longest lasting of any Chinese dynasty, the framework of classical poetry, philosophy and art was constructed. After the fall of the Zhou came the imperial age, presided over by a succession of dynasties beginning with the Qin in the second century BCE and ending more than two thousand years later with the Qing in the twentieth century. It is a history without parallel.

What has characterized China over the past three millennia is a combination of constant tumultuous change and historical continuity, a combination distinct from that in Europe. One of the themes of this book is that cultures and civilizations are not self-enclosed entities. They all borrow, steal and remake each other's jewels. The more frenetic the borrowing and stealing, the more fertile the ground for innovation. The Eastern Mediterranean was a forge for civilizations because it was also a furnace for cultural and intellectual melding.

China was a continental, not a maritime, nation. Chinese rulers and thinkers were well aware of the world, and of the cultures and civilizations beyond. They traded in goods and ideas just as the Greeks and Persians and Phoenicians did. India and Afghanistan, Korea and Japan, Persia and Arabia, Greece and Rome – Chinese emperors, merchants and scholars knew of all these and many more, and there was considerable dialogue and bartering. But in China, the primary trade was not with peoples beyond but with peoples within. The Zhou Dynasty, during the early part of its rule, expanded aggressively into neighbouring territory. Zhou rulers gave relatives and followers control over fiefdoms in an effort to maintain authority over vast lands. Inevitably, over time, central authority weakened, and the state disintegrated into many warring factions. The rulers of every Zhou splinter continued, nevertheless, to see themselves as inheritors of a common culture, a jealously guarded possession that linked them to each other and to their common past. This sense of cultural unity was to shape the development of Chinese society and thought. It allowed for the free interchange of ideas throughout the territory, but led also to a greater suspicion of, and need for, exchange with outsiders.

This process of continuity and change, of political fragmentation and cultural stability, shaped Chinese history and politics and helped forge a distinct form of ethical thought. 'The wise man delights in water; the good man delights in mountains. The wise move; the good stay still. The wise are happy; the good endure.' So wrote Kongzi, better known in the West as Confucius, the first and, for some, the greatest Chinese philosopher. Kong, who was born a century before Socrates, had no knowledge of the Greeks. The twentieth-century Chinese philosopher Fung Yu Lan, who played an important role as a philosophical bridge between China and the West, took Kong's aphorism to be prophetic, however, about the distinction between Greek and Chinese moral traditions. The Greeks, Fung wrote, were a maritime people, whose civilization was forged out of communication with other peoples, cultures and traditions. That interaction helped construct a treasure house of knowledge and foster a love of learning for its own sake. The Chinese, on the other hand, a continental people whose interactions with the outside world were restricted by geography, who inhabited a land politically fragmented but bound by the perception of a common civilization, saw learning in more instrumental terms. Chinese philosophers, Fung insisted, have tended to avoid the abstract, showing little interest in metaphysics or pure logic, pouring their energies instead into developing more down-to-earth, practical, political arguments. They were, he suggested, 'concerned chiefly with society and not with the universe', more preoccupied with defining how to live rather than in discovering how things are. Or, as another Chinese philosopher Y.L. Chin has put it, 'Chinese philosophers were all of them different shades of Socrates'.[1]

Not just geography, but language, too, Fung suggested, made Chinese philosophy distinct. The Chinese corpus contains few great philosophical tracts. There is little to compare with Aristotle's *Metaphysics* or Aquinas's *Summa Theologica* or Kant's *Critique of Practical Reason*. Chinese philosophy tends rather to be poetic, aphoristic, suggestive. The very language of the Chinese, many argue, has lent itself to aphoristic philosophy and discouraged long, finely argued theses. A written language based on the alphabetic system, and with a tight grammatical fabric, as came eventually to be used in the West, provides useful material from which to fashion an argumentative treatise. A language that is constructed from symbolic characters that are not susceptible to considerations of singular or plural, or of past, present or future tenses, and most of which can equally be a noun, a verb, an adjective or an adverb, but whose connotation changes according to the other symbols alongside which it sits in a sentence, is necessarily more ambiguous and allusive in meaning. Chinese language is, the philosopher Laurence Wu suggests, 'an excellent tool for poetry but not for systematic or scientific thought'. There is in Chinese philosophy 'profound insights, brilliant aphorisms, interesting metaphors, but few elaborate arguments'.[2]

The cleavage between the Chinese and Western traditions is not, in fact, as great as many suggest. Within the European tradition, the differences between Aristotle, Aquinas, Descartes, Hume, Hegel, Nietzsche, Russell, Heidegger and Singer are huge. So are the differences within the Chinese between Kongzi, Mo Tzu, Meng Ke, Hsun Tzu, Zhu Xi and Fung Yu Lan, all figures whose work I will discuss. Many of these Chinese philosophers probed deep into metaphysics as well as ethics. There have been many poetic and aphoristic strands of European philosophy. Nor are the differences that do exist simply the result of geography or language; indeed, how much difference geography or language makes is a matter for considerable debate. Nevertheless, distinctions do exist between European and Chinese traditions. Perhaps the most important of these for the story I am telling lies in the social role of ethics. Morality occupies a uniquely important place in Chinese history. Religion, certainly in the way it is understood elsewhere in the world, for centuries played only a minor role in China. Ethics, not religion, provided the spiritual basis of Chinese life. The teachings of Kongzi helped cement that unique role of ethics.

2

Kongzi, or 'Master Kong', was born as Kong Qui around 551 BCE in Zou, in the state of Lu on the eastern seaboard. He lived at around the same time as the Buddha, though neither, of course, knew of the other. It was a time of great conflict between the fragmenting parts of the Zhou Dynasty and between fiefdoms inside and outside Zhou territory. By the time of Kong's birth Lu was in a state almost of anarchy.

Little is known of Kong's background or early life. It is likely that he was born into an impoverished branch of minor nobility and eked out a living as a petty official. Frustrated, he became in his fifties a peripatetic teacher. He soon gathered large numbers of students around him, perhaps eventually as many as three thousand.

Like most Chinese philosophers, Kong was concerned primarily with ethics rather than metaphysics. The central theme of his philosophy is the behaviour needed to create a harmonious society. At the heart of it are two human qualities: *ren* and *li*.

Ren, the highest Confucian principle, is perhaps best translated as humaneness, or loving kindness. It is related to the Greek concept of *agape*, the Christian notion of 'love' and Kant's idea of 'goodwill'. An individual who possesses *ren* possesses sympathy for others and empathy for their needs and desires. But he or she must possess much more than simply that. *Ren* embodies all the qualities necessary for one human being to express ideal behaviour towards another. Asked if there was a single act that one should practise throughout one's life, Kong responded, 'Do not inflict on others what you yourself would not wish done to you.'[3] It is a version of the 'Golden Rule' that appears many times in Kong's teachings.

For Kong, ideal behaviour could not be behaviour that was universal, as perhaps it was for a Stoic or a Christian. Rather, it expressed precisely how one individual ought to behave towards another given their respective social roles. And this takes us to the second of the two pivots of Confucian ethics, *li*, meaning propriety, the following of tradition, ritual and conventional mores. 'If one is courteous but does without ritual, then one dissipates one's energy,' Kong suggested; 'if one is cautious but does without ritual, then one becomes timid; if one is bold but does without ritual, then one becomes reckless; if one is forthright but does without ritual, then one becomes rude.'[4]

Kong is expressing here two distinct ideas. The first is the belief that nothing should be done in excess, a notion reminiscent of Aristotle's 'doctrine of the mean', and of *li* as the means by which to ensure moderation. Second, Kong is suggesting also that accepting the social structure defined by *li* is crucial to be able properly to express *ren*. To be humane is not only to show empathy and love towards others; it is also to perform the duties and obligations required of one's role or station in life. Kong called this 'the rectification of names', meaning that there should be a correspondence between a person's title and his or her behaviour. 'Let a ruler be a ruler,' he wrote, 'a subject a subject, a father a father, a son a son.'[5] The whole of Confucian teaching is focused upon the cultivation of the moral character necessary to rule, to administer and to follow.

There were for Kong five relationships (*wu-lun*) critical for the maintenance of social harmony and order: those between father and son, husband and wife, older brother and younger brother, older friend and younger friend, and ruler and subject. Out of these relationships society was built, and in them were incubated the duties and obligations upon which harmony was founded. Each of these relationships Kong understood in terms of the traditional Chinese contrast between yin and yang, concepts shared by different schools throughout the history of Chinese philosophy. Yin and yang refer to the complementary forces – dark and light, hot and cold, weak and strong, active and passive – through the interaction of which the universe operates at every level of existence. In each of the *wu-lun* relationships, Kong sees one partner as yin, the other as yang, one as dominant, the other as submissive. A son must be submissive to his father, a woman to her husband, a subject to his ruler. Dominance and submissiveness are aspects not of an individual but of the social role. The same individual can be dominant as a father but submissive as a subject. Submissiveness, in particular, was a requirement of *li*, and without being properly submissive an individual could not express his or her *ren*. 'To subdue oneself and return to ritual', Kong insisted, 'is to practise humaneness.' Living as he did in a period of great social turmoil, Kong worried that many in society, women and the poor in particular, were incapable of subduing themselves and behaving with propriety. 'Women and small men [men of low birth] seem difficult to look after,' he observed. 'If you keep them close, they become insubordinate; but if you keep them at a distance, they become resentful.'[6]

The practices of *li* had emerged in the early Zhou Dynasty through the ritualization of ancestor worship, and of sacrifice. Such worship and sacrifice were rooted in the belief that the spirits of deceased ancestors would look after the family and take an interest in the affairs of the world, and that they possessed the ability to influence the fortunes of the living. Over time, the ruling class established a set of rules and practices by which the veneration of ancestors was formalized. Everyone had ancestors; but only the nobility had ancestors whom they could trace and name through a family tree. *Li* became therefore also a mandate for rule, as only the ruling class could perform the rituals.

The significance of Kong lay in his expansion of the meaning of *li*, in his application of the concept not simply to a small set of practices by which the king and the nobility found justification for their rule but to all activities in life. There were rules about how a son greeted his father, and a husband his wife; rules about how to bow when meeting a stranger; rules about what colour of clothes to wear on certain days; rules about how to eat certain foods; and so on. *Li* was a form of etiquette by which life was structured, relationships regulated and harmony established. But it was far more than simply etiquette. Through *li* all of life began to take on a religious, ritualized quality. All of life became, in a sense, 'sacred'. Through *li* Confucian ethics took on the aura of a religion.

3

The notion of humaneness, as it developed in Greek, Christian and, to a certain extent, Buddhist, thought, was closely related to the desire to break down social barriers, to the development of ideas of universalism and cosmopolitanism. For Kong, and for his successors, such cosmopolitanism was contrary to both nature and to the ground rules of propriety. As Hsun Tzu, a third-century BCE philosopher and one of the most important early interpreters of Kong, put it, what makes 'man truly man' is that 'he makes social distinctions':

> Birds and beasts have fathers and offspring, but not the affection between father and son. They are male and female, but do not have the proper separation between males and females. Hence in the Way of Humanity there must be distinctions. No distinctions are greater than those of society. No social distinctions are greater than the *li*.[7]

It was through another Chinese philosophical tradition, the Mohist school, founded a century after Kong by the philosopher Mo Tzu, that universalist ideas emerged. Mo taught that *ren* should be shown to others without distinction or favouritism, and that the needs of distant strangers should rank as highly as those of family or clan. It was a remarkable argument made four centuries before similar ideas began to develop in the Greek and Christian traditions.

Where exactly Mo was born remains uncertain, as do the exact dates of his birth and death. He possibly hailed from the state of Lu, Kong's birthplace, and he probably lived in the second half of the fifth century BCE, and perhaps into the early part of the fourth; in other words, at around the same time as Socrates, Plato and the later Sophists in Greece. This was the Era of the Warring States in China, where the disintegration of the Zhou Dynasty had led to all-out conflict between a number of different states, in particular Jin, Chu, Qin and Qi. The turmoil ended in 221 BCE, more than a century after Mo's death, with the victory of Qin, the unification of the various warring fragments and the founding of the first Chinese imperial dynasty (though the Qin Dynasty itself lasted only fifteen years). 'Mo' is an unusual surname, Chinese for 'ink'. Some scholars have speculated that it was an epithet given to him for having once been a slave or a convict, whose faces were often branded or tattooed with dark ink. Others suggest that Mo took on the name as a way of identifying with the lowest class of people. Most historians now believe that Mo was a member of the lower artisan class who managed to climb his way to an official post. Fung Yu Lan suggested that Mo was a *hsieh*, a hereditary warrior who had lost his position and title, and made a living by offering his services to those who would employ him. He is certainly thought to have founded a highly organized, quasi-religious military community that came to the aid of small states under threat, a practical expression of the Mohists' opposition to military aggression.

Today we know of Mo's philosophy primarily through a text called *Mozi*, which was probably written not by Mo Tzu himself, but by successive groups of disciples. The original consisted of seventy-one chapters, of which only fifty-three remain. The social turmoil that beset China over several centuries had led Kong to stress tradition and ritual as a means of assuring order and harmony. It led Mo to argue for the opposite.

Mo distinguished between two principles: that of 'partiality' and that of 'universality'. Someone who held to the principle of partiality, as Kong did, discounted the moral interests of other tribes or other states, or hated or despised them because they were of other tribes or other states. To adopt the principle of 'universality' did not mean, as some have suggested of Mo, that one should love strangers as much as one loves one's family, but rather that the moral interests of strangers, and of other tribes and states, must concern us as much as those of our family, that one should 'regard others' states as though regarding one's state, regard others' families as though regarding one's family, and regard other persons as though regarding one's person'. How, Mo asks, do these two approaches explain 'the current calamities of the world', in particular 'great states attacking small ones, great families overthrowing small ones, the strong oppressing the weak, the many harrying the few, the cunning deceiving the stupid, the eminent lording it over the humble'? Such calamities have not arisen out of people 'loving others and trying to benefit them'. Rather, they have 'come from hating others and trying to injure them'. Therefore, 'partiality is wrong and universality is right'. 'If men were to regard the states of others as they regard their own', Mo asks, 'then who would raise up his state to attack the state of another? It would be like attacking his own.' Adopting the principle of universality would ensure that 'Others will be regarded as the self' and so the need for wars would be greatly reduced, even disappear.[8]

Mo's philosophy was not a warm, fuzzy embrace of an 'All you need is love' attitude. He was much more hard-headed and pragmatic. Why, he asked, should I act to embrace others and to benefit them rather than simply to benefit myself? Because 'He who loves others, must also be loved by others. He who benefits others, must also be benefitted by others. He who hates others, must also be hated by others. He who injures others, must also be injured by others.'[9] There are echoes here of utilitarian ideas, and of evolutionary notions of 'reciprocal altruism', developed two millennia later.

Mo rejected what he regarded as Kong's fetishization of ritual, which, he argued, was merely for show and detracted from the changes necessary to bring about a truly harmonious society. What people required was food, clothing, work and peace, not elaborate funerals or rules of etiquette. Mo was even hostile to the playing of music, which, he thought, provided amusement for the ruling class but not bread or peace for ordinary folk.

Despite Mo's pragmatism, there remains something implausible both in his ethical utopianism and in his vision of human nature and of human relationships. Modern universalism is primarily a social and political claim. It requires the acceptance that whatever an individual's background, and whatever we may personally feel about him or her, we accord that individual the same rights as we would do anyone else, that in meting out justice we do not discriminate on grounds of race, ethnicity, nationality, gender, sexuality, and so on, and that there are certain values, institutions and forms of governance under which all humans best flourish. Insofar as such universalism is plausible, it is because society is well enough developed to be able to steamroller traditional inequalities, differences and hierarchies, to afford equal treatment to all, and to be able to think practically of common forms of governance across national and cultural boundaries. It was different in the premodern world. Inequality and hierarchy were essential to the functioning of such societies. The possibilities of social transformation, and of the creation of a society built on the equal treatment of all, would have appeared to most people as fantastical. Universalists were inevitably seen as dreamers and utopians; and dreamers and utopians they were. Universalism necessarily had primarily to be not social but psychological in form, an argument less about how society should be constructed than about how we should regard others. Given the constrained character of society, universalist ideas about regarding others as we regard ourselves could have seemed only fanciful. However pragmatic and utilitarian Mo Tzu's philosophy might have been, this was true of his claims too. But while Mo's psychological vision might have appeared implausible, his ethical vision was crucially important, and in many ways more developed and 'modern' than those of Stoics or Christians almost half a millennium later.

Mo criticized Kong not simply for his conservative adherence to tradition and his support for social discrimination but also for his rejection of God. Growing disbelief in the power and providential character of God and of the spirit world had, he wrote, led to widespread immorality and social chaos, both because it coarsened human behaviour and ethical thinking and because it 'displeased' God and the spirits. God's will, Mo insisted, was that all humans should love one another. He rewarded with good fortune those who obeyed His commands, punished with calamity those who defied His will. There is something of the Old Testament about Mo's vision of a personal, judgemental, vengeful God who sets in stone the meaning of right and wrong, punishing the wicked and rewarding the faithful. And yet Mo's faith was quite unlike that demanded by the Old Testament. Good and bad, for Mo, were not simply arbitrary notions defined by God. That which is good is good because it promotes peace, harmony, order and proper governance. Had he been faced with Socrates, Mo's answer to the Euthyphro dilemma would have been clear. What is right is right not merely because heaven intends it. Rather, heaven intends it because it is right.

Kong was not a humanist in the modern sense, but he talked little of God or of the spirit world, and neither played a role in his moral philosophy. What he was, was a deeply conservative thinker who sought to rationalize the ways of the past. 'I transmit but do not create,' he wrote. 'Being fond of the truth, I am an admirer of antiquity.'[10] For Kong, truth was to be found by excavating the past, and reason was a means of ensuring that social mores were not overturned. Mo possessed a mystical view of God, and of the spirit world. But he was forcefully radical, challenging traditional mores and trying to develop a rational argument for a deep-rooted universalism. The relationship between Kong and Mo expresses the complexity of the relationship between faith, reason and morality, particularly in the premodern world.

For all his radicalism, there was also something quite authoritarian about Mo's morality. We can see this most clearly in his fascinating parable about the origins of, and the necessity for, the state. Through the parable Mo set out a political argument superficially similar to that of Thomas Hobbes almost two millennia later. Both Mo and Hobbes saw humans, in the state of nature prior to the creation of society, as living in a condition of constant warfare. But where Hobbes saw conflict as arising out of the untrammelled pursuit of self-interest, Mo saw it as the consequence of discord over values. 'Before there were any laws or governments, every man's view of things was different,' wrote Mo. 'One man had one view, two people had two views, ten men had ten views – the more men, the more views. Moreover, each man believed that his own views were correct and disapproved of those of others.' As a result people were 'unable to live in harmony' and 'people all resorted to water, fire, and poison in an effort to do each other injury'.[11]

To overcome this disorder, 'the most worthy and able man in the world was selected and set up as Son of Heaven'. There could be only one standard of morality in this state, based on the principles that 'What the superior considers right, all shall consider right. What the superior considers wrong, all shall consider wrong', and 'Always agree with the superior; never follow the inferior'.[12] This Mo calls 'conforming upwards'. Mo's state is absolutist, and the authority of its ruler absolute.

Like the implausibility of Mo's conception of human nature, so the authoritarian character of his ideal state reveals the limitations upon ethical thinking in the premodern world, largely the result of constraints upon social possibilities. In a world in which neither the understanding of the self nor the potential for social transformation were well developed, the concept of individual rights had no more meaning to Mo than it did to most ancient thinkers, and universalism could only be understood in terms of social order imposed by fiat.

There is an argument to be made for thinking of Mo Tzu, rather than Kong, as China's first philosopher. He, not Kong, was, as the philosopher Chris Fraser observes, 'the first Chinese thinker to engage, like Socrates in ancient Greece, in an explicit, reflective search for objective moral standards and to give step-by-step, tightly reasoned arguments for [his] views'. He, not Kong, 'formulated China's first explicit ethical and political theories', and he advanced the world's earliest form of consequentialism, remarkably sophisticated for its time.[13]

Mo was, however, one of history's losers. During the Era of the Warring States, Mohism was influential, vying with Confucianism for the ear both of rulers and the masses. With the unification of China in 221 BCE, and the creation of imperial rule, Kong's star rose, while Mohist ideas were seen not just as irrelevant but as dangerous too. The conservatism of Confucianism, its appeal to tradition and ritual, its usefulness in helping train government officials, all found favour with the imperial court. Kongzi became, as the literary critic and human rights activist Liu Xiaobo observes, the 'court guard dog' for two millennia.[14] Mo's radicalism, and his distaste for *li* and for traditional concepts of order, provoked fear. Under the Han Dynasty that followed, Confucianism was adopted as the official imperial ideology, while Mo's teachings were suppressed. Kong came to be venerated as China's greatest sage, even as a god. In the 450s the imperial government built the first Confucian temple, and within a century no city of respectable size was without its temple to Kong. New temple rituals were established to celebrate everything from Kong's birthday to the spring equinox to success in civil service exams. Mo Tzu and his school fell into neglect and obscurity, their texts largely unread. The *Mozi* was nearly lost to history. Paradoxically, it was growing familiarity with Western philosophy in the nineteenth century that led many Chinese scholars to excavate their own intellectual history in a search for untapped intellectual resources within their own traditions, and to rediscover Mo Tzu's legacy.

4

Yin and yang may have been a way for traditional Chinese philosophy to characterize the interplay of forces in the universe. It is also a good metaphor for the structure of traditional Chinese philosophy. If Confucianism was the yin, Daoism was the yang.

The origins of Daoism lie way back in Chinese history, in forms of shamanism and folk religions. It expressed as much an attitude and a way of life as a philosophy, and its threads can be found in many religions and worldviews. Its formal roots lie in two literary classics. The first is *Dao De Jing*, a book that, with the *Analects*, is regarded as the highest peak of classical Chinese literature. By tradition the *Dao De Jing* was written by Lao Tzu in the sixth century BCE. Lao Tzu, or 'great master', is probably a figure of myth. The book was most likely compiled some two centuries later; the earliest copy we possess today dates from around 200 BCE. The second classic Daoist work is the eponymously titled *Chuang Tzu*. Unlike Lao Tzu, Chuang Tzu was a historical figure, who lived at the end of the fourth century BCE. How much of the book, if any, he actually wrote is unknown.

There is virtually no traditional Chinese philosophy that does not make use of the concept of the 'Dao'. In Confucian writing, the 'Dao' means 'the Way', the proper form of conduct for individuals and of governance for rulers. In Mohism, Dao is akin to a guide to moral wellbeing. In Daoism, it refers to the very being of the universe, the source of all that exists. It is loosely related to the Hindu concept of *brahman*, the ground of being; but *brahman* is both definable in human language and recognizable as the same spirit that is manifested in the *atman*. The Dao is unknowable, mysterious, at one and the same time a metaphysical reality, a natural law, and the inevitable pattern of human life. The famous opening lines of the *Dao De Jing* express the mystery and mysticism at the heart of Daoism: 'The Dao that can be spoken of is not the true Dao. The name that can be named is not the eternal Name.'

Whatever we make of the metaphysical claims of Daoism, its ethical ideas have been influential, not just in China and not just in the ancient world. At the heart of Daoist ethics is the acceptance of nature as perfect and as complete in itself. Any attempt to change or improve upon the perfection of nature, any attempt at 'civilization', can result only in disaster. This vision leads to the doctrine of *wu-wei*, fundamental to Daoist ethics. The more that we strive to change something, the more it remains the same. Real change occurs only when we let go of thinking and reflecting, and simply follow where the Dao takes us. 'Leave all things aside to take their natural course and do not interfere,' as Lao Tzu put it.[15] It is an idea that echoes the Buddhist insistence that one must let go of the illusion of the self (and, indeed, the ideas of Chuang Tzu were to be highly influential in the development of Buddhism in China). The unexamined life is very much worth living, is, in fact, the only life worth living. And the inactive life too: at its most extreme, attachment to *wu-wei* leads to the belief that doing nothing achieves everything.

5

The Silk Road ran from the Chinese seaboard to the Mediterranean and the Black Sea. It was not a single road but a network of trade routes, extending some four thousand miles. First constructed in the Han Dynasty, around the first century BCE, it became the superhighway of the ancient world, linking the civilizations of China, India, Persia, Arabia, Greece and Rome. Along it were traded gold, jade, spices and, of course, silk. Along it were traded, too, ideas, philosophies and religions. It was along the Silk Road that Buddhism came to China.

When exactly China encountered Buddhism is lost in the myths of history. It was probably in the latter half of the first century BCE; and the first Buddhists probably came not from India, but from Central Asia. China had suffered considerable turmoil between the collapse of the Han Dynasty in 220 CE and the establishment of the Tang Dynasty in 618. In those centuries of mayhem Buddhism found a foothold.

In India, during the first century BCE, Buddhism had split into two schools, the *Theravada* and the *Mahayana*, meaning respectively 'teaching of the elders' and 'greater vehicle' (Theravada is sometimes referred to, derogatorily, as *Hinayana*, or 'lesser vehicle'). Where Theravada insisted on a literal interpretation of Buddhist teachings, Mahayana was more relaxed and open to change. It developed in north-west India and south India, the two areas where Buddhism was most exposed to foreign influences, in particular Persian and Hellenistic ideas, not least through Alexander the Great's attempted invasion in 326 BCE. Theravada Buddhism became confined largely to India; Mahayana, having absorbed outside influences, confidently burst forth beyond India's boundaries.

Buddhist scripture, many Mahayanas came to believe, had become fossilized. From the second century BCE onwards there was, in the Mahayana tradition, an explosion of new writing. All these new texts were nevertheless presented as the very words of the Buddha himself. The Mahayanas depicted the Buddha less as a historical figure than as a timeless embodiment of *dharma*, who lived on beyond his enlightenment and provided a succession of Revelations throughout history.

In the Theravada tradition, the ideal Buddhist is the *arhat* ('worthy one') who has lost the fetters of ordinary existence, such as belief in the self or a desire for sex, a 'person all of whose impurities are dissolved', and 'who has laid down his burden, attained his goal, and freed his mind through perfect understanding'.[16] He has, in other words, achieved nirvana. The Mahayana ideal is the *bodhisattva*, or 'enlightened being', who has gained enlightenment but voluntarily postpones his or her final entry into nirvana until everyone else has also become enlightened. The *arhat* seeks only his liberation, the *bodhisattva* the liberation of all. In Theravada only monks can achieve buddhahood;

in Mahayana all can potentially do so. It is a more social gospel, evincing greater compassion for the poor and the needy. For Mahayanas, compassion ranked equally with wisdom as a means of achieving salvation. More flexible about the demands of scripture, more willing to adapt the Buddha's teachings to local sensitivities, more attuned to social needs, it was unsurprisingly Mahayana Buddhism that travelled better beyond the boundaries of India. Virtually all Buddhist communities outside India – in Nepal, Tibet, Mongolia, Korea, Japan and China – are Mahayanan.

By 500, Buddhism was flourishing throughout China, with hundreds of monasteries and temples, and thousands of works translated into Chinese. For a religion that was often hostile to the very notion of *li*, that appeared indifferent to family life, and whose belief in rebirth was dismissed by many almost as occultist, it was a remarkable story of success. But if Buddhist ideals were often at odds with Confucian mores, they nevertheless meshed sympathetically with Daoist philosophy. The denial of the self, the importance of meditation, the renunciation of ritual, the oneness with nature, the view of nirvana as 'emptiness' – all appealed to the Daoist mind.

It was not simply its philosophical affinity to Daoism that attracted many towards Buddhism. It was also its ability to address social issues that neither Confucianism nor Daoism could, and to address issues that mattered to both the ruling class and the masses. The ruling class valued the Buddhist stress on peace and its disapproval of violence and disorder. At the same time, the poor and the dispossessed were drawn to the *bodhisattva* ideal, the belief that enlightenment was possible for even those on the lowest rung of the social ladder.

The influence of Daoism helped create in China a new form of Buddhism, called *Ch'an*, more commonly known in the West by its Japanese name, Zen. Its aim is enlightenment as experienced by the Buddha under the Bodhi-tree. More than any other Buddhist school, it embraces meditation as the road to nirvana. Ch'an explicitly rejects intellectual debate as a means to enlightenment, a rejection illustrated by the importance of *koans* in Ch'an meditation. A koan is a fragment of a story, a dialogue, a question or a statement that is supposed to foster doubt and to reveal the limits of language and of reasoning. One famous koan is called 'A Philosopher asks the Buddha':

> A philosopher asked the Buddha: 'Without words, without the wordless, will you tell me truth?' The Buddha kept silent.
>
> The philosopher bowed and thanked the Buddha, saying: 'With your loving kindness I have cleared away my delusions and entered the true path.'
>
> After the philosopher had gone, Ananda asked the Buddha what he had attained. The Buddha replied: 'A good horse runs even at the shadow of the whip.'

Such koans aim to force adherents to abandon language and reason, and to take a leap into the intuitive. It was this approach that eventually made Zen so appealing to hippies and New Agers in the West.

6

The rise of Daoism, and even more of Buddhism, posed new challenges to Confucianism. Kong's philosophy had come by the sixth century to be ill-placed to defend its rational, reforming, this-worldly outlook against the mystical, quietist, other-worldly vision of Buddhism. As the official ideology of the empire, Confucianism had stultified; many of the literati had learnt Kong's teaching not truly to understand it, but merely as a necessity to pass civil service exams. At the same time, Buddhism appeared to possess both a deeper emotional call on people and a much sharper intellectual edge; there was, for instance, in Buddhism a cosmology and a metaphysics that Confucianism appeared to lack, and that many found both attractive and spiritually necessary, particularly during the social turmoil of the Period of Disunion between the fall of the Han in the third century and the establishment of the Tang in the seventh. By comparison Confucianism appeared to many to be a barren and passionless philosophy.

The response by Confucianists to these various challenges was the remaking of the tradition between the ninth and the twelfth centuries. The European Jesuits who arrived in China in the sixteenth century labelled this reworking of Confucian thought 'Neo-Confucianism'. The most important Neo-Confucian thinker, and possibly the most influential Chinese philosopher of the second millennium, was Zhu Xi (1130–1200). He redefined the tradition, restoring its original focus on moral cultivation and realization, wrenching it from the more bureaucratic approach of the preceding centuries, and drawing upon rival philosophies to create a new metaphysics and cosmology within which to root reworked Confucian ideas of morality and human nature.

Zhu was born in Fujian province on the south-eastern coast of China. A precocious child, he is supposed by the age of eight to have read the Confucian classics. His sharp mind and equally sharp tongue, and his willingness to criticize court policy, led to his dismissal from several imperial administrative posts. He became instead a temple guardian and a teacher at a Confucian academy, posts that shielded him from the cut-throat politics at court, and gave him the leisure to become a productive scholar.

At the heart of Zhu's philosophy was a reformulation of the traditional concepts of *li* and *qi*. For Zhu, *li* meant not just propriety, the obligatory order of social relations and the rituals and etiquette necessary to maintain that order. It meant also the essence of an object or phenomenon. It is what makes a thing that which it is. *Li* is the 'dogness' that makes a dog a dog or the 'bookness' that makes a book a book. A book is a book because it embodies the essence of a book and not that of a dog or a rose or a chair.

Zhu then adds a second concept: that of *qi*. *Li* gives the dog its dogness, a book its bookness. *Qi* is the material that makes manifest the dogness and the bookness, that turns the abstract essence into an actual dog or a book. It is not the same as matter or stuff, but is more like a 'cosmic force' or energy. Nor is it merely things that possess *li*; relations, actions, events, situations – every phenomenon is defined by its *li*. The relationship of father to son or husband to wife, the Era of Warring States and the Period of Disunion, the Zhou and the Han – each has its own essence, just as a dog or a book does. In this way, Zhu links the traditional Confucian view of ritual and social order to a metaphysics of cosmic order. It is no longer merely tradition or reason that anchors Confucian arguments about moral behaviour; it is also nature and the structure of the universe.

The ultimate principle, the 'essence' of the universe, is what Zhu calls 'the Supreme Ultimate'. It is abstract, beyond time and space, the source of things and forces and phenomena in the universe. 'The Supreme Ultimate', Zhu wrote, 'is what is highest of all, beyond which nothing can be. It is the most high, most mystical, and most abstruse, surpassing everything.'[17] Zhu's Supreme Ultimate is reminiscent of the Dao as Daoists understood it, or the Plotinus' One in the Neoplatonic tradition. Having been spurred into action by the need to defend the rationality and this-worldliness of Confucianism against the mysticism and other-worldliness of Buddhism, Neo-Confucianists ended up by drawing upon Buddhism and Daoism to make Confucianism more mystical and other-worldly.

In humans, *li* was, for Zhu, the essence of being human; it was, in other words, the abstract expression of human nature. As such, the *li* for all humans was the same. *Li*, Zhu insisted, 'is nothing but good, for since it is *Li*, how could it be evil?' So why are some humans bad? Why does evil exist? Because, argues Xhu, *li* – human nature – has to be embodied in *qi* – the material or force that actually makes up a human individual. 'Those who receive a *Qi* that is clear are the sages in whom the nature is like a pearl lying in clear cold water. But those who receive a *Qi* that is turbid are foolish and degenerate in whom nature is like a pearl lying in muddy water.'[18]

Zhu is addressing here a question that had troubled Confucianism from the beginning: is human nature good or bad? The two philosophers who, in the two centuries after Kong, developed his ideas most systematically and are regarded as the most important early Confucian thinkers gave contrary answers. Meng Ke (c372–c289 BCE), better known in the West by his Latinized name Mencius, whose work is usually seen as the orthodox interpretation of Kong, insisted on the innate goodness of every human individual. It was poor social influence, he believed, that was the cause of bad moral character. Hsun Tzu (c312–c230 BCE) had a more pessimistic view, seeing all humans as being born evil. The existence of human desires that cannot be satisfied creates 'disorder' and thereby the need for *li*.

Zhu married these two arguments. He agreed with Meng Ke that human nature is fundamentally good, because *li* 'is nothing but good'. But like Hsun Tzu he saw human desire as the root of immorality. Such desire was to be found not in human nature – *li* – but in the material from which humans are made – *qi*. According to Zhu, *ren* – humaneness, the highest of Confucian principles – is *li* as it is 'originally inherent in man's mind'; that is, *li* perfectly materialized in *qi*. For most humans, however, *li* is obscured by 'selfish desires'. 'When selfish desires can be entirely eliminated', Zhu writes, 'and the principle of Nature operates freely, that is *ren*.'

Zhu's work is perhaps the high point of Chinese philosophy, a sophisticated melding of traditional Confucian ethics with an elaborate metaphysics and cosmology. It is a synthesis that held for most of the second millennium. Not till dynastic rule itself crumbled in the twentieth century, and Confucianism lost its privileged place in society, were Zhu's theories dethroned.

The centuries enveloping the turn of the millennium were notable not simply for the development of philosophy but also for the flowering of learning and the advance of technology. The invention of woodblock printing – which made printed books common in China long before Gutenberg's movable type transformed European literary life – gunpowder, the compass, the spinning wheel, and new techniques of agricultural irrigation all put China at the cutting edge of technological innovation. Major advances in mathematics, especially algebra, and in physics, astronomy and geography were matched only by those in the Islamic world. Chinese social organization, and in particular the organization of governance, was without comparison – a strong state, a huge, efficient, well organized bureaucracy, a civil service that chose its candidates not through the whim of the ruler but rationally and equitably through a rigorous examination system. As late as the eighteenth century China was still the largest economy in the world.

But the left hand of China's medieval greatness was the undoing of its right. The strength and solidity of the bureaucracy that initially laid the basis for growth and innovation came eventually to stifle both. Stability gave way to stagnation, economic, social and intellectual. The fact that Zhu's Neo-Confucian synthesis still dominated Chinese philosophy even at the turn of the nineteenth century was a source of pride and identity for many in China. For others, it was a source of regret and despair at the failure to develop and innovate the nation's intellectual heritage. In Europe tumultuous social, political and economic changes overthrew the old order and created fertile ground for new scientific, political, philosophical and ethical thinking. That never happened in China.

CHAPTER SEVEN

Faith and power

1

Mecca was a desolate place, a bleak, windswept town set in desert sands and encircled by barren mountains. It was deep inside the Arabian Peninsula, a land of tribes surrounded by a world of civilizations. To the north was the Fertile Crescent, gateway to two great empires divided by the River Euphrates. On one side of the Euphrates stood Byzantium, the eastern half of the Roman Empire, the half that most engaged with the Greek tradition. On the other side of the river was the land of the Sasanians, whose domain, which extended over what is now Iran and Iraq, had emerged out of the old Persian Empire. To the south, on either side of the Red Sea, lay Ethiopia, an ancient Christian kingdom, and Yemen, a land of fertile mountain valleys, and a point of transit for long-distance trade. Further to the east lay the great civilizations of India and China. Beyond Byzantium, to the west, was the other half of the Roman Empire, which eventually became the centre of Christendom.

In between the empires of the north and the kingdoms of the south lay the desert of Arabia, at the centre of the ancient world, but on the edge of civilization. It was a tribal land, dominated by bedouins, nomadic herders who incessantly criss-crossed the sands from oasis to oasis. A few had adopted a more settled way of life, farmers cultivating grain or palm trees in oases, craftsmen and traders plying their trade in villages and small market towns. Even in the settled communities people followed a way of life shaped by bedouin traditions. They lived in tribal units, looked to the elders for direction and protection, and defined their lives through ideals of courage, honour, loyalty and dedication to the collective wellbeing of the tribe. It was a way of life that would have brought a gleam of recognition to the eyes of ancient Canaanites and Homeric Greeks.

As Arabia was at the edge of civilization, so Mecca was at the edge of Arabia. The town was far from the main trading routes in the area, primarily those linking Yemen to the Fertile Crescent. What it possessed, however, was the Ka'ba: a small, squat, cube-shaped, grey-stone roofless building in the heart of the town that for centuries had been seen as a sanctuary for gods. The people of the desert worshipped many gods, each affording protection to their family or tribe. And eventually every one of these possessed an idol in the Ka'ba.

The origins of the Ka'ba lay deep in ancient Arabian history. Its fortunes, and that of Mecca, too, were transformed through the rise of the Quraysh tribe in the fourth century CE. The Quraysh leader Qusai ibn Kilab knitted together various warring clans and, through a mixture of diplomacy and force, managed to take control of the Ka'ba, recognizing that in that unprepossessing building lay both commercial and political power. He reconstructed the sanctuary from a state of decay and strengthened its role as the dominant place of worship in the region, placing within it idols of all the gods of neighbouring tribes, and turning it into a universal shrine, home to more than three hundred deities. Peoples from across the Arabian Peninsula felt a spiritual obligation to the Ka'ba and to the city that protected the god that gave them protection. The annual pilgrimage to the Ka'ba was transformed into the principal religious festival of the region, the Haj.

By tradition, the area surrounding a religious shrine was sacred ground, on which no fighting was permitted. Qusai took advantage of the peace that surrounded the Ka'ba to encourage trade. In a region in which bloodletting was a form of life, merchants were eager to find protection from violence, and happy to make a detour from the usual caravan routes to be able to conduct business in tranquillity. Qusai taxed all trade within Mecca's borders, bringing new riches to the town, and creating a template for a new form of religious economy.

The renovation of the Ka'ba transformed the fortunes of Mecca. It also eroded the tribal ethic. Tribal life had never been egalitarian. An individual's moral worth was, as in most ancient societies, defined by his or her social status. Nevertheless, the ethos of the collective good ensured that the tribe took care of every member. Mecca's growing affluence acted as an acid to this philosophy. The riches from the Ka'ba accrued to only a few families and helped create an ever more stratified society. The weak, the infirm and the dispossessed were denied not simply access to the new-found wealth but to the protection that came from the old tribal ideals too.

It was into this world in transition that a trader called Muhammad was born. And it was out of this world in transition that his Revelations materialized, Revelations that would forge a new, world-changing, world-shaking religion – Islam. Every Ramadan, a pagan festival of fasting and restraint, Muhammad was in the habit of seeking solitude on the slopes of nearby Mount Hira, to meditate and spend nights alone in a cave, a habit not unusual among Arabs of that time. He was a tortured soul, a successful businessman disturbed by the levels of poverty and inequality in his community. One year, around 610 CE, on one of those nights alone in his cave, Muhammad was overwhelmed by a terrifying experience, of the kind that had previously confronted Paul on the road to Damascus and Augustine in the garden in Milan. An invisible presence within the cave seemed to crush him in its embrace, squeezing the breath out of his body. Just as he was about to surrender to the certainty of his death, the darkness of the cave was broken asunder by a visionary light and a terrifying voice rolled over him 'like the break of dawn'. 'Recite,' it commanded. 'I am not a reciter,' Muhammad pleaded. Whereupon the invisible being 'took me and whelmed me in his embrace until he had reached the limit of mine endurance'.[1] More than once this happened. More than once the force in the cave embraced him to the point of expiration. Finally it released him, and Muhammad felt 'written on my heart' a divine verse:

Recite thou in the name of thy Lord who created;
Createth man from a clot of blood:
Recite thou! and thy Lord is the Most Beneficent,
Who hath taught by the pen;
Hath taught man that which he knoweth not.[2]

The voice was that of the Angel Gibreel, or Gabriel, the words those of God and the verse the first of the Qur'an. That moment in the cave was, the writer Reza Aslan observes, 'Muhammad's burning bush',[3] the moment in which he ceased being a businessman and became a prophet. Over the next twenty-one years, the Qur'an, which means 'recitation' in Arabic, was revealed to Muhammad, line by line, verse by verse, sura by sura.

That, at least, is the traditional Islamic telling of the tale. The historical roots of Islam have been far less studied than those of Christianity. There is little contemporaneous evidence; the traditional story of Muhammad and the founding of Islam was written down a century after the events, by writers who, as in the case of Christianity, had an interest in creating particular myths. Modern, particularly Western, scholars, such as John Wansbrough, Patricia Crone and Michael Cook, have begun challenging the traditional accounts. More recently, the British historian Tom Holland has courted controversy by suggesting that Muhammad was born and preached not in Mecca but much further north in Avdat on the desert borders of Palestine.[4] The questions raised by such scholars are important for the historical story of Islam (though I remain unconvinced by some of the answers, including the relocation of Muhammad's birthplace). For the story I am telling in this book, however, the story of the quest for the moral compass, the Muhammad of myth is as important as the historical figure. Just as the myths about Moses are vital to Judaic ethics, and those about Jesus crucial to Christian ethics, so, too, are the legends about Muhammad vital to Islamic ethics. There was no burning bush on Mount Sinai. There was no resurrection three days after the crucifixion. And there was no Angel Gibreel in a cave on Mount Hira. But the belief that there was has, in each case, helped shape not just a faith but a moral outlook too.

2

If you open the Qur'an today, the first verse is al-Fatiha, the Opening, a prayer recited in Muslim worship:

Praise be to God, Lord of the Worlds!
The compassionate, the merciful!
King on the day of reckoning!
Thee only do we worship, and to Thee do we cry for help.

The verse that Muhammad found impressed in his heart in that cave on that fateful night does not appear until sura 96. The Qur'an does not follow the chronology of God's visit to Muhammad. Rather, after the opening sura, it is arranged by length of verse, the longest ones first, the last of the 114 the briefest. The Qur'an has a different texture to the Torah or the Bible. It is full of stories, many of them, from Adam and Eve to the birth of Jesus, taken from the Judaic and Christian canons, though often told differently. But it does not disclose a story. It is, rather, a series of episodic meditations on humanity's relationship with God, and on human beings' relationship with each other. The rhythm of the Qur'an is distinct too. There is a crushed, fractured character to the language that lends the work an austere, poetic beauty, a beauty that is for Muslims itself an expression of the text's divine provenance.

The idea of the Qur'an as the perfect, uncorrupted word of God is, for Muslims, strengthened by the fact that Muhammad was illiterate, a condition that possesses the same emotional charge in the Islamic tradition as Mary's virginity does in Christian belief: it is both evidence of a divine miracle and an expression of the Prophet's personal purity. Muhammad's Revelations were passed by word of mouth, initially around close family and friends, and then as word spread, and the Prophet took openly to preaching his new-found word of God, to increasingly wider circles of Meccan society. By the time of his death in 632 there were numerous copies of various sura, written down by his literate followers on animal skins or papyrus, but as yet no such thing as the Qur'an.

The process of creating the Qur'an began around a decade after Muhammad's death, during the reign of the Caliph Uthman ibn Affan, who had been a companion of the Prophet. He commissioned Zayd ibn Thabit, one of Muhammad's scribes, to collate an official written copy. Zayd collected the various suras, discarded some, arbitrated between differing versions, ordered them into a single work and generated the Qur'an. Zayd's manuscript was declared the authentic, official text, to which nothing could be added and from which nothing could be subtracted, the template for all subsequent copies of the Qur'an, the pure, uncorrupted, untouched word of God.

3

Like many around him, Muhammad was sorely troubled by the erosion of the traditional norms of tribal society, the wearing down of the idea of the collective good and the growing immiseration of large sections of the Meccan population. Verse by verse as the Qur'an was revealed to Muhammad, so it became a response to this sense of a breakdown in moral life. The social crisis that afflicted Mecca was different from that which had afflicted Israel in the sixth century BCE or Palestine in the first century CE. But like Judaism and Christianity, Islam emerged out of an attempt to address that crisis, an attempt that transformed the landscape of faith, and the social and political landscape too.

Two themes dominated Muhammad's Revelations: the religious and the social. Humanity's destiny, Muhammad insisted, lies with God and one is lost if one thinks otherwise. The name that Muhammad gave his God – Allah – was the name by which Arabs already knew their god. He was, however, not a tribal deity, but a universal power. There was, for Muhammad, only one God, omniscient, omnipotent, yet, in the words of the opening sura, 'compassionate' and 'merciful'. Muhammad's new kind of God demanded not simply submission (the literal meaning of Islam) but also a new kind of society. Like Jesus on the Mount, Muhammad, in some parts of the Revelation at least, denounces the actions and attitudes of the rich and the powerful and decries the mistreatment and exploitation of the weak and the oppressed:

> Woe to every Backbiter, Defamer!
> Who amasseth wealth and storeth it against the future!
> He thinketh surely that his wealth shall be with him for ever.
> Nay! for he shall be flung into the Crushing Fire.[5]

There was nothing about Muhammad's monotheism that would have surprised or scandalized Arabs. The Arabian Peninsula was home to significant

Jewish populations, whose presence could be traced back to the Babylonian exile. Indeed, so close was the relationship between Jews and pre-Islamic Arabs that Arabs considered themselves to be descendants of Abraham, or Ibrahim as they knew him, whom they thought had built the Ka'ba and to whom an idol had been dedicated in the sanctuary. Even before Muhammad, there had been a succession of Arab prophets, called *hanifs*, who preached the virtues of a single God.

What made Muhammad different was the marriage of belief in a single, transcendent, omnipotent God to a social ethic that echoed traditional tribal ideas of virtuous behaviour but that also challenged the mores of the Meccan ruling elite, and that appealed to large sections of a society disenchanted with the transformation of their world. Muhammad's social ethic gave his God moral content. His God gave his social ethic a sense of power.

As Muhammad's following swelled, inevitably he came into conflict with Mecca's ruling families. He was eventually driven out of the city in 622 and found a new power base in a small agricultural oasis 250 miles to the north of Mecca called Yathrib. It was soon given a new name: Medinat an-Nabi, the City of the Prophet, or more simply Medina. The secret journey of Muhammad's followers from Mecca to Medina, the *Hijra*, marks for believers the beginning of Islam as a community, the abandonment of a wicked, pagan society and the creation of a new people living according to the moral guidance of Allah, the first day of the Muslim era. From his Medina power base, Muhammad was drawn into an armed struggle with the Quraysh, especially over the all-important trade routes. He triumphed in a series of battles through which he established control over Mecca and the surrounding areas.

It was in this period of conflict that the Prophet's Revelations took their final form and out of which Islam acquired its initial shape and temper. In traditional Arab tribes, power was distributed within a collective leadership. In Medina, power was vested solely in Muhammad, a man whose authority as Prophet and Lawgiver came from God and so could not be challenged. As Muhammad's power as Lawgiver became unquestioned and unquestionable, so the character of Gibreel's Revelations changed. There was now much greater concern with defining ritual observances and with social rules governing property, marriage, inheritance, the role of women and relations between the sexes, many in response to a debate among the faithful. Increasingly Islam became a religion not simply of compassion and benevolence but also of struggle and expansion. Allah provided divine permission for war, violence and even slaughter. When the Quarayzah, one of Medina's Jewish tribes, sided with Mecca during the Battle of the Trench, a fortnight-long siege of Medina in 627, Muslim forces imposed upon them the most savage of punishments. Muhammad's men laid siege to Medina's Jewish quarter for twenty-five days until the Quarayzah unconditionally surrendered. Every one of the surviving men was executed, every woman and child enslaved. The eighth-century Muslim historian Ibn Ishaq described the slaughter of the men:

> They surrendered . . . Then the Apostle went out to the market of Medina (which is still its market today) and dug trenches in it. Then he sent for them and struck off their heads in those trenches as they were brought out to him in batches.[6]

Such savagery was not uncommon in seventh-century warfare and, shocking though it was, the slaughter in the marketplace tells us more about the premodern moral universe than it does about the distinctive character of Muhammad's ethics. But the fact that it does not tell us much that is distinctive about the ethics of Islam is itself revealing. Muhammad breathed in the moral air of seventh-century Arabia. There was in Mecca unhappiness at the impact of the Ka'ban taxes and a sense of moral drift that Muhammad sought to address. He did so not by creating a novel moral framework but by drawing upon pre-existing notions of right and wrong and of virtuous behaviour. This is as true of what we now see as Muhammad's 'good' ethical injunctions – to be compassionate, benevolent, generous, merciful – as of what we recognize as the bad, such as his savagery towards those whom he regarded as enemies.

Islam transformed the moral landscape in the same way as Christianity had – through establishing not so much a set of new moral rules as a new reason for being moral. Morality was anchored in Allah's will. Prayer and alms-giving were required by God. So was the annihilation of enemies. The butchering of the Quarayzah was, in Muhammad's eyes, a moral necessity, an act sanctified by God. This is not to say that Islam did not have a major impact on moral life. The acceptance of a monotheistic god transformed, as it did in the case of

Christianity too, the idea of belongingness and the moral shape of the community. A traditional Arabian tribe had been a closed unit; only those born into it could become members. In Medina, Muhammad's followers defined themselves as the *ummah*, whose boundaries were set not by race, ethnicity or descent but by conviction. Anyone could join Muhammad's community by avowing that 'There is no god but God and Muhammad is God's Messenger'. Here was crafted a new kind of tribe, a universal tribe, a community defined by tribal norms, rules and rituals, and yet one that appealed not to a restricted group but to the whole of pagan Arabia, and, eventually, to the whole of the world. It was not universalism in a modern secularist sense – moral worth was defined by a willingness to submit to Allah – but nevertheless Islam continued the development of the idea of a universal community that had begun with the Stoics and been further elaborated by Christians.

As with Christianity, Islam's insistence on a single transcendent, omniscient, omnipotent, absolutely good God helped consecrate the idea of a rule-based morality. Goodness was to be found not in the cultivation of laudable habits, or in the aspiration to wisdom through self-examination, but in the ability to accept unconditionally God's law and to follow faithfully the rules that He set down for entry to heaven. As with Christianity, Islam combined an ethics as malleable as clay with the iron rod of God's word.

4

The first stone was laid in 689, upon ground that could barely have been holier, at least for Jews. It was the very place at which, in Judaic tradition, Abraham had prepared to sacrifice his only son Isaac, having been commanded so to do by God. It was also the very place where once had stood Solomon's Temple and later Herod's Temple, both destroyed by the wrath of Gentile invaders. But this was no Jewish shrine that was now rising on this holiest of mounts. It was the Dome of the Rock, the first, and perhaps greatest, of all Muslim shrines, built not in Mecca or Medina but in the heart of Jerusalem.

Within two years the Dome of the Rock had been completed, an extraordinary building quite unlike either earlier Arab architecture or the later Muslim design. Both the octagonal structure of the building and the dome that capped it are drawn from the Byzantine style, as is the mathematical rhythm of the proportions that enhances its visual impact. At the heart of the shrine is the sacred rock, from which the building gets its name. For Jews, this is the rock on which Abraham prepared to sacrifice Isaac. For Muslims, it is the rock from which Muhammad's winged horse leapt into the sky, accompanied by the Archangel Gibreel, on the Night Journey to heaven. A small hole in the rock leads to a cavity beneath known as *Bir el-Arwah*, the 'Well of Souls', in which, it is said, the voices of the dead mingle with the falling waters of the lower rivers of paradise as they drop into eternity. It is, for Jews, the spiritual junction of heaven and Earth.

It was for more worldly reasons, though, that the Caliph Abd-al Malik ibn Marwan ordered the construction of the Dome. Ostensibly designed to provide a shelter for Muslim pilgrims, its true purpose was far grander and more political. The Dome of the Rock symbolized the new power of Islam. Barely half a century after Muhammad had been forced to flee a small town in the middle of a desert at the edge of the civilized world, his followers had carved out a great empire and now controlled the holiest of all cities. And in building the Dome at that particular place, on Temple Mount, in the heart of Jerusalem, Abd-al Malik physically established Islam's place in the lineage of Abraham, while both distinguishing Islam from the spiritual legacy of Judaism and Christianity and challenging the temporal power of the other two monotheistic faiths.

The death of Muhammad in 632 had unleashed a power struggle, religious and secular, both within the new Muslim community and between that community and its external foes. These struggles came to define the character of the faith in its early days. The first question to settle was that of who should become *Khalifat Allah*, or 'Deputy of God' (a title that later became *Khalifat Rasul Allah* – 'the successor to the Messenger of God'), or Caliph. The Companions, Muhammad's closest followers who believed they had a special understanding of the Prophet's thoughts, the Medinan tribes who had given him succour in his hour of need, and the Quryashi aristocracy in Mecca that first rejected Muhammad and later embraced him all became locked in a power struggle.

The obvious choice of successor appeared to be Muhammad's cousin and son-in-law Ali ibn Abi Talib. But many of the more powerful clans, especially among the Qurayshi, feared that if such a close relative of Muhammad's were to become Caliph, he would hold in his hands not just the reins of political authority but also the mantle of prophethood, and so upset the delicate power relations between clans. It was important for them to establish a distinction between the religious authority of the Prophet and the secular authority of the Caliph. The first three Caliphs were all chosen as much because they were not Ali as for any personal qualities they possessed. Ali eventually became Caliph at the fourth attempt in 656. His accession to the caliphate sparked the first Muslim civil war. He was eventually murdered while praying in a mosque.

Right from the beginning, then, Islam cleaved along political lines. What began as political faction fighting mutated over time into theological distinctions. The Sunnis and the Shia, for instance, grew out of the early power blocs that fought over Muhammad's succession. The *Shi'atu Ali* ('the party of Ali') wished to restrict the caliphate to Muhammad's descendants. The Sunnis emerged in part out of another early power bloc, the *Shi'atu Uthman* ('the party of Uthman'), that took a more pragmatic view, arguing that leadership should be vested with those politically most capable of maintaining order and stability in the *ummah*.

The political challenge to the early Caliphs came not just from power blocs in Mecca and Medina but also from tribes that, after Muhammad's death, no longer felt they owed allegiance to the *ummah*. Tribal leaders throughout the Arabian Peninsula began imitating Muhammad's project, each declaring himself God's messenger, each receiving his own Revelations, each establishing his own divinely inspired state, each creating his own private *ummah* bound by its own particular ethic. The first Caliph, Abu Bakr, sought to affirm his authority within the *ummah* by taking up arms against the 'false prophets'. The wars of the Ridda, as they were called, helped create a much more militarized society, not to mention a battle-hardened army, and the momentum of action generated by the struggle against the false prophets carried the *ummah* to the borders of the great empires that surrounded Arabia and then, eventually, into their very hearts. Barbarian invasion, agricultural collapse, plague and war had all sapped the strength of the old Mediterranean world. The Sasanid and Byzantine Empires were no match for the vigour and vim of

Arab armies, sinews stiffened by God. By the end of the second Caliph Umar's reign, barely a decade after Muhammad's death, the whole of the Arabian Peninsula, Mesopotamia, Persia, Syria and Egypt had been conquered. By the early eighth century the Muslim Empire stretched from Sindh in the east to Iberia in the west.

The creation almost overnight of a new empire confirmed for Muslims the divine power of their God. It also exacerbated the political struggles within the *ummah*. These were no longer local to the Hijaz region of Arabia but enveloped elites from Hispania to the Hindu Kush. The Caliphs became little more than figureheads as local dynasties developed, each running their own mini-empires. The size of the empire, its fragmentation, the remoteness of rulers from their subjects and, ironically, the very secular character of his office, all made Islam increasingly indispensable to the Caliph. Caliphs claimed to rule by divine edict, in accordance with the Qur'an and by the rules of right conduct as defined by the Prophet's behaviour. As a secular power, the Caliph lacked the authority to justify his divine right to rule or to establish how one ought to live according to the Qur'an. So a new class of religious scholars emerged to perform that function. The *ulama* or 'learned ones' took upon themselves the responsibility of guiding the *ummah* according to God's will. They came to hold extraordinary power in shaping the beliefs and practices of the Muslim community.

The *ulama* wielded its power in a different way to Christian clergy. In Christianity, faithfulness was defined primarily through correct belief, hence the fractious debates and schisms over doctrines such as the divinity of Christ and the nature of the Trinity. Belief is clearly important within Islam, too, but faithfulness is defined less by right belief than by correct practice. It is a distinction between what philosophers call *orthodoxic* and *orthopraxic* faiths. The one and only belief required of a convert to Islam is simple – 'There is no god but God, and Muhammad is God's messenger'. Al-Ghazali, one of the most important philosophers of traditional Islam, set out three basic beliefs that could not be challenged: belief in a single God; belief in the Qur'an as God's word as revealed to Muhammad; and belief in the existence of an afterlife. Beyond these beliefs what is truly demanded of Muslims is that they are faithful to the practices required of them – in particular the Five Pillars, the basic obligations that every Muslim must satisfy to live a good and responsible life, and sharia, the comprehensive body of rules guiding the life of all Muslims. It was through establishing and policing these practices that the *ulama* gained its power. 'Caliphs will come and go, and the caliphate as a civil institution will rise and fall in strength,' Reza Aslan observes, 'but the authority of the Ulama and the power of their religious institutions will only increase with time.'[7]

CHAPTER EIGHT

Reason and Revelation

1

He is born to a princess who had secretly married her lover. Fearful of what might happen if the king should learn about her son, the princess places the infant in a little boat and casts him out to sea. He is eventually washed up on a distant uninhabited island where he is found by a gazelle whose own fawn had been devoured by an eagle.

The gazelle nurtures the infant as her own. The boy initially lives as a beast, but begins to recognize that he is different from all the other creatures on the island. The deer that had nursed him eventually dies. In great distress, the boy begins to ponder the mystery of death. Gripped by a 'vehement desire to find, if possible, that part where the defect was, that he might remove it, and she return to her former State, of Life and Vigour', he dissects the gazelle's body. He comes to realize that the cause of her death was the result of the dissolution of soul and body, the departure of a spirit that 'once dwelt here, but has now deserted his Habituation and left it empty'.[1] The boy now sets out on a journey of inquiry and self-discovery, slowly unravelling the ultimate mysteries of the cosmos through rational contemplation.

So begins Abu Bakr ibn Tufail's extraordinary twelfth-century novel *Hayy Ibn Yaqzan*, whose enigmatic title translates as *Living, Son of Wakeful*. The first ever philosophical novel, and the first to strand its hero upon a desert island, there are few books that today lie as neglected as *Hayy Ibn Yaqzan* and yet historically have been more influential. Translated into Latin in 1671, and later into English, it became a bestseller in Europe, influencing novelists and philosophers, its echo to be heard in books such as Daniel Defoe's *Robinson Crusoe* and in concepts including the *tabula rasa* and the noble savage that helped shape the Enlightenment.

Ibn Tufail was born in the first decade of the twelfth century near Granada in Muslim Iberia. He studied philosophy and medicine and is said to have written numerous works on both subjects as well as astronomy. Almost all are lost, with the notable exception of *Hayy Ibn Yaqzan*. It is a novel infused with the ideas of Plato and Aristotle – or, at least, with the ideas of Plato and Aristotle as filtered through the Neoplatonism of Plotinus. It is one of the first explorations of human life in the 'state of nature', a form of imaginary reconstruction that was to become important in the Enlightenment. Perhaps its greatest significance lies in its belief in the ethical importance of rational contemplation, and in its insistence that such contemplation could, unaided, reach out to all the truths of the world. Reason, Ibn Tufail suggests, is instantiated in human nature, and there is a natural progression of the human mind towards the discovery of truth.

Through his investigations, Hayy is led to the discovery of the spiritual world, of a world beyond that of the senses, a world of transcendent Forms that can be 'apprehended by Intellectual Speculation' alone.[2] He comes to recognize the necessity of a Creator, and for such a Creator to exist outside of time and space. True happiness comes only through people acknowledging their kinship to the Creator and in diligently contemplating Him. The journey of Hayy toward a Neoplatonist vision of the cosmos mirrored that of the Muslim world itself. It was only in the eighth century that the Arab world discovered Plato and Aristotle. That discovery transformed the Arab world, and its understanding of God, humanity and morality. It was eventually to transform the rest of the world too.

2

The expansion of the Islamic Empire from India to Iberia created new political tensions and theological dilemmas. It created also new kinds of administrative problems, the most pressing being the difficulty of collecting taxes, keeping accounts and maintaining records of state in an empire consisting of dozens of languages, forms of law and administrative styles. In the early eighth century, Caliphs decided that Arabic should be the common language of the empire, and the one in which public records and accounts were to be kept. So there began the so-called 'translation movement', a huge project to translate local records into Arabic. Soon the translation movement spread its wings. The new empire had within its borders a treasure house of philosophical, scientific and religious texts, mainly Greek and Persian. The Arab world discovered Plato and Aristotle, Euclid and Ptolemy. Much of the translation was undertaken not by Muslims but by Christian scholars, particularly in Syria. Just as later the work of Muslim philosophers such as Ibn Rushd would transform the Christian and Judaic traditions, but largely be ignored within Islam, so the work of Syriac Christian translators transformed the intellectual standing of the Islamic Empire, at a time when learning in Christian Europe was languishing.

The acquisition by Arabs of the philosophical jewels of the Greek and Persian worlds helped transform the intellectual culture of the new empire. In the mid-eighth century, the Caliph al-Mansur built the new city of Baghdad to be his imperial capital. And here his great-grandson, the Caliph al-Ma'mun, created the 'House of Wisdom', a celebrated library and centre for scholarship that turned Baghdad into the world's greatest intellectual centre of the time, and helped launch a cultural tradition as lustrous as that of ancient Athens before or Renaissance Florence after. Centred first in Baghdad and then in Cordoba, in Muslim Iberia, Arab philosophy and science played a critical role not just in preserving the gains of the Greeks but in genuinely expanding the boundaries of knowledge. It also laid the foundations for the European Renaissance and the Scientific Revolution. Neither happened in the Muslim world, but without the Muslim world, neither may have happened at all, at least in the form they did.

By the second half of the tenth century, the translation movement had come to an end largely because all the great works had already been translated and studied. By now a new movement had begun – that of original Arabic scholarship. Over the next three centuries there was in the Muslim world a remarkable flourishing of science and learning. Arab scholars revolutionized astronomy, invented algebra, helped develop the modern decimal number system (a rudimentary version of which they had discovered in India), established the basis of optics, and set the ground rules of cryptography.

The translation into Arabic of Aristotle, Plato and other Greek philosophers helped create a fissure that was to run throughout Islamic intellectual history. On the one side stood the Rationalists, dedicated to the ideal of *falsafah*, by which they meant not simply the discipline of philosophy, but also a way of living rationally in accordance to the laws of the cosmos. The *faylasufs* saw learning as an ethical duty. They took from the Greeks both their spirit of rational inquiry and their faith in the almost boundless power of the human intellect. Most were deeply pious, and accepted the Qur'an as the word of God. But they challenged the idea that religious truths could be accessed only through divine Revelation, insisting that reason alone would suffice. Every human, in other words, had inside him or her an inner Hayy. Most *faylasufs* insisted, too, that all theological arguments must adhere to the principles of rational thought. Even the interpretation of the Qur'an and the Sunna were, in Rationalist eyes, subordinate to human reason.

On the other side of the divide were the Traditionalists, for whom human reason was as weak and corrupt as human beings themselves, and for whom Revelation and scripture were the only sure paths to truth. The theology of the Traditionalists was different to that of Augustine, but their views of human nature and of God's power bore striking similarities. Traditionalists were often forced to engage with Rationalists on philosophical ground, and appropriated many arguments from the ancient philosophers. Perhaps the greatest of all Traditionalist philosophers, Abu Hamid Muhammad ibn Ghazali, or al-Ghazali, used the method of *falsafah* to attack its content, attempting to show rationally the incoherence of the Rationalist arguments. But more often than not, Traditionalists dissociated themselves completely from *falsafah* on the grounds that it was either impious or foreign, or both. 'Rationalist' and

'Traditionalist' are, of course, loaded terms, and not necessarily how the two sides in the debate would have understood themselves or their opponents. Nevertheless, used carefully, they help illuminate a crucial debate that took place in the early centuries of Islamic philosophy.

The earliest of the Rationalist movements was the Mu'tazilite. Founded by the theologian and jurist Wasil ibn Ata (c700–48), it flourished mainly in Baghdad and Basra, but its influence was far-reaching. At its heart was a revolutionary defence both of human reason and of the rationality of God's ways. Since God was entirely rational, so His laws could be substantiated intellectually, as Hayy had done, without necessarily either leaning upon or repudiating the authority of scripture.

The early insights of the Mu'tazilah were continually developed in the Rationalist tradition through a line of philosophers beginning with al-Kindi, continuing with al-Farabi (c872–951), often regarded as the founder of the *falsafah* school and known as the 'Second Master' (second, that is, after Aristotle), and culminating in the work of the two most important Muslim philosophers, Ibn Sina and Ibn Rushd, known respectively in the West as Avicenna and Averroes. This tradition of Muslim Rationalism is these days barely remembered in the West. Yet its value and significance, not least to the so-called 'Judaeo-Christian' tradition, is difficult to overstate.

Ibn Sina wrote more than four hundred works, probably the most important and influential of which was *Kitab al-Shifa*, or *Book of Healing*. A philosophical encyclopaedia, it is divided into four parts that deal with logic, physics, mathematics and metaphysics. Ibn Sina summarizes here the rational argument about God and faith, making a case not just for the existence of God but also for Islamic social and ethical practices. He does so, however, with barely a mention of the Qur'an. Rather he stands his argument unaided upon reason.

Abu al-Walid Muhammad bin Ahmad bin Rushd, or Ibn Rushd (1126–96), was the supreme Muslim interpreter of Aristotle and the Muslim philosopher with the greatest influence upon the non-Muslim world. He was born in Cordoba into a family of distinguished scholars and jurists. Among his early mentors was Ibn Tufail, who inspired him to write his famous commentaries on Aristotle. Working at a time when the Rationalists were already on the defensive in the Muslim world, Ibn Rushd came to wield far more influence within Judaism and Christianity than within Islam. It was largely through Ibn Rushd that Western European philosophers rediscovered their Aristotle, and his commentaries shaped the thinking of a galaxy of thinkers from Moses Maimonides to Thomas Aquinas. In *The Divine Comedy* Dante places him with the great pagan philosophers whose spirits dwell not in Hell but in Limbo, 'the place that favour owes to fame'. Raphael depicts him with Aristotle, Plato and Socrates in his painting *The School of Athens*.

The starting point for most of the Rationalists was God's truth as revealed to Muhammad. But the stress they placed upon reason raised questions about the very nature of, and indeed need for, Revelation. A coherent account of the universe, the Rationalists insisted, required a God, an Unmoved Mover that was the cause of all matter and motion but was itself uncaused, a being that by definition had to be outside of space and time for He was the cause of space and time. It was a God modelled partly on Aristotle's Unmoved Mover. Behind every change in the universe, Aristotle had insisted, must lie a chain of causes. But that chain cannot extend for ever. The first link in the chain, as it were, was the Unmoved Mover. It was a God modelled also on Plotinus' concept of the One that transcends thought and being altogether.

The Rationalist God was an all-powerful, all-knowing, completely good being, wholly simple in the sense that He possessed no parts, no body, no physical existence. He was immutable, unchangeable, necessary, a God not unlike the Allah imagined by most Muslims. But the implications the Rationalists drew from the nature of God were distinct and revolutionary.

As an expression of perfect unity, God was not divided in any way. He had no brain through which to think, no soul through which to express Himself, no limbs through which to act, no vocal cords through which to speak. Hence, for the Rationalists, God possessed no attributes, either in terms of physical form, such as a body or a face, or in terms of more abstract qualities of mind or character such as wisdom or will. These, the Rationalists suggested, were simply human ways of thinking because humans possessed no language through which to describe God as a Being-in-Himself.

Reason led the Rationalists to see the necessity for God. But reason also led them to insist that it was impossible rationally to define God, and to deny that God could intervene in the mundane aspects of human affairs. A simple being, outside of time and space, and without physical or mental attributes, could not act upon space and time. God, Ibn Sina suggested, is far too exalted to partake in the humdrum reality of human life. He is the condition of being of the cosmos, and He apprehends everything that has emanated from Him and that He has brought into being. But He knows the human world only in general and universal terms. God does not deal in particulars. Nor can humans talk positively of God. They can only define what God is *not* – He is not human, He is not material, He does not consist of parts – not describe what He is.

Both the idea of a simple God, and that of the *via negativa* – the insistence that it was not possible to speak positively of God – became highly influential, not just in Islam, but in Judaism and Christianity too. Muslim Traditionalists were, however, aghast. They accepted the simplicity, purity and unity of God. But they could not imagine Allah as possessing no attributes or as being unable to intervene in human life. The Qur'an describes a God that walks, talks, wills and judges, a God that possesses bodily parts and sits upon a throne. How could a being outside of time and space, completely unified and possessing no parts also have a face, a body, sit on a throne and be wise and judicious? The Traditionalists' answer was to shrug their shoulders. '*Bila kayfa*,' they said – 'Don't ask how.'

For the Rationalists such an answer was incoherent and unacceptable. In making God so transcendent, pure and good that He could only be spoken of in the negative, and in insisting that God was reason itself, the Rationalists paradoxically both diminished the status of God and exalted that of humans. Human reason had to be powerful enough to divine God's message and human will had to be strong enough to act upon it. Divine justice had, for the Rationalists, to be as pure as God Himself. God could do no evil. The Traditionalists accepted that God alone defined good and evil. That which God had decided to be good or evil may sometimes seem arbitrary or unjust but it is not for humans to question. *Bila kayfa*. The Rationalists, on the other hand, insisted that God could not do that which was contrary to reason or act with disregard for the welfare of His creatures. No omnipotent deity could act in violation of the precepts of justice and righteousness by, say, torturing the innocent, or demanding the impossible, simply because He was God.

Good and evil were not arbitrary demands but rational categories that could be established through unaided reason.

This debate returns us to the dilemma that Plato raised in *Euthyphro*. Either goodness is divinely defined but arbitrary, or it is rational but exists independently of the gods. The Traditionalists were happy to accept the seeming arbitrariness of God's commands so long as believers unquestioningly accepted those commands as divine law. The Rationalists could not accept the idea of God making irrational moral demands. But this was to question the very belief that God defined goodness and badness. Or, to put it another way, the idea of a rational morality and that of a rational God came to pull Rationalists in two different directions.

3

At the end of *Hayy Ibn Yaqzan*, Asal, a religious figure from a neighbouring land, arrives on Hayy's island. The two men come to meet and to recognize the similarity between the Revelation of scripture and the ideas to which Hayy had been led by contemplation. Asal understands that references in scripture to angels, prophets, heaven and hell were mere representations in sensible terms of the spiritual realities that Hayy had perceived on his own and that 'the Original and the Copy did exactly agree together'. Hayy realizes, in turn, that the claims of revealed scripture conform with his own experiences of this world and of the world of spirit. Muhammad truly was 'a Messenger sent from his Lord; and he believ'd him, and affirm'd his Veracity and bore Witness to his Message'.[3] He could have complete faith in God's law as laid down by the Prophet.

For Ibn Tufail the meeting of minds between Hayy and Asal underscores both the power of reason and the authority of scripture, revealing one to be the mirror of the other. But it also raises the question: why do we need scripture? Why not simply rely on human reason? The conventional Rationalist explanation was put forward by Ibn Rushd. Most people, he suggested, are not capable of exercising reason. God created scripture for the unreasoning masses. He intended the Qur'an to be read in one of two ways. The learned, the *falsafah*, read it allegorically. 'Anyone who is not a man of learning', however, 'is obliged to take these passages in their apparent meaning.' 'Allegorical interpretation' of the Qur'an is, for the masses, Ibn Rushd suggested, the same as 'unbelief because it leads to unbelief'.[4] Allegorical interpretations ought to be discussed only in philosophical texts that learned men and no one else could comprehend. This is an aristocratic view of morality, part of a long thread that stretches back to Plato and forward into the modern world. The idea that scripture should be read differently by the learned and by the masses was already an important theme in Christianity and was to become even more so. Some Muslim Rationalists adopted, however, a more democratic view of morality. In so doing, they took the argument about the relationship between reason and Revelation much further, denying the very need for scripture and resolving the conflict between the idea of a rational morality and that of a God, by abandoning God.

There was during the Abbasid period (750–1258) an extraordinary flourishing of freethinking, of a kind unseen since the height of Greek philosophy, and that would be unseen again until the Enlightenment. Dubbed *ziddiqs*, or 'heretics', by the authorities, many posed an open challenge to Islamic dogma. The most celebrated of the freethinkers was Abul Ala al-Ma'arri (c973–1058), sometimes known as the Eastern Lucretius for his unflinching religious scepticism:

> They all err—Moslems, Jews,
> Christians, and Zoroastrians:
> Humanity follows two world-wide sects:
> One, man intelligent without religion,
> The second, religious without intellect.[5]

Born in Syria, al-Ma'arri was struck down at an early age by smallpox, which was eventually to lead to blindness. He is one of the greatest poets in the Arab tradition. His most famous work, *The Epistle of Forgiveness*, in which he describes visiting paradise and meeting Arab poets of the pagan period, bears comparison to Dante's *Divine Comedy*.

Not Revelation, nor tradition nor authority but only reason, al-Ma'arri insisted, should guide human life:

> Traditions come from the past, of high import if they be True;
> Ay, but weak is the chain of those who warrant their truth.
> Consult thy reason and let perdition take others all:
> Of all the conference Reason best will counsel and guide.

Religion, al-Ma'arri insisted, was like a 'pasture full of noxious weeds', a 'fable invented by the ancients', to hold the masses in thrall:

> O fools, awake! The rites you sacred hold
> Are but a cheat contrived by men of old,
> Who lusted after wealth and gained their lust
> And died in baseness—and their law is dust.

There was in al-Ma'arri's poetry a deep and enveloping pessimism that harked back to a Stoic view of the world. He had a great belief in the sanctity of life – he became a vegetarian, not wishing to harm other living creatures – but seemed sometimes to be overwhelmed by the ephemeral, pain-filled character of human life. Life's two gifts, it seemed to him, were pain or death:

> Over many a race the sun's bright net was spread
> And loosed their pearls nor left them even a thread.
> This dire world delights us, though all sup—
> All whom she mothers—from one mortal cup.
> Choose from two ills: which rather in the main
> Suits you? —to perish or to live in pain?

There is in al-Ma'arri's work a pervasive sense that it would have been better had humans never been created:

> Better for Adam and all who issued forth from his loins
> That he and they, yet unborn, created never had been!
> For whilst his body was dust and rotten bones in the earth
> Ah, did he feel what his children saw and suffered of woe.

The almost unplumbable darkness of al-Ma'arri's vision reveals the difficulty of living without God in tenth-century Arabia. Modern humanism has its material roots in the ability of humans to transform their world, a world in which the great revolutions – scientific, industrial and political – have provided concrete meaning to the idea of human-driven progress. This was not al-Ma'arri's world. He lived in an age in which life seemed forever static and immovable, constrained by the brute facts of nature, in which the idea that humans could refashion the world for the better would have seemed not merely hubristic but irrational and insane, in which grief and anguish were as much a natural, ineradicable part of life as the sun rising in the morning and the leaves falling in the autumn. His was a world in which there seemed no possibility of comfort and solace without God, no prospect of infusing life with a sense of meaning, no hope of recompense for a life of pain and torment. In such a world it took immense courage to look into the void and accept the darkness, to examine one's life and acknowledge unflinchingly its unremitting pain. Most Rationalists leavened that pain by accepting God's existence and viewing reason, not as a challenge to scripture, but as an alternative path to scripture's truths. Not so al-Ma'arri.

4

Ibn Rushd and al-Ma'arri represented the two poles of the Rationalist worldview, the one establishing reason as the equal of Revelation, the other dismissing Revelation in its entirety. Both were to be influential, but neither within the Islamic tradition. Ironically, it was in Christian Europe that their philosophies found their greatest following.

Islam came eventually to define itself not through rationalism, whether of the restrained kind espoused by Ibn Sina and Ibn Rushd, or the more exuberant freethinking of al-Ma'arri, but through mysticism, on the one hand, and a more literal understanding of Revelation on the other. The most significant critic of the Rationalists, al-Ghazali, helped shape the development of both these approaches.

Born in Tus, in what is now north-eastern Iran, al-Ghazali (c1056–1111) came to be one of the most important philosophers, theologians and jurists of medieval Islam. Appointed to the prestigious Nizamiyya Madrassa in Baghdad, he published a series of books challenging the *falsafah* school. What distinguished al-Ghazali from the myriad other critics of *falsafah* was his use of the method of the *faylasufs* to attack the content of their arguments. Rationalist claims about God, the cosmos and human nature, he insisted, were wanting in reason.

In his book *The Incoherence of the Philosophers*, al-Ghazali set out twenty key teachings of the *faylasufs* that he believed could not be rationally sustained. Most posed no problem for Islamic doctrine and, while, in his eyes, incoherent, could nevertheless be tolerated. Three key *falsafah* claims were, however, contrary to Islamic belief: the idea that the universe had no beginning and had always existed; the claim that God's knowledge included only universals and not particulars; and the insistence that after death the souls of humans would not return to their bodies. Al-Ghazali imposed a *fatwa* declaring all those who publicly defended these three *falsafah* concepts to be unbelievers and apostates whom righteous Muslims had a moral duty to kill. Here were defined starkly the boundaries of religious tolerance in Islam. In a subsequent work, al-Ghazali elucidated three other principles, opposition to which constitute apostasy and unbelief: acceptance of monotheism, of Muhammad's Revelation as the word of God and of the Qur'anic descriptions of life after death.

Al-Ghazali's intervention signalled the end of the great period of debate and freethinking within the Muslim world. Rationalists came to be hunted down, persecuted, killed. Politics, even more than theology, contributed to the demise of the Rationalists. In 833 the Abbasid Caliph al-Ma'mun instigated what came to be called the *al-mihna*, or 'inquisition', to force religious scholars to adopt a Mu'tazilite, or Rationalist, view about the creation of the Qur'an. Scholars were dragged before a specially convened court, interrogated over their beliefs, and those who gave the wrong answers were imprisoned.

Al-Ma'mun died a few months after launching the *al-mihna*, but his immediate successors shared his enthusiasm and the inquisition lasted for another sixteen years. Eventually, in 849, the Caliph al-Mutawakkil ended the persecution, released the non-complying *ulama* from prison and restored many of the refuseniks to positions of authority.

The *al-mihna* may appear at first glance to have been a theological struggle between the Rationalists and the Traditionalists. It was, in fact, a political struggle between the caliphate and the *ulama*. Since the days of the first Caliph, Abu Bakr, there had been a cleavage between the secular power of the caliphate and the religious power of the *ulama*, a cleavage deliberately established to prevent the concentration of power in a single hand. The *al-mihna* was a shot at a power grab by the Caliph, an attempt to claim authority over both secular and religious spheres. Its failure ensured that, as professor of Islamic history Ira Lapidus has put it, 'the caliphate would evolve . . . as a largely military and imperial institution' while the religious elites 'would develop a more complete authority over the communal, personal, religious, and doctrinal aspects of Islam'.[6]

Having established distinct spheres of interest for the caliphate and the *ulama*, both sides came to recognize that Rationalist views about human nature, moral character and free will were corrosive of a fixed social order. Too much reason brought too much scrutiny and too great a challenge to authority. Just as Roman emperors had backed Augustine against Pelagius, so Caliphs backed the Traditionalists against the Rationalists.

It took more than two centuries of struggle for the Traditionalists to establish themselves as the custodians of Sunni orthodoxy. But by the time Ibn Rushd challenged al-Ghazali in the twelfth century, his book *The Incoherence of the Philosophers*, rebutting many of al-Ghazali's anti-Rationalist arguments, the Rationalists were already firmly on the defensive, and the Traditionalists and the conservative *ulama* entrenched in power.

At the very moment that the Muslim Empire turned its back on the Rationalist tradition that it had nourished, Christian Europe, which for a millennium had supped upon shrivelled scraps of Socrates, Plato and Aristotle, rediscovered that heritage in large part through the scholarship of the thinkers that Islam had now rejected. The rationalist spirit that had been carried first by the Greeks, and then by Muslims, now found a new home in Christian Europe. The irony is that whereas in Islam the separation of faith and state had helped empower the conservative *ulama*, within Christian Europe it was the rationalist challenge to religion that helped separate faith and state in a new way, and in so doing opened the door to a new form of progressive politics and ethics.

5

'God shrivelled my tongue until I was prevented from giving instruction. So I used to force myself to teach on a particular day for the benefit of my various pupils but my tongue would not utter a single word.'[7] Shortly after completing *The Incoherence of the Philosophers*, al-Ghazali seems to have suffered a mental breakdown. His autobiography, *al-Munquidh min al-Dalal*, a tortured, moving work that bears comparison to Augustine's *Confessions*, tells the story of al-Ghazali's spiritual torments and intellectual doubts, his discovery of his inability to teach, his renunciation, at the height of his fame, of his Baghdad career, his wanderings through Syria, Palestine and Hijaz, and his eventual resumption of teaching, eleven years later, at Nishapur, in eastern Iran.

Al-Ghazali discovered the truths he was seeking in Sufism, in the 'light which God infused into [my] heart'.[8] The transcendent, he came to believe, could neither be apprehended by the senses nor described by human language, nor yet discovered through reason, but was ineffable. The ultimate goal of the seeker of truth was the pure beatific experience that comes with the annihilation of the self and its absorption into God. Reading Sufi literature, al-Ghazali writes in his autobiography, made him realize that both theological convictions and good deeds were by themselves insufficient for gaining redemption in the afterlife. Good spiritual being was necessary too. This conviction led al-Ghazali to write his masterpiece, *The Revival of the Religious Sciences*, a comprehensive guide to ethical behaviour in everyday life.

Like most Traditionalists, al-Ghazali insisted that reason was neither sufficient nor relevant to the making of moral judgements. Only God could determine whether an action was good or bad. Good actions are those that are rewarded in the afterlife and bad actions those that are punished. The connection between human actions and reward or punishment in the afterlife can be learnt only from Revelation. Yet, while al-Ghazali accepted the Traditionalist idea of good and bad as divinely given, rather than rationally determined, he came to be critical of traditional Sunni ethics. Morality, he argued, is not simply about doing the right thing but also about being the right person. Traditional ethics is limited paradoxically because it is too closely defined by *fiqh*, Islamic jurisprudence. Its aim is to make people comply with the demands of sharia, and to follow the example of the Prophet, rather than to transform their inner character. There is an echo here of Jesus' criticism in the Sermon on the Mount that what is important is not simply to follow God's law but also to do so for the right reasons. There is more than an echo of Aristotle's understanding of virtues.

The Nicomachean Ethics had been translated into Arabic at the end of the ninth century, and had an immediate impact particularly on the thinking of the Rationalists. The Rationalists had been grappling with the question of good and evil: if God was absolutely good, and His laws were incorruptibly rational, how did evil exist? The question of evil posed as great a problem for Muslims as it did for Christians and Jews, and it led to similar kinds of arguments. For some, God's will was unfathomable. Humans could not understand why evil existed or what role it played in God's plans. Just as in Christianity, various forms of Islamic theodicy developed. For others, such as the Rationalists, it was possible rationally to understand evil, but only as a human creation.

For the Rationalists, since God was to no degree malevolent, the presence of evil had to be explained through the activities of humans. The corollary of the absolute goodness of God was the free will of humans. With the Muslim discovery of *The Nicomachean Ethics*, the Rationalists combined the defence of free will with an Aristotelian view of virtues to develop a distinctive narrative of moral life.

Al-Farabi, Ibn Sina and Ibn Rushd all adopted versions of Aristotelian virtue ethics. The most important moral thinker of the period was, however, Ahmad ibn Muhammad Miskawayh (c940–1030). A contemporary of Ibn Sina, Miskawayh was born in Rayy, near Teheran, into an aristocratic family and became librarian, secretary and treasurer to a number of viziers. What sets humans apart from other animals, Miskawayh argued in his most influential book, *The Cultivation of Morals*, is their capacity to reflect and deliberate and to act upon such reflection and deliberation. Like Aristotle, Miskawayh saw human beings as rational animals for whom happiness, or *eudaimonia*, was an expression of the degree to which they had achieved the goal for which they had been created. Where they disagreed was upon the nature of that goal. For Aristotle the ultimate end for humans was 'the life of activity expressing reason well'. For Miskawayh it was a life of intimate union with God. Humans act morally, and make themselves happier, when they use their 'will and initiative', to live their lives as they were 'destined to by the Creator'. An individual acts badly, and reduces his capacity for happiness, when he behaves in a fashion that would 'hinder him from attaining those desirable ends'.[9]

Many Traditionalists were also drawn to virtue ethics but were wary of the concept of free will, and of the insistence that one could define virtue through reason. Both were central to Rationalist ideas of virtue, but both suggested limitations on God's will and power. For Traditionalists, the will of God was supreme and He was the Creator of all human acts, whether evil or good; nothing could happen on Earth that contradicted His will. Humans were not creatures defined by their ability to choose right and wrong but creatures designed to obey God. All that was important was whether humans obeyed or disobeyed God, not why they did so.

It was the idea of goodness as deriving simply from performing the right acts that al-Ghazali challenged. It was important, he insisted, not just to do the right thing but also to possess the right character. But he, like most Traditionalists, was suspicious of notions of free will, and of humanly created limitations on God's power. So his was a virtue ethics in which the path to a virtuous life was defined by God, not determined by humans. Humans, he believed, are born deficient and ignoble. Only through discipline, training and faith could individuals develop virtuous traits. But the ability of humans to educate and discipline themselves was not, as it was for Aristotle, an expression of their natural capacity to develop rationality, but rather an indication of God's power and guidance. Goodness was not about nurturing a rational soul but about surrendering the self into a union with God through living a simple, pious, ascetic life.

The two major strands of Islam – Sunni and Sufi – reflect the two sides of al-Ghazali's argument. The one enforced piety through policing the strict observance of God's law as defined by the Qur'an, Sunna and sharia; the other sought a more mystical, esoteric route to the divine, seeking 'the reparation of the heart' by 'turning it away from all else but God'.[10] Insofar as the Rationalist tradition maintained a presence in Islam, it was within Shi'ism. Shia doctrine, in contrast to Sunni, tends to emphasize human responsibility and free will and deny predestination. It is, however, a highly aristocratic version of

Rationalism. The real power rests with the clergy, and in particular the Grand Imam, who is considered sinless and infallible, and who interprets God's will.

The marginalization of Rationalism helped create an ethical universe within which there was little room for a concept such as *eudaimonia*. Questions of right and wrong behaviour were determined primarily by legal scholars, and the debate about morality transformed from the realm of ethics to that of law. The concern of legal scholars was with moral action and religious duty rather than individual happiness and human flourishing, and with exhorting moral behaviour rather than justifying it.

CHAPTER NINE

The human challenge

1

One summer afternoon in 1054, just as a service of the Divine Liturgy was beginning in Hagia Sophia, Constantinople's Church of the Holy Wisdom, the Papal envoy Cardinal Humbert, accompanied by two other legates, entered the building and made his way up to the sanctuary. He placed a Bull of Excommunication upon the altar. The three men then marched out. The following day, the Patriarch of Constantinople, Michael Caerularius, burnt the Bull and himself excommunicated Humbert and his companions. In that moment many Christians see the great schism that rent their Church between the Greek East and the Latin West.

The divorce of the Eastern and Western Churches came, in fact, not in a moment of pique in Constantinople but in the course of a centuries-long process of separation. The bickering couple found theological reasons for the break-up, in particular the famous '*filioque*' dispute, which rested upon the wording of the Nicene Creed, the foundational text that had established the doctrine of the Trinity. In truth, the divorce had less to do with arcane doctrinal matters than with questions of power. The separation in faith shadowed a political separation between the two halves of the Roman Empire, as the Mediterranean world fragmented.

The death of the Roman Empire might have been scripted by Quentin Tarantino. It was bloody, messy and drawn out. It began in the third century with a fifty-year civil war. In 285, in the wake of that war, Emperor Diocletian restored some stability to the empire by creating the 'Tetrarchy' – the rule of four – by which the empire was carved into two halves, each ruled by two emperors, one senior and one junior. The junior emperor was expected to succeed to full power on the death of his senior colleague. Over the next two centuries the empire swung from being a single entity, whenever an emperor was strong enough to reunite the various parts of his dominion, to fragmenting under weaker rulers.

The eastern half of the empire was more prosperous than the western half, its political structure more stable, its intellectual achievements more entrenched, its cultural sophistication more polished. Constantinople, the new capital built by Constantine, not only shifted the balance of power to the East, but its very existence spoke of Rome's decline.

The prosperity of the Eastern Empire enabled it to maintain a large army, and to pay ransom to its enemies. The poorer Western Empire was less able to protect its borders. Visigoths, Huns, Vandals, Suebi, Alans – all grabbed chunks of territory. Visigoths sacked Rome in 410 and the Vandals did so again in 455, events that shocked contemporaries and signalled the disintegration of Roman authority. Romulus Augustus, the last of the Western Roman emperors, was deposed in 476 by Odacer, leader of the federated Germanic troops within the Roman army. His fall traditionally marks the end of the Roman Empire in the West and the beginning of the Middle Ages.

As the Western Roman Empire declined, the Eastern Empire was able to ward off challengers, and even to expand across Europe, transforming itself into what historians now call the Byzantine Empire. Greek was readopted as the language of government and Latin influence waned. Then, Byzantium came under attack not from small-scale tribes but from a far more formidable foe – the new Islamic Empire. Eventually, in 1453, after two centuries of warfare between Byzantium and the Ottoman Turks, who had seized control of most of the Muslim realms, Constantinople fell, marking the final end of the Byzantine Empire.

2

In the West, tribal attacks tore at the very fabric of Roman life. The empire had been lived in its cities, which now fell into disrepair, as did the roads that connected them and the workshops and warehouses that served them. Life became ruralized, but rural life itself fell apart. Technology regressed, agriculture decayed, populations plummeted, trade declined.

The very precariousness of life in the West was, paradoxically, the making of Christianity. As the authority of imperial institutions collapsed – indeed, as the institutions themselves collapsed – the Church was left as almost the only body capable of maintaining some semblance of social order within the boundaries of the disintegrating empire. Increasingly it took over many of the functions previously performed by the imperial government. Not just taxation and policing but cultural life, too, came within the Church's domain. The clergy was left as the sole literate class in the Western world and the Church as the lone patron of knowledge and the arts.

The new-found status of the Church was enhanced by the conversion to Christianity of many of the rulers of the new kingdoms founded upon the ruins of the Western Empire, and of their subjects too. Even as the Roman Empire disintegrated, the spiritual empire centred on Rome expanded. Through that expansion came the fusion of the spiritual and the secular. In the course of the first millennium, the Western Church consolidated its power, becoming a political as well as a religious empire. It also asserted its independence from the Eastern Church; so much so that in 1204, during the Fourth Crusade, Western forces turned from their assault on Muslims to sack Constantinople.

The first half of the Middle Ages, from the collapse of the Roman Empire to the turn of the millennium, saw the rise of Islam, the consolidation of Byzantium and the retrenchment of Western Christendom. Byzantium and the Islamic Empire absorbed and developed the learning of the ancient Greeks, as well as the other traditions with which they came into contact, including that of Persia, Babylonia and India. It was the very fact of mixture that all the great empires of the Eastern Mediterranean – Greek, Macedonian, Persian, Muslim and Byzantine – found so intellectually fruitful.

Western Christendom was cut off not simply from the cultural admixture that defined Byzantium and Islam, but also from the Greek tradition itself. This was not the 'Dark Ages' of myth, a millennium without learning. Christian philosophers in the West such as Boethius, Philoponus and Alcuin, for instance, produced important work. And yet, while Christian thinkers recognized that they had been graced by the spirit of Greek philosophy, and Christian monasteries kept alive elements of that tradition, there was also ambiguity about the merits of pagan learning. 'What is there in common between Athens and Jerusalem?' asked Tertullian, the first significant Christian theologian to write in Latin, adding, 'Away with all projects for a "Stoic", "Platonic" or "dialectic" Christianity'.[1] The most significant casualty of the Christianizing of learning was Aristotle, whose empirical, this-worldly approach to knowledge was most at odds with the dictates of faith. Plato, with his other-worldly philosophy of Forms, was transformed into an honorary Christian. Even Plato was known primarily for *Timaeus*, his account of the creation of the universe and of humanity by the Demiurge or 'Master Craftsman' written late in life, a text that is among Plato's more obscure, mystical works. For early Christian theologians, its appeal lay precisely in that it was more mystical than philosophical.

In the latter part of the Middle Ages, the relationship between the three main successors of the Mediterranean ancient world was transformed. Byzantium was swallowed up by the Ottoman Empire, Constantinople falling in 1453 to Mehmet II. The Ottomans continued to expand their empire, absorbing much of the old Islamic realms and marching into Europe. But by the time that Suleiman the Magnificent reached the gates of Vienna in 1529, the intellectual and spiritual boundaries of his empire had already begun to shrink. The Rationalists had long since lost their struggle with the Traditionalists, and what physicist and historian Jim al-Khalili has called 'the golden age of Arab science' was over.

At the very time that Byzantium collapsed and Islam faltered, Western Christendom revived, economically, socially and intellectually. The fixed world of the old feudal order started giving way to something new. The Frankish king Charlemagne in the eighth century, and the German king Otto, a century later, fought a series of bloody wars to unite the disparate lands of Western Europe, Christianizing them and creating an alliance with the Papacy. On Christmas Day 800, Pope Leo III crowned Charlemagne Emperor of the Romans. In 962, Otto was given the title *Imperator Romanus Sacer*, or Holy Roman Emperor, by the Vatican. This consolidation of territory allowed Europe to achieve a degree of political stability after centuries of war, invasion and dislocation. Populations grew, agriculture was revitalized, urban life became more vibrant, craft guilds were formed to organize artisan life in the now-flourishing towns, new technologies, such as the windmill and the waterwheel, were developed, and long-distance trade revived. Contact with the Islamic and Byzantine worlds became more frequent, through which the Christian West renewed its relationship with the Greek tradition, a development that both encouraged and was encouraged by the growth of an increasingly literate upper class.

3

At the beginning of the twelfth century the only works of Aristotle known in Latin were the *Categories* and *De Interpretatione*. By the second half of the century virtually all his work preserved within Islamic and Byzantine scholarship had been translated into Latin, together with much of the learned Arabic commentary upon them. Central to this transformation was one of the great innovations of twelfth-century Europe: the university. The first university had been established in Bologna at the end of the eleventh century. Paris soon followed, as did Oxford, Cambridge, Salamanca, Montpellier, Toulouse and Padua. Each was a self-regulating community of teachers and students, built on the model of a medieval artisan guild, all bound together by a shared language (Latin) and a common syllabus. Students and masters could move easily from one to another, so that every university was a genuinely international institution bringing together scholars from all over Western Christendom. But perhaps what most bound together the medieval universities into a common project was the dazzling re-encounter of Western Christendom with ancient Greece, the reinvigoration of a culture that for centuries had known of Greece primarily through a mangled image of Plato now being confronted once more by the full majesty of Aristotle.

If the university created the space for the second coming of Aristotle, one scholar above all filled it: Thomas Aquinas. No figure better embodies the new spirit of inquiry now coursing through Europe. No philosopher played a greater role in transforming Aristotle into a Christian thinker. Today we think of Aquinas as the towering figure of medieval philosophy, certainly outside of the Islamic world, and, together with Augustine, as the greatest of Christian thinkers. He was not always seen so. In 1277, just three years after Aquinas' death, many of his doctrines were denounced as heretical by both the Bishop of Paris and the Archbishop of Canterbury. The universities of Paris and Oxford banned much of his teaching. Yet within forty years Pope John XXII had made Thomas into a saint. The shifting fortunes of Aquinas following his death, journeying from heretic to saint within half a century, reveal the difficulties faced in interweaving pagan philosophy and Christian theology.

Aquinas was born in 1225 into feudal nobility in the Italian town of Roccasecca, then part of the Sicilian Empire, now in the region of Lazio. At the age of five he was sent by his father to be brought up by the Benedictine monks of the great abbey of Monte Cassino. At the age of nineteen, however, much to the distress of his family, Thomas abandoned the socially acceptable Benedictines to become a Dominican monk. The Dominicans were a new order, and one that was little concerned with material wealth – friars begged for their living – but much taken with reading, learning and teaching.

Aquinas' family was so appalled that a son of his background and breeding should join the begging friars that for more than a year it imprisoned him in various family castles and villas, even attempting to break his monastic resolve by hiring a prostitute to seduce him. When she entered his room, so the story goes, Thomas snatched a brand from the fire and drove the poor woman out. He then traced a cross on the wall with the charred end of the stick and fell to his knees. Henceforth, according to his earliest biographer, Thomas lived a life of chastity 'avoiding the sight and company of women . . . as a man avoids snakes'.

In 1252 Aquinas moved to Paris, initially as a student, rising through the academic ranks, and eventually taking a chair in theology. In 1274, on the way to the Second Council of Lyon, set up to find a way of reuniting Western and Eastern Christendom, Thomas, riding a donkey, struck his head on the branch of a tree, became seriously ill and died a few weeks later.

Aquinas was one of the most prolific of philosophical writers, producing several million words, which, though little read, have proved immensely influential. His two key works are *Summa Contra Gentiles*, a defence of Christianity written as a missionary tract for those working with Muslims and pagans, and his masterpiece *Summa Theologica*, a comprehensive synthesis of Christian belief. Aquinas found in Aristotle both an argument for and a means to transform the traditional relationship between reason and faith in Christian theology. For Augustine and early Christian theologians, reason was subservient to faith. The yen for knowledge had led to Original Sin and Original Sin had corroded human intellect and will. Aquinas, echoing the arguments of the Muslim Rationalists, reversed the relationship between reason and faith. Reason was not a corrupting expression of human hubris, but a divine gift to enable humanity to understand God, and bring them to Him. The first three books of *Summa Contra Gentiles* deal entirely with reason and nature, as had Ibn Sina in *Kitab al-Shifa*. Only in the fourth and final book does Aquinas introduce those Christian doctrines sustainable solely by faith, including the Trinity, the Incarnation and the creation of the universe by God *ex nihilo*, 'out of nothing'.

Just as Augustine and early Christian thinkers had made Plato palatable, so Aquinas cleaned up Aristotle for Christian tastes. He did not reject Plato, on whom he leaned, as much as did earlier theologians, for his understanding of the transcendent. But Aquinas's philosophy was much more this-worldly, and just as Plato was his guide to the next world, so Aristotle was to this world.

Aquinas' relationship with Aristotle was similar to that of Ibn Sina and Ibn Rushd. Aquinas agreed with Aristotle that humans are rational animals and that to fulfil one's function as a human being one had to actualize one's capacity for reason. He agreed, too, that the life of happiness is the end goal for human beings. But, like the Rationalists, he disagreed with Aristotle over what constituted a rational life and what was the nature of the ultimate end. For Aquinas, as for Ibn Sina and Ibn Rushd, the point of an ethical life was not merely rational flourishing but also intimate union with God. 'God alone', Aquinas wrote, 'constitutes man's happiness.'[2]

Aristotle had insisted that having the right moral character was necessary for human flourishing and that the right use of reason would reveal the means of developing such a suitable character. For Aquinas, there was more to moral education and a virtuous character than simply the good life on Earth. They were means of preparing humans for union with God. Only imperfect happiness – what Aquinas called *felicitas* – was possible in this world. Perfect happiness – *beatitudo* – was possible only in the afterlife. Whereas Aristotle believed that complete happiness was possible in this lifetime, Augustine taught that happiness was impossible and that our main pleasure consists in the mere anticipation of the heavenly afterlife. In Aquinas, Aristotle and Augustine fuse in the search for a rational underpinning for faith.

4

Aquinas's ethical view emerged from his view of the nature of God, of human nature and of the structure of nature. His God was the all-powerful, all-knowing, completely good, wholly simple being that had already been described by the Muslim Rationalists. He was the condition of being for all that exists. He was also, however, the God of scripture, who far from being outside of space and time, actively intervened in both, a being that was immanent as well as transcendent.

This idea of a God outside of space and time acting upon space and time posed the same problem for Aquinas as it had for Muslim philosophers. To resolve the conundrum, Aquinas suggested that God may act timelessly to bring about an effect within time, an argument of which even the sympathetic theologian Peter Vardy says that 'It is, admittedly, hard to understand what a timeless action involves'. The tension between Aquinas' two Gods, between the wholly simple God and the loving, acting God of scripture, between the idea of God as the condition of being and God as lawmaker and judge, lies at the very heart of Christianity. In Islam that same tension was resolved to a certain degree in the separation between Rationalists and Traditionalists. There was within Christianity the equivalent of Rationalist and Traditionalist strands, but the tension between the two kinds of God did not separate out, as it did in Islam, into distinct theological threads but remained at the heart of the faith. That tension became one of the springs for the transformation of Christianity and eventually for the formation of a secular tradition very different to that found in Islam.

Aquinas' God stood at the summit of a hierarchy of being. The place of any object in that hierarchy was determined by the extent to which it resembled God. Just below God came the angels; at the foot of the ladder, furthest from the divine, was brute matter, matter that had not yet taken form. All life slotted in between these extremes.

Humans stood at a significant point in the hierarchy, the point at which material beings gave way to immaterial beings, and at which non-thinking objects transmuted into entities possessed of intellect. Of all entities in the cosmos, humans alone possessed both physical bodies and immaterial minds. They lived in two worlds: the physical world of rocks and trees and dogs and the spiritual world of ideas and thoughts and minds.

Aquinas drew upon Plato's tripartite division of the soul. Humans, he believed, possessed three sets of fundamental capacities: the vegetative, the sensory and the intellectual. Inanimate objects enjoy none of these attributes. All living entities possess vegetative powers, the ability to nourish themselves, grow and reproduce. Most animals possess sensory capacities. The creatures capable of engaging with the world most fully are intellective beings, since intellective creatures can know and love the beings around them in a way similar to God's knowledge and love. Humans have a weak intellect. So unlike higher, non-material beings such as angels, humans require their sensory and vegetative powers to be able to survive and function; their intellect cannot acquire knowledge if it exists on its own. Whereas Plato and Augustine had looked upon the body as a burden upon the soul, Aquinas, like the Muslim Rationalists, considered it necessary for the intellect to function, helping the soul carry out its proper activity by providing it with information gathered through sense perception. There was little in Aquinas of the moral distaste for bodily functions and sensuous actions that we find in Augustine.

Aquinas linked the relationship between the material and the immaterial, and between the intellect and the sensory, to a third and, perhaps, most important contrast: the distinction between actuality and potentiality, concepts that Aquinas once more derived from Aristotle. Potentiality, for Aristotle, was the capacity of an entity to be in a more completed state, to become what it could be in actuality and thereby to realize its intrinsic function. The function of an acorn is to become an oak. The 'potentiality' of being an oak was always within that acorn. The state of being an oak tree constitutes the actualization of the potential within the acorn. If an acorn does not become an oak tree then its potential is not actualized and its function remains unfulfilled.

For Aquinas, God was 'actuality itself', and possessed no potential. As a wholly perfect being, He could not change or be any different. Everything aside from God was a composite entity, existing 'both in actuality and in potentiality'. The more actualized a being is, the closer it is to God.

The relationship between actuality and potentiality defined not just a being's closeness to God but also its goodness. For Aquinas, an entity, living or non-living, was good insofar as it was able to fulfil its nature. The more that it could transform potential into actuality, the more that it was a fully actualized member of its natural kind, the more it could be said to be good. A good knife is sharp and slices through bread or meat. A bad knife is blunt and incapable of cutting that which it should, and hence unable to fulfil its natural function.

Unlike objects that possess only vegetative or sensory powers, such as knives, or trees or cats, rational agents possessed of intellect, including humans, have a degree of control over how, or even whether, they actualize their capacities. Humans can be bad in the sense of being unable physically to function as fully actualized members of their kind. They might be blind, for instance, or have injured an arm or suffer from schizophrenia. In this sense they fail to transform potential into actuality in the way a blunt knife fails to do so.

Rational agents can, however, be bad in another sense, too, a sense that is denied to knives or trees or cats. Possessing intellect and will, they can *choose* not to actualize certain capacities. They can decide to be lazy, or to be mean or to commit murder. Blindness is a shortcoming, but not a moral shortcoming. Being deliberately blind to the needs of others is, however. Morality for Aquinas is a matter of properly actualizing the capacities humans possess by nature and can control. Free will is that which allows us to choose how we are going to actualize and direct those capacities. An immoral person is someone who *chooses* not to actualize his or her God-given capacities. There are two ways, then, that humans can fall short of a life of flourishing. One is as a result of natural incapacity, the other of moral irresponsibility.

5

Aristotle had argued that human beings possessed a natural impulse to desire the good. Aquinas similarly believed that God had crafted human nature to have an instinctive understanding of right and wrong. The natural, God-given understanding of what constitutes the good, and the desire to act in a moral fashion, Aquinas called 'natural law', a concept borrowed from the Greeks. The principles of natural law are akin to the laws of human nature, the first and most fundamental of which is 'Good is to be done and pursued and evil is to be avoided'.[3] But if humans are naturally inclined to the good, why then do they act badly or do evil? Aquinas gives a very Christian answer. Human nature is disordered by Original Sin. Before the Fall, human actions – that is, those of Adam and Eve – were entirely in keeping with the fundamental laws of human nature. Once humans had fallen into sin, their natures became disordered and disabled. Aquinas did not take an Augustinian view of Adam's misdeeds as having corrupted human nature to its core; but corrupt it, they had.

To the extent that human nature is both limited and disordered, natural law has to be augmented by three moral props: virtue, law and grace. Virtues are habits that individuals learn that help 'perfect' human nature and order his or her action to help achieve the ultimate end of union with God. Intellectual virtues are habits that ensure a better understanding of truth. Moral virtues – such as generosity, honesty, gratitude and chastity – help order and perfect the appetites.

Seven virtues were of particular importance to Aquinas. Four were the cardinal virtues: prudence, justice, courage and temperance. 'Cardinal' comes from the Latin *cardo*, meaning 'hinge'. These are the habits upon which moral life hinges; the cardinal virtues work together to support an individual's pursuit of that which reason has judged to be good.

The hinge of moral life they may be, but for Aquinas the cardinal virtues are not the most important ones. Beyond them lie the three theological virtues: faith, hope and charity. The cardinal virtues help us to be good in this world. The theological virtues prepare us for the next world, indeed permit us a glimpse of that next world, by allowing humans to be 'partakers of the divine nature', as Aquinas put it, quoting St Peter. Unlike other virtues, which bring us closer to God by promoting the good, the theological virtues have union with God as their direct object. The highest of the theological virtues is charity because it 'directs the acts of all other virtues to the last end'.[4] Charity, in other words, orients all human action towards knowing and loving God.

There is an even more elemental difference between cardinal and theological virtues. Cardinal virtues are acquired habits – we can learn to be prudent, just, courageous and temperate through education, practice and experience. Not so with faith, hope and charity. They are gifts from God 'infused' into the soul. The theological virtues, Aquinas suggests, 'should properly be called not human virtues, but superhuman or god-like virtues'. Humans only become faithful, hopeful and charitable insofar as they participate in the divine nature. And by participating in the divine nature, humans can reach a happiness 'surpassing man's nature, and which man can obtain by the power of God alone'. This is a fundamentally different vision from that of Aristotle. For Aristotle, the idea of a virtue as something that 'God works in us without us', that 'cannot be caused by human acts, the principle of which is reason, but is produced in us by divine operation alone',[5] would have made little sense. For Aquinas it was an expression of the disorder of human nature, of the necessity for God's grace.

Virtue and grace are two means of ordering the disordered human nature, the one internal to the soul, the other external. The third is law. Before the Fall, natural law would have been sufficient to maintain humans on the path of the good. After the Fall, human nature was no longer a reliable guide to natural law. Natural law had therefore to be supplemented by other kinds of law. The most important of these was 'eternal law', another name for God's master plan by which He organized the workings of the natural world and the inclinations of the human mind, guiding and ordering everything to its proper purpose. Divine law is that part of eternal law that God explicitly reveals, primarily in scripture. For Aquinas, the Ten Commandments were a reiteration of what humans could have known through natural law had they not been corrupted by sin.

Human law, that which political leaders make and judges uphold, derives from natural law. It is 'a dictate of the practical reason' that specifies how natural law best applies to a given community. Natural law defines a crime; human law establishes how it should be punished. When humanly made laws depart from natural law, they forfeit any genuine moral authority. But they often do so because of the disorder of human nature. Variation in human laws, Aquinas believed, is a reflection of 'the uncertainty of human judgement'. Such uncertainty reveals the need 'for man to be directed in his proper acts by a law given by God', a law that 'cannot err'.[6] The 'light of grace' must brighten the 'light of nature'. For all Aquinas' defence of reason, in the end divine Revelation is the foundation of his moral framework. And yet Aquinas also does something novel with the Christian moral framework. He grasps the tension at the heart of Christian belief between human agency and the consequences of the Fall and, unlike Augustine, tries to rethink that tension to minimize human degradation and maximize the possibilities of reason.

6

> Through me the way into the city of woe:
> Through me the way into eternal pain:
> Through me the way among the lost.
> Justice moved my maker on high
> Divine power made me,
> Wisdom supreme, and primeval Love.
> Before me nothing was but things eternal
> And eternal I endure.
> Abandon all hope, ye who enter here.[7]

So is inscribed the archway above the gates of Hell, in Dante's *Inferno*. Through those gates walk Dante and his guide, Virgil. The *Inferno* is the first part, or canticle, of *The Divine Comedy*, Dante's great triptych of journeys through the next world that takes the poet down to the depths of Hell, where he comes face to face with Lucifer, and then up through the mountain of Purgatory, before finally realizing ultimate happiness through union with God in Paradise. The *Comedy*'s imaginative re-creation of the physical and the moral universe, and of the interlacing of the two, infused medieval culture and allowed Europeans to understand both their place in the physical architecture of the cosmos and their duties in the moral architecture of Christian society.

Born in Florence in 1265, Dante was more than simply a poet, albeit the greatest of his age. He had a thorough grounding in the latest philosophical and scientific theories, was familiar with Arab translations of Aristotle and Ptolemy and possessed a deep appreciation of the theology of Thomas Aquinas. He was also intimately involved in the turbulent politics of his native city. In 1300 Dante became one of the six Priors of Florence, who helped govern the city. The tortuous politics of his age pushed him eventually into conflict with the Vatican. In 1301 a *coup d'état*, engineered with the assistance of Pope Boniface, ousted Dante's party from power. Dante himself was banished from Florence, never again setting foot in his beloved city of birth.

Dante's poetry was cut through with both his philosophical learning and his political leanings, and no work more so than his masterpiece, *The Divine Comedy*. The structure of the *Comedy* seamlessly blends the physical and the ethical, as two aspects of the divine order. At the centre of Dante's universe, both physical and moral, lies the immobile Earth. Around the Earth revolve nine concentric celestial spheres, seven carrying the sun, the moon and the five planets then known. The eighth sphere is that of the fixed stars, the ninth an invisible crystalline heaven, the *Primum Mobile*. The tenth, all-embracing sphere, the Empyrean, is the seat of God and, unlike the other nine, is at perfect rest. The architecture of Dante's cosmos was drawn sphere for sphere from the work of Ptolemy, the Hellenistic Egyptian astronomer whose treatise, *Almagest*, on the structure of the universe was the most influential scientific work before modern times. It had recently been rediscovered in Western Europe through a Muslim translation and both Dante and Aquinas moulded it into the Christian story.

If Dante finds in Ptolemy the structure of his cosmos, the geography of the Earth and of Hell he borrows from Greek mythology, Christian doctrine and medieval prejudice. In the *Comedy*, only half the Earth, the northern hemisphere, is inhabited. The limits of the civilized world are the Ganges to the east and the Pillars of Hercules to the west. At the centre of civilization, not just metaphorically but physically, too, lies Jerusalem. Beneath the ground, like a funnel narrowing down towards the centre of the Earth, lies Hell; in its deepest part sits Satan, enchained.

When Satan fell from Heaven he bored deep into the Earth, pushing aside an enormous portion of the interior and driving it upward, creating the great mountain of Purgatory, the abode of souls headed for Paradise but still in need of purification. On the summit of the mountain, the point where the Earth comes closest to the lowest celestial sphere, lies the Earthly Paradise, where Adam and Eve lived before the Fall. Above lies true Paradise.

The physical structure of Dante's universe reflects the moral structure of human activity. The geography of Hell mirrors that of the Heavens. It consists of nine concentric circles, each representing a gradual increase in wickedness. At the very centre of Hell is Satan, a giant, terrifying beast with three faces, a parody of the divine Trinity. He stands waist deep in ice, forever beating his six giant wings as if trying to escape. And 'In each mouth he was chewing with his teeth / A sinner'.[8] Suffering the torment with Judas were Brutus and Cassius, punished for their assassination of Julius Caesar, the founder of the Roman Empire, which Dante viewed as an essential part of God's plan for human happiness.

Having survived the terrors of Hell, Dante and Virgil ascend through the gloom to the mountain of Purgatory on the far side of the world. Just as there are nine circles down to the depths of Hell, so there are seven terraces cut into the mountain of Purgatory, together with an ante-Purgatory at the foot and the Garden of Eden at the summit. In each terrace are found sinners who have committed one of the seven deadly sins – pride, envy, wrath, sloth, covetousness, gluttony and lust – though their crimes were not as monstrous as those of the poor souls who languished in Hell.

At the summit of Mount Purgatory lies the Garden of Eden. As Dante has journeyed up the mountain, so he has attempted to recapture the innocence that had existed within humanity before Adam and Eve's Fall, and it is here in the Garden that he discovers that state of grace. Here also Dante meets Beatrice, the great love of his life, and his muse, who had died in 1290, almost twenty years before he began work on the *Comedy*. She is the soul who will guide the poet through Heaven, into which Virgil, as a pagan, cannot step.

Beatrice leads Dante through the nine celestial spheres of Heaven to the Empyrean, the abode of God. While the circles of Hell and the terraces of Purgatory had been structured by sin, the spheres of Paradise are defined by virtue – the four cardinal virtues of prudence, justice, temperance and courage and the three theological virtues of faith, hope and charity. From the ninth, and final, sphere of the physical universe, the *Primum Mobile*, a sphere moved directly by God, and home to angels, Dante ascends to a region beyond physical existence, the Empyrean. Beatrice is transformed to a figure more beautiful than ever before so that 'only her maker could enjoy it perfectly'. Dante himself becomes enveloped in light that 'left me wrapt in such a veil of glory / That nothing was visible to me'. The light helped 'make the candle ready for the flame', rendering Dante fit to see God, who now appears in the form of three inextricably but ineffably linked circles. With this poetic vision of the Trinity, neither the rational nor the poetic understanding of which was 'a flight for my wings', Dante ends his journey and the *Comedy*.

The Divine Comedy is perhaps the most important work of Christian imagination (arguably more so than Milton's *Paradise Lost*), a brilliantly poetic allegorical telling of Christian doctrine, a way of rendering in the effable language of this world the ineffable and inexplicable myths of the Christian story from Satan to Eden to the angels to the Trinity. It is, however, far more than that. Dante was not merely a poet of the religious imagination, nor even simply the greatest Christian poet. He was also, as the German critic Erich Auerbach put it in the title of a famous study, a 'poet of the secular world'. *The Divine Comedy*, despite its focus on the eternal and immutable features of the other world, is at heart a very human exploration of this world.

In all previous imaginings of heaven and hell, Auerbach observed, the dead were either immersed 'in the semi-existence of the realm of shades, in which the individual personality is destroyed or enfeebled' or else the good and the saved were separated from the wicked and damned 'with a crude moralism which resolutely sets at naught all earthly relations of rank'.[9] In Dante's other world, the souls retain their this-worldly forms and thoughts and desires and sins and virtues. The human takes centre stage in *The Divine Comedy*, in a way that had not happened previously in Christian thought. In this, Dante looks forward to the poets and artists of the Renaissance and beyond, to Michelangelo's *David* and *Adam*, to Botticelli's *Venus*, to Shakespeare's Hamlet and Falstaff.

At the heart of the *Comedy* is a tension between the concept of fate and the moral agency of the individual, a tension that had existed from the time of Homer onwards, but which in Dante has become like a violin string made taut almost to breaking point. Human action, Dante insists, is not predetermined but is freely chosen. In Purgatory, Dante enters into a discussion about sin, virtue and free will with a figure called Marco who observes that

> You who are living attribute all causes
> To the stars above, as if everything there is
> Had of necessity to move with them.
>
> If it were so, that would mean the destruction
> Of your free will, and it would not be just,
> For good to be rewarded, and sinners punished.[10]

Without free will, in other words, there could be no moral judgement. And 'if the present world is going off course', as Dante believes, then, Marco insists, 'The reason is in you and should be sought there.' In fact, for Dante, the real issue was not the moral failure of ordinary people but the moral corruption of ruling institutions. As Marco puts it,

> You can easily see that bad government
> Is the cause that has made the world wicked,
> And not your nature, corrupted though it may be.[11]

And the most corrupt institution of all was the Church:

Rome, which was the maker of the good world,
Used to have two suns, by which could be seen
Both the road of the world and the road to God.

One has put out the other; and the sword is combined
With the pastoral crook; the two held together,
It must of necessity be that things go badly . . .

. . . the Church of Rome
By confounding two powers within itself,
Falls in the muck and dirties itself and its load.[12]

The Church had debased itself and sullied the moral landscape by confusing its secular and religious roles, by fusing the vengeful sword and the pastoral crook. Dante's was an astonishing attack on the Papacy, though explicable given the political turmoil in Florence and his exile from the city. It was also an understanding of good and evil distinct from the Augustinian view that had shaped Christian attitudes for a millennium. Augustine saw humans as indelibly depraved, whose only salvation lay in God's grace and obedience to God's representatives on Earth, the Church of Rome. For Dante, the Church was irretrievably corrupt and salvation could only come through individuals taking action to root out that corruption and cut down the power of the Church. Dante unquestioningly accepted the doctrine of Original Sin. Yet he was able to arrange the pieces of the Christian story and of Greek philosophy in such a way that Adam's sin became almost irrelevant to his understanding of moral corruption. Sin and virtue were no longer simple and monochrome, and corruption was not just, or even primarily, of the human soul as a result of Adam's sin but also of human institutions because of the failure to wield in separate hands the sword and the crook ('. . . bad government / Is the cause that has made the world wicked, / And not your nature, corrupted though it may be').

Dante was a poet, not a moral philosopher or a theologian. Yet in his poetic imagination he found a language through which to glimpse – and through which others could glimpse – the new moral landscape that Aquinas had begun to sketch through his rethinking of the relationship between faith and reason, and that would soon transform ideas in Western Europe about human nature and ethical conduct. Dante, perhaps even more than Aquinas, did not just occupy the high point of medieval scholarship but was bursting out to worlds anew.

CHAPTER TEN

The revolutionary spirit and the reactionary soul

1

In the late Middle Ages, a new kind of intellectual traveller took to the roads of Europe. They were collectors tramping from monastery to castle, from library to palace, searching for rare manuscripts, lost documents and unknown texts. They came to be known as 'humanists', not because they rejected revealed religion, as humanists do today – they were, in fact, often extremely devout men – but because they yearned to resurrect the intellectual spirit and educational values of the *literae humaniores* ('humane letters') of the Greek and Latin classics. Previous generations of Christian and Muslim scholars had, they believed, mistranslated them, misunderstood them and hence corrupted the public stock of knowledge.

The most important of these early collectors was the Italian poet Francesco Petrarca, known in English as Petrarch, who is often called the 'father of humanism'. Petrarch it was who coined the term 'the Dark Ages' to describe the millennium that separated the end of antiquity and the beginnings of the Renaissance. It is to Petrarch, too, that we owe the word 'Renaissance', the 'rebirth' of culture and learning after the Dark Ages had expunged the flame lit by the great poets of Greece and Rome.

Few historians today would countenance the term 'Dark Ages'. There is little doubt that there was through the disintegration and collapse of the Roman Empire a decline in the culture of learning in Western Europe.

Scholarship was of a different quality to that which had flourished previously in Greek and Hellenistic cultures, on the one side, and would again in the European cultures of the later Middle Ages. It was not in Western Europe but in the Islamic Empire that the most significant minds of this period flourished. Nevertheless, the idea of the 'Dark Ages' is a self-serving phrase that later thinkers employed to elevate the intellectual standing of their own era by suggesting that, between the glories of Greece and Florence, there had been nothing but cultural darkness. While the first half of the Middle Ages may have lacked intellectual spark – though it was never a 'dark age' entirely bereft of the light of learning – the culture of Europe after the turn of the millennium, a culture that produced Aquinas and Ockham, Giotto and Dante, was unquestionably sophisticated, restless and curious. The Renaissance was not created, like the Christian universe, *ex nihilo*, but emerged from an age that was already vibrant and creative, and that had already rediscovered the philosophical and literary legacy of Greece and Rome.

Yet, for all that, there was something unquestionably extraordinary about the Renaissance and about the humanists. Their accomplishments are wondrous enough without having to disparage the previous age as one of darkness. The theologians and Scholastics of the later Middle Ages had been obsessed by Aristotle and by questions of God and of logic. The humanists of the Renaissance marvelled at that which the Scholastics had barely noticed: the poetry, the oratory, the rhetoric, the grace and the style. Humanists treasured the beauty of words and savoured the art of elegant argument. The beauty and the art they desired they found in Plutarch and Cicero, Epictetus and Marcus Aurelius, Seneca and Lucian, Virgil and Livy, Horace and Homer. They devoured those texts of which Scholastics had little knowledge, and for which they had even less respect: essays, letters, histories, biographies. And when it came to philosophy, the humanists were enthused less by Aristotle's dry treatises than by Plato's stylish dialogues. They established a new model of intellectual excellence that emphasized literature, philology, oratory, history, ethics and politics – the *studia humanitatis*, or the 'humanities' as we now call them, the disciplines that they believed to be essential in preparing young men to work in princely councils, city chanceries and Papal offices.

The humanists were humanist in a different, and more modern, sense too.

At the heart of their writing was a new appreciation of the importance of humanity, and in particular of what many called the 'dignity of man'. In contrast to the traditional Christian view of humans as fallen creatures unable to redeem themselves by their own works, a view to which even the most rational and optimistic of believers such as Aquinas and Dante subscribed, humanists saw them as self-creating agents, free to transform themselves and the world through their actions.

The aphorism of the Greek Sophist Protagoras that 'Man is the measure of all things' became the motif of the Renaissance. But Renaissance humanists read the maxim differently to the Sophists. For Protagoras it was an argument against the possibility of objective truth. For the humanists it was an expression of the creativity of human reason.

Perhaps the most famous expression of this came in Giovanni Pico della Mirandola's celebrated oration on 'The Dignity of Man'. Born into nobility, Pico was, like most humanists, a man of immense intellectual curiosity who studied theology, was immersed in philosophy and wrote poetry, a man who mixed rationalism and mysticism, read Greek, Latin, Hebrew, Arabic and Aramaic, and had an unquenchable belief in the moral importance of the human quest for knowledge. In 1486, at the precocious age of twenty-three, Pico invited scholars from all over Europe for a public disputation of 900 theses derived from Greek, Latin, Hebrew and Arabic writers that he intended to defend. He composed an oration in which God addressed Man:

> Thou, constrained by no limits, in accordance to thine own free will, in whose hand We have placed thee, shalt ordain for thyself the limits of thy nature. We have set thee at the world's centre that thou mayest from there more easily observe whatever is in the world.[1]

Pope Innocent III halted the proposed debate and denounced the oration as heresy that did 'nothing but reproduce the errors of pagan philosophers'.[2] Pico was imprisoned for a short period, and forced to recant. Despite his formal recantation, Pico never changed his views, even writing an *Apologia* defending his arguments.

If Pico was the voice of the Renaissance, Erasmus was its soul, the most brilliant, learned, revered and influential humanist of his age. Born in Rotterdam around 1467, Erasmus was the illegitimate son of a priest. Both his parents died of the plague while he was still a boy. His guardians packed him off to a monastery believing it to be the best hope of providing him with education and security. In later life, once he had achieved fame, Erasmus received Papal dispensation from his monastic vows.

Like all humanists, Erasmus had a great love of Greek and Latin learning and he became perhaps the most famous and sought-after translator of ancient texts, producing important translations of Euripides, Cicero, Lucretius and Plutarch among others. His real innovation was the application of humanist learning to Christian works. Erasmus produced new editions of key early Christian manuscripts that had been written in Greek, the most significant of which was his 1516 edition of the Greek New Testament. It became the source of most of the vernacular Bibles over the next few centuries, including Martin Luther's famous German version of 1522. These vernacular Bibles made for new ways of reading the Gospels. They were also expressions of the burgeoning nationalist sentiment that had begun to grip much of Europe, and a challenge to the authority of the universal Church. At the same time, Erasmus' careful scholarship revealed the errors to be found in previous translations, especially in the Vulgate edition produced by St Jerome at the end of the fourth century that had become the definitive Catholic Bible and formed the basis of much Christian theology. Erasmus' translation revealed, for instance, that the original Greek Bible contained no reference to purgatory. The issue of purgatory, and of indulgences, payments made to the Church to ensure that souls went straight to heaven, had become an indispensable feature of the medieval Church and a source of considerable disaffection, one of the crucial issues at the heart of the great rebellion that was to become the Reformation. This new translation emboldened the rebels and added to their theological ammunition.

The relationship between Erasmus and Martin Luther, the greatest of all the Reformation rebels, was fraught. Both were severely troubled by corruption within the Church and both sought to transform the religious institutions of their age. But where Erasmus sought reform from within, Luther demanded the ripping up of the old foundations and the creation of the new.

Where Erasmus saw humanism as the means of the regeneration of faith, for Luther the humanist celebration of the pagan world and its anti-Christian philosophy was at the heart of the problem. Most of all, where Erasmus, like all humanists, proclaimed the dignity of Man, and from it drew his faith, Luther saw humans as wretched beings possessed of no dignity, whose very wretchedness revealed the need for faith.

2

'Here I stand. I can do no other.' Martin Luther's famous response to the Holy Roman Emperor Charles V, defending his right to challenge the authority of the Pope on the basis of his personal convictions, sounds to a modern reader like a ringing endorsement of personal conscience, individual freedom and free will. Whether Luther actually spoke those words remains uncertain. What is certain, though, is that it was never his intention to defend freedom of will. Luther dismissed as blasphemy the very concept. 'Free will, after the Fall, exists in name only, and as long as it does what it is able to do, it commits a mortal sin,'[3] as he put in his Heidelberg Disputation, a famous debate within the Augustinian Order. Indeed, he barely believed in any kind of freedom. When Luther insisted that 'I can do no other', he was defending not his independence of will but his lack of freedom to believe and to act. He could do no other because he was compelled to do as he had.

The Reformation, that deep schism in sixteenth-century Western Christendom out of which Protestantism emerged, is usually seen as the great leap forward, not just in Christianity but also in modernity. 'Why can't Islam have its own Reformation?' is a common question asked by those who wish to suggest how backward Islam is compared to Christianity. The Reformation was, however, a deeply contradictory movement, or set of movements. It was as reactionary as it was revolutionary, as constraining as it was liberating. Luther's view of human nature and of human freedom was as earth to the fire of Pico and Erasmus. And yet the Reformation he launched helped create a society in which Renaissance values could bear fruit.

Luther was born in 1483 in Eisleben in the Holy Roman Empire, in what is today eastern Germany. His father, a miner and smelter, had hoped better for his children and provided them with an education. Martin had been training for the law when, according to his own account, he was, on a summer's day in 1505, caught in a horrific thunderstorm. Afraid that he was going to die, he screamed out a vow, 'Save me, St Anna, and I shall become a monk.' St Anna was the mother of the Virgin Mary and the patron saint of miners. He survived the storm and kept his vow. Within two weeks Luther had entered the Augustinian monastery at Erfurt.

Luther's thunderstorm story is in keeping with the Christian tradition of theatrical conversions to a life of faith, such as that of Paul and of Augustine. As with Paul and Augustine, the drama of a sudden religious transformation provided a means of making sense of a longstanding personal trauma, a personal trauma that came also to have historical resonance because the psychological agony of the individual mirrored a deep-rooted social distress.

Europe in the fourteenth century was a devastated continent. The Black Death had killed some 75 to 200 million people worldwide. In Europe, in the space of just four years between 1348 and 1352 more than a third of the population was wiped out by the plague. In parts of Southern Europe that figure was closer to 60 per cent. One can barely conceive the fear and desolation that such horror would have instilled. The irony of the Renaissance was that its beauty and light emerged from the depths of continental darkness and despair. But that darkness and despair left an indelible mark, especially as the plague returned regularly well into the sixteenth century. There was a widespread obsession with death and salvation, a pervasive sense of insecurity and despond. Luther's personal demons echoed Europe's social desolation.

Luther had long been haunted by insecurity about his personal salvation, and driven by a sense of his own worthlessness. In the monastic life he discovered the stability and assurance that seemed lacking outside. Salvation, Luther came to believe, was not something that humans could strive for, but was simply a gift of God. 'Faith alone', he wrote, 'makes someone just and fulfills the law.'[4]

The story that almost everyone knows about Martin Luther is of his nailing the famous *Ninety-Five Theses* to the door of Castle Church in Wittenberg. This was a public challenge to the Pope from which there could be no going back, the moment at which the division of Western Christendom became inevitable, and the Reformation was launched. Except that it did not happen like that, or at least it did not happen as it is portrayed in the myth.

At the heart of *The Ninety-Five Theses* was a stinging criticism of the practice of granting indulgences, remission of temporal punishment for sins granted after the sinner had performed good work which increasingly included a payment to the Church. It was through such payments that the Church financed many of its great building projects. In 1516 the Pope dispatched to Germany a Dominican friar, Johann Tetzel, to sell indulgences to raise money to help rebuild St Peter's Basilica in Rome. Luther was outraged. He wrote to his bishop, Albert of Mainz, protesting at what he saw as the purchase of salvation. Enclosed with his letter was a document entitled *Disputation of Martin Luther on the Power and Efficacy of Indulgences*, which we now know as *The Ninety-Five Theses*. 'Why does the Pope, whose wealth today is greater than the wealth of the richest Crassus, build the basilica of St Peter with the money of poor believers rather than with his own money?'[5] she asked in one of the theses.

In 1520 Pope Leo X issued a rebuttal, *Exsurge Domine*, demanding that Luther retract forty-one errors. Luther refused. The following year he was excommunicated. Luther publicly burnt the Bull of Excommunication in Wittenberg, cheered on by a large crowd of townsfolk to whom he had become a hero. Luther was ordered to appear before the Diet of Worms, a general assembly of the estates of the Holy Roman Empire, in the Rhineland town of Worms, over which Emperor Charles V presided. Again Luther refused to recant. The Diet declared Luther an outlaw, banning his literature, requiring his arrest and making it a crime for anyone to give him food or shelter. The verdict was unpopular with German princes, many of whom sympathized with the religious rebel. Frederick, the Elector of Saxony, arranged for Luther to be given safety in Wartburg Castle, where he began his great German translation of the Bible.

3

'I am bound by the Scriptures I have quoted and my conscience is captive to the Word of God. I cannot and will not recant anything, since it is neither safe nor right to go against conscience.'[6] So declared Luther at the Diet of Worms. This was a challenge not just to the Pope and to the Holy Roman Emperor, but also to Aristotle and Aquinas. Aquinas had seen reason as a spark illuminating the path to God. Not so, insisted Luther. Reason may be used to question human activities and institutions, but not to light up the divine. Humans could learn about God, Luther maintained, only through Revelation. His was a view of human nature darker even than Augustine's. Humans were degenerate to the last fibre of their being. Neither desire nor reason could be trusted to lead humans to moral safety, for both had been corrupted in the Fall. 'If we believe that Christ redeemed men by his blood, we are forced to confess that all of man is lost,' Luther thundered; 'otherwise we make Christ either wholly superfluous or else the redeemer of the least valuable part of man only; which is blasphemy and sacrilege.'[7]

The only true moral rules are divine injunctions, such as the Ten Commandments. These had to be accepted on faith and unquestioningly followed. It was an argument similar to that of the Islamic Traditionalists in their struggle with the Rationalists. There could be no rational accounting of God's word. Human reason was too weak to comprehend God's plan. Luther added a Christian twist to the argument. Human reason cannot understand God's commands because it has become enslaved by sin. Nor could following God's moral rules ever satisfy our desires, for our desires, too, have been corrupted with the rest of human nature. There always exists an antagonism between what humans want and what God commands humans to do.

Strict adherence to God's law is, nevertheless, insufficient to ensure salvation. Nothing humans do can assure a place in heaven. Salvation is not a state to be achieved; it is a state to be received through God's grace. God's law allows human communities to survive by limiting moral chaos and the consequences of sinfulness. It does not make humans moral. It simply constrains their capacity for immorality. All humans can do is close their eyes, shut out reason and desire, accept God's word on faith, and hope for the best in the next world.

Do the gods love the good because it is good, Socrates had wondered in Plato's *Euthyphro*, or is something good because it is loved by the gods? Luther's answer, like that of Muslim Traditionalists, was unambiguous. There was no rhyme or reason to God's law. Humans had to accept God's idea of the good simply because God tells us it is good, not because they could justify it through reason or through any external measure. Morality was indeed arbitrary. That was the whole point of it.

4

The Reformation was an intensely conservative religious reaction against the spirit of reason that Aquinas had introduced into Christianity, a reaction that found its voice in the terrifying, transcendent God of the Old Testament, the God that had thundered at Moses, 'Draw not nigh hither.' Aquinas believed that all humans participated in God's nature and that all possessed a certain God-given autonomy of will. The reformers insisted on the absolute sovereignty of God over His creation and saw the human race as a 'teeming horde of infamies', as John Calvin put it, whose innate sinfulness degraded any autonomy except for the autonomy to be wicked.

And yet, despite the Reformation's mordantly reactionary soul, its rebellion against the Catholic Church was also the source of a radical revolution, the harbinger of a liberal modernity. The paradox of the Reformation is that a movement that deprecated autonomy and will, insisted on the unlimited sovereignty of God and sought solace in unquestioning faith also helped create a world that came to celebrate individualism, foster agency and take secularism to be the social norm.

Luther insisted on the 'priesthood of all believers'. Religious authority was torn away from any external institution and rested solely in the individual believer, each interpreting the Bible according to his or her own private conscience, each fostering his or her own personal relationship to God. For all his dismissal of free will, Luther's rebellion was an assertion of individual conscience against the monolithic authority of the institutional Church. The Reformation, as historian Richard Tarnas has observed, 'marked the standing forth of the individual in two senses – alone outside the Church and alone directly before God'.[8]

It was, of course, not just Luther who could hear the inner voice. The individual, and his conscience, was looming large throughout sixteenth- and seventeenth-century culture, fostered by the Renaissance celebration of the dignity of Man. The entanglement of the Reformation and the Renaissance limited the Augustinian bleakness of the Lutheran vision. Protestantism flourished in many forms, and many Protestants had a view of human nature less dark than Luther's. At the same time, the social changes engendered by the Reformation eased the way for the more optimistic Renaissance vision.

The biggest social change came out of a second paradox at the heart of the Reformation. A movement that sought to restore faith to the centre of life helped ironically to engineer the modern secular world. For Luther, little that humans did on Earth was relevant to what happened to them in the next world. Neither good works, nor moral acts nor yet penitence provided the key to salvation. Faith and grace were all that mattered. So what sort of laws should guide human conduct in this world? Since there was no point in designing rules of conduct to get humans into the next world, such rules could reflect the needs of this one. Hence the Reformation created the possibility of a secular space defined by laws that defended political rather than divine order.

It was an argument that clearly appealed to monarchs and princes chafing at the constraints imposed by Papal power. By the thirteenth century the Church had achieved an unprecedented level of political authority in Western Europe. It was also riddled with corruption, shot through with sleaze, and had become a machine for minting money and grasping power. In 1492 Pope Alexander VI, a member of the Borgia family, had artfully bribed his way to the Papacy, despite having several mistresses and at least seven known illegitimate children. Forty years earlier, Duke Amadeus VIII of Savoy had managed to get his eight-year-old son appointed as the Bishop of Geneva. If the higher clergy were lacking in any sense of moral virtue, the lower clergy were often illiterate, uncouth and ignorant. Little wonder that huge resentments had built up against Papal power. The so-called 'magisterial Protestantism', the Protestant rebellion led by the elite, swept through much of Northern and Central Europe, from the Swiss cantons, and the German-speaking lands of the Holy Roman Empire, to Bohemia, Poland and the Baltic states to the east and through the Netherlands to England to the north.

As the new faith spread, it diversified and new forms of Protestantism emerged. On mainland Europe, Lutheranism was joined by the Reformed Church, rooted partly in the ideas of the Zurich priest Huldrych Zwingli, and Calvinism, which grew out of John Calvin's teaching in Geneva and soon became the dominant Protestant movement on the continent. There were smaller movements, too, such as the Huguenots in France and the followers of Jan Hus in Bohemia. In England a highly distinctive form of Protestantism – Anglicanism – evolved that spoke to local political and social needs and that maintained many of the traditions and practices of the Catholic Church. England's imperial expansion over the next few centuries would eventually make this provincial version of Protestantism one of the most influential.

Magisterial Protestantism wrenched power away from the Pope to carve out a space for secular rule. It did not, however, abandon the idea of God as the ultimate source of political authority. Rather, God was now called upon to authorize the rule of His secular representatives on Earth. Monarchs claimed absolute sovereignty by virtue of the 'divine right of kings' to rule. It was righteous, Aquinas had suggested, to depose an unjust king. Not so, argued the new Protestant monarchs who insisted that they were not subject to the will of the people, or of any other Estate of the realm; only God could judge the king. Attempts to unseat the king or to restrict his powers ran contrary to the will of God and hence were sacrilegious. Catholic kings, too, such as Louis XIV of France, now rested their authority upon the doctrine of divine right.

There was another paradox too. Luther had insisted that actions in this world had no bearing on one's reception in the next; hence the possibility of creating a secular space. In practice, however, the spread of Luther's message led to the greater fusion of Church and State. As kings and princes cleaved to the Reformation as a means of gaining power, so the institutions of faith and the institutions by which they enforced their rule became barely distinguishable. A movement that began by asserting the right of every individual to interpret the Bible as he or she wished soon realized that this would lead to religious and social anarchy. Each of the various strands of Protestantism established its own institutions to enforce its particular doctrines and rituals and to eliminate heresy, often on the pain of death. A movement that had begun by challenging the corruption of the Catholic Church through its acquisition of secular power, and had insisted on the distinction between divine law and worldly law, soon fused Church and State as a means of defending the power of both, the Church sheltering in the bosom of princely power, the State gaining legitimacy through the licence of God.

There were more revolutionary versions of the Protestant rebellion too. Inspired by ideas of individual conscience, many sought to challenge the power not just of Popes but of monarchs as well. Perhaps the most important of these were the Anabaptists, so called because their reading of the Bible led them to insist that no divine warrant existed for the practice of infant baptism and that all adults had to be re-baptized.

The differences with magisterial Protestantism were far greater than such seemingly trivial doctrinal distinctions. The Anabaptists saw the social order as being as corrupt as Luther had seen human nature. Most Christians viewed the conversion of the Roman Emperor Constantine as a watershed in the history of the Church; imperial patronage had allowed Christianity to emerge from the margins and become a social force. The Anabaptists also saw Constantine's conversion as a turning point but for the opposite reasons. It was the moment in which Christianity had compromised its integrity through an accommodation with imperial power. To cleanse themselves of that compromise, Christians would have to disengage from the social order. Anabaptists refused to swear oaths to a secular authority, opposed the death penalty, decried wars, and condemned private property as unchristian.

The Anabaptists built up a strong following in German-speaking lands and in the Low Countries, even taking control of the town of Münster in 1534. Similar movements flourished in other countries, such as, for instance, the Levellers and the Diggers in England a century later. The Levellers were a political movement during the English Civil Wars that emphasized popular sovereignty, extended suffrage, equality before the law and religious tolerance, and a notion of 'natural rights'. The Diggers were a group of agrarian communists. 'In the beginning of time God made the earth,' their leader

Gerard Winstanley argued in his pamphlet *The New Law of Righteousness*. 'Not one word was spoken at the beginning that one branch of mankind should rule over another, but selfish imaginations did set up one man to teach and rule over another.'[9]

The emergence of such movements was particularly unsettling to the Protestant elite. Luther was as conservative in his politics as he was in his faith, and supported the ruthless suppression of the revolutionary movements. In 1524 the Peasants' War broke out, a popular revolt in German-speaking lands against oppressive taxes and land laws. Some three hundred thousand peasants took part, demanding the end of serfdom, the abolition of cattle tithes and death taxes and the right to use 'common fields, forests and waters'. The uprising was brutally put down by the ruling classes, with some hundred thousand peasants losing their lives in the slaughter.

The peasants had used the Bible to support their grievances and, in turn, to justify their rebellion. Poorer clergy, led by Thomas Müntzer, championed the peasants' demands and encouraged their revolt. But the leaders of the magisterial Reformation, Luther and Calvin in particular, took up arms against the peasants. In 1525 Luther published his essay *Against the Murdering Thieving Hordes of Peasants*, berating the rebels for the use of violence but defending the right of princes to employ force to suppress the revolt because the peasants had 'become faithless, perjured, disobedient, rebellious, murderers, robbers, and blasphemers, whom even a heathen ruler has the right and authority to punish'.[10]

In time, Protestant ideas of 'justification by faith', of individual conscience and the 'priesthood of believers', and of the separation of secular work and divine salvation, all helped feed the radical democratic spirit. But fusion of the reactionary soul and the revolutionary spirit that drove Luther's rebellion ensured that modern liberal democratic societies developed as much in spite of the Reformation as because of it.

CHAPTER ELEVEN

The human triumph

1

In 1948 Berthold Brecht revived Sophocles' play *Antigone* at the Chur Stadttheater in Switzerland in one of the most celebrated theatrical productions of the twentieth century. The last of the Theban Plays (though the first to be written), through which Sophocles reworks the tragedy of Oedipus, the mythical king of Thebes who unknowingly kills his father and marries his mother, and whose family is fated to be doomed for three generations, *Antigone* tells of the confrontation between the eponymous heroine, the daughter of Oedipus, and Creon, the current king of Thebes. Just before the play opens, Oedipus' two sons, Eteocles and Polynices, have killed each other. The two brothers had shared the throne of Thebes, each ruling in alternate years, until Eteocles had refused to turn over power at the end of his annual term. Polynices gathered an army and attacked the city in furious retaliation. The brothers died at each other's hands in single combat. Creon, their uncle, the new king of Thebes, decides that Eteocles should be buried with full honours as a defender of the city. The body of Polynices will, however, be left outside the city gates, to rot unmourned as a traitor. Anyone who would honour him with a burial, Creon decrees, would be put to death. Antigone, sister to both Eteocles and Polynices, defies Creon's decree. She scatters funeral oil and earth over her brother's body. A furious Creon condemns Antigone to be buried alive, letting the gods dispose of her as they will.

To the modern mind, Creon is a brutal tyrant and Antigone an unalloyed heroine, defending her rights and the honour of her family, and of her people, against her antagonist's savage megalomania. That was certainly how Brecht saw it. In his *Antigone*, over which the shadow of the Holocaust inevitably looms, the prologue is set in a Berlin air raid shelter. Creon struts like a manic Hitler, Antigone embodies the spirit of popular resistance. But this was not Sophocles' Antigone, nor his Creon. Sophocles viewed Creon not as a tyrannical brute but as the unbending defender of the polis, as the eloquent champion of the overriding claim of the city upon the loyalty of its citizens, particularly in times of danger:

> . . . Remember this:
> our country is our safety.
> Only while she voyages true on course
> Can we establish friendships, truer than blood itself.
> Such are my standards. They make our city great.[1]

If Sophocles' Creon appears in the glow of patriotic virtue, his chorus shows little sympathy for Antigone. 'You went too far, the last limits of daring – / smashing against the high throne of Justice!' it insists. 'Your own blind will, your passion has destroyed you,' it taunts her.[2]

The chasm between Sophocles' Antigone and Brecht's is the chasm between the ancient world and the modern, between the ancient concept of the primacy of the polis and the modern view of individual liberty. A seventeenth-century audience may have found glimpses of understanding in both Antigones and perhaps, at times, found both baffling too. For the seventeenth century was the hinge between the ancient and the modern, when many of the developments that had been maturing over centuries now decisively transformed moral and political conceptions.

In the ancient world, Aristotle, who found *Antigone* perplexing and did not regard it as a great work of tragedy, nevertheless agreed with Sophocles that no citizen 'should think that he belongs just to himself'. All citizens belonged to the polis and 'the responsibility for each part naturally has regard to the responsibility for the whole'.[3] For Aquinas, a millennium and a half later, living at the very edge of the ferment that would first rediscover Aristotle and then sweep away his world, 'the uncertainty of human judgement' had led to 'different and contrary laws', requiring humans to be directed 'by a law given by God'.[4] For Aristotle, the warrant for moral rules and right conduct came from nature and from the community. For Aquinas, it came from God. For Aristotle, to be moral was to be part of a community through which our desires and dispositions could be formed and trained toward the pursuit of commonly acknowledged goods. For Aquinas, moral law rested in God's will.

The rise of the market economy, the dissolution of traditional communities and the growth of religious scepticism had, through the early modern period, corroded the ability of both God and community to warrant moral behaviour. Who or what could now authorize moral rules? This was the question facing moral philosophers in the seventeenth and eighteenth centuries. Many suggested a revolutionary answer: humans could. Human nature, needs, desires, aspirations and possibilities would act as the warrant for the moral good. How human nature would play this role remained perplexing given the 'uncertainty of human judgement' that Aquinas had observed in making his case for the necessity of God's law.

Two seventeenth-century philosophers provided different responses to this challenge. One was the waspish Englishman Thomas Hobbes, the other the quiet Dutchman Baruch Spinoza. Hobbes helped launch a British tradition of moral philosophy; in his wake come Locke, Hume, Bentham and Mill. Spinoza helped shape what is now often called the 'Continental' tradition. Thinkers as diverse as Rousseau, Kant, Hegel, Marx and Nietzsche are all in his debt. The distinctions between the two traditions are often overplayed. Nevertheless, the ideas of Hobbes and Spinoza were to shape the way that the modern world was to approach the question of moral rules, and to mould different answers as to what should warrant moral behaviour.

Hovering over both Hobbes and Spinoza was the work of a third seventeenth-century philosopher, whose ideas about the individual and individual consciousness have probably had a greater influence on modern thinking than that of any other figure, who not only gave philosophical shape to the new idea of the 'inner self' but in doing so helped lay the ground for modern philosophy and establish the key modern conundrum about human nature: René Descartes.

2

Descartes was born in 1596 into a family of minor landed gentry in La Haye, a small village near the Loire that was later renamed after its most famous son. Trained by Jesuits at their renowned Collège Royal Henry-le-Grand in La Flèche, Descartes went on to study law at the University of Poitiers.

It was a time of great religious turmoil in Europe, the continent torn asunder by faith wars between Catholics and Protestants. Descartes enlisted on both sides of the great religious divide, first as a volunteer in the army of the Protestant Prince of Orange, then in the army of the Catholic Duke Maximilian of Bavaria. The Europe of Descartes was beset by intellectual turmoil too. The Renaissance and the Reformation had helped erode the medieval Christian worldview. The growth of the empirical study of nature, encouraged by the Renaissance, and transformed in the Scientific Revolution, was undermining faith in both Aristotelian and Biblical accounts. The erosion of the authority of the Church, and the emergence of the idea that every individual had to find his or her own relationship with God, encouraged scepticism. The old sources of authority could no longer be trusted and yet there was no new criterion of truth. The burgeoning age of exploration, exemplified by the voyages of Columbus, Magellan and Vasco de Gama, had further weakened traditional ideas of right and wrong by bringing to the attention of Europeans different cultures and moralities and suggesting to some that, in the words of the great sixteenth-century French humanist and essayist Michel de Montaigne, 'The laws of conscience which we say are born from nature, are born of custom'. There was, for Montaigne, no absolute truth.

In such a time of doubt, of what could we be certain? This was the question that Descartes addressed in his most famous work, *Discourse on Method*. Published in 1637, its influence is matched by only a handful of philosophical texts. It contains perhaps the best known line in all of philosophy: *cogito ergo sum*. 'I think, therefore I am.' Paradoxically, Descartes observed, the very fact that he was able to doubt revealed the one thing of which he could be sure: that he existed, and existed as an entity that could think. For if he doubted, he must exist in order to doubt.

This method led Descartes to two fundamental principles that shaped his entire work and much of modern thinking about human nature and our moral lives. The first was the importance of the self both as a defining feature of a human being and as a means of acquiring truth. Prior to Descartes, scholars discussed reason as a general condition of being, not as the product of an individual's mind. When Descartes writes that 'I' did this or that, he does so in a much more modern sense – as a personal reflection on his thoughts and the workings of his own mind. The *Discourse* is written almost as a narrative, with Descartes himself as the hero, in search of the Holy Grail of truth. With Descartes the mind became fully interior and the private possession of the individual.

If human beings were thinking substances, nature was a machine. This was the second principle that permeated the work of Descartes. It was a view in direct contrast to that of Aristotle, for whom the cosmos was more like an organism than a machine. In the new philosophy articulated by Descartes the teleological view of nature was banished. The Aristotelian universe, full of purpose and desire, gave way to an inert universe composed of purposeless particles each pursuing its course mindless of others. Here were the philosophical foundations of modern science.

What Descartes is best remembered for, however, is neither his concept of ego and agency, nor his clockwork universe, but rather his failure to connect the two. Mind and matter, for Descartes, inhabited radically different realms and comprised distinct substances. Matter was knowable to humans using science and reason. Mind was foreclosed to human inquiry, at least through scientific means. Cartesian dualism still shapes much of the way we think about the world and humanity's place in it, but the sharp distinction that Descartes drew between the material world and the world of the mind has long been criticized. It was, the American philosopher Richard Rorty has suggested, 'an unfortunate bit of residual Aristotelianism'.[5] In fact, Cartesian dualism was both much more and much less than that. It expressed a fundamental conundrum that the modern world faces in thinking about what it is to be human. On the one hand, science has taught us to perceive nature in largely mechanistic terms, a process that has driven out magic and mysticism and 'disenchanted' the natural world. Humans, too, have become part of the natural order and amenable to be understood naturalistically – that is, independently of divine grace. On the other hand, we now view humans as possessing consciousness and agency, qualities difficult to express in physical terms. We are happy to view human bodies – including human brains – as machines but what we value about our fellow humans is that they do not act as machines but as people. If they did act as machines we would think that there was something wrong with them, that they were not quite human. The very idea of morality relies on viewing humans not as machines but as conscious agents capable of making choices and taking responsibility for their actions. This conflict between scientific mechanism and human exceptionalism has haunted thinking about the human condition from Descartes' day to ours, not least the work of Hobbes and Spinoza.

3

In 1629 Thomas Hobbes published a translation of Thucydides' *History of the Peloponnesian War*. Born in Athens in 460 BCE, the year that the first Peloponnesian War between Athens and Sparta broke out, Thucydides had spent much of his life contemplating the nature of war and the role of human nature in war. His account of the conflict between Athens and Sparta is often seen as the first 'scientific history' and the first work of political realism. The moral of Thucydides' tale was the political corrosiveness of democracy. Athens had fallen thanks to the moral laxity of the Athenian masses. It was not the only lesson that Hobbes absorbed from the Greek historian. Thucydides had adopted a materialist view of history and of human nature. Most importantly, he had built a theory of morality from a vision of humans as they had existed in the state of nature. Moral laws and powerful rulers were, Thucydides insisted, necessary to keep in check the natural impulses of humans to dominate each other, impulses that ensured that life in the original state of nature was brutal and chaotic. This was to be Hobbes' starting point in the work that was to confer upon him philosophical immortality – *Leviathan*.

Hobbes was born in 1588, the year of the Spanish Armada. The son of a disreputable village vicar, he studied at Oxford thanks to the benevolence of a rich uncle. He eventually became tutor to William Cavendish, the soon-to-be second Earl of Devonshire, and an immensely wealthy man. It was a post that Hobbes held for the rest of his life and that furnished him with the time and space to read, think and write.

Hobbes' work, like that of Descartes, was shaped by the unprecedented upheaval, political and religious, military and economic, of his time. England stood divided against itself. The nation found itself on the verge of a market economy, with many people making great fortunes, and others losing everything. The first land enclosures were driving tenant farmers off their plots and privatizing common land, creating hardship and famine. Accompanying the economic turmoil was political turmoil, and growing class conflict as the interests of the monarchy, the nobility, a nascent bourgeoisie and the rural poor came increasingly to clash. The struggle for power culminated in the English Civil Wars, which began in 1642 and did not finally finish till 1651, and in the midst of which Charles I was executed in 1649. A staunch Royalist, Hobbes fled to Paris in 1640, and there he remained for a decade. By the time of his exile he had become the most famous of English philosophers and he was, for a while, tutor to the future Charles II, who had also been forced to flee to the French capital.

Hobbes' stature was such that, even before leaving England, he was one of a handful of philosophers to whom Descartes turned to comment upon his 1641 work, *Meditations on First Philosophy*, which expanded upon the metaphysical system he had introduced in the *Discourse*; both the comments and Descartes' replies were published with the book. Hobbes loathed the work. Like Descartes, he despised Aristotle. Like Descartes, he viewed nature as a piece of clockwork. But, unlike Descartes, Hobbes rejected the distinction between mind and matter. For him there was no such thing as a non-bodily substance and no possibility of non-corporeal entities, whether angels or souls. His answer to the question of how to find certainty in an era of turmoil was different.

It was in his last years in Paris, as the threads of feudal society were coming unpicked in his native England, that Hobbes wrote *Leviathan*. His starting point, like that of Thucydides, was 'natural man' – humanity as it existed in the state of nature, outside of society. His state of nature is, again like that of Thucydides, a bleak, unforgiving landscape, a place of unremitting war of all against all. Since all humans are roughly equal in their natural powers of body and mind, and all desire the same goods, so they all inevitably end up fighting each other. In such a world, human existence could only be, in Hobbes' celebrated words, 'solitary, poore, nasty, brutish and short'.[6]

There are no laws in the state of nature, because laws only come with society. But if there are no humanly created laws, there are laws of nature, key among which is the principle of rational self-interest. It is a principle that leads humans to give up some of the unfettered liberty they possess in their natural state in return for safety, to 'be contented with so much liberty against other men, as he would allow other men against himself'.[7] This is the covenant between all citizens out of which society is born. To police the covenant, people transfer their rights, save that of self-defence, to a central power that ensures that no one reneges on their agreement to limit their own rights, and is able to enforce law by punishment. This central authority Hobbes calls the Commonwealth. The supreme ruler is himself not party to the covenant and so is incapable of breaching it. Such a sovereign is the source of law and property rights in the new society, and it is his function to enforce the covenant and protect his subjects.

Hobbes accepted that the supreme power could be an 'Assembly of men' or of 'one Man'. But even an assembly would be no democracy. The power of the ruler, whether an individual or an assembly, had to be absolute. The only liberty a subject possessed was the liberty to do anything not regulated by the sovereign. Even in society, however, the right of every individual to self-preservation is absolute. If the sovereign threatens this right to self-preservation, then the subject had 'the Liberty to disobey'.

Hobbes was the first of the modern 'social contract' theorists, for whom society is created through voluntary agreement between its members. The origins of the argument lie, as we have seen, way back in history, with the Greek naturalists, and in particular Thucydides. For Thucydides, as for Hobbes, the covenant displayed both a pessimistic view of human nature and a deep disdain for democracy. In the modern world, social contract theory became a key component of liberalism. What early liberals took from Thucydides and Hobbes (later liberals developed different arguments) was the idea of the individual as existing prior to society, conceptually if not historically, and of society as the product of voluntary, rational agreement between its members. In this liberal view, the individual arrives on the stage with his or her psychological dispositions fully formed, and with his or her moral ends and social aims already given.

Critics pointed out that it made no sense to think of the individual as existing prior to society, either historically or conceptually. For Hobbes, the contract is the foundation of all social life; before the contract there are no shared rules or standards. The contract is the explanation of how such shared rules and standards came into being. Yet without some shared rules and standards, how is it possible to establish a contract in the first place? As the critics observed, humans are not individuals who become social. They are social beings whose individuality emerges through the bonds they create with others. Psychological dispositions and desires are not fixed but are shaped by the social institutions and relations in which individuals are immersed, as are the answers to questions such as 'What are my ends?' and 'How should I live?'

Hobbes' theory is unconvincing also in its impoverished view of human motives and desires. There is something Lowry-like about his picture of human psychology. Humans are driven by the urge to satisfy their desires, on the one hand, and by the need for self-preservation on the other. What is missing is not simply the vastness of the ocean of human emotional life but also the very question that lies at the heart of all moral existence: what kind of life do I want? Hobbes dismisses the idea that there is any such thing as '*finis ultimus* (utmost aim) or *summum bonum* (greatest good), as is spoken of in the books of the old moral philosophers'.[8] Rather, 'The Passions that incline men to Peace are, Fear of Death; Desire of such things as are necessary to commodious living; and a Hope by their Industry to obtain them.' But what such 'commodious living' amounts to, Hobbes never says. Rather, humans, in his account, seem to swing from desire to desire without ever asking themselves, 'Is that desire good or bad?' 'Would I be better off desiring something different?' 'What should be the end point of all my desires?' Such questions made little sense for Hobbes because he saw desires as a given. The consequences of human desires could be managed through a strong sovereign, but the desires themselves could neither be educated nor transformed.

For ancient philosophers, Eastern and Western, and for Christian (and Muslim and Jewish) theologians, the structure of society was fixed but the structure of human nature was malleable. Humans had to be educated in their desires, so that desires could fit in with the broader concept of the good. In the premodern world, morality grew inevitably out of the structure of society. The concept of the individual was ill-developed because the individual was ill-developed as a social actor. When people thought of individuals, they thought of them only in the context of the community to which they belonged and the roles they played in that community.

By Hobbes' time, the individual was emerging as a new kind of social actor. 'With money in the pocket one is at home anywhere,' as Moll Flanders puts it in Daniel Defoe's eponymous novel. The new individual arrived on the scene both as the consequence of the dissolution of old social forms and as an agent of that dissolution. The transformation of the relationship between the individual and society made more plausible the idea of an individual who stood outside of society and whose needs and desires could be understood in their own terms. It also gave credibility to the idea that society was malleable but that human nature was fixed. Rather than the structure of society being a guide to moral rules, the structure of human nature now became a guide to the nature of society. From Adam Smith to Francis Fukuyama, from Herbert Spencer to Friedrich Hayek, the appeal to 'human nature' as fixed and immutable has in the post-Hobbesian world become a means to rationalize a particular social order.

4

In the summer of 1661 Henry Oldenburg, the newly appointed secretary of the Royal Society in London, was visiting the Netherlands. Amidst his official appointments, he made an arduous detour to the village of Rijnsburg, near Leiden, to visit a young philosopher who held no academic position, had published nothing, and was an outcast in his own community. Yet, even then,

Baruch Spinoza was recognized as one of the finest philosophical minds of his age, a mind worth travelling a mighty distance to meet.

Spinoza's stock is today not very high. In the pantheon of great seventeenth- and eighteenth-century philosophers, such as Descartes, Hobbes, Locke, Hume and Kant, Spinoza is usually seen as hovering in the back row. He is surprisingly little known, often regarded as a philosopher difficult to understand and possessed of little influence. Yet he is arguably the philosopher who more than most has shaped modern thinking about freedom and equality and the possibility of a secular morality. No one else, the historian Jonathan Israel suggests, 'during the century 1650–1750 remotely rivalled Spinoza's notoriety, as the chief challenger of the fundamentals of revealed religion, received ideas, tradition, morality and what was everywhere regarded . . . as divinely constituted political authority'.[9]

Baruch Spinoza was born in Amsterdam in 1632 into a prosperous Jewish merchant family that had migrated from Iberia at the end of the previous century. He attended a rabbinic school and learnt the Bible and the Talmud. By his teens, Spinoza had become sceptical of Jewish theology and on becoming an adult gave up much of Jewish practice. In 1656 he was excommunicated from the synagogue for his 'evil opinions', 'abominable heresies' and 'monstrous deeds'.[10] Devout Jews were forbidden from talking to him.

Cut off from the community that had nurtured him, Spinoza moved from Amsterdam to the village of Rijnsburg, where Oldenburg visited him, and then to Voorburg, another small village near The Hague. He lived largely in isolation, training himself to make lenses and manufacture optical instruments. Spinoza, who never occupied an academic post, became the first major philosopher since antiquity to have earned his living working with his hands.

By 1675 Spinoza had finished his masterpiece, *Ethics Demonstrated According to the Geometrical Order*. Warned by his friends not to publish it as he risked being prosecuted as an atheist, it was not published until after his death in 1677. Spinoza opens the *Ethics* with a discussion of metaphysics, moves to explore human psychology, and concludes with an ethics of human freedom derived from the metaphysics and the psychology. Spinoza models his argument on that of Euclid's geometry. Each of the five parts of the book begins with a set of definitions and axioms and proceeds to offer formal proofs of numbered propositions. The geometrical method bears little scrutiny. But the philosophical arguments, stripped of their Euclidean pretensions, were to be immensely influential.

Spinoza's ideas were shaped by Descartes and his mechanical universe. In fact, in 1663 he had published his *Principia philosophiae cartesianae* ('Principles of Cartesian Philosophy'), a geometrical exposition of Descartes' *Discourse*. Spinoza's views of the cosmos and of human nature are, however, very different to those of Descartes, largely because, like Hobbes, he took Descartes' mechanistic philosophy much further than Descartes himself was willing to. For Descartes there were two fundamental kinds of substance, mental and material. Spinoza insisted on but one reality and one set of rules governing the whole of that reality, of which humans were an intimate part. There existed a single substance, which Spinoza called *Deus sive Natura* – 'God or Nature' – a substance that possessed the attributes both of thought and of space. Mind and body do not, as in the Cartesian universe, belong to separate realms; they are inseparable from each other and from the rest of reality.

Having established the character of reality, mind and matter, Spinoza moves in the third book of *Ethics* to a discussion of human passions. Like Hobbes, he begins with an egoist's view of human nature. The aim of human life is self-preservation. Human beings, like all other beings, are driven to stay alive and to repel anything that might injure or destroy them. The consciousness of this drive we call desire. When the drive for self-preservation operates freely we feel pleasure; when it is impeded we feel pain. Our judgements of good and evil, and our moral actions, are determined by our desires and aversions.

Passions can be passive or active. Passive emotions, like fear, jealousy and anger, are generated by external forces. They trap those who have no rational understanding of their emotions and their causes, tossing unenlightened individuals like rudderless ships upon the ocean of their desires. Emotions of which an individual has a rational understanding, Spinoza calls 'active'. Like Socrates, Spinoza sees good and evil in terms of knowledge and ignorance. Knowledge is liberating because the more we know about ourselves and about the human condition, the more we are able to recognize that we love or hate or find joy or feel pain as the result, not of free choice, but of chance and history and accidental association and past conditioning. Once we realize that, we can stop blaming others for their actions, for these are absolutely determined. We can stop blaming ourselves, too, for our actions are also equally determined. Hate, envy and guilt vanish. There is in Spinoza's argument a clear echo of the Stoics, and of Buddhists, though it is unlikely that Spinoza ever read any Buddhist texts. To take a God's-eye view of human life, to see ourselves and others as part of a natural system of necessity is, for Spinoza, to set ourselves free. Self-knowledge liberates, replacing passive emotions with active ones. Knowledge, and in particular self-knowledge, is the foundation of virtue and of happiness.

Moral liberation and human freedom depend, paradoxically, then, on accepting the necessity of all things, on acknowledging that things cannot be otherwise. But there is another paradox here. Spinoza insists that the world, and the actions of individuals, cannot be otherwise and that freedom comes from accepting the system of necessity. But in accepting that the world cannot be otherwise, we are demonstrating that it can. Spinoza believes that we have a choice: either we accept that the world cannot be otherwise and in so doing achieve freedom and demonstrate virtue, or we continue to rage against necessity, becoming trapped in our impotence, and prey to destructive passions such as anger, hatred and jealousy. The choice we have is to accept that we have no choice.

This is a paradox at the heart of all ethical claims, from Stoicism to many contemporary naturalistic theories, that deny free will but accept the possibility of moral transformation. Such claims are faced with the other side of Descartes' dilemma. In separating mind and matter, Descartes found himself unable to explain how mind influenced body, or indeed how one could rationally explain the mind and its products. Spinoza insisted on a naturalistic understanding of the human condition, including of the mind, but could not explain how humans could choose to transform themselves. In that paradox lies also the significance of Spinoza's theory. Just as the two irreconcilable sides of Descartes' theory – a mechanistic view of the universe and an almost mystical view of the human agent – have both come to inform the way we think of the world and our place in it, so too have the seemingly irreconcilable dual sides of Spinoza's theory, the naturalistic view of the human condition and the insistence on the importance of freedom and of self-transformation.

The importance of Spinoza lies not in his claim that things cannot be otherwise but in his belief that the human condition can be rationally understood and that out of this understanding emerge the tools with which we can transform ourselves. Spinoza agreed with Hobbes in his acceptance of a mechanical universe, in his dismissal of Cartesian dualism, in his naturalistic understanding of the human condition, in his scepticism of religion – but not in his vision of human nature. More than any other moral philosopher before him, more even than Aristotle, Spinoza saw human nature as malleable, and emotions and desires not as given but as transformable. The most significant transformation, for Spinoza, was from being a slave to one's passions to being an agent of one's change. The development of human powers becomes the end of moral and political life. This vision of human transformation not only distinguished Spinoza from Hobbes but also made him the patron saint – if anyone so Godless could be described as a patron saint – of the radical wing of the intellectual storm that was to sweep through eighteenth-century Europe: the Enlightenment.

5

About a week before his death in 1804, the great German philosopher Immanuel Kant received a visit from his physician. Kant rose to thank him, in disconnected words, for taking time from his busy schedule. The doctor tried to persuade his patient to sit down, but Kant waited until his visitor was seated and then, collecting his powers, said with some effort, '*Das Gefühl für Humanität hat mich noch nicht verlassen*' – 'The feeling for humanity has not yet left me'. The physician was almost moved to tears.[11]

The story might seem charming but inconsequential. Yet Kant's struggle, even on his deathbed, to give expression to his 'humanity' reveals the degree to which this idea was central to the consciousness of his age. In the Enlightenment, that intellectual wind of change that blew through Europe in the eighteenth century, the humanist sensibility that had emerged in the Renaissance found full flower.

To the question 'What is Enlightenment?', Immanuel Kant responded that it was 'Man's emergence from his self-incurred tutelage', from the 'lack of courage to use one's own mind without another's guidance'.[12] For Kant and Voltaire, for Hume and Diderot, and all the *philosophes*, the importance of the Enlightenment was that it cleansed the European mind of medieval superstition and allowed the light of reason to shine upon human problems. This was, of course, a self-serving definition, and one that airily dismissed pre-Enlightenment intellectual traditions upon many of which the *philosophes* drew, but it was also one that gave a sense of the historical significance of the Enlightenment.

Through much of the second millennium, a series of intellectual and social developments had begun to transform European culture. This was the period in which the modern idea of the self, and of the individual as a rational agent, began to develop; in which the authority of custom and tradition weakened, while the role of reason in explaining the natural and social world was vastly expanded; in which nature became regarded not as chaotic but as lawful, and hence amenable to reason; and in which humans became part of the natural order, and knowledge became secularized. It was in the Enlightenment that these changes fused, transforming in Jonathan Israel's words a culture 'based on a largely shared core of faith, tradition and authority' into one in which 'commonly received assumptions about mankind, society, politics and the cosmos' came to be questioned. The Enlightenment 'not only attacked and severed the roots of traditional European culture in the sacred, magic, kingship, and hierarchy, secularizing all institutions and ideas, but (intellectually and to a degree in practice) effectively demolished all legitimation of monarchy, aristocracy, woman's subordination to man, ecclesiastical authority, and slavery, replacing these with the principles of universality, equality and democracy'.[13]

The notion of 'humanity' possessed, in the eighteenth century, a number of different meanings, some harking back to old definitions, some carving out new ones. From the late Middle Ages on, humanity had been synonymous with gentleness, courtesy and politeness. As Kant's response to the physician reveals, this meaning was still important to the Enlightenment, though it had acquired a new resonance. Enlightenment thinkers set great store by civility and manners because these expressed respect for other human beings.

Humanity was an expression not merely of civility but also of civilization. Closely intertwined with these meanings was the idea of humanity as representing the qualities, especially the moral and ethical qualities, that pertain specifically to humans. Humanity in this sense was distinct from barbarity. The moral dimension of being human was of immense importance to Enlightenment *philosophes*.

But, perhaps most importantly, there developed during this period a new meaning of humanity as that which is distinct from the divine. To be human meant to have the power and capacity to be master of one's own destiny, independently of divine intervention. Whereas for previous generations nature made sense as God's order, for many Enlightenment *philosophes* only humans infused it with meaning. 'If we banish man, the thinking and contemplating being, from the face of the earth,' the French *philosophe* Denis Diderot claimed, 'this moving and sublime spectacle of nature will be nothing more than a sad and mute scene.' It was 'the presence of man which makes the existence of beings meaningful'.[14]

The exalted humanism of men such as Diderot was the product of a new spirit of optimism that infused the age (*optimisme* itself was a word that first entered the French language in the eighteenth century). It was an attitude that rested partly on a new belief in progress. The historian Gilbert Murray described the decline of the Roman Empire and the emergence of the Christian worldview as the 'rise of asceticism, of mysticism, in a sense, of pessimism; a loss of self-confidence, of hope in this life and of faith in normal human effort; despair of patient inquiry, a cry for infallible revelation'. This he christened 'a failure of nerve'. In contrast, Peter Gay vividly describes the experience of the eighteenth century as 'the recovery of nerve'.[15]

There were, in fact, two Enlightenments, as Jonathan Israel points out in his magnificent trilogy, *Radical Enlightenment*, *Enlightenment Contested* and *Democratic Enlightenment*, through which he rethinks the history of the Enlightenment and of its impact upon the modern world. The mainstream Enlightenment of Kant, Locke, Voltaire and Hume is the one of which we know and which provides the public face of the 'Age of Light'. But it was the Radical Enlightenment, shaped by lesser-known figures such as d'Holbach, Diderot, Condorcet and, in particular, Spinoza, whose atheism, monism and radicalism turned him into the driving force of the Radical movement, that provided the Enlightenment's heart and soul. The two divided, according to Israel, on the question of whether reason reigned supreme in human affairs, as the Radicals insisted, or whether reason had to be limited by faith and tradition – the view of the mainstream. This distinction, Israel suggests, was to shape the attitudes of the two sides to a whole host of social and political issues such as equality, democracy and colonialism. The mainstream's intellectual timidity constrained, in Israel's view, its critique of old social forms and beliefs. By contrast, the Radical Enlightenment 'rejected all compromise with the past and sought to sweep away existing structures entirely'. The Radicals were driven to pursue their ideas of equality and democracy to their logical conclusions because, having broken with traditional concepts of a God-ordained order, there was no 'meaningful alternative . . . to grounding morality, political and social order on a systematic radical egalitarianism extending across all frontiers, class barriers and horizons'. In Israel's view, what he calls the 'package of basic values' that defines modernity – toleration, personal freedom, democracy, racial equality, sexual emancipation and the universal right to knowledge – derives principally from the claims of the Radical Enlightenment.[16]

The intellectual and political divide between the Radicals and the mainstream was never as sharp as Israel suggests. Hobbes was an atheist and a materialist but a political authoritarian. Hume, too, was an atheist but politically and socially a conservative. Rousseau and Kant were theists but supportive of revolutionary thinking. Many revolutionaries, such as Tom Paine, rejected institutionalized religion but accepted a Deistic idea of God. The roots of the revolutionary idea of equality lie not in the Radical Enlightenment but in religiously shaped movements that emerged from the radical wing of the Reformation, such as the Levellers. Ideas and beliefs never cleave cleanly, especially in an age as questioning as the Enlightenment. Historical roots are inevitably tangled and knotted. Nevertheless, however fuzzy the boundaries may be, and however difficult it may seem to pigeonhole individual philosophers, the distinction between the Radical and the mainstream Enlightenment remains important and illuminating. It provides a powerful and cogent framework through which to understand intellectual and social conflict both in the Enlightenment and in the post-Enlightenment world.

What Jonathan Israel's distinction expresses, in part, is the new relationship between morality and politics, between moral claims and the structure of society. As the old social order crumbled, so moral transformation rested on the possibility and the necessity of social transformation in a way that had previously seemed unimaginable. All the *philosophes* recognized that to create a more moral society one had to create a more rational one. Only those who followed in the footsteps of the Radicals accepted that to create such a rational society would require root and branch transformation.

Descartes, Hobbes and Spinoza were, none of them, moral philosophers. Yet in their ideas we can see a decisive turn in the quest for the moral compass. They helped shape modern moral philosophy because they helped shape new ways of thinking of what it is to be human. In so doing, they also threw up a host of questions and conundrums. Can the mind be understood scientifically, and morality objectively? Can morality be reduced to the pursuit of rational self-interest? Are desires and dispositions naturally given or socially created? Do humans possess moral choice? Can we transform human nature? None of these were new questions. But they acquired new meaning as the understanding of what it is to be human was transformed – and as new possibilities of social transformation opened up too.

CHAPTER TWELVE

Passion, duty and consequence

1

> In every system of morality, which I have hitherto met with, I have always remark'd, that the author proceeds for some time in the ordinary way of reasoning . . . when all of a sudden I am surpriz'd to find, that instead of the usual copulations of propositions, *is*, and *is not*, I meet with no proposition that is not connected with an *ought*, or an *ought not*. This change is imperceptible; but is, however, of the last consequence.[1]

So wrote David Hume almost as an afterthought in his *Treatise of Human Nature*. An afterthought it may have been, but there is arguably no single paragraph that has more resonated through modern ethics. Hume's famous distinction between *is* and *ought* – between the world as it exists and the world as we would wish it to be – and his wrenching apart of the realm of facts and the realm of values has indelibly stamped itself upon modern ethical debates and established one of the key distinctions between modern and ancient ethics. Many have come to read Hume as meaning that *ought* cannot be derived from *is*, that values do not derive from the facts of the world. That was neither likely to have been Hume's intention nor the necessary consequence of his argument. Nevertheless, from Hume comes one of the defining features of modern ethics: the separation of facts and values.

David Hume was born in 1711 into minor Scottish nobility. At twelve he went to Edinburgh University to study literature and philosophy. He trained as a lawyer before trying his hand in commerce with a sugar company. Neither life suited him. So he took himself off to France where, for three years, he lived in La Flèche. There, in the library of the Jesuit college at which Descartes had been educated, Hume wrote his first work, *A Treatise of Human Nature*. He published the book on his return to England, but was so dissatisfied with its reception and with what he regarded as the defects of his own style of writing, that he rewrote parts of the *Treatise* in a more popular fashion, publishing them as *An Enquiry Concerning Human Understanding* and *An Enquiry Concerning the Principles of Morals*. He even took out a newspaper advertisement beseeching readers to ignore the original and read the later works. But whatever the immediate reaction, the *Treatise* came in subsequent centuries to be seen as perhaps Hume's most important work, and one that helped define his approach to knowledge and to morality.

Like Spinoza's *Ethics*, the *Treatise* opens with a discussion of the character of reality and of mind, moves on to explore the psychology of the passions, and concludes with a consideration of morality derived from his understanding of reality, mind and the passions. But whereas for Spinoza reason, will and the structure of the cosmos were the keys to comprehending morality, for Hume it was the structure of the mind and the nature of the passions.

Traditional moral philosophy, Hume wrote, had depended 'more upon Invention than Experience'. From Socrates onwards every moral philosopher had 'consulted His Fancy in erecting schemes of Virtue & of Happiness, without regarding human Nature'. In contrast to all this, Hume resolved to make human nature 'my principal Study, & the Source from which I wou'd derive every Truth'. 'The foundation of ethics' is 'a question of fact, not of abstract science'.[2] But if the foundation of ethics is 'a question of facts', why is Hume so seemingly concerned at philosophical attempts to derive *ought* from *is*, that is to derive ethics from facts?

In the first part of the *Treatise*, Hume sets out to produce an account of the relationships between ideas that would mirror Isaac Newton's account of gravitational attraction between bodies. The most innovative and important section is the discussion of induction – the process of reasoning from the observed behaviour of entities to their behaviour when unobserved – and of causation. Humans, Hume argued, tend to look for regularity in the world and to believe in the persistence of such regularity through space and time. Over the past year the sun rose in the morning and set in the evening. We assume that it will do so over the next year too, and we assume that it will do so in Australia as well as in America, even if we have not been to either place. Humans, in other words, tend to believe that patterns in the behaviour of entities in the observed present will persist into the future, and throughout the unobserved present. But, Hume insisted, we cannot rationally justify that belief. It is not reason but natural instinct, the given way our minds work, that leads us to make such inferences.

Similarly with causation. Just as humans have a tendency to search for regularities in the world, so they have a tendency to see the world in terms of cause and effect. However, as with inductive inference, our perception of causation is, Hume insists, a product of the way our minds work, not of the external world. Ideas of necessary causation, as Hume puts it, are 'qualities of perceptions, not of objects, and are internally felt by the soul, and not perceiv'd externally in bodies'.[3]

If all human knowledge comes through observation, and yet the regularities that one observes are simply the products of the mind, and the inferences one draws from those regularities cannot logically be justified, then there can be no certain knowledge. Having begun by insisting that a true 'science of man' could be established only 'by following the experimental method' that had served the natural sciences so well, Hume seems to have cast into doubt the very possibility of scientific knowledge. Hume, following in the footsteps of English-speaking philosophers such as Francis Bacon, John Locke and Bishop Berkeley, advanced empiricism to its logical and sceptical conclusions. If all that I know of the world I know through observation, then what can I know beyond the contents of my own mind? The 'disastrous conclusion' from Hume's impeccable logic seemed to be, as Bertrand Russell put it, 'that from experience and observation nothing is to be learnt'.[4]

Hume was, however, far more than simply the logical dead-end of empiricism. Having accepted the sceptical conclusions of empiricism, Hume set out to show that they need not indeed be 'disastrous'. For Hume, as the philosopher David Fate Norton observes, 'the most important remaining task of philosophy, given these well-established and obvious conclusions, was to show how we are to get on with our lives'.[5] Nowhere was this more evident than in his discussion of morality.

2

In the second book of the *Treatise*, Hume moves on to discuss the passions, or what these days we might call emotions, feelings and desires. The passions are the bridge between Hume's scepticism and his moral ideas. Traditionally philosophers had been hostile to the role of passions in human life, believing them to be a burden upon reason. Hume, however, not only viewed the passions as a vital and integral part of human nature, he also attributed to them many of the functions that previous philosophers had considered to be in the province of reason – the ability to make causal inferences being only the most striking example. The importance of the passions to morality is that, for Hume, reason is impotent to produce any action. Only the passions, aroused by the prospect of pleasure or pain, can drive humans to act. 'Reason is and ought only to be the slave of the passions,' Hume insisted in one of his more notorious formulations.[6] Whereas for Spinoza, reason is a means of transforming our desires, for Hume desires are the means of motivating reason.

The whole purpose of moral judgements is to guide our behaviour. Since reason cannot move us to action, so moral judgements cannot be the product of reason but must be the consequence primarily of the passions. Hume does not erase reason entirely from the picture. Reason provides information, especially about how to effect the means to our ends. But only the passions can set those ends. Morality, as Hume put it, 'is more properly felt than judg'd of'.[7] From Socrates to Spinoza, moral philosophers had viewed wrongdoing as the product of ignorance, a failure of reason. Not so for Hume; reason, he believed, had little to do with distinction between right and wrong, virtue and vice.

When Hume turns in Book III of the *Treatise* to explore the 'moral sense', he introduces a new term – 'sentiment'. It is through sentiment that we are able to make moral evaluations of other people and their characters and to distinguish between virtues and vices. A virtue is a character trait, the disinterested contemplation of which produces approval, a vice one that elicits disapproval. Approval gives us pleasure, disapproval creates pain. Moral sentiments are the means by which humans are able to engage in such disinterested contemplation; that is, the means by which they can distinguish between right and wrong, virtue and vice.

A moral sentiment is, as Hume explains it, a complex psychological disposition. It is like a passion in that it provides motive for action. It is also more than a passion, for it involves an important element of judgement. The sentiments of moral approval and disapproval are caused by the operation of 'sympathy', which is not a feeling but rather a psychological mechanism that enables one to participate in the emotional life of others; today we would probably talk of 'empathy'.

Sympathy allows us to share in the pleasures and pains that are the effects of those traits that we disinterestedly contemplate. When we feel pleasure, too, we approve of that trait, and view it as a virtue. When we feel pain, we disapprove and view the trait as a vice. We approve of generosity because we can identify with the pleasure it nurtures. We abhor malice because we, too, can feel the pain that malicious action can cause. Judgements about virtues and vices become resolved, therefore, into experiences of pleasures and pains.

Not every action or person that gives us pleasure is, of course, necessarily virtuous. Cocaine might give an addict pleasure. A sadist might find pleasure in inflicting pain upon others. And most of us might find it pleasurable to stay in bed all day or painful to have to put in a full day's shift. So how do we distinguish those pleasures that are virtuous and those that are merely hedonistic? By judging them pleasurable or painful from a disinterested viewpoint, argues Hume. Through the mechanisms of sentiment and sympathy, we view pains and pleasures not simply from a subjective viewpoint, but also from the viewpoint of common humanity.

A disinterested view of pain or pleasure could apply equally to aesthetic as to moral judgements. There is little in Hume's argument that allows us to distinguish between *morality* and *taste*. Subsequent philosophers came, indeed, to view morality as a kind of statement of taste. At the same time, the idea of a 'disinterested' view suggests the possibility of objective criteria for evaluating pleasure and pain, and hence virtue and vice. These may be criteria rooted in human nature or in the structure of the society. If that is the case, why then cannot reason evaluate vice and virtue? Or, to put it another way, if there are objective criteria for evaluating good and bad, criteria rooted in the facts of the world, both natural and social, should we not accept that values, in some sense at least, do derive from facts? Hume, in other words, can be, and has been, read in highly contradictory ways. For some he looked upon morality as a form of subjective taste. For others he viewed it as a phenomenon rooted in objective facts.

Hume believed that some virtues are natural in the sense that they are dispositions embedded in human nature. These include benevolence, generosity, clemency, moderation, temperance and frugality. Every human being, Hume suggests, from primitive times to the present, has been motivated by these characteristics. Such dispositions produce good on each occasion of their practice and are approved of on every occasion.

Other virtues, however, are not natural but artificial, not traits embedded in human nature but behaviours and rules created and developed through human history. Whereas natural virtues are always good – there are no instances Hume can imagine in which benevolence and generosity are not beneficial – and always win approval, artificial virtues are not necessarily always good or acclaimed. The most important of the artificial virtues is justice. In primitive society, Hume argues, people were motivated to act with benevolence and generosity but had no need for rules of justice, natural dispositions being sufficient to maintain order in small, kinship-based units. But as societies grew larger and more complex, and as certain goods came to be in short supply, so they began to recognize that their interests would be best served by a form of co-operation that led to the development of conventions and rules that we now call justice. What began as a purely self-interested concern that the rules of justice be followed becomes over time, largely through the mechanism of sympathy, a moral concern for the welfare of others. Sympathy leads us to feel pleasure in response to any act that maintains the system of justice, and hence promotes the public good, and to feel pain in response to actions that break the rules of justice and endanger the welfare of others. Through his artificial virtues, Hume marries Aristotle and Hobbes, virtue and self-interest.

For Hume, then, moral duties and obligations cannot be rationally deduced from purely factual premises. Hence the failure of much traditional moral philosophy that sought through reasoned argument to deduce *ought* from *is*. He does not argue, however, that values cannot derive from the facts of the world, nor that there is an unbridgeable chasm between facts and values. Distinctions between good and evil, right and wrong, were, for Hume, the products not of reason but of a moral sense. But moral sense was itself a natural disposition, an aspect of human nature. Indeed, Hume claims that '*no action can be virtuous, or morally good, unless there be in human nature some motive to produce it, distinct from the sense of its morality*'.[8]

3

Hume, like Plato and Aristotle, saw morality in terms of virtues and vices. Plato and Aristotle, however, unlike Hume, had felt no compulsion to explain the mechanism through which humans came to express what Hume called 'fellow feeling'. They saw virtue and vice in terms purely of the happiness of the individual. This was not because their ethical world was centred around the individual but, paradoxically, precisely because it was not. 'The whole must be prior to the part,' Aristotle insisted, and the community 'prior to the individual'.[9]

The Ancients had an almost visceral attachment to the common good and to the sublimation of individual interests to those of the community. They took for granted that the individual only had meaning in the context of the community. To judge an individual good was to judge him as manifesting dispositions, or virtues, that enabled him or her to play a particular role in a particular kind of social life. For the Ancients, happiness was defined in terms of satisfactions that emerged, and emerged only, from given forms of social life. The break-up of traditional forms of social life, and the rise of individualism, necessarily transformed the meaning of happiness. Eventually the very idea that morality should be seen in terms of virtues and vices came to be challenged. Initially, however, the disintegration of feudal social life was reflected through an impassioned debate about how to define the public good and how that good related to the psychology of the individual. It was a debate that required a radical rethinking of psychology and the creation of a whole new apparatus of appetites, passions, inclinations and sentiments. The concept of appetites and passions was, of course, borrowed from the Greeks; the idea of 'fellow feeling', and of sympathy with other human beings by virtue of their being human, came from the Stoics, distilled through Christianity. But in a world in which the individual had come to mean something very different, so necessarily did his or her psychological traits. This shift in the meaning of appetites and passions was made particularly acute by the emergence of science and of the belief that science should apply to the inner world as well as the world outside, giving impetus to ethical naturalism – the claim that the ideal of the good life is to be derived not from divine precept but from a description of human nature.

Nowhere was the debate about the relationship between individual psychology and social need more intense than in Britain. The debate about enlightened self-interest that Hobbes had unleashed with *Leviathan* was accentuated not just by the British obsession with empirical science but also by the rising power of the forces of commerce and the political needs of nascent capitalism. The growth of a market economy gave legitimacy to the Hobbesian idea of morality as mere self-interest. The Hobbesian idea of morality as self-interest helped give legitimacy to capitalist exploitation.

This interleaving of commerce and self-interest found its sharpest expression in philosopher and satirist Bernard Mandeville's *Fable of the Bees* in which he drew upon a Hobbesian vision of human nature to upend traditional concepts of morality. The poem, first published in 1705, told the story of 'A Spacious Hive well stock'd with Bees, / That lived in Luxury and Ease' but which worried that it lacked virtue. Irritated by the bees' constant grumbling, God decides to make them virtuous, to ensure that 'Honesty fills all their Hearts'. The hive falls into apathy and all industry vanishes.

The moral of the poem, as Mandeville explained, is 'the Impossibility of enjoying all the most elegant Comforts of Life that are to be met with in an industrious, wealthy and powerful Nation, and at the same time be bless'd with all the Virtue and Innocence that can be wish'd for in a Golden Age'. For Mandeville, what are traditionally called virtues, being 'contrary to the impulse of nature', undermine all social and intellectual progress. The vices, on the other hand, by which Mandeville meant the expression of Hobbesian self-interest, stimulate society into action and progress. Hence, in Mandeville's view, 'private vices are public benefits'. Mandeville's assault on the very idea of virtue caused scandal. In England, the Grand Jury of Middlesex declared it a 'public nuisance' because of its immoral desire 'to run down Religion and Virtue as prejudicial to Society, and detrimental to the State',[10] while in France, the translation was burnt by the public hangman.

The philosophical challenge to Mandeville and his Hobbesian view of human nature came primarily through the idea of 'moral sense', developed by a series of anglophone philosophers, including the Earl of Shaftesbury, Joseph Butler and Francis Hutcheson, the last and most important of whom was David Hume. The term 'moral sense' was first used by Anthony Ashley, the third Earl of Shaftesbury (1671–1713), a pupil of John Locke's. The distinctions good and evil, Shaftesbury insisted, 'have their foundation in nature'.[11] It is because we are social beings that we acquire the sense of right and wrong. Moral sense is embodied not merely in individuals but also in human nature and the nature of our common humanity. Shaftesbury derived these themes, in part, from the seventeenth-century German jurist, philosopher and statesman Samuel von Pufendorf. In his 1671 book *The Law of Nations and Nature*, Pufendorf argued that society is not created through a social contract but emerges out of the natural bonds that exist between human beings as a consequence of 'human nature belonging equally to all men'. This was an idea, Pufendorf suggested, that came 'close to the very reasonable theory of the Stoics', whereas Hobbes 'serves up a *réchauffé* of Epicurean theories'.[12] The belief that the notions of sentiment, sympathy and moral sense derived from the Stoics became a powerful theme in the Enlightenment.

Shaftesbury's writings reflect the optimistic hue both of the British moralist tradition that he helped found and of much of the philosophy of the Enlightenment, of which the moral sense thinkers were an important current. Hobbes, Shaftesbury believed, had a blinkered view of human nature. Selfishness was not the only natural passion. Benevolence, generosity, sympathy and gratitude were far more important natural feelings, constituting an 'affection for virtue', or moral sense, through which was created a natural harmony between virtue and self-interest and through which humans were naturally led to promote the public good. Morality might be intimately linked to the passions but, Shaftesbury insisted, morality was also peculiar to rational beings. Reason is both crucial to human moral life, and makes moral life peculiarly human, because it is through reason that humans develop a 'conscience', the faculty that allows them to sift right and wrong, and to reflect upon their actions.

The significance of the moral sense school lay in the seriousness with which it approached the question of individual moral psychology, and its success in developing a naturalistic ethics, rooted not in God but in human nature. Its weakness was that, for all its dismissal of Hobbesian ideas, moral sense theorists still clung to the notion of the individual as a figure with an existence prior to, and distinct from, society, a weakness that has continued to dog much subsequent moral thinking. This was particularly so as two key ideas developed by the moral sense theorists, that of the individual conscience and of happiness as a measure of moral goodness, came to inspire the two schools of thought that would dominate nineteenth-century moral thinking, and still do today – Kantianism and utilitarianism.

4

Immanuel Kant was born in 1724 in Königsberg, then the capital of Prussia, today the Russian city of Kaliningrad. Brought up in a devoutly Lutheran household in which faith, humility and a literal interpretation of the Bible were all-important, he received a strict, punitive education that stressed religious instruction and knowledge of Latin over mathematics and science. He studied philosophy at the University of Königsberg, where he was eventually to teach and, indeed, to spend his entire academic career. Kant never married and never travelled, so it was said, more than ten miles from his place of birth.

The whole of Kant's philosophy can be seen as an attempt to address the challenge of Hume's scepticism. Hume had seemed to question the very possibility of objective knowledge, and to reject the idea of an objective morality. Kant suggested that the conflict between empiricism and rationalism – between the idea that all knowledge came through the senses and the claim that the mind can create knowledge through reason and its own inner workings – may be resolved if we recognize that the mind is not a passive recipient of sensation but an active organizer of sense impressions into knowledge. The mind creates the concepts and categories through which we can organize perceptions and make them meaningful. We know the world within a framework of space, time and substance. But space, time and substance are not objective realities that exist 'out there', independently of us, but categories created through intuitions or reason without which we could not comprehend the world. The empiricist mind was like an old drawer into which all manner of odds and ends had been thrown without thought. The rationalist mind was akin to a beautiful museum exhibition case but without any objects. Only a Kantian mind was both rich in treasure and well ordered. 'Concepts without percepts are empty,' as Kant put it; 'percepts without concepts are blind.'[13]

The concept of the active mind lay at the heart of Kant's moral beliefs too. He rejected the idea that moral values came from outside, from God, or from nature. The only source of morality for Kant was the moral agent himself. 'Each man his own moralist,' as he put it. The idea of the active mind expressed itself in Kantian morality primarily through the notion of duty. Throughout virtually the whole history of ethics, the ultimate goal of the good life had been happiness. Kant broke decisively with that tradition. Duty, not happiness, was the measure of the good.

Happiness and duty were for Kant not just different measures of goodness but also conflicting motives. For Aristotle a truly virtuous man was one who enjoyed being kind, generous, courageous and magnanimous. One could only be virtuous by acting with the grain of human nature, not against it. For Kant, on the other hand, duty stands in conflict with our naturally given desires and inclinations. The more that human reason 'concerns itself with the aim of enjoying life and happiness', he wrote, 'the farther does man get away from true contentment'.[14] It is the painfulness of acting to the good that is the real mark of virtue. Kant never adopted his family's strict Pietism; yet the spirit of Luther (and of Augustine) clearly inhabits his moral thought.

Most of the ends that traditionally were seen as 'good' were not, in Kant's eyes, necessarily good at all. Fortune, power, intelligence, courage – all the traditional virtues can be used to bad ends. Even happiness can be corrupting. The only indisputably good thing is a good will. The goodness of a good will is given not in what it achieves but simply in the fact that it is. Even if will 'is entirely lacking in power to carry out its intentions', Kant wrote, 'if by its utmost efforts it still accomplishes nothing, and only good will is left', it would still 'shine like a jewel for its own sake as something which has its full value in itself'.[15] A good will is good by its very existence – and it is the only thing that is good by its existence alone. The good will is the highest good and the condition of all other goods, including happiness.

What does it mean to possess a good will? It means to be motivated by duty and by duty alone. For Kant, the role of reason is not to inform the will how best to choose the means to some further ends, as it was for Hume for instance, but is rather to produce a will that is motivated solely by duty and hence is good in itself. A will, then, is good only when motivated by duty. But what does it mean to be motivated by duty? It is far more than to do something that is morally right. Someone may act in a way that appears to be, perhaps even is, his or her duty, and yet does so from quite different motives. Suppose a customer inadvertently, and unknowingly, overpays a shopkeeper. The shopkeeper runs after him and returns the money. She does so because she thinks that honesty will pay dividends: that the customer is more likely to return to the shop, and that his friends may well come too. For Kant, that is not to act in a moral fashion.

It is not just acting in self-interest, however, that conflicts with morality. Acting altruistically may do so too. Suppose the shopkeeper had returned the money not because she calculated that it would be profitable to do so, but simply because she happened to have an honest and generous nature. In that case the shopkeeper was following her inclinations rather than her duty. And that too, for Kant, does not count as a moral deed. Inclinations, he argues, are built into our nature. They are absolutely determined. We cannot choose them. What we can choose is to do our duty. Even when the outcome might be the same, an act is only moral if I have followed my duty, not my inclination, for only in the former case have I *chosen* to act in that fashion. The most moral person is the one who wrestles with his or her natural desires and chooses to act against them, knowing it is his or her duty to do so.

To explain what he means by 'duty', Kant makes a distinction between hypothetical and categorical imperatives. An imperative is a directive about what one should do. A hypothetical imperative is a conditional directive. It takes the form, 'If you want X, you must do Y.' 'If you want to be popular, be generous with your friends.' 'If you want good publicity for your shop, be honest with your customers.' It is about the means by which to arrive at a particular end.

A moral act is driven not by a hypothetical but by a *categorical* imperative. Categorical imperatives are absolute, not conditional, insisting that 'No matter what your desires are, or what you wish to achieve, you must do this and only this'. It is, in other words, an injunction but not towards a particular end. 'Don't ever lie.' 'Always give to charity.' There are, of course, many kinds of unconditional imperatives that make immoral demands: 'Cheat whoever you can'; 'Never serve black people.' What, then, defines a categorical imperative that makes it moral and transforms it into my duty? Kant gives several answers, the most important of which are that they can be made universal and that they do not confuse means and ends.

For an action to be moral, the maxim (a 'maxim', for Kant, is the underlying principle for an act) had to be one that could apply to everyone – including oneself. Suppose I cannot pay my rent and am about to be evicted. I borrow some money from a friend, promising to pay her back, but knowing that I will be unable to. I reason, however, that it is not immoral to do that, as otherwise I will be homeless. But if everyone followed the maxim of making promises and breaking them, then social life itself would break down. At the same time, it is not the way that you would wish someone else to act towards you. A categorical imperative is one of which you would be happy to be the object as well as the subject.

The second important feature of the categorical imperative is that it treats other people as ends, not means. In one sense, of course, no society can function without using people as a means to an end. I use a train driver as a means of getting from London to Manchester. I use my lecturer as a means of getting a better degree. Kant's distinction between means and ends speaks, however, to a far more profound notion of what it means to be human. Humans possess an intrinsic worth by virtue of being human, a worth that cannot be diminished simply to enhance someone else's worth.

Kant revolutionized moral thinking. His ethics of duty was the first true challenge to the idea of *eudaimonia* and to the virtue ethics of Plato and Aristotle. His idea of moral autonomy and of human dignity became central to modern perceptions of human worth and of human rights. Yet Kant's concepts of duty and of autonomy can also be deeply troubling. First, they can appear like empty vessels. The categorical imperatives tell us what not to do; they tell us not to lie, not to commit murder, not to break promises. But they seem reluctant to tell us what we should do, still less what should be the moral ends that we should pursue. So long as an individual keeps promises, tells the truth, does not commit murder, and so on, he or she seems free to pursue any form of life. Since Kant cannot tell us how to live, so the categorical imperatives must rely upon another moral code to do so.

Categorical imperatives can also force the agent into irrational, indeed immoral, actions. There are many cases in which, for instance, it may be moral to lie, immoral to tell the truth. Imagine a young child whose mother requires a surgical operation. Should the parents tell the child about it? The answer is not clear – as always, it depends upon the context. There may be many situations in which it would be immoral to tell the truth. But the whole point about the categorical imperative is that it is independent of context. It is categorical and does not allow for exceptions.

Context matters because we live in an imperfect world. It is that imperfection, of the world and of human nature, that creates the very need for morality. It is also the reason that such morality cannot be categorical. The question that Kant never adequately answers is how far a good individual should modify his or her conduct to meet the needs of an imperfect world, to account for the existence of badness, and indeed simply for the fact that the world is complex; a world in which people fall ill, in which children are psychologically vulnerable, in which it often requires the use of deceit or violence to catch or vanquish those who would do harm, whether petty criminals or genocidal warlords. Kant recognized, of course, that we lived in such a world. In practice, in his discussion of politics, for instance, he could be flexible, even pragmatic. But flexibility is the death of the categorical imperative. Kant's theory suffers from the same predicament as all rule-bound moral codes. The rules are an attempt to bring moral order to the chaotic imperfection of the world. But it is precisely that very same chaotic imperfection that renders such rules unusable.

There is a final problem with Kant's argument that is all too rarely reflected upon. For Kant, every human being is an autonomous moral agent subject only to his or her own maxims. But equally for Kant, I as a human being am not only an end in myself but also a member of 'the kingdom of ends', a 'systematic union of rational beings under common objective laws'.[16] These two claims seem difficult to reconcile. Being a rational being, every member of the kingdom of ends is, like me, subject only to laws made by himself. Yet, being rational, those laws are universal and hence apply to all. The laws of rational beings inevitably coincide, Kant argued, precisely because they are made by rational beings. Where there are disagreements, then rational arguments will resolve them. It is a view that is certainly more attractive than Mandeville's notion of morality as self-interest. But the idea that all the different individual maxims will magically cohere into a harmonious system of universal law is no more plausible than Mandeville's claim that the invisible hand of the market will turn individual selfishness into social benefit. It is no more plausible for the same reason. Both Kant and Mandeville, in their very different ways, think of morality as the morality of the individual isolated from society. The tension in Kant's work between legislator and subject implicitly acknowledges that individual moral agency can only be understood in its social context. But he lacked the philosophical framework through which to pursue this idea. It took a different moral tradition, one that saw humans as both inherently social beings and as moral agents, a tradition developed by Rousseau, Hegel and Marx, among others, to rethink the relationship between humans as legislators and subjects, between humans as agents of free will and as objects bound by natural and social laws.

5

Kant challenged the idea that happiness should be the supreme goal of moral life. Eighteenth-century British philosopher and social reformer Jeremy Bentham restored happiness to the heart of his moral code. In doing so, however, he challenged the second key theme that had distinguished traditional morality: the insistence that morality was defined through character and motive. This idea lay at the core of virtue ethics. A good man was marked out by a good character; a good act was an act done for good motives and by a man of good character. Bentham paid little heed to character or motive. All that mattered, he insisted, was the *consequence* of any act. What determined the moral character of such consequences was the principle of utility, by which Bentham meant not usefulness, but the capacity to engender happiness, both in the individual and in society. In utilitarianism, the moral school he founded, the measure of a moral act is that it increases happiness.

Many of these ideas had already emerged out of the moral sense school. Francis Hutcheson coined the phrase that came to define utilitarianism, suggesting that the ultimate criterion by which we should judge an act is whether or not it 'procures the greatest happiness for the greatest numbers'. But while such thoughts were already in the air, it was Bentham who caged them in a philosophical framework and transformed utility and 'the greatest happiness for the greatest numbers' into the criteria through which to make moral judgements.

Bentham was born in 1748, the son of a prosperous London lawyer. He himself was destined for a legal career, but came so much to despise both the profession and the legal system that he abandoned it to take up a life of writing and the pursuit of social and legal reform, and in particular of prison reform. He became the spirit of non-conformist radicalism in early nineteenth-century Britain, forming around himself a group of supporters called the 'Philosophical Radicals', who in 1823 founded the *Westminster Review* as a journal to promote their causes. These included the abolition of the monarchy and the House of Lords, the introduction of annual parliaments elected by universal suffrage, and the disestablishment of the Church of England. Bentham proposed a new, science-based national curriculum for schools and helped set up University College, London, the first British university to admit students irrespective of their faith, or lack of it.

Bentham's first book, *Fragment on Government*, published in 1776, the year of the American Revolution, introduced the maxim that 'it is the greatest happiness of the greatest number that is the measure of right and wrong'. Thirteen years later, in 1789, the year of the French Revolution, Bentham published his second, and most important, work, *Introduction to the Principles of Morals and Legislation*. Nature, he famously wrote in the opening lines, 'has placed mankind under the governance of two sovereign masters, *pain* and *pleasure*. It is for them alone to point out what we ought to do, as well as to determine what we shall do.'[17]

By pleasure, Bentham did not mean simply the pleasure gained from eating or drinking or sex. Pleasure is also the happiness that comes from making millions on the stock market or from writing the *Principia Mathematica*. But while happiness is at the heart of Bentham's philosophy, it is a strikingly different kind of happiness to that of the Ancients' *eudaimonia*. For Aristotle, happiness, the form of human flourishing, and pleasure, sensual gratification, are distinct states. Bentham, by contrast, saw the two as indistinguishable. To maximize pleasure is to maximize happiness.

For Aristotle the value of any kind of pleasure was intrinsically bound to the value of the activity through which that pleasure derives. The pleasure of reading Aristotle is necessarily greater than the pleasure of reading Dan Brown because the value of reading the one is greater than the value of reading the other. Not so for Bentham, for whom the value of each and every pleasure was the same no matter how it was gained. The quality of the pleasure was irrelevant. All that mattered was the quantity. 'Prejudice apart,' as he put it, 'the game of push-pin is of equal value with the arts and sciences of music and poetry.' And 'If the game of push-pin furnish more pleasure,' he suggested, 'it is more valuable than either.'[18] He would, undoubtedly, have made a good *X-Factor* judge.

What was crucial for Bentham, then, was to be able to quantify pain and pleasure, to determine, in the same way as one can determine how hot or cold it is by looking at a thermometer, how much pleasure or pain any action creates by reading off an objective scale. Bentham created a 'felicific calculus' that measured pain and pleasure according to a list of seven criteria, including intensity, duration, certainty, fecundity, purity, immediacy and extent. To work out the moral worth of an act, we have to sum up, on the one side, the values of all the pleasures produced by that act and, on the other, the values of all the pains. 'The balance, if it be on the side of pleasure', then the act is good. If it falls 'on the side of pain', then the act is bad.

Bentham was concerned not simply with private pleasure. A social reformer, he wanted to quantify pain and pleasure to transform public policy. Indeed, the notion of 'the greatest good for the greatest number' made no sense if all we measure is pain and pleasure in one individual rather than in all. How do we find out if a particular act is good or bad for the community? We simply add up the pleasures and pains of every individual affected by the act and see on which side of the balance the aggregate rests.

The idea that humans are motivated simply by pain and pleasure is, as the English philosopher Roger Scruton has put it, not so much a distinctive theory of human nature as an 'attempt to describe the whole of morals and politics without one'.[19] It squeezes the rich complexity of human emotions and needs into an accountant's grid. Contemporary critics were wont to dismiss Bentham's utilitarianism as 'pig philosophy', as Thomas Carlyle dubbed it in his *Latter-day Pamphlets*. If the quantity of pleasure was all that mattered, then would it not be more morally satisfying to be a pig, contentedly rolling around in the mud of the sty, than to be a Jeremy Bentham, anxious and dissatisfied by thoughts not fully formed, projects not quite fulfilled, a life that remained imperfect?

For Bentham, a moral society was one in which the greatest happiness accrued to the greatest number. But the greatest number of what or whom? Citizens or men or humans or sentient creatures or living beings? At different times over the past two centuries, each of these has been proposed as the community whose happiness should be maximized. In choosing a different community, we establish different moral rules and different notions of happiness. In recent years, thanks largely to the work of the Australian philosopher Peter Singer, the community has come to be defined as the community of sentient beings. This is perhaps the biggest impact of utilitarianism upon moral thinking: gaining widespread acceptance both among moral philosophers and the general public that the moral community should be extended beyond humans to all sentient beings, and in so doing helping to launch the 'animal rights' movement (though utilitarians, of course, believe that there are no such things as 'rights', which Bentham dismissed as 'nonsense on stilts').

Once the 'community of happiness' has been defined, another question arises: in measuring happiness, do we consider only the total happiness or should we also consider average happiness? Should we take into account the distribution of happiness as well as its quantity? Suppose that we have succeeded in establishing an objective scale for the measurement of happiness, a scale on which 0 represents absolute misery and 10 represents total bliss. And suppose we have to choose between two political policies. The first policy will lead to 60 per cent of the population scoring 6 on the happiness index and 40 per cent scoring 4. The second policy will lead to 80 per cent scoring 10 and to 20 per cent scoring 0.[20] Which policy should we choose? The second creates a greater amount of total happiness than the first, but it also creates a greater amount of misery for a minority. The first creates less overall happiness, but a fairer distribution. And, most importantly, it does not confine any humans to absolute misery.

This is not an abstract question. Slavery subjects a minority (occasionally even a majority) of people to absolute misery so that the rest can benefit. A utilitarian might argue that a slave society is not one that maximizes overall happiness. Perhaps so, though we can certainly imagine slave societies that do. Should utility be the only argument against slavery? If so, if there is a slave society in which slavery does maximize overall happiness, would the enslavement of humans then be moral? If not, what does that say about the claim that utility should be the moral measure of an act?

Similarly, questions can be raised with many other social practices, such as torture, or barbaric punishments such as amputating the hands of a thief. Historically, the reason for opposition to both slavery and torture was the recognition that it was immoral to sacrifice in this fashion the interests of the few to improve the happiness of many. Why? Because human individuals possess certain rights and dignities that should not be breached precisely because they are human individuals. This was the very argument that Bentham had rejected as 'nonsense on stilts', as most utilitarians and consequentialists continue to do. The notions of 'natural rights' and 'natural law' are, as Bentham observed, problematic concepts. But just because the idea of natural rights is problematic, it does not mean that the very notion of rights or of humans as moral agents, who possess certain rights and dignities by their existence as moral agents, should be jettisoned. Utilitarianism, as Roger Scruton points out, rejected the concept of the rational agent 'not because it had been examined and found wanting, but because it had not been examined'.[21]

For all the flaws in Bentham's theory, he remains an important moral philosopher, whose work transformed ethical thinking in two ways. First, the insistence that good and bad, right and wrong, should be defined not by motive or intention but by consequence was historically revolutionary. In the two centuries since Bentham, a whole host of consequentialist theories have emerged, each of which evaluates consequences according to different criteria. Utilitarianism – which judges consequences according to the degree of happiness or unhappiness, of pleasure and pain, produced – is only one kind of consequentialist theory, but the most influential. Non-utilitarian consequentialists may evaluate an act in terms not of pleasure and pain but of other goods such as justice, fairness or equality.

Second, Bentham challenged the idea, which had previously dominated moral thinking, that certain kinds of actions are intrinsically wrong and should never be performed, irrespective of the consequences. He challenged, in other words, the idea of the moral absolute. He was not the first to do so, of course. Greek Sophists, the sixteenth-century French philosopher and essayist Michel de Montaigne, Hobbes and even Spinoza had all issued the same challenge. So had many of the moral traditions of India and China – most strands of Buddhism and Daoism, for instance, challenge the idea of eternally fixed moral laws. It was Bentham, however, who, in the Western tradition, most helped transform the thought into a philosophy.

Even those critical of utilitarianism have been forced to take on some of its insights. Yet, so glaring are the flaws in Bentham's theory, that for much of the 200 years since Bentham published his *Introduction*, those who have followed in his footsteps have been forced to spend most of their time rethinking his basic concepts. The most important of the rethinkers was John Stuart Mill, eldest son of the Scottish philosopher, historian and economist James Mill, perhaps the fiercest advocate of Bentham's theory.

6

John Stuart Mill was born in London in 1806. His father gave him what one can only call a rigorous upbringing, deliberately shielding him from other children of his own age, and setting out to fashion an intellectual genius who could continue the cause of utilitarianism after he and Bentham had died. Mill junior was never allowed a holiday 'lest the habit of work should be broken, and a taste for idleness acquired'.[22] Mill senior clearly believed that on the felicific calculus, the misery wrought on the boy was more than balanced by the intellectual rigour created in the man.

A notably precocious child, Mill was learning Greek by the age of three. By the age of eight he was reading Plato, Herodotus and Diogenes, mastering Euclid and algebra, and composing poetry. Despite his prodigious talents, Mill never went to university. He refused to study at either Oxford or Cambridge because both required him to take Anglican orders, which he was unwilling to do. Instead he followed his father to work for the East India Company. His object in life, he tells us in his autobiography, was to be 'a reformer of the world'.

In 1826 Mill suffered a mental breakdown and fell victim to a deep depression. He was rescued from his crisis, on his own account, on reading the poetry of Wordsworth and Coleridge. The Romantics opened up vistas of human life, and of human emotions, that had no place in Bentham's system. 'What made Wordsworth's poems a medicine for my state of mind', Mill wrote in his autobiography, 'was that they expressed, not mere outward beauty, but states of feeling . . . a source of inward joy, of sympathetic and imaginative pleasure, which could be shared in by all human beings.' Mill continued to venerate Bentham, but he became convinced that Bentham's utilitarianism needed modification. Pleasures were not simply quantitatively different, but qualitatively too. There were higher and lower pleasures. 'It is quite compatible with the principle of utility', Mill wrote, 'to recognize the fact that some kinds of pleasure are more desirable and more valuable than others.' This distinction allows Mill to deal with the jibe that Bentham's theory is a form of 'pig philosophy'. What distinguishes humans from swine is that only humans desire higher pleasures. And humans do so even when lower pleasures might give a higher reading on the felicific calculus. 'It is better to be a human being dissatisfied than a pig satisfied,' Mill observed. It was also better, he insisted, 'to be Socrates dissatisfied than a fool satisfied'.[23]

It is questionable whether every human would agree with Mill that it is better to be an unhappy philosopher than a happy philistine. But even if they did, it raises an awkward question for utilitarians. Why is it better to be an unhappy human than a happy pig? And why is it better to be Socrates dissatisfied than a fool satisfied? Aristotle and Plato, Augustine and Aquinas, Hume and Hutcheson, Spinoza and Kant could all have given an answer, though each a different one. It was much more difficult for a utilitarian to do so. Mill suggests that a pain for Socrates has a higher value than a pleasure for a fool. This, of course, runs against the grain of utilitarian thinking. The problem is not just that from a utilitarian viewpoint it is difficult to explain why a higher pleasure should be higher than a lower one. It is also that, as Seth Payne has put it, 'if we accept the notion that pleasures involving the "higher faculties" are more valuable than more "base" pleasures, then it becomes all too easy to exclude the concerns and happiness of beings incapable of utilizing the higher faculties'.[24] Making a distinction between higher and lower pleasures might help resolve some of the problems of 'pig philosophy' but it also undermines one of the most attractive aspects of Bentham's utilitarianism – the insistence that all members of a moral community be treated equally, and that the welfare of all, whether black or white, men or women, rich or poor, clever or stupid, be taken into account in determining whether an act is good or bad.

There is in Mill the early intimations, too, of another distinction that has become important in consequentialist theory – that between an act and a rule. Like the distinction between higher and lower pleasures, the cleft between act and rule was hewn to overcome another of the fundamental problems of Bentham's framework. If all that matters are the consequences of an act, then what is moral may turn out to be bizarre and, indeed, immoral. There is, in Bentham's world, no *a priori* reason for not imagining that the entire pleasure of an individual or even of a group may not be sacrificed for the greater benefit of humanity. Rule consequentialists, of whom the most important were the twentieth-century philosophers R.M. Hare and Derek Parfit, attempt to overcome such problems by suggesting that we should evaluate the consequences not of specific acts but of social rules. Actions are moral when they conform to the rules that lead to the greatest good or, to put it another way, they are immoral if they are forbidden by rules that themselves are justified by their consequences. The rules may be of the kind 'Murder is wrong' or 'You must not drive at more than 70mph on a motorway' or 'Give to charity'. But what if the consequences of following a rule, even one designed to lead to a greater good, are worse than breaking it? Most rule consequentialists would accept that it would be moral to break a rule in such circumstances. If that is the case, however, then rule consequentialism all but collapses into act consequentialism.

Another form of consequentialism, championed by R.M. Hare and Peter Singer, suggests that the good is defined in the satisfaction of an individual's interests or preferences, the bad in their frustration. A 'preference' is defined not as a sensation but, rather, as a desired state of affairs, such as finding a job or falling in love. A moral act is one that maximizes the preferences of an individual or of a community. The philosophical stock of preference consequentialism has risen in recent years, boosted not least by Peter Singer's support. It is, nevertheless, an outlook that is confronted with many of the same problems as more traditional forms of consequentialism. How, for instance, should we calculate the value of preferences, and how do we weigh the value of one against the value of the other? How is Salman Rushdie's preference to publish *The Satanic Verses* to be weighed against the desire of Muslims not to be offended? If sufficient numbers of Muslims wish *The Satanic Verses* to be banned, and their preferences outweigh that of free speech advocates, would censorship then be a moral good? Are different kinds of preferences to be given the same weight? Should someone's desire to stay in bed all day have the same preferential weight as another's to spend the day reading Kant's *Critiques*? There are, of course, many workarounds for such problems, and many have been proposed. Richard Brandt, for instance, suggests preferences should be limited to informed desires that remain informed desires after a course of cognitive therapy. But why (from a consequentialist viewpoint) should the ability to survive therapy be the criterion of a good preference? Even if such questions are answered satisfactorily, the cumulative impact of such workarounds is to diminish the consequentialism of consequentialist theory. What comes to matter is less the consequences of the action than its intrinsic value. What the history of consequentialism reveals is the difficulty in thinking about moral acts without passing judgement on the intrinsic worth of those acts.

CHAPTER THIRTEEN

The challenge of history

1

'When did I lose my freedom?' asks Sammy Mountjoy. Free will, he observes, 'cannot be debated but only experienced, like a colour or the taste of potatoes'. As a child he could see colours and taste potatoes. He remembers sitting in a bright, sunlit park, where 'there was no guilt but only the splash and splatter of the fountain at the centre'. He was wondering what to do next. Several gravel paths led away from where he sat in the park. And all at once he was 'overcome by a new knowledge'. He could take whichever path he wanted. 'I danced down one for joy in the taste of potatoes,' remembers Mountjoy. 'I was free. I had chosen.'

Once, then, Sammy Mountjoy had been free. He had had the power to choose. But no longer. How did he lose his freedom? That is what he wants to know. To find out, he has to retrace the story of his life to discover what freedom is and how he came no longer to possess it.

So begins *Free Fall*, William Golding's extraordinary, haunting, allusive fable of free will, a retelling through the life of Sammy Mountjoy of the Christian story of Original Sin, of the Fall and of redemption. The German philosopher Georg Hegel spent his philosophical life being a Sammy Mountjoy in reverse. The question with which he wrestled was not 'How did I lose my freedom?' but 'How did humanity gain it?' To answer this, he, like Mountjoy, 'must go back and tell the story over'. Not the story of his life, but the story of the life of humanity. 'The history of the world', Hegel wrote in the introduction to his *Philosophy of History*, 'is none other than the progress of the consciousness of freedom'.[1] What distinguished Hegel's thinking was, as Friedrich Engels was later to put it, 'the exceptional historical sense underlying' it.[2] It was Hegel who, above all others, wove history into philosophy, and into human nature, insisting that neither could be understood without seeing both as phenomena that come to be, rather than just exist. In this he posed a challenge not simply to the Hobbesian idea of a static, given human nature that had dominated much of eighteenth-century thought, but also to virtually the whole of moral philosophy.

Georg Wilhelm Friedrich Hegel was born in 1770 in Stuttgart. He studied theology at the Tübinger Stift, a Protestant seminary attached to the University of Tübingen, where he became close friends with the poet Friedrich Hölderlin and the philosopher Friedrich Schelling. All three shared an enthusiasm for the French Revolution, the drama of which unfolded while they were still students, and which Hegel described as 'a glorious mental dawn'. After leaving the theology college, Hegel became a private tutor to aristocratic families in Bern and in Frankfurt, before securing, in 1801, a post at the University of Jena. Five years later, just as he was putting the finishing touches to his first major work, *Phenomenology of Spirit*, Napoleon crushed Prussian forces at the Battle of Jena, just outside the city, leading to the French conquest of Prussia. Hegel's admiration for Napoleon was unbounded. Nevertheless, Napoleon's victory forced Hegel to flee the city. Desperately short of money, he worked as an editor of a local paper and then became the headmaster of a gymnasium in Nuremburg before, in 1816, taking up a post at the University of Heidelberg, and subsequently being offered the chair of philosophy at Berlin University, the most prestigious position in the German philosophical world. By the time Hegel died in 1831 he had been transformed from a penniless, obscure philosopher into the most fêted thinker of his day. The denseness of his writing (which, depending on your point of view, is a mark either of the profundity of his ideas or the shallowness of his thought) makes them open to many readings. In the two centuries since his death, his reputation has taken a battering, particularly in the English-speaking world. Yet it is difficult to overestimate his influence, in establishing a historical understanding of knowledge, and in shaping many currents of modern thought, including Marxism, idealism, existentialism, phenomenology and the 'Continental tradition'. Indeed, this book itself, in insisting that moral claims do not exist in a sphere of their own, nor are fixed and eternal, betrays, in its own way, a Hegelian spirit.

2

'It's really hard to design products by focus groups,' the late Steve Jobs, founder of Apple, once observed. 'A lot of times, people don't know what they want until you show it to them.'[3] I doubt that Jobs would have seen himself as a Hegelian. I am not sure that he ever read Hegel. Yet there is a Hegelian spirit in that observation. Before Hegel, human desires were seen as fixed and immovable. Hobbes and Hume, Mandeville and Mill, Spinoza and Kant all wrote as if the individual arrived on the social stage, fully pumped and primed, ready for his wants and desires to be satisfied. But an individual's passions and the ends for which he yearns, Hegel observed, are not, and could not be, ready-made to be used 'out of the box'. They must also be shaped by the social milieu in which he finds himself and the possibilities that present themselves to him. The desire to live in one way rather than another, Hegel recognized, cannot be the same in all societies, in all ages.

Human societies, Hegel suggested, develop through a succession of forms from the most primitive to the most advanced. Each social form throws up internal contradictions, the resolution of which leads to its inevitable transformation into the form that succeeds it. Here, Hegel introduces the idea of the dialectic, which is a way of understanding change, whether in history or in logic. Its formal logical pretensions have long since been punctured, but as a metaphor for social, historical or intellectual change the dialectic has proved highly influential. Every state of being, Hegel argued, whether social, historical, intellectual or logical, brings forth its opposite state from contradictions within itself. These two states he called the 'thesis' and 'antithesis'. The interaction between these opposites then generates a third stage, in which thesis and antithesis are integrated, each in the process being both overcome and fulfilled, into a higher and richer synthesis. The synthesis then becomes the raw material for a new cycle of change, the thesis that generates an antithesis, the two of which are subsequently integrated into a new synthesis. And so on.

History, for Hegel, is neither, as Macbeth says of life, 'a tale told by an idiot, full of sound and fury, signifying nothing', nor, as Henry Ford would have it, 'one damn event after another'. It is, rather, like a story that writes itself, where the events that unfold in one chapter are the inevitable consequences of the tensions revealed in the previous one, and in which the denouement is inescapable and yet cannot be written, nor indeed discerned, until the plot has reached the final chapter. The story that writes itself, Hegel called *Geist*, which roughly translates as 'spirit' or 'mind'. Cosmic history consists in the life story of the *Geist*. The internal development of Spirit manifests itself in concrete reality. The motive force of history is Spirit's drive to actualize its potential.

Hegel's historical view of ideas was part of a broader cultural shift, the emergence of the Romantic sensibility. Romanticism emerged out of the growing volatility of late eighteenth-century Europe. The tolerance, egalitarianism and optimism that had characterized the Enlightenment derived, at least in part, from the relative stability of Europe. This stability gave rise to the classic liberal providential view of Man in which individual aspiration and social needs were seen as seamlessly compatible. The second half of the eighteenth century saw the rise of new tensions and conflicts, culminating in the epic drama of the French Revolution. Such conflicts made the inevitable correspondence of individual and social needs sound less plausible. Whereas Enlightenment *philosophes* had seen human nature as constructed by external factors, physical nature and social institutions, and hence amenable to elucidation by the tools of science, the Romantics placed stress on self-expression and the active creation of the human spirit and of human nature.

The Romantic stress on the inner world of humans helped elevate emotion above reason, imagination above science. It also helped create a new vision of humans as active creators of the world, of humans as crafting history through their own activity. Human nature, in the Romantic view, was not just naturally given, but historically constructed, the idea that was central to Hegel's moral philosophy. Hegel's relationship with Romanticism was complex. He was often critical of the Romantic approach and fell out with many of its leading figures, including Schelling. In his idealism and his historical sense, however, he stood in the shadow of the movement.

The belief that history could illuminate the human condition was not new. We can glimpse flashes of this sentiment in Herodotus and Thucydides, in Montesquieu and Gibbon. Romantic historical consciousness was different. It was a sensibility that suffused every crack and crevice of the intellectual and cultural imagination. History, for the Romantics, was not the unpeeling of the past but the breathing in of the living foundations of the present.

3

Two men meet on the battlefield in a struggle to the death. For one, honour is more important than mere animal existence. He is willing to risk death. The other is not. Inevitably, on that battlefield, the warrior risking death is the victor. The vanquished, for whom survival is preferable to honour, is reduced to an animal existence, a slave, little more than a beast of burden to the victor, who is now the Master.

Yet, the Master is not quite the master and the Slave is not quite the slave. The Master wants to be freely recognized as Master. But the Slave only acknowledges him as such because he is enslaved. Recognition is not freely given. The Master controls the Slave. But the Slave, in making himself the physical form of the Master's will, in turn exercises control over the Master. It is his work that makes the Master's life possible. The Master is increasingly alienated from the world that the Slave creates for him, precisely because it is a world created by another. The Slave, on the other hand, begins to see himself reflected in the world he is creating and, unlike the Master, finds recognition through his labour. The Master, having become wholly dependent upon the world created by the Slave, finds himself enslaved by that world. The Slave is still a slave, with no freedom. The Master is the master, with total freedom. And, yet, their relationship has subtly and profoundly changed, as have the meanings of freedom and enslavement.

Hegel's celebrated discussion in *Phenomenology of Spirit* of the Master and Slave is one of his most important and influential, and yet also most ambiguous, passages, a wonderfully rich, allusive study of the development of human self-consciousness.[4] (Hegel actually talks of 'Lord' and 'Bondsman' but the two actors have become almost universally known as 'Master' and 'Slave'.) Philosophers before Hegel had simply assumed the existence of the human subject. Hegel insisted that the human subject had to be created. An isolated individual could not be truly self-conscious, nor act as an agent. I become conscious of my self only as I become conscious of others and of my relationships with them. Humans are not individuals who become social but social beings whose individuality emerges through the bonds they create with each other. Psychological dispositions and desires are not fixed but are shaped by those bonds, as are the answers to questions such as 'What are my goals?' and 'How should I live?' Freedom can never be simply that of the individual, but must also be at the same time social.

Hegel's allegory of the Master and the Slave is a story of individual development and, more importantly, of humanity's development. He traces through history, in a highly caricatured form, the journey by which humans come to be truly self-conscious or, to put it in more Hegelian terms, by which Spirit achieves self-realization. At first, the Slave decides to embrace his servitude manfully, viewing his enslavement as a matter of fate to be borne with tranquillity. This is the attitude of the ancient Stoic. In looking only within for the resources through which to endure injustice and a denial of recognition, the Stoic is unable to resolve the contradictions within the Master–Slave relationship. At the next stage, the Slave acts like a Cynic or sceptic, viewing the external world as an illusion. He outwardly conforms to society's demands while inwardly denying the norms that society proclaims. The contrast between the inner and outward attitudes becomes intolerable and consciousness passes dialectically into a third stage, which Hegel calls 'the unhappy consciousness', by which he means Christianity, or more broadly monotheistic religion.

Religion provides the recognition that it is the spiritual, not natural, world that is the true home of human beings. Humans may live, like animals, in the natural world but, unlike animals, they are spiritual beings. Without that recognition humans remain trapped in the natural world, in an animal existence. Religious consciousness is, however, a consciousness torn between two radically distinct realms, the earthly realm of the corruptible and changeable, and God's realm of the unchangeable and essential. A believer is forced to live with knowledge of the gap between his imperfect self, a false self, and an ideal self, a true self but one as yet unrealized. An individual's consciousness becomes divided, and the believer becomes 'alienated' from it. Yet, if religion expresses in the most extreme form the alienation between self and world, it also, in Hegel's eyes, provides the means to overcome that alienation. What is required is not simply an inward transformation, as in a more pious heart, but also an outward revolution, in which the external world becomes made anew into a stage that satisfies the needs of humans as spiritual beings.

The key moment for Hegel was the Reformation, the greatness of which was its insistence that the individual conscience is the ultimate judge of truth and goodness. In this way, the Reformation had unfurled 'the banner of Free Spirit' and proclaimed as its essential principle that 'Man is in his very nature destined to be free'. History, in the wake of the Reformation, was defined by the attempt to transform the world in accordance with this principle, and to ensure that all social institutions are made to conform to reason, and hence are fit for human freedom. The Enlightenment, the French Revolution and the Declaration of the Rights of Man were all moments in this transformation. Yet, while supportive of the Revolution, Hegel was also deeply ambivalent about it, and particularly about its descent into the Terror. The problem was that the Revolutionaries had attempted to put into practice purely abstract philosophical principles, without paying regard to the real, concrete disposition of the people.

How could the principles of freedom be reconciled with the concrete reality of human needs? Why, in the Prussian state, of course. Over the years Hegel had become increasingly conservative, and by the time he had achieved fulfilment as Prussia's most revered sage, he had also discovered that the Spirit had found self-realization in Prussia, that ideal combination of freedom and stability. There was in the Prussian state no contradiction, so no further historical change, no new synthesis, was possible. The Spirit had come to rest, and history had come to an end.

Hegel's consecration of the Prussian state did not simply reflect the way that he had by now become a crusty reactionary. It also signified his attempt to resolve two key problems raised by the introduction of history into moral thought, and by the challenge that this posed to the idea of a fixed human nature. What is the relationship between individual freedom and the community out of which the individual emerges? And how can we think of values as historically flexible and yet sturdy enough to provide the foundations of moral life? If nature and moral evaluations are not fixed, how can we ever define what is right? In trying to answer these questions, Hegel drew upon arguments developed by the Swiss philosopher Jean-Jacques Rousseau. Today Rousseau is viewed as, at best, naively eccentric, at worst dangerously deluded. The idea of the 'noble savage', for which Rousseau is perhaps best known, is portrayed as a romantic celebration of primitivism. The concept of the 'general will', by which Rousseau meant the authority to which individuals within a collective must accede, is often seen as paving the way to totalitarianism. In fact, Rousseau was far subtler in his arguments than modern critics allow. Though indelibly associated with the concept of the noble savage, Rousseau neither used the phrase nor believed in the idea. And while the notion of the 'general will' does have totalitarian implications, it is also part of the late eighteenth-century attempt to think anew the relationship between the individual and the collective.

4

Born in Geneva in 1772, the son of a watchmaker, Rousseau was brought up a Calvinist but converted to Catholicism in his teenage years. Moving to Paris, he became friends with leading *Encyclopaedists* including Diderot, d'Alembert and Voltaire. Rousseau found himself increasingly alienated from their easy optimism, and drawn towards a darker view, not of human nature, such as that possessed by most pre-Enlightenment thinkers, but of civilization, which the *philosophes* had seen as the tool for human betterment. In this he anticipated the Romantics.

The starting point of Rousseau's philosophy, as it was for most seventeenth- and eighteenth-century theorists, was human nature as it had originally existed. Unlike a philosopher such as Hobbes, Rousseau neither saw humans in the natural state as given simply to self-aggrandizement nor viewed human nature as fixed and unchanging. The solitary human, Rousseau observed, cannot be selfish. Selfishness can only express itself in a social setting because it has meaning only in a world in which it is possible also to be altruistic. One is selfish only if one has the opportunity to be altruistic and refuses to take it. Unlike Hobbes, Rousseau insisted that selfishness does not exist prior to society, but emerges through society. 'Society must be studied in the individual and the individual in society,' he wrote. 'Those who desire to separate politics from morals will understand neither.'[5]

Like earlier thinkers, Rousseau believed that social life emerges as humans come to recognize the value of co-operation. The creation of society also leads, however, to the institutionalization of private property in which Rousseau finds the source of inequality, oppression and enslavement. Imagine, Rousseau wrote, 'The first man who, having fenced off a plot of ground, took it into his head to say *this is mine* and found people simple enough to believe him.' What crimes, wars and horrors would the human race have been spared, he wondered, by 'someone who, uprooting the stakes or filling in the ditch', had 'shouted to his fellow men: Beware of listening to this imposter'.[6]

The claim of Rousseau's many detractors that he wanted to restore the original state of nature, that he wanted, in Voltaire's mocking words, to return to walking on all fours, is, the intellectual historian O.J. Lovejoy observes, 'one of the most persistent historical errors'.[7] In the state of nature, Rousseau argued, humans are essentially animals desiring only 'food, a female and sleep' and fearing nothing other than 'pain and hunger'. Nevertheless, they possess dispositions for empathy and co-operation, dispositions that eventually enable social life. It is through the creation of society, of education and of law, that humans truly become human. Here is another reason why selfishness and altruism are not, for Rousseau, the opposites that Hobbes imagined. The self-realization of human individuals happens only through others. The distinction that Rousseau introduces between 'selfishness' and 'self-realization' is significant. 'Selfishness' conveys the idea that individual interests are expressed through the individual alone, that they would and do exist independently of society, and that social interests comprise an aggregate of individual interests. 'Self-realization' is the recognition that individual interests can be expressed only through society, that one only comes to realize what one's interests are in relation to others, and that while individual interests may well conflict with those of society, they cannot exist independently of them. It is a distinction that is still little understood and too often ignored.

Like Hobbes, Rousseau accepted that moral norms had no meaning in the state of nature. Before private property had created inequality, there was no need for the concepts of justice and injustice. These ideas only emerge with society. As society develops, so more complex virtues evolve through the education of simpler moral feelings. Unlike Hobbes, Rousseau also argued that with the emergence of society there develops not merely morality but immorality too. Just as selfishness and altruism are both the products of society, so too are good and bad.

The ills born of moral depravity and the ills deriving from private property create the desire for political institutions that emerge through a social contract between members of a society. Every individual now finds herself 'under the supreme direction of the general will'. The notion of the 'general will' did not originate with Rousseau. Earlier *philosophes*, such as Diderot and d'Holbach, had used the term to define the idea of a common good and to express the notion of sovereignty as residing with the people and not with a monarch or a Hobbesian-style authoritarian ruler. In Rousseau, as in Diderot and d'Holbach, Jonathan Israel observes, 'the general will has a thoroughly equalizing role: all citizens are equally subject to, and benefit from, its sway'.[8] Rousseau, however, reconfigures the concept in new ways. The general will imposes order upon society, dampens down the turmoil arising from social inequality, and is the collective moral body through which individuals find freedom and self-expression. Every individual is both a citizen, insofar as he or she shares in the sovereign authority, and a subject who owes obedience to the laws of the state.

For Rousseau, humans find self-fulfilment not through the assertion of self-interest but in the performance of social roles. At the same time, the collective 'general will' is not simply a restraint on freedom but a means of forging new ones, freedoms not of the isolated individual, but of the individual as part of a collective. That is the positive, progressive reading of Rousseau's argument. There is, however, a negative, reactionary side to it too. The will demands 'the total alienation of each associate, together with all his rights, to the whole community'. What the general will is not is an expression of the democratic spirit. Rousseau was sceptical about the merits of democracy. 'If there were a people of Gods, they would govern themselves democratically,' he wrote. But 'so perfect a Government is not suited to men'. The general will, Rousseau argued, 'is always right and tends to be to the public advantage; but it does not follow that the deliberations of the people are always equally correct. Our will is always for our own good, but we do not always see what the good is.'[9] Here emerges the woefully undemocratic aspect of Rousseau's thought, ideas that may be rightly condemned for their authoritarian, even totalitarian, spirit. Yet, even here, the issue is not simply that of Rousseau. The conflict between the defence of human freedom, and of self-realization, on the one hand, and the insistence that the interests of the individual must necessarily be alienated to that of the community, on the other, is a conflict that lies at the heart not just of Rousseau's thought but also of the very conception of freedom in the modern world. Because the community is not a given, and there is no set relationship between the individual and society, so that relationship appears continually conflictual. It was to Rousseau's credit that, unlike previous thinkers who had simply assumed a reconciliation between the individual and the community, he attempted to think through how such a reconciliation might be achieved.

Hegel took from Rousseau's understanding of the relationship between the individual and the collective both its progressive and its reactionary aspects. The story of the Master and the Slave was a way metaphorically of revealing the importance of others for the realization of an individual's freedom and identity. Hegel recognized that only through social institutions could others become the means by which I realize myself. But in elevating the state to the high point of history, and in regarding its creation as the moral end for which the Spirit uses individuals as its instrument, Hegel took the anti-democratic threads of Rousseau's vision and wound them into a despotic knot. Even more than Rousseau, Hegel conflated 'society' and the 'state', and in so doing legitimized the coercive powers of the state as the paradoxical means through which the individual achieved freedom.

After his death, Hegel's followers divided themselves into Old, or Right, and Young, or Left, Hegelians. The Right Hegelians followed their master in believing that the dialectic of history had come to an end and that reason and freedom had found their greatest concrete expression in the Prussian state. The idea that the present is the inevitable culmination of the unfolding of history has since found many proponents, the most notable being perhaps Francis Fukuyama with his 'End of History' thesis, which claimed that the fall of the Berlin Wall in 1989 had triumphantly brought history to its culmination in liberal capitalism.

For those on the right, self-realization came to be seen primarily in terms of 'my station and its duties', as the influential English nineteenth-century Hegelian F.H. Bradley put it; in other words, in terms of one's social role and the duties and obligations that flow from it. 'To know what a man is', Bradley wrote, 'depends on what his place is, what his function is, and that all comes from his station in the organism.'[10] This might appear to hark back to the ancient Greek ideal of human flourishing as developing out of the fulfilment of one's role in the community. But in ancient Greece, the community was a given. In Bradley's world, society was a battlefield. Revolution was in the air, and the fear of revolution could be tasted like potatoes, as Sammy Mountjoy might have said.

Bradley's starting point was not, as it was for Homer and Plato and Aristotle, the solidity of the community but rather its brittleness, not the certainty of seeing moral rules as ineluctably flowing from social roles, but the fragility of the modern understanding of morality and of its relationship to society. Hence Bradley's insistence that the relationships out of which an individual's identity emerges are not so much the informal associations of private life or of civil society, but the institutional interactions that bind together the state and lash people to it. 'A man's life with its moral duties', he wrote, 'is in the main filled up by his station in that system of wholes which the state is, and that this, partly by its laws and institutions and still more by its spirit, gives him the life that he does live and ought to live.'[11]

The Right Hegelians drew also upon the ideas of the Irish philosopher Edmund Burke, the founder of modern conservatism. Society for Burke was akin to an organism, and as in an organism, all the parts needed to operate in harmony with each other. Burke rejected the abstract conception of 'natural rights'. On the contrary, he argued, an individual possesses only those rights and privileges that prevail in a given community and which allow that community to progress in a harmonious fashion. Status and hierarchy were essential to society. Burke feared that equality would destroy the natural and time-honoured agencies through which social stability was maintained. A nation, he wrote, 'is not an idea of only local extent and individual momentary aggregation', but also 'an idea of continuity, which extends in time as well as in numbers and in space'.[12]

History, for Burke, was not a process of social change but a means of maintaining social stability, a mechanism for distilling the essence of a people. Morality was not about conscience and choice but about obligation and obedience. Burke was no Hegelian. But the Right Hegelians were fervently Burkean in their understanding of the state and an individual's relationship to it, and of the meaning of morality. 'The state', Bradley wrote, 'is not put together, but it lives.' It is not a 'machine' but it possesses a 'soul'. 'In the activity of obedience', Bradley ominously insisted, the state 'bestows individual life and satisfaction and happiness'.[13] It is striking how many modern conservative critics of Rousseau's 'totalitarianism' are drawn nonetheless to Burkean notions of tradition, hierarchy and moral obedience.

Whereas the Right Hegelians took from Hegel the importance of 'my station and its duties', the Left, or Young, Hegelians took from him the image of history as an avenging angel, of history as having, in the words of the modern conservative philosopher Roger Scruton, 'replaced eternity as the key to our salvation'.[14] They drew upon Hegel's idea that the purpose and promise of history was the negation of all that which restricted freedom and reason, not to defend God and nation, but to mount radical critiques first of religion, then of the Prussian political system and, finally, of capitalism itself. The most important and significant of these was Karl Marx.

5

In 1864 Karl Marx was one of a number of revolutionaries attempting to set up a Workingmen's International Association (which eventually came to be known as the First International). He was unable to attend the first meetings in London that discussed the Association's declaration of principles. When he finally saw the draft that had been drawn up in his absence, Marx was shocked. It was, he wrote in a letter to friend and comrade Friedrich Engels, 'a fearfully cliché-ridden, badly written and totally unpolished preamble pretending to be a declaration of principles'. Marx redrafted the declaration, as well as a set of rules for the new Association. His fellow revolutionaries, he told Engels, 'adopted all my proposals. I was, however, obliged to insert two sentences about "duty" and "right", and ditto about "Truth, Morality and Justice" in the preamble to the rules, but these are so placed that they can do no harm'.[15]

Marx's aversion to ideas of duty, right, truth, morality and justice could not have been made clearer. They are concepts that may have to be acknowledged for form's sake, but must always be hidden away where 'they can do no harm'. The German sociologist Werner Sombart, an early Marxist of whom Engels said that he was the only person who understood *Capital*, wrote that 'Marxism is distinguished from all other socialist systems by its anti-ethical tendency. In all of Marxism from beginning to end, there is not a grain of ethics, and consequently no more of an ethical judgment than an ethical postulate.'[16]

Why, then, talk of Marx in a book about morality? The question of Marx's relationship to moral thought has been deeply controversial, particularly among Marxists. Many view Marxism, as Sombart did, as rejecting the very idea of ethics. Morality, Leon Trotsky wrote in his essay *Their Morals and Ours*, 'more than any other form of ideology has a class character'. The ruling class 'forces its ends upon society and habituates it to considering all those means which contradict its ends as immoral'. The capitalist class 'could not have endured for even a week through force alone. It needs the cement of morality.'[17] Morality, as Thrasymachus might have said, is a scam, a set of rules invented by the ruling class to promote its own interests and to keep everyone else in check.

Yet, it is taxing to imagine a critique of capitalism that is not in some way *moral*. As Terry Eagleton has written of attempts to drive morality out of Marxism, it is then difficult to see 'why tackling famines, combating racism or disarming nuclear missiles should be described as good'.[18] Marx himself, for all his dismissal of bourgeois morality, liberally used normative language, condemning 'robbery', 'slavery', 'suffering' and 'subjugation', describing capitalism as 'exploitation', 'brutalization' and 'inhuman', and celebrating 'freedom'.

Marx, the ethicist George Brenkert observes, did not reject morality as such. Like Hegel, he saw morality not as fixed and timeless, standing above human societies, but as historical and changing, the product of social development. Unlike Hegel, however, Marx did not see history as the unfolding of the Spirit. Rather, in Engels' memorable phrase, Marx 'set Hegel on his feet', transforming Hegel's idealism into a materialist vision of history. The driving force of history was human endeavour and, in particular, the class struggle. Nor did Marx see, as Hegel did, the Prussian state as the towering monument to the end of history. Rather, Marx insisted, capitalism had raised class struggle to its highest pitch, and the contradictions inherent in the capitalist mode of production would eventually see its overthrow and its replacement with communism. What was important to Marx was not, as it was for most moral philosophers, to define how people should behave in this society, but rather to consider how they should act to create a new one. Any notion of morality had to be inextricably linked to the idea of social transformation. Marx refused to deal directly with the traditional moral questions that occupied Kant, Hume, Mill and other modern moral philosophers because such questions were irrelevant to the task of transcending capitalism.

Marx was not, however, an amoralist or an anti-moralist. He rejected morality based on ideas of duty or utility or self-interest or moral sense. He rejected the morality of 'thou shalt' and 'thou shalt not'. He did not reject morality as such. His critique of capitalism was rooted in large part in his moral disgust at its impact upon the human spirit. To be human was, for Marx, to possess the capacity consciously to act upon and transform the natural world, to use one's hands and mind in productive activity. Only through such activity, he suggested, do humans develop themselves. Marx, like Rousseau and Hegel, placed self-realization at the heart of his moral thinking. But humans, in his eyes, realized themselves specifically through their labour. By 'acting on the external world and changing it', he wrote, the human being 'at the same time changes his own nature. He develops his slumbering powers and compels them to act in obedience to his sway.'[19]

Under capitalism, labour becomes something to be despised rather than to be embraced. A worker, Marx writes, 'does not confirm himself in his work, but denies himself, feels miserable and not happy, does not develop free mental and physical energy, but mortifies his flesh and ruins his mind'. To be human is to occupy one's hands and mind. But under capitalism when one does this, when one works, one feels most estranged from oneself. The worker, Marx writes, 'only feels himself freely active in his animal functions – eating, drinking, procreating'. But 'in his human functions he no longer feels himself to be anything but an animal'. Hence in a capitalist society, 'What is animal becomes human and what is human becomes animal.'[20]

Far from dismissing moral claims, Marx was keenly driven by questions of human flourishing, of how humans can truly realize themselves, about the kind of life best suited for a human being. For Marx, what makes communism the 'good society' is 'the creative manifestation of life arising from the free development of all abilities of the whole person'.[21] Many people would, of course, snort at the idea of this being any description at all of a communist society. Others might dismiss it as a hopelessly romantic vision. Such criticisms are, however, immaterial to an understanding of Marx and morality. This is how Marx defines a good society, and he does so not in terms of duty or consequence or self-interest or moral sense but in terms of the development of the whole person. It is a concept of morality distinct from that of modern philosophers such as Locke or Kant or Bentham or Mill, but one close to that of Aristotle and the virtue ethicists. For Aristotle, as for most Greek philosophers, the central issue of morality was indeed that of the 'development of all abilities of the whole person'. For Marx, however, unlike for Aristotle, the key question was not about how best to foster human flourishing in this society within a given structure. It was, rather, about the kind of society necessary to allow humans to flourish in this fashion. This was why his attitude to morality can appear so ambivalent.

6

Karl Marx was born in 1818 into a relatively prosperous family in Trier, an ancient Catholic city in the deeply Lutheran German Rhineland. His father was a liberal Jew who had converted to Christianity so that he could pursue his career as a lawyer in the face of Prussia's anti-Jewish laws. Marx studied first law, then philosophy, at the universities of Bonn and Berlin. Having read every word of Hegel when an illness confined him to bed, Marx became a confirmed Young Hegelian. His radicalism denied him the possibility of an academic post, so he took up journalism instead, writing for, and eventually editing, a local liberal newspaper, the *Rheinische Zeitung*. After it was shut down by the censors in 1843, he moved to Paris, where he edited the first issue of a new journal-in-exile, *Deutsch-Französische Jahrbücher*, before (as he often did) falling out with his benefactor, Arnold Ruge, who suspended publication. It was in Paris that Marx met his lifelong friend, comrade and personal banker, Friedrich Engels, with whom he wrote many of his early works. Marx was, inevitably, expelled from Paris. He found refuge first in Brussels, where he became a leading figure of the Communist League, and then in London, where he was to spend the rest of his life, often in abject poverty.

'All that is solid melts into air,' Marx wrote in the *Communist Manifesto* of the impact of capitalism, 'all that is holy is profaned.' Few in mid-nineteenth-century Europe would have disagreed. This was the age of Isambard Kingdom Brunel and Baron Haussmann, of the Eiffel Tower and the Crystal Palace, of railways and sewage systems, of pasteurization and the anaesthetic. It was also the age of the urban slum and the 'dark satanic mills', of the cholera epidemic and the workhouse, of the Peterloo Massacre and the Chartist rebellion. The price of progress had been brutal repression and almost unimaginable immiseration. Engels, son of a textile manufacturer who owned factories in Manchester, painted a devastating picture of urban life in his book *The Condition of the Working Class in England*, published the year before he met Marx. This is his description of 'Little Ireland', a Manchester slum:

> The cottages are old, dirty, and of the smallest sort, the streets uneven, fallen into ruts and in part without drains or pavement; masses of refuse, offal and sickening filth lie among standing pools in all directions; the atmosphere is poisoned by the effluvia from these, and laden and darkened by the smoke of a dozen tall factory chimneys. A horde of ragged women and children swarm about here, as filthy as the swine that thrive upon the garbage heaps and in the

> puddles . . . The race that lives in these ruinous cottages, behind broken windows, mended with oilskin, sprung doors, and rotten door-posts, or in dark, wet cellars, in measureless filth and stench, in this atmosphere penned in as if with a purpose, this race must really have reached the lowest stage of humanity. This is the impression and the line of thought which the exterior of this district forces upon the beholder.[22]

Shame about such conditions drove the philanthropic movement and the demand for social reform and change that marked late nineteenth-century liberalism. Anger about them inspired revolutionary movements. In 1848 a series of revolts and insurrections swept through the length and breadth of Europe, largely in response to political tyranny and economic impoverishment. They were crushed, often brutally.

Already by 1848 Marx had produced much of the work in which, driven by Engels' excoriation of the factory system, he laid out his moral critique of capitalism, though many of his early works, such as *The German Ideology* and *The Paris Manuscripts of* 1844, remained unpublished for almost a century. At the heart of Marx's moral critique is his understanding of human nature and of what he regarded as the alienation of humans from their nature. Marx never uses the phrase 'human nature'. He talks rather of *Gattungswesen*, a concept he borrowed from a fellow Young Hegelian, Ludwig Feuerbach, and which is usually translated as 'species-being' or 'species-essence'. The distinction between human nature and species-being is a distinction between a view of human drives and dispositions as fixed and eternal and a view of the human essence as not simply given by nature but also as shaped by history. It is also a distinction between the idea of humans as individuals who happen to live in societies and that of humans as social beings whose individualism only becomes expressed through society. In turning 'Spirit' into 'species-being', Marx 'set Hegel on his feet' and saw both history and human nature in materialist, not idealist, terms.

In the premodern world, Marx argued, nature dominates human society and human self-awareness is little developed. Capitalism transforms humanity's relationship to nature. It raises the productive forces making possible hitherto undreamed-of social development, accomplishing 'wonders far surpassing Egyptian pyramids, Roman aqueducts and Gothic cathedrals'. But it also separates humanity from nature and human beings from each other. The market economy emerged in part through the pitiless enclosures of the common land, which helped create a class of landless labourers who had nothing to sell but their labour. For the first time in history, the majority of people in society were denied direct access to the means of production and subsistence. Labour became a commodity, sold on the market, much like the products of labour, whether apples or cars, jeans or sofas. Workers no longer enjoyed the right to dispose of the goods they produced. They had become separated from the products of their labour. In feudal society, humans were dominated by nature, and the peasant was subordinate to his master, often in a most inhumane fashion. Yet the peasant generally worked his own land and produced most of the things he needed for himself and his family. Whereas a premodern craftsman 'makes use of a tool' and becomes part 'of a living mechanism', in the factory system, 'the machine makes use of him'; factories 'mutilate the labourer into a fragment of a man, degrade him to the level of an appendage of a machine'.[23]

The worker becomes 'alienated' from his nature. Again, Marx 'sets Hegel on his feet'. Hegel had seen alienation in terms of estrangement from God. Alienation arose from humanity's dependence on a being that lay in a transcendent sphere, a sphere of perfection that human consciousness could never reach. Marx regards the worker as alienated from the object he produces because it is owned and disposed of by another, the capitalist. He is also alienated from himself because the product of his labour 'exists *outside him*, independently, as something alien to him' and 'it becomes a power on its own confronting him' so that 'the life which he has conferred on the object confronts him as something hostile and alien'.[24]

Capitalism makes people appear like objects, and objects to possess agency and power. In a capitalist society, individuals relate to other individuals less through mutual personal relations than through the buying and selling of the commodities they produce or consume. In a feudal society, social relationships were often relationships of domination and subordination, but they were obviously relationships between concrete individuals. Under capitalism, however, the thousands of people who enter an individual's life every day do so not directly but rather through the commodities they produce and she consumes – through the clothes she wears, the food she eats, the technologies she uses. Commodities, at the same time, appear to take on a life of their own. It is through them that humans relate to each other and it is through them that life appears to possess both meaning and shape. We talk of markets making decisions, or of oil prices dictating government policy.

Marx's critique is powerfully moral, not in the sense of establishing rules of right and wrong conduct but in the older sense of describing what it is for humans to be able to flourish, to be able to realize themselves fully. It was also cynical about the very idea of morality, or rather of what it had come to represent. For Marx, the concept of alienation, and of human flourishing, could not be wrenched away from the project of social transformation, of the overthrowing of capitalism itself.

7

For Marx, the point of revolutionary change was to create the conditions for self-realization. In reality, the revolutions made in Marx's name formed societies that, far from fostering self-realization, estranged and alienated their citizens, denying them basic freedoms and liberties. From the Soviet gulags to the killing fields of Cambodia, from the tyranny of East Germany to the medieval horrors of North Korea, communism in practice has been, by almost any moral standards to which one might subscribe, undeniably immoral.

The reality not just of communism but also of the process of achieving it, some suggest, raises deep problems for the idea of a Marxist morality. 'The claim of Marxism to be a morally distinctive standpoint', argues Alasdair MacIntyre, for many years a Communist Party member, 'is undermined by Marxism's own moral history.' Whenever 'Marxists have had to take explicit moral stances', they have 'always fallen back into relatively straightforward versions of Kantianism or utilitarianism'.[25] There is in Marx, MacIntyre suggests, an absence of thought about the moral underpinnings of the project of social transformation. Marx excoriated the moral consequences of capitalism. He wrote of how human nature might flourish under communism. But he wrote little of the norms by which revolutionary social movements should be judged. One result was the wrenching apart of politics and morality in those movements and societies influenced by Marx. Social change came to be seen purely in political terms and its moral content defined solely in terms of the success of its political ends. The moral case for any action was that it furthered the cause. As a result, MacIntyre suggests, there is a moral hollowness to Marxism that could only be filled by looking elsewhere for moral answers, in particular to utilitarian ideas that the revolutionary means were justified by the revolutionary ends.

Whatever the criticisms thrown at Marxism, and at its moral qualities, Marx's critique of capitalism seems to many as vital today as it was in the days of the 1848 revolutions. Indeed, the financial collapse and economic crisis of 2008–9 led even the most hardened capitalists to pull off their bookshelves cobwebbed editions of *Capital* and *Grundrisse*. Barely a week went by without a newspaper op-ed piece or a TV interview declaring that Marx had been right all along.

Yet in the very resurrection of Marx was revealed also his weakness. 'Philosophers have hitherto only interpreted the world in various ways,'[26] Marx had famously written in his *Theses on Feuerbach*; 'the point is to change it.' It is a line inscribed on his grave. For Marx, self-realization was only possible through the overthrow of capitalism. By 2008, however, the possibility of change (at least in the way that Marx would have understood it) had become negligibly small. The depth of the economic crisis led to talk of a 'crisis of capitalism'. And yet there was no political challenge to capitalism. Workers' organizations had been destroyed, the left had imploded, as had the idea that there could be an alternative to the market system. The resurrection of Marx challenged none of this. Those who turn to Marx these days look upon him not as a prophet of capitalism's demise but as a poet of its moral corruption. But to what extent does a moral critique that is explicitly hitched to a social critique remain meaningful when the possibilities of acting upon that social critique seem so to have faded? That, perhaps, is the most difficult question to be asked of Marx's thought.

CHAPTER FOURTEEN

The death of God, the end of morality

1

On 21 May 1924 two Chicago teenagers, Nathan Freudenthal Leopold and Richard Albert Loeb, lured into their car a fourteen-year-old schoolboy, Robert 'Bobby' Franks, the son of a millionaire. They struck him over the head with a chisel, stuffed a sock into his mouth, poured hydrochloric acid over the lifeless body, and dumped it in a culvert under some railway tracks. They then had supper before phoning their victim's parents to tell them they had kidnapped their son and to demand a ransom. The boy's disfigured body was soon discovered, and Leopold and Loeb arrested.

The trial of Leopold and Loeb was a sensation, the first 'Trial of the Century', though inevitably not the last. The boys came from two of the wealthiest families in Chicago, and their motive for the murder was not money, but simply the thrill of the kill and the desire to commit the 'perfect crime'. They were defended by Clarence Darrow, perhaps the most famous attorney of his day, who the following year would be the defence lawyer in the notorious Tennessee 'monkey trial', the next 'Trial of the Century', in which teacher John Scopes was prosecuted for teaching Darwin's theory of evolution.

In his twelve-hour concluding argument, Darrow pinned the blame for the murder not on the two teenagers but on the philosopher Friedrich Nietzsche. At an age at which most 'healthy boys were playing baseball or working on the farm, or doing odd jobs', Darrow told the court, Leopold 'was reading

Nietzsche' with whom he had become 'enamored', but whose philosophy 'a boy should never have seen . . . at that early age'. Nietzsche 'held a contemptuous, scornful attitude to all those things which the young are taught as important in life', believing that 'man has no obligations; he may do with all other men and all other boys, and all society, as he pleases'. Nietzsche's philosophy, Darrow claimed, 'was a criticism of all moral codes as the world understands them; a treatise holding that the intelligent man is beyond good and evil', and is 'exempted from the ordinary laws which govern ordinary men'.[1]

The Leopold and Loeb trial was probably the first time that Nietzsche had been called upon as a defence alibi. It was certainly not to be the last. 'Nietzsche made me do it' has become commonplace. Among the latest is Jared Lee Loughner, the man who opened fire at a Democratic Party political rally in Tucson, Arizona, in January 2011, killing six people, and injuring fourteen others including Congresswoman Gabrielle Giffords. He was said to be a nihilist who drew his inspiration from Nietzsche's *The Will to Power*. Nor is it just the defence that has fingered Nietzsche. When Norwegian gunman Anders Behring Breivik went on a murderous rampage through Oslo and Utøya in July 2011, he claimed to be protecting Christian values. Horrified Christians accused him of following in the footsteps not of Jesus but of Nietzsche. Similarly, American conservatives have accused the perpetrators of the Columbine High School massacre of being influenced by Nietzsche's philosophy even though there is no evidence that they had ever read or even heard of him.[2]

Nietzsche has become over the past century a byword for immorality. He has also come to be embraced as a cultural hero. Painters and poets, musicians and novelists, psychologists and sociologists, historians and philosophers have all drawn inspiration from his work. From Adler to Zweig, from Camus to Yeats, from Foucault to Strauss, Nietzsche's ability to mine into the soul of twentieth-century thought and culture has been astonishing. What is it about Nietzsche that allows him to occupy such an extraordinary place in modern culture?

2

Friedrich Nietzsche was born into a devout Protestant family in Saxony in 1844, heir to a long line of Lutheran pastors reaching back to the seventeenth century. Despite, or perhaps because of, such an upbringing, by his teens he had ceased to be a believer. Nietzsche attended the universities of Bonn and Leipzig, studying philology, a subject for which he displayed such facility that he had become a full professor by the age of twenty-four, even before he had completed his doctorate. After ten years, he left his post largely because of illness, having been plagued since childhood by headaches, indigestion and moments of blindness, all possibly psychosomatic. Leaving academia, he lived a peripatetic existence, spending summers near St Moritz and winters in Genoa, Rapallo, Turin and Nice, searching for a climate to suit his frail constitution. Working as an independent author, Nietzsche now produced many of his greatest works, including *The Gay Science*, *Beyond Good and Evil*, *On the Genealogy of Morals* and *Twilight of the Idols*. In January 1889 Nietzsche suffered a mental breakdown from which he did not recover. He died in August 1900.

Nietzsche never trained as a philosopher and his writing is quite unlike traditional philosophical work, whether the dry, rigorous plodding of an Aristotle or a Kant, or the flights of sometimes unintelligible fancy that mark the work of Hegel. It is, rather, frothy, pithy and aphoristic, often fragmentary, usually poetic, always provocative. He himself saw his work neither as philosophy nor as literature, but as 'declarations of war'. He was not a writer, nor even a prophet, but a 'battlefield' on which was being fought the struggle for Europe's soul. There was always a touch of the megalomaniac fantasist about Nietzsche.

Beneath the light and the froth and the absurd self-regard lay an engagement with the most powerfully unsettling issues of the day: the 'death of God' and the moral chasm that now seemed to have opened up. Nietzsche gave voice with startling insight to the spiritual disorientation of fin-de-siècle Europe. Few spoke to the dilemmas of modern nihilism with as much force and clarity. One of his last books, *Twilight of the Idols*, is subtitled 'How to Philosophize with a Hammer'. Nothing could better express both Nietzsche's method and his impact on subsequent moral thinking.

Nietzsche's starting point was the recognition that the death of God had created a moral vacuum. Traditional values had ceased to make sense, and philosophy was in a state of crisis, faced as it was by an inherently meaningless universe. This was not, as Dostoevsky, whom Nietzsche greatly admired, thought, because without God everything was permitted. It was, rather, because religion, and Christianity in particular, had itself destroyed morality. Christianity was, for Nietzsche, at the core of the modern sickness – 'the one immortal blemish of mankind', he called it. While Christian belief in the next world led to a moral devaluation of this one, and hence to a false spirituality, it had also come to embody values destructive of moral life.

The death of God had opened up exhilarating new possibilities for humankind. But it had also created a great despond. Humans could not exist without attributing meaning to their lives. For more than two millennia that meaning had derived from an individual's relationship to God. Now that this relationship had been ripped asunder, little wonder that Europe felt itself as if trembling at the edge of a moral chasm. Worse, while God might be dead, 'there will perhaps be caves for millenniums yet, in which people will show his shadow'. Modern moral thought, from Kantian notions of duty to utilitarian concepts of happiness, and contemporary political demands, from the liberal belief in democracy to socialist ideals of equality, were simply reworked forms of Christian eschatology. It was necessary not simply to kill God, but 'to overcome his shadow' too.[3]

The roots of the moral malaise of the modern world lay, for Nietzsche, in the triumph of Christianity over the Greeks. In that victory the very idea of morality, and of good and bad, became overturned, or 'transvalued'. To understand how this had come about, it was necessary to understand the history of moral thinking. Nietzsche, like many post-Romantic thinkers, was driven by the idea that the past held the key to the present and to the future.

In *On the Genealogy of Morals* Nietzsche laid out his history of morality. It is a highly original work, in which philosophy, psychology and philology interweave in Nietzsche's quest to trace the origins of Western moral thought. In the modern world, Nietzsche observes, we think of 'good' as meaning an act that is altruistic or just, or in Nietzsche's language 'unegoistic', and 'bad' as describing that which is cruel or unjust. It is morally good to protect the weak, give alms to the poor, treat all people with dignity and respect. It is morally bad to be self-regarding, to be cruel to those with less power, deliberately to harm or injure. These, however, were not the original meanings of good and bad. For the early Greeks, the ones of whom Homer wrote, 'good' and 'bad' referred to different types of humanity. The nobility was 'good', as were the dispositions of character necessary to be noble and aristocratic, dispositions such as courage, strength and pride. 'Bad' referred to the 'herd', and to the characteristics of the masses, such as vulgarity, untruthfulness and cowardice. This was the world of Achilles and Agamemnon, of Hector and Odysseus.

The celebration of nobility Nietzsche calls the 'master morality'. It began to erode within Greek culture itself. In his first published work, *The Birth of Tragedy*, Nietzsche draws a contrast between two aspects of the Greek psyche: the wild irrational passions personified in Dionysus and the disciplined and harmonious beauty represented by Apollo. The triumph of Greek culture was to achieve a synthesis between the two. Dionysus is the explosive, ungoverned force of creation, Apollo the power that channels that force into creative wonders. The Greeks were at once cruel and creative, brutal and innovative, physically savage and aesthetically sensitive. Abandon the brutality, Nietzsche suggests, and one foregoes the creativity. As the eponymous prophet puts it in *Thus Spoke Zarathustra*, 'The greatest evil belongs to the greatest goodness: but that is creative.'[4]

One is reminded here of the lines spoken by Orson Welles in Carol Reed's film *The Third Man*. Welles plays Harry Lime, a drug racketeer in postwar Vienna who has made a fortune out of death and misery by stealing penicillin from hospitals, diluting it and selling the adulterated drug on the black market. He is tracked down by his old friend Holly Martins for a confrontation on the Riesenrad, Vienna's giant Ferris wheel. Martins is outraged at the immorality of Lime's actions. 'In Italy for thirty years under the Borgias they had warfare, terror, murder, and bloodshed,' Lime responds with a smile, 'but they produced Michelangelo, Leonardo da Vinci, and the Renaissance. In Switzerland they had brotherly love – they had 500 years of democracy and peace, and what did that produce? The cuckoo clock.'

It is with Socrates, Nietzsche suggests, that the rot set in. Socrates was driven neither by Dionysus nor Apollo, but by reason and dialectics. Socratic reason crushes Dionysian passion, enchains it, and so leads to the disintegration of Greek art and drama and, eventually, of Greek civilization itself. Reason, for Nietzsche, is superficial. What really drives human beings are passions and instincts. 'Everything good is instinct,' he wrote in *Twilight of the Idols*. 'Every mistake', on the other hand, 'in every sense, results from a degeneration of instinct, a disgregation of the will'.[5]

Socratic reason began the process by which heroic values were tamed. It took the monotheistic religions truly to replace the 'aristocratic morality' of self-affirmation with the 'slave morality' of envy. In this process the meanings of good and bad become transformed. 'It was the Jews', Nietzsche writes, 'who, with awe-inspiring consistency, dared to invert the aristocratic value equation (good = noble = beautiful = happy = beloved of God)', establishing in its place 'the principle that "the wretched alone are the good"' while 'the powerful and the noble, are, on the contrary, the evil, the cruel, the lustful, the insatiable, the godless to all eternity, the unblessed, accursed and damned'. With the Jews 'begins the slave revolt in morality, a revolt which has a history of two thousand years behind it and which we no longer see because it has been victorious'.

If the slave revolt began with the Jews, it was left to the Christians to bring it to fruition by exalting the virtues of the weak, the humble, the poor, the oppressed. With Christianity, the distinction between 'good' and 'bad' became transmuted into that between 'good' and 'evil', a distinction primarily not between different kinds of characters but between divinely sanctioned and divinely forbidden behaviours. Christianity, Nietzsche observes, 'presupposes that man does not know, cannot know, what is good for him, what is evil: he believes in God, who alone knows it.'[6]

Christianity, in Nietzsche's eyes, was driven not by a love of the poor and the dispossessed but by a rancorous hatred of nobility and strength. Nietzsche describes this as a process of *ressentiment*, a term he borrowed from the Danish Christian philosopher Søren Kierkegaard, and by which he meant the projection onto an external scapegoat of the pain that accompanies one's sense of personal inferiority. It is not simply a psychological process. It is also the means by which the inferior being substitutes an inverted, and perverted, moral code for the values of the superior being. The success of Christianity led to the degeneration of civilization and, indeed, of the human race. Pity, for Nietzsche the archetypical Christian value, was a poison that had infected the healthy body of civilization with a horror of suffering. Compassion for the weak was debilitating for the strong. Contemporary humans had lost the will to be truly human. 'The strongest and most evil spirits', Nietzsche observed, 'have so far done the most to advance humanity'.[7]

Nietzsche's is an audacious account of the history of morality that possesses a kernel of historical truth, but a truth degraded and distorted by his particular prejudices and preoccupations, in particular his scorn for democracy, his contempt for the 'herd', his veneration of aristocratic morality and his visceral disgust of Christianity. The key turning points that Nietzsche identifies – the emergence of the classical Greek philosophical tradition, the triumph of monotheistic religion, the breakdown of the religious moral framework – are also important turning points in the story told in this book. In place of the complexities of Greek, Jewish and Christian history, however, Nietzsche creates a stark black and white contrast between the original Greek aristocrat and the slave-loving Jew and Christian. It is a story in which historical truth becomes so interwoven with Nietzsche's moral obsessions that Socrates, for instance, comes to be seen not as laying the groundwork for a new, more reflective form of moral thought, but as signalling the corruption of the very idea of morality.

Nietzsche's genealogy reflects his own preoccupations, but also those of the age in which he was writing. It expresses his own prejudices, but also the pessimism of the late nineteenth century. Nietzsche's relationship to his age was highly ambivalent. He was acerbically hostile to many of the major tendencies of his time, whether progressive or reactionary: imperialism, nationalism, anti-Semitism, liberalism, socialism, Kantianism, utilitarianism. Yet he both nurtured and was nurtured by the ground soil in which many of these tendencies flourished. It was an age shaped not simply by a crisis of faith, but also by a 'crisis of reason'[8] – the ebbing away of Enlightenment optimism, the disenchantment with ideas of progress, the disbelief in concepts of truth. No one expressed that twin disenchantment more acutely than Nietzsche.

In one sense Nietzsche's deicide completed the task begun by Spinoza, Hume and Marx. Yet Nietzsche's excoriation of Christianity had little in common with the anti-clericalism of the Radical Enlightenment or the humanism of the Young Hegelians. For the Radical *philosophes*, opposition to God was rooted in their commitment to reason and emerged out of their desire for social progress. For Marx, too, challenging religion was only a side-show to the task of transforming society and establishing it on a more rational basis. Nietzsche was as dismissive of the Enlightenment *philosophes*, and of socialist ideologues, as he was of God and of religion. He might have been the high priest at God's funeral. He was also the chief celebrant at reason's wake. The death of God was part of a broader estrangement in the nineteenth century from classical notions of truth, reason and universal human values, notions that were embodied in certain strands of traditional religion and in the Enlightenment critique of faith. It was not until the following century that such disaffection would fully blossom. Nietzsche's brilliance at giving voice to the growing disaffection with faith and reason would eventually turn him in the twentieth century into a key figure of the postmodern assault on the Enlightenment project.

3

'What really is it in us that wants "the truth"?' Nietzsche asked in *Beyond Good and Evil*. '*Why not rather* untruth? And uncertainty? Even ignorance?' Truth was not unimportant for Nietzsche. But he believed it was overvalued. The obsession with truth rips away the beautiful untruths necessary for a fulfilled human life. In any case, the 'drive to knowledge', Nietzsche believed, had never been the 'father of philosophy'. Philosophy is not the will to truth; it is a manifestation of the will to power. Philosophers are 'cunning pleaders for their prejudices which they baptize "truths"'. What we call 'truths' are nothing more than '*irrefutable* errors'. There is no single way to truth, only 'a perspective seeing, only a perspective "knowing"'.[9]

Some, such as contemporary postmodernists, have read Nietzsche as meaning that all truth is relative. Others, naturalistically inclined philosophers such as Brian Leiter and Maudemarie Clark, for instance, claim Nietzsche as an exponent of scientific rationality for whom different perspectives are merely different ways of accessing the single, objective truth. Both views, as Nietzsche himself might have argued, provide different perspectives on his philosophy and neither constitutes the truth.

The problem of truth for Nietzsche was not, in any case, simply that of perspective. It was also that the very search for truth often obscured the values by which humans had to live their lives. Meaning does not exist in the world, to be discovered as one might discover scientific facts, but must be invented by humans. 'A "scientific" interpretation of the world', Nietzsche suggests, might 'be one of the *most stupid* of all possible interpretations of the world, meaning that it would be one of the poorest in meaning.' A world in which all we knew was scientific truth would be 'an essentially *meaningless* world'. In antiquity, 'the striving for virtue' came before the search for facts; knowledge was seen as 'the best means to virtue'. With modernity 'knowledge wants to be more than a mere means'.[10] The problem with the modern world was that truth had become not a means to an end, but an end in itself.

Good values are distinguished from bad not by their ability to conform to factual truth but by their capacity to affirm life. 'The falseness of a judgment', Nietzsche wrote, 'is not . . . necessarily an objection to a judgment.' What matters is the extent to which such judgement 'is life-promoting, life-preserving, species-preserving, perhaps even species-breeding'.[11] In one sense, Nietzsche stands in the tradition of the Sophists and Thrasymachus. Morality is an expression of power, power is the assertion of morality. Unlike Thrasymachus, however, Nietzsche possessed not a cynical, but a Romantic, vision of power. Power and domination are valuable not for their own sake but as an affirmation of life. And no Nietzschean figure more expressed this sensibility than his *Übermensch* or Superman.

4

Zarathustra, a prophet of great wisdom who lived alone in the mountains, grows weary of his solitude. He decides to 'descend into the depths', leaving his mountain paradise for the world of men. Arriving at the nearest town, he finds people assembled in the market square. Zarathustra begins to preach to them:

> *I teach you the Superman.* Man is something that should be overcome. What have you done to overcome him?
>
> All creatures hitherto have created something beyond themselves, and do you want to be the ebb of this great tide, and return to the animals rather than overcome man?
>
> What is the ape to men? A laughing-stock or a painful embarrassment. And just so man shall be to the Superman: a laughing-stock or a painful embarrassment.[12]

So begins *Thus Spoke Zarathustra*, the most celebrated, and contentious, of Nietzsche's works, the one in which appears the *Übermensch*, the most infamous and puzzling of his creations. If *On the Genealogy of Morals* was a work of intellectual archaeology, unearthing the roots of the modern world's moral malaise, *Thus Spoke Zarathustra*, published four years earlier, was a work of ethical reconstruction, showing that which was necessary to save humanity from moral dissolution. To create a new moral order, the values of Christianity had to be reversed and a second transvaluation of values effected. Humanity had to create a 'higher type' of human, capable of such transvaluation, an *Übermensch*, a figure 'who transcends'.

Having already achieved a higher stage of existence, Zarathustra's aim was to educate humans to become higher beings themselves. Humans are not an end but a bridge, a transition between apes and the *Übermensch*. Where *On the Genealogy of Morals* is the most pedagogic of Nietzsche's work, *Thus Spoke Zarathustra* is the most impressionistic, a poetic novel rather than a philosophical discourse, an expressive attempt to recreate aristocratic morality. At its heart lies the concept that Nietzsche was to develop through much of his later work: that of the 'will to power', the unquenchable, inexhaustible, life-affirming desire for domination that is as inextricably woven into the fabric of life as breathing and breeding.

The will to power was a concept that Nietzsche had discovered in Arthur

Schopenhauer, perhaps the most pessimistic of all philosophers. Writing a generation before Nietzsche, Schopenhauer believed that the universe and everything within it is driven by a primordial will to live, a blind striving that imbues all living creatures with a desire to avoid death and to reproduce. Will is insatiable, leading to never-satisfied desires, aspirations and cravings, and making a burden out of one's existence. Its insatiability makes it the source of all evil and suffering. Life, for Schopenhauer, is hell. There is no escape from the flames; all that is possible is to hide under a blanket as far away from the furnace as possible. An atheist influenced by Eastern philosophies, in particular Buddhism, Schopenhauer became the apostle of renunciation – a life of self-sacrifice and self-imposed poverty, a rejection of bodily desires, the extinguishing of one's will to live. He was not the kind of philosopher you would want to invite to your wedding feast.

Like Schopenhauer, Nietzsche insisted on the primacy of the will. But he rejected Schopenhauer's the-world-is-a-vale-of-woes pessimism, and his philosophy of renunciation, which Nietzsche found too close to the Christian slave mentality. Nietzsche's will to power is a life-affirming view; living beings affirm themselves through their instincts to acquire power and dominance. Suffering is not an evil but a necessary part of existence that must be embraced. Happiness and self-fulfilment derive from living according to one's instincts and through the ability to exert one's will to power. 'What is good?' Nietzsche asked. 'Whatever augments the feeling of power, the will to power, power itself, in man. What is evil? Whatever springs from weakness.'[13]

Zarathustra insists again and again that there are two types of humanity: the weak, docile rabble and the aristocratic elite who alone possesses the will to affirm life and extend it to its fullness. The elite is not constrained by such slave demands as 'Thou shalt not rob' and 'Thou shalt not kill' because it recognizes that 'all life itself comprise robbing and killing'. In the words of Raskolnikov, the anti-hero of Dostoevsky's *Crime and Punishment*, who like Loeb and Leopold kills an old woman just because he can, the masses 'exist merely for the sake of bringing into the world by some supreme effort . . . one man out of a thousand who is to some extent independent'. And such independent men 'all transgress the law and are all destroyers'.[14] For Nietzsche, too, a healthy aristocratic society 'accepts with a good conscience, the sacrifice of innumerable men who, *for its sake*, have to be suppressed and reduced to imperfect men, into slaves and instruments.' The aristocrats' 'fundamental faith must be that society should *not* exist for the sake of society but only as foundation and scaffolding upon which a select species of being is able to raise itself to its higher task and, in general, to a higher *existence*.'[15]

5

In November 1933 Adolf Hitler paid a visit to the Nietzsche-Archiv in Weimar. The archive had been founded forty years earlier by Nietzsche's sister Elisabeth who had taken on the task of keeper of his legacy. Elisabeth Förster-Nietzsche, and her husband Bernhard Förster, whom Nietzsche loathed, were vicious anti-Semites. In 1887, with fifteen other German families, they set up Nueva Germania, a 'pure' Aryan colony in Paraguay. The scheme went so badly that Förster poisoned himself and Elisabeth scuttled back home within two years. In 1930 Förster-Nietzsche joined the Nazi Party. After Hitler came to power, the German government poured money into the Nietzsche-Archiv, in return for which Förster-Nietzsche bestowed her brother's considerable prestige upon the regime.

The Nazis' celebration of Nietzsche has led many to view him as the driver of nineteenth-century racism and anti-Semitism, and as a precursor of twentieth-century Nazism. Nietzsche, the Marxist philosopher Georg Lukacs wrote in his magnum opus *The Destruction of Reason*, 'foreshadowed in the most concrete fashion possible Hitler's fascist ideology'.[16] More recently, Nietzsche has become adopted by many on the left, from French poststructuralists, such as Michel Foucault and Jacques Derrida, to American naturalists, including Brian Leiter and Maudemarie Clark. Such left-wing champions of Nietzsche insist that while the philosopher's legacy might have been appropriated by the Nazis, it was only because Elisabeth Förster-Nietzsche had used her control of the Archiv to censor Nietzsche's work, interpreting the idea of the will to power and his fascination with war and violence as prefiguring Nazi ideology, and so shaping public perceptions. Nietzsche, they insist, unlike his sister, was no anti-Semite. He was critical of German nationalism and was more hostile to Christianity than to any other religion. Nietzsche's radical supporters point out that *Thus Spoke Zarathustra* is the least philosophical of his works, and that the concept of the *Übermensch* is barely mentioned in Nietzsche's later books. They argue, too, that Nietzsche was apolitical, unconcerned with social or political transformation. 'Throughout his career', Leiter suggests, Nietzsche expressed 'sustained hostility to politics'. What he called for was not 'a *political* transformation, but an *individual* one, that of the nascent higher human being'.[17]

Much of this is true, though Nietzsche himself saw *Thus Spoke Zarathustra* not as a literary cul-de-sac, but as his masterpiece, with which, he proclaimed with typical understatement, he had presented 'humanity the greatest gift it has ever been given'.[18] Yet, even if we accept that the *Übermensch* was not essential to Nietzsche's philosophy, the aristocratic contempt for the herd and the venomous hostility to democracy certainly were. Such aristocratic contempt was also at the heart of nineteenth-century conceptions of race. Today the concept of race is so intertwined with the idea of 'colour', and with the distinction between the European and the non-European 'Other', that it is often difficult to comprehend how nineteenth-century Europeans understood the notion.

Nineteenth-century ideas of race developed in response to a key contradiction of the post-Enlightenment world – the contradiction between an abstract belief in equality, which was fundamental to Enlightenment philosophy, and the reality of unequal societies. The Enlightenment had been more than an intellectual movement. The belief in equality and a common humanity had been the ideological embodiment of a wider social and political movement through which the feudal order had crumbled and a new society – capitalism – had emerged. Out of the complex interaction between the ideology of equality and developing capitalist social relations had emerged the concept of race. Capitalism had destroyed the parochialism of feudal society but it had created divisions anew; divisions that, moreover, seemed as permanent as the old feudal ones. As social inequalities persisted in the new society, and acquired the stamp of permanence, so these inequalities began to present themselves as if they were natural, not social.

Enlightenment *philosophes* had believed that social progress would heal the divisions between social groups. Nineteenth-century thinkers discovered that in reality progress seemed to exacerbate such differences, revealing even more sharply the vast gulf that existed not just between Europe and America and the rest of the world but also within Europe itself. The nineteenth century was the great age of nation-building in which countries such as France, Italy and Germany emerged as fully fledged nations. But the very process by which nationhood was constructed was also the process through which was revealed the deep divisions within each nation. In an address to the Medico-Psychological Society of Paris in 1857, the Christian socialist Philippe Buchez considered the meaning of social differentiation within France:

> Consider a population like ours, placed in the most favourable circumstances; possessed of a powerful civilisation; amongst the highest ranking nations in science, the arts and industry. Our task now, I maintain, is to find out how it can happen that within a population such as ours, races may form – not merely one but several races – so miserable, inferior and bastardised that they may be classes below the most inferior savage races, for their inferiority is sometimes beyond cure.[19]

The dilemma faced by a man such as Buchez was this. He, like many of his class and generation, had a deep belief in equality, a belief inherited from the *philosophes*. Buchez trusted in progress and assumed that potentially all human beings could develop into a state of civilization. In practice, however, social divisions seemed so entrenched and unforgiving that they appeared permanent, as if rooted in the very soil of the nation. How could one rationally explain this? As they wrestled with this dilemma, many prominent thinkers came to the conclusion that certain types of people were by nature incapable of progressing beyond barbarism. They were naturally inferior. Racial ideology was the inevitable product of the persistence of differences of rank, class and peoples in a society that had accepted the concept of equality.[20]

While Nietzsche's philosophy was not a precursor of Nazism, his aristocratic reaction was at the very heart of racial thinking. Contempt for the herd was the common currency of elite discourse. Nietzsche's fear of moral degeneration was also a central feature of nineteenth-century racial thought. In the second half of the century, the cultural historian Daniel Pick observes, the idea of degeneration 'moved from its place as occasional sub-current of wider philosophies and political and economic theories, or homilies about the horrors of the French and Industrial Revolutions, to become the centre of scientific and medical investigation'.[21]

The division of humans into the aristocrats and the herd, the human and the sub-human, gave justification to the greatest of immoral acts. 'The party of life', Nietzsche wrote in *Ecce Homo*, must 'take in hand the greatest of all tasks, the higher breeding of humanity, together with the remorseless destruction of degenerate and parasitical elements'. 'What signify these dark races to us?' the British racial scientist Robert Knox had asked almost forty years earlier. 'Destined by the nature of their race to run, like all other animals, a certain limited course of existence, it matters little how their extinction is brought about.'[22] Less than a century later, the Nazis built their gas ovens.

'It is easy to scoff' at Nietzsche's aristocratic reaction, Roger Scruton suggests, but 'there is no coherent view of human nature (other than a theological one) which does not have some such ideal of excellence as its corollary'.[23] For religious thinkers such as Scruton, *Übermensch* is the inevitable consequence of the death of God. It is true that the death of God had raised the question about how, and in what, to root morality. But Nietzsche's was not the sole answer. The Radical Enlightenment had already offered an alternative account in which a radical view of human equality provided the ground soil for a new moral vision. It was not simply the death of God that gave rise to Nietzsche's *Übermensch*. It was also his rejection of equality and democracy.

The Nazis, the intellectual historian Richard Wolin observes, 'tried to render Goethe and Schiller serviceable for their cause' but failed because 'their attachment to the traditional ideals of European humanism represented a formidable hurdle'. In Nietzsche's case no such hurdle existed. 'Was it really so far-fetched,' Wolin asks, 'as Nietzsche's defenders have claimed, that a thinker who . . . flaunted the annihilation of the weak, toyed with the idea of the Master Race, and despised the Jews for having introduced a cowardly "slave mentality" into the heretofore aristocratic discourse of European culture . . . would become the Nazis' court philosopher?'[24]

CHAPTER FIFTEEN

The anguish of freedom

1

'Take now thy son, thine only son Isaac, whom thou lovest,' God tells Abraham, 'and get thee into the land of Moriah; and offer him there for a burnt offering upon one of the mountains which I will tell thee of.' So Abraham 'clave the wood for the burnt offering', saddled his ass, took with him his son Isaac and 'went unto the place of which God had told him'.[1]

The Biblical tale of Abraham, and of God's demand that he sacrifice his only son Isaac to reveal his faith, is one of the great stories about the dilemmas of moral choice and the painfulness of religious duty. For some there is something tragically heroic in Abraham's willingness to sacrifice his son, a son for whom he had waited eighty years, and for whose sake he would gladly have given his own life. For others there is something truly monstrous about a God that could make such a demand. For some the story reveals the depth of commitment required by religious belief, for others, the immorality of the demands made by such faith. Perhaps no philosopher has explored more subtly both the story and its meaning than Søren Aabye Kierkegaard.

Kierkegaard was born in Copenhagen in 1813 into an affluent family, but one steeped in misfortune and tragedy. His father Michael, a wealthy hosier, was possessed of a sharp intellect, a deep melancholy and a fathomless well of guilt. Sternly religious, he believed himself to have been cursed by a blasphemy he had uttered long ago as a shepherd boy, and thought all his children to be doomed to die by the age attained by Jesus.

Kierkegaard studied philosophy and theology at Copenhagen University. Like his father he came to possess a highly austere vision of Christianity, but one that was married to a Socratic ideal of philosophy. 'What I really need', he wrote, 'is to get clear about "what I am to do" not "what I must know"'.[2]

Kierkegaard is as much a poet as a philosopher. He attracts the reader as readily by the fluency of his words as he does by his argument. He possesses the poet's desire to explore the unsayable and the unknowable. His philosophy begins and ends with the individual and with the moral choices that an individual has to make. He rejected the idea that there could be an objective or rational basis for moral claims. Rational argument could do no more than present us with alternatives between which we must decide, using criteria beyond, and behind, reason. Suppose, Kierkegaard argued, that one looks to reason to justify a particular moral claim. In reasoning our way to a moral stance, we start with certain premises from which we derive a particular conclusion. But those premises themselves must be justified. We may justify them rationally by deriving them from more fundamental premises. But then the same problem reappears, for those more fundamental premises themselves have to be justified. At some point, Kierkegaard insisted, the chain of reasoning must end, and that end comes when we simply choose to stand by certain premises. Aristotle had argued that in the physical world, the chain of causation must end somewhere, and that somewhere is God. Kierkegaard similarly argued that in the moral world the chain of reasoning has to end somewhere, and that somewhere is the human agent. At that point, choice has replaced reason.

Kierkegaard explored this idea in a series of works in the 1840s, many published under different pseudonyms. *Either/Or*, his first major work, contrasts two different ways of life, the 'aesthetic' and the 'ethical'. The aesthetic life is one in which the only goal is that of personal satisfaction. The aesthete is governed by his feelings but is blind to spiritual values. He is a cultured and considerate individual who pursues his pleasures with impeccable taste and elegance. But he eschews any commitment, whether personal or social, that might constrain his ability to indulge in his pleasures.

The aesthete imagines himself as living a life of freedom. He is deluded. He is, writes Kierkegaard, like a man who owns a mansion, but finds his freedom living in the cellar, having no desire, or ability, to explore the other floors. He is in a state of 'despair'; not because he is despondent or depressed – indeed, he may think of himself as being happy, even ecstatically so – but because he lacks the awareness that a higher, spiritual self is possible. This, for Kierkegaard, is the state in which most people find themselves.

One floor up from the aesthetic cellar is the ethical stage. The ethical life is one not of pleasure but of duty, a duty not externally imposed but internally realized. Unlike Kant, Kierkegaard sees the universal law not as realized through reason but rather as freely chosen, by a self that has undergone spiritual development. Of course, this does raise the question of why such a law should be 'universal'. Why should I make one choice rather than another? Why should the ethical stage be seen as higher than the aesthetic stage? In what way does the aesthete have a less developed self? Kierkegaard never satisfactorily answers these questions.

What the argument does reveal is the importance of the self to Kierkegaard, as the agent that can make choices. But the ethical sphere is not, for him, the highest stage, nor does the ethical person possess the most developed self. There is another floor in the mansion, but one cannot get there by climbing the stairs. One needs to make a 'leap of faith'. That leap of faith Kierkegaard explored in *Fear and Trembling*, a guide to the higher floor of the human house.

2

Fear and Trembling opens with four retellings of the story of Abraham and Isaac. In the first version, Abraham decides to kill Isaac in accordance with God's will, but tells his terrified son, who 'clung to Abraham's knees, pleaded at his feet, begged for his young life', that he is committing murder by his own will, not by God's. It is, Abraham tells God, and himself, 'better that he believe I am a monster than that he lose faith in Thee'.

In the second version, a sullen, silent, traumatized Abraham is about to kill Isaac, when he sees a ram and sacrifices that beast instead. Even though the ram had been left there by God, Abraham loses faith. 'From that day on', Kierkegaard writes, 'Abraham became old, he could not forget that God had demanded this of him'.

In the third story, Abraham decides not to kill Isaac. But he is tormented and can find 'no peace'. Abraham 'could not comprehend that it was a sin to have been willing to sacrifice to God the best he owned'. And 'if it was a sin, if he had not so loved Isaac, then he could not understand that it could be forgiven; for what sin was more terrible?'

In Kierkegaard's fourth retelling, Abraham makes 'everything ready for the sacrifice, calmly and quietly', but cannot go through with the killing. As he turns away 'Isaac saw that Abraham's left hand was clenched in anguish, that a shudder went through his body'. His father's unwillingness to follow God's command leads Isaac himself to question his faith.[3]

In these retellings, Kierkegaard draws out the conflicting demands on Abraham. Had Abraham refused to sacrifice Isaac, he would have disobeyed God and foresworn his religious duty. Had he been prepared to kill his son, he would have been ready not only to commit murder, but also to sacrifice his most sacred ethical duty. There is no greater ethical claim than that of a child upon its parent. Yet, conflicting though these demands are, Kierkegaard has no hesitation in insisting that Abraham should have done what he actually does in the Bible. He should have followed God's command, blindly and in faith. Abraham acted as he did not because he failed in his ethical duty but because he chose to transgress the humanly created moral order to grasp at a higher end beyond it. Socrates, a true ethical hero for Kierkegaard, was willing to lay down his life rather than betray his principles, willing to accept the ultimate punishment for the sake of a universal moral law. Abraham was a different kind of hero, monstrous in the light of worldly ethical conduct, but heroic in God's radiance. His heroism lay precisely in his willingness to abandon his ethical duty to maintain his obedience to God's command.

God, for Kierkegaard, could not simply be the personification of ethical duty. If God has to have any meaning, it can only be if there is a higher sphere than the mere ethical, if the demands He places through His unique relationship with every believer can override any commitments that believer has from moral law. 'For faith is this paradox,' as Kierkegaard observed, 'that the particular is higher than the universal.'[4]

In Kierkegaard, Luther's Protestant celebration of faith over reason is taken to its extreme. Religion is not simply an act of faith, based on no reason or moral law, it is also necessarily offensive to reason, including moral reason. Kierkegaard is critical of Hegel because of his attempt to present religion in rational terms. Through Revelation, Kierkegaard believed, religion brings to reason a truth that reason does not inherently possess. But in insisting that neither individual choice nor God's demands can be justified by worldly reason, Kierkegaard transforms Christianity into a sealed vessel, meaningless except to those who are willing to believe without reason. Abraham had kept his plan secret from Sarah, Isaac and his friends because there was no human language through which to explain it. Indeed, Abraham could not rationally justify his actions to himself. He could only leap blindly. So, Kierkegaard suggests, does every human, making every decision.

But the idea of a leap of faith anchored by nothing beyond that faith itself, the idea of a God who can call upon any individual to violate any ethical law on grounds that cannot be justified in worldly terms, is deeply troubling. How can we tell a genuine call from a delusion? We cannot. In the post 9/11 age, that cannot but seem a terrifying moral black hole.

3

How does Abraham know that it is God who is telling him to act? If I hear voices, who can prove that they proceed from heaven and not from hell?

So asked Jean-Paul Sartre in his influential 1946 lecture *Existentialism is a Humanism*. Philosopher and novelist, playwright and publisher, cultural critic and political activist, Sartre is, with Wittgenstein, perhaps the best known of twentieth-century philosophers, but a philosopher whose ideas are better savoured in his novels and plays, which often possess immense psychological power, than in his dry, abstract philosophical tracts. At the heart of Sartre's work, philosophical and fictional, was both an acknowledgement of the loneliness and alienation that inevitably accompany individual freedom, and a demand for responsibility, commitment and action. So central were these themes to twentieth-century consciousness that Bernard-Henri Lévy, one of France's so-called 'new philosophers', and one especially hostile to Sartre, nevertheless labelled the twentieth century 'Sartre's century'.[5]

Sartre was born in Paris in 1905. He studied at the prestigious École Normale Supérieure, where he met the writer and social philosopher Raymond Aron, the phenomenologist Maurice Merleau-Ponty, and his lifelong friend, muse and lover Simone de Beauvoir. After teaching philosophy in a lycée in Le Havre, he moved to Berlin in 1933 to study at the French Institute. There he discovered phenomenology, a new philosophical approach to the study of consciousness and mental phenomena, pioneered by Edmund Husserl and his student Martin Heidegger, both of whom came to exercise great influence over Sartre. He seems barely to have noticed the rise to power of the Nazis. Shortly before the outbreak of the Second World War he returned to France. Whether he actually joined the Resistance has been a matter of much debate. Mostly he was preoccupied with his existentialist magnum opus *Being and Nothingness*, which he published in 1943. In the postwar years, Sartre became increasingly drawn to Marxism, working closely for a while with the Parti Communiste Français (PCF), though never formally joining it. The Soviet invasion of Hungary in 1956 led him decisively to break his links with the PCF, though he renounced neither his Marxism nor his political activism. Sartre became an unswerving supporter of the struggle for Algerian freedom, a brave stance for a public intellectual in 1950s France. He was a staunch opponent of the Vietnam War, too, and was later involved in the *événements* of May 1968. In 1964 he turned down the Nobel Prize for literature because, he said, 'a writer must refuse to let himself be transformed into an institution'.[6]

The intellectual fruits of Sartre's Marxism came in his second major work, *Critique of Dialectical Reason*, published in 1960. A long, rambling, difficult text, it is an attempt to marry Marxism and existentialism, to incorporate a philosophy of individual responsibility into a politics of class relationships, to give ideas of historical and collective struggle a moral dimension. Sartre was highly critical of those strands of Marxism that saw history in determinist terms, waiting for the inevitable overthrow of capitalism. It is a view, he insisted, that denies human responsibility for *making* change.

4

'Existence comes before essence'. So wrote Sartre in *Existentialism is a Humanism*. It is a phrase that gets to the heart of his understanding of human nature and of human freedom. Humans do not possess a given nature, an unchanging essence, from which their capacities, personalities and values derive. Rather humans create themselves and their nature by acting upon the world.

This, for Sartre, was the inevitable conclusion to be drawn from a Godless world. 'When we think of God as the creator,' Sartre observed in *Existentialism is a Humanism*, 'we are thinking of him, most of the time, as a supernal artisan.'[7] But what if there is no God? Then there can be no God-created human nature. More, there can be no human nature at all. The only coherent way in which we can speak of a distinctive human nature is as a preconceived creative plan for human beings, just as the only way we can speak of a knife is as a consciously manufactured artefact. If we do not believe in God, we cannot believe in human nature. For Sartre, the death of God provided also the last rites for human nature.

The idea that without God there can be no human nature might seem a strange view, especially for an atheist, in the post-Darwinian world. The publication in 1859 of Darwin's *On the Origin of Species* had transformed the debate on human nature by suggesting in evolution by natural selection a mechanism by which to create without a Creator, to design without a designer. In the decades that followed, Darwinism came to be seen, however, as a mechanism through which to understand not the human essence but human differences. The idea of race, and of innate, evolved group differences, dominated discussions of human nature. With the exception of one or two isolated figures, it was not till the 1970s that serious consideration began to be given to the concept of an evolved common human nature. Sartre, in his discussion of existentialism and humanism, was engaging with the ghosts, not of Darwin, but of Aristotle and Descartes. He was challenging not so much the idea of a biologically defined human nature as of a determinist view of history.

The key distinction for Sartre was that between *people* and *things*. Things have a definable essence, exist to perform a function, follow natural laws, and are determined by prior causal conditions. Persons have no definable essence, but define and redefine themselves constantly, and are radically free.

For Aristotle, an object could only be understood in relation to its purpose or function. Humans had been designed to exercise reason. To flourish, humans had to act in accordance with reason. Sartre dismissed this vision of human function and human flourishing. Humans, and only humans, could define for themselves their function, their role in life. 'Man', as Sartre put it, 'is nothing else but what he makes of himself.'[8]

Sartre's vision is, in one sense, quite Cartesian, an image of a world divided between people and things, between a mechanistic nature and self-conscious humans, who could not be understood in terms of mechanistic nature. This affinity was, perhaps, inevitable; Sartre had, like virtually all modern French philosophers, supped from the earliest days on the milk of the *Discours*. In another sense, however, Sartre was proposing a startlingly anti-Cartesian view. For Descartes, the only thing of which I can be sure is that I exist. The ego is the one unquestionable truth in the universe, existing before consciousness, and responsible for consciousness. For Sartre, to the contrary, consciousness helps create the ego. This might seem, at first hand, a strange way of looking at the issue. Sartre is suggesting that I don't create my thoughts; my thoughts create me. This, however, is the way that many contemporary philosophers and neuroscientists understand the notion of the self. The self is not a thing, or an object, that makes us conscious of the world. Rather, the disparate strands of our consciousness unify into the self. For Sartre, as for a contemporary philosopher such as Daniel Dennett (who is no existentialist), 'I' come to be in that unity.

Unlike many contemporary philosophers, however, Sartre does not conclude from this that the 'I' is a fiction and 'free will' an illusion. Rather the opposite. The fact that the ego is contingent upon consciousness suggests to Sartre that humans are radically free and that this radical freedom, not any pre-given essence, defines what it is to be human. Radical freedom arises out of the very nature of the human condition. 'There is no difference', as Sartre puts it, 'between the being of man and his being free.'[9]

For Sartre, the question 'How shall I live?' cannot be answered by appealing to a fixed human nature or essence, to a pre-existing ego that helps define our thoughts, beliefs and values. Neither God nor human nature, neither science nor theology, nor yet philosophy, can set out the answers to the fundamental questions of existence. Only I can determine how I should live; I alone am responsible for the decisions that I make. 'Man', Sartre concluded, 'is condemned to be free.' Why condemned? Because, Sartre observed, 'he did not create himself, yet is nevertheless at liberty, and from the moment he is thrown into the world he is responsible for everything he does.'[10]

5

Imagine, Kierkegaard wrote in his pseudonymously published *The Concept of Anxiety*, a man standing at the edge of a cliff. When he glances over the edge, he is overcome with dread, not just because he is filled with fear at the thought of falling, but also because he is seized by a terrifying impulse deliberately to leap. What grips that man, Kierkegaard suggests, is dread of the possibilities open to him; what he experiences 'is the dizziness of freedom'.[11]

Sartre, too, sees what he calls 'anguish' as the condition of human freedom. Since nothing can determine our choice of life for us, neither can anything explain or justify what we are. There is no inherent meaning in the universe. Only we can create meaning. Albert Camus, the French-Algerian novelist and fellow existentialist, called this sense of groundlessness the 'absurdity' of life. There is, Camus observed, a chasm between 'the human need [for meaning] and the unreasonable silence of the world'. Religion is a means of bridging that chasm, but a dishonest one. 'I don't know whether this world has any meaning that transcends it,' he writes. 'But I know that I do not know this meaning and that it is impossible for me just now to know it.'[12] Camus does not know that God does not exist. But he is determined to *believe* it, because that is the only way to make sense of being human. The only way to find meaning, the only way to bridge the chasm between the cold, silent world and the human need for moral warmth, is to create our own meaning, our own values. Sartre similarly sees the world as absurd in the sense that there is no meaning to be found beyond that which humans themselves create. The price of making meaning is anguish.

A wholly authentic or truly human life, Sartre suggests, is only possible for those who recognize the inescapability of freedom and its responsibility and are happy to live with anguish. But humankind, Sartre agrees with T.S. Eliot, mostly 'cannot bear too much reality'. They fear, they dread, they feel enchained by, the responsibility of freedom. Humans try to avoid the anguish that comes with looking over the cliff edge by hiding the truth from themselves, by pretending that there is no cliff, that something or someone has erased that edge. There are, Sartre suggests, many ways in which people do this. The most important, and the idea for which Sartre is probably most celebrated, is that of 'bad faith'. People often try to evade the terrifying realities of the human condition by ordering their lives according to some preordained social role, in essence by turning themselves into objects, in an effort to deny the burden of subjectivity.

Sartre's most famous illustration of bad faith is of a waiter who exaggerates his every movement, who embroiders all his conversations, so as to appear more 'waiteresque'. He is just too eager to please, too ostentatious in his deportment, too Uriah Heepish in the way he demeans his own status. Everything about him suggests that he thinks of himself as entirely circumscribed by his role as a waiter. And yet his exaggerated behaviour reveals not just that he is play-acting, but also that he is aware that he is play-acting, aware that he is more than merely a waiter. He self-consciously denies that something more, turning himself into an object in the world, an automaton whose essence is to be a waiter. This conscious self-deception Sartre calls 'bad faith'.

The existential conception of the good life is, then, an authentic life, a life defined by the pursuit of consciously self-chosen values and purposes for which the chooser takes full responsibility. This seems to suggest the good life is distinguished not by *what* is chosen, but by the *manner* in which it is chosen. But can this be true? Can it really be the case that a heroin dealer and a neurosurgeon can both be said to live the good life if both chose to be what they are freely, honestly and in good faith? Suppose the heroin dealer chose to act as he did, while the neurosurgeon took up her scalpel for the 'wrong' reasons. Should we really say that the heroin dealer is the better person? Or take Nazi Germany. Some people joined the Nazi Party because they truly believed in exterminating Jews and in creating the thousand-year Reich. Others did so because they wanted an easy life, to gain promotion, or to gain access to goods and services that might otherwise be denied them. Were those who joined the Nazis because they truly believed in its evil aims really more moral than the time-servers?

Few existentialists would, of course, agree with such a proposition, least of all Sartre. His life of political activism was testament to the importance he placed upon the content of values expressed, not just the manner in which it was expressed. It was testament, too, to the importance he placed upon struggle. In his book *The Myth of Sisyphus*, Camus retells the ancient Greek tale as a metaphor for the making of meaning. Having scorned the gods, Sisyphus is condemned by them to spend eternity in the Underworld forever rolling a rock to the top of a mountain, only for it to roll all the way down again, forcing him to begin his labours once more, and to continue to do so for eternity. Meaning, Camus insisted, can come only through struggle, even if that struggle appears as meaningless as that of Sisyphus. For Sartre, too, struggle was central to his vision of how to infuse the world with meaning, but there was more to struggle than simply acting upon the world. Struggle was to act not simply for the sake of it but for a reason; and that reason was social transformation. The early Sartre saw freedom and agency as ends in themselves. The later Sartre saw the importance of freedom, and the responsibility it placed upon humans, as inextricably linked to the project of social renewal. It was this idea that led him to Marxism. Some former friends, such as Aaron and Camus, found Sartre's dalliance with Marx inexplicable. Partly they were repulsed by the kind of social change demanded by communism and by the socialism being practised in the Soviet Union. Partly also they found it impossible to imagine how the idea of individual subjective freedom, which was at the heart of existential philosophy, could be reconciled with a materialist view of history. For Sartre, it was precisely his desire to understand individual freedom against the background of historical change that drew him to Marxism. It was for him a recognition that existentialism could not simply be a philosophy of the individual or the subjective, and that freedom was collective as well as individual.

As so often, Sartre best expressed these ideas through an illustration rather than an argument. There are, he observed, two kinds of crowds. One is like the queue that forms every morning at a bus stop on the Place Saint-Germain in Paris, the other like the revolutionary mob that had stormed the Bastille. The bus queue is an expression of seriality, of a 'plurality of isolations'. It is a crowd in the sense that individuals who share the same objective – to get on the bus – come together in the same physical space. But every individual in that queue tends to see every other as a potential competitor for a limited resource – a seat on the bus. Each is an obstacle to the aims of the others. The crowd that stormed the Bastille also comprised individuals in the same physical space. But every individual, rather than competing with every other to achieve the same objective, necessarily had to assist each other. The bus queue is devoid of any wider meaning, united by nothing more than every individual's subjective desires. The storming of the Bastille was resonant with wider symbolism. The mob only formed because of wider aims, aims that were social and historical rather than individual and personal. It was a 'fused group', not a 'seriality'.

Freedom, Sartre came to believe, derived not simply from individual choices but from the way that individuals co-operated to achieve their ends. The individuals in a bus queue passively accept the given conditions and hence limit their freedom and capacity for choice. In storming the Bastille, the crowd was acting as a battering ram upon history, choosing consciously to transform its conditions, and hence transforming the possibilities of freedom. Sartre rejected the idea, held by many, perhaps most, Marxists, that history had a preordained end that it was possible to know, and to which the unfolding of history inevitably led. There was, for Sartre, no inevitability about history, no predetermined course or conclusion. How history developed depended upon the choices people made and the actions in which they engaged. In storming the Bastille, the crowd was attempting to shape the course of history, to bend it to its will. Hence its historical, and existential, importance.

'Men make their own history,' Marx had written, 'but they do not make it as they please; they do not make it under self-selected circumstances, but under circumstances existing already, given and transmitted from the past.'[13] Sartre borrowed this idea and transformed it into a framework for moral thought. His starting point was the recognition that in politics questions of morality could never be brushed aside. Every time we act upon the world, we make a choice, and in so doing we take a moral stance. But if morality can never be evaded, neither can it ever be understood in its own terms. People act not upon a world that they have created but a world, and a history, institutions and traditions, that already exist. This did not mean that humans are prisoners of their history or their culture. It meant simply that choices are made not upon a blank slate but upon one on which others have already written. We are not merely the products of our circumstances but can make choices within those given circumstances. Indeed, we have to.

Sartre called the background against which we make choices 'facticity'. The aim of social transformation is to transform facticity, and hence the possibilities of the choices we are able to make. Social transformation, the conscious remaking of society, the collective attempt to shape history, was for Sartre the means of bridging individual subjective choice and the objectively given environment.

6

Existentialists face a similar kind of problem to consequentialists. Consequentialism reduces the complexity of moral debates into a measure of moral worth that is often abstractly rational but is rarely reasonable within the framework of actually lived human lives. To overcome the problem, consequentialists have advocated all manner of workarounds, from J.S. Mill's distinction between 'higher' and 'lower' pleasures to Richard Brandt's suggestion that preferences be limited to the informed desires that remain after a course of cognitive therapy. The cumulative impact of such workarounds is to diminish the consequentialism of consequentialist theory.

Similarly with existentialism. Existentialists foreground a crucial aspect of our lives, without which moral choice would become meaningless – freedom and responsibility. But in turning every moral choice into a 'leap of faith', in unstitching choice from the rest of the architecture of our lives, existentialists transformed an important insight about the significance of human agency into an implausible demand detached from the reality of the human condition. Sartre turned to Marx to find a means of bringing existentialism back to earth, of relating individual freedom to the collective structures of society. He scaffolded existentialist ideas of freedom with a materialist understanding of history and infused the concept of agency into Marxist theories of social transformation, challenging determinist notions of historical change. All this only raised new questions about Sartre's existentialism and about his Marxism.

The later Sartre seems almost to reverse the argument about human freedom proposed by the earlier Sartre. 'It would be quite wrong to interpret me', he wrote in *Critique of Dialectical Reason*, 'as meaning that man is free in all situations as the Stoics claimed. I mean the exact opposite: all men are slaves insofar as their lives unfold in the practico-inert field.'[14] The 'practico-inert field' is a very Sartrean term to describe the kind of human group that acts more like the bus queue than like the crowd storming the Bastille. It is, in Sartre's view, characteristic of capitalist society. In describing humans as 'slaves', Sartre does not mean that they possess no capacity to act freely. It is, nevertheless, a claim difficult to reconcile with the idea of radical freedom, of humans as beings who can make and remake themselves almost at will. Nor is it easy to reconcile with the existential belief that 'There is no difference between the being of man and his being free'.[15] For the later Sartre there clearly *is* a difference between the being of man and his being free, since true freedom is only possible under certain social conditions, that is, under certain conditions of being.

Sartre was confronted, too, by many of the same questions as Marx had been, though with even greater force since the reality of revolutionary transformation had become so much clearer. From the Soviet Union to Cuba, the challenge to capitalism had not freed people from 'slavery' but had created societies less free, less moral and less conducive to self-realization. The tyranny of the Soviet Empire, and of the other communist states, did not of itself discredit either Marxism, or Sartre's fusion of Marx and Kierkegaard. But it did pose difficult questions for a moral theory that freedom required the overthrow of capitalism. Nor was it just that alternatives to capitalism appeared less attractive; it was also that they appeared less achievable. By the time Sartre died in 1980 there was already growing disenchantment with the very possibility of social transformation. Within a decade, the collapse of the Berlin Wall marked the end of the Soviet Empire. It signalled also the fading of the dream of an alternative to the market system.

For Sartre, as for Marx, social transformation was the link between the subjective and the objective, between individual moral choice and the objective needs of society. Through mass movements, individual desires became transformed into historical possibilities. As such movements disintegrated in the last decades of the twentieth century, as the very possibility of such transformation seemed to ebb away, so the question was posed: if freedom is defined through struggle and through conscious social transformation, what does freedom mean in those conditions in which such struggle and such transformation no longer appear plausible?

This was a question posed not simply to Sartre. Through the twentieth century, moral arguments came increasingly to be seen either as purely subjective or as purely objective. On the one hand, human agency came to be seen increasingly in terms of subjective desires; on the other, morality was viewed as determined entirely by facticity. That which Sartre had tried to bring together increasingly pulled apart.

CHAPTER SIXTEEN

The ethics of liberation

1

Aimé Césaire, the Martinique-born poet and statesman, once wrote of Haiti that it was here that the colonial knot was first tied. It was also in Haiti, Césaire added, that the knot of colonialism began to unravel when 'black men stood up in order to affirm, for the first time, their determination to create a new world, a free world'[1]. In 1791, almost exactly three hundred years after Christopher Columbus had landed there, a mass insurrection broke out among Haiti's slaves, upon whose labour France had transformed Saint-Domingue, as it called its colony, into the richest island in the world. It was an insurrection that became a revolution, a revolution that today is almost forgotten, and yet which was to shape history almost as deeply as the two eighteenth-century revolutions with which we are far more familiar – those of 1776 and 1789.

Slaves had always resisted their enslavement. What transformed that resistance in Haiti into something more historic was another revolution 5,000 miles away. The French Revolution of 1789, and the Declaration of the Rights of Man and of the Citizen that followed, provided the moral argument for revolutionary change in Haiti. Adopted by the French National Assembly in August 1789, the Declaration defined a single set of individual and collective rights for all men, universal in scope and valid in all times and places. 'Men are born and remain free and equal in rights', declared Article 1. According to

Article 6, 'The law is the expression of the general will'. It 'must be the same for all, whether it protects or punishes', and 'All citizens, being equal in the eyes of the law, are equally eligible to all dignities and to all public positions and occupations, according to their abilities, and without distinction except that of their virtues and talents.' Four years later, in 1793, a second, more radical and egalitarian version was adopted.

The Haitian slaves were led by Toussaint L'Ouverture, a self-educated former slave, well read, highly politicized and possessed of a genius for military tactics and strategy. His greatest gift, perhaps, was his ability to see that while Europe was responsible for the enslavement of blacks, nevertheless within European culture lay also the political and moral ideas with which to shatter the bonds of enslavement. The French bourgeoisie might have tried to deny the mass of humanity the ideals embodied in the Declaration of the Rights of Man. Indeed, thanks mainly to the influence of colonial planters, the Declaration of the Rights of Man did not specifically revoke the institution of slavery. But L'Ouverture recognized in its spirit a weapon more powerful than any sword or musket or cannon.

The Saint-Domingue slaves rose in rebellion on 24 August 1791. In the space of twelve years they defeated, in turn, the local French garrison and planters, a Spanish invasion, a British expedition of 60,000 men, and a French force of similar size led by Charles Victor Emmanuel Leclerc, Napoleon Bonaparte's brother-in-law. Slaves who, just months earlier, had trembled in their hundreds before a single master, had been transformed into a people able to organize themselves and defeat the most powerful European nations of their day. In 1803 the only successful slave revolt in history gave Haiti its independence.

There was, the historian Robin Blackburn observes, 'a universalistic emancipatory element in the French Revolution, but those who issued the Declaration of the Rights of Man were by no means always aware of it, or willing to follow through its logic'. For the emancipatory logic to be fulfilled, 'there was needed the independent action of formerly excluded, oppressed and exploited social layers'.[2] The Haitian revolution embodied a moral claim – the insistence that the Rights of Man applied to all. That moral claim could find expression only through social transformation. Here was revealed the new relationship between morality and politics that had emerged in the transition from the premodern to the modern world. In the premodern world, morality and politics were inextricably linked because social structures were a given. In the modern world, morality and politics are inextricably linked because social structures are *not* fixed. Morality helps define our vision of the good society. Moral claims emerge not out of a fixed set of social institutions but through social struggle. In the modern world, as Blackburn observes, it is only through the articulation of social power that moral claims find concrete expression.

2

Few people these days remember the Haitian revolution or recognize its significance. That any do so at all is largely due to the work of Aimé Césaire's Caribbean contemporary, C.L.R. James. Césaire was perhaps the greatest poet of the anti-colonial movement. It was James, however, who most eloquently captured the poetry of the Haitian revolution in his magnificent masterpiece *The Black Jacobins*. An extraordinary synthesis of novelistic narrative and factual reconstruction, it is a book that helped transform both the writing of history and history itself. Three decades before historians such as Christopher Hill, Eric Hobsbawm and E.P. Thompson began writing 'history from below', James told of how the slaves of Haiti had not simply been passive victims of their oppression but active agents in their own emancipation. And in telling that story, he created a work that was to become indispensable to a new generation of Toussaint L'Ouvertures that, over the next three decades, helped lead anti-colonial struggles in Africa, Asia, Latin America and the Caribbean.

Born in 1901 in Trinidad, Cyril Lionel Robert James is one of those towering figures of the twentieth century who, like the revolution he so eloquently depicted, is all too rarely recognized as such. Novelist and orator, philosopher and cricketer, historian and revolutionary, Trotskyist and Pan-Africanist – there are few modern figures who can match his intellectual depth, cultural breadth or sheer political contrariness. At the heart of all his work is the distinction he found in L'Ouverture, the distinction between the immorality of European colonialism and the moral necessity of many of the ideas that flowed out of Enlightenment culture. Indeed, L'Ouverture was significant to James not just because he had led the first great slave revolution, but because, in so doing, he had made concrete that distinction. James was attempting to address a challenge posed for liberation struggles by a shift in the way that the Western elites had come to view the 'Other'.

In the nineteenth century ideas of race and class had been tightly fused. By the twentieth century race had become a means not of explaining social distinctions within Europe but of branding the non-European Other. The contempt for the herd so fervidly expressed by nineteenth-century thinkers had not disappeared but race was now primarily a means of explaining and justifying imperial power. 'What *is* Empire but the predominance of race?' the English liberal imperialist and prime minister Lord Rosebery observed.[3] By the eve of the First World War, most of the world had come under the direct rule or indirect political control of a handful of European states and the USA, confirming a sense of inherent superiority. It confirmed also a sense of the moral worthlessness of the Other. All must appreciate the 'race importance' of the struggle between whites and the rest, wrote the soon-to-be US president Theodore Roosevelt in 1896; the elimination of the inferior races, 'whose life was but a few degrees less meaningless, squalid and ferocious than that of the wild beasts', would be 'for the benefit of civilization and in the interests of mankind', adding that it was 'idle to apply to savages the rules of international morality that apply between stable and cultured communities'.[4]

The issue of imperialism, and of the struggle against it, rarely makes an appearance in discussions about morality, especially in the West. Yet, as the Indian novelist and essayist Pankaj Mishra observes, 'The central event of the last century for the majority of the world's population was the intellectual and political reawakening of Asia and its emergence from the ruins of both Asian and European empires';[5] the intellectual and political reawakening, indeed, not just of Asia, but of much of the non-European world. It is difficult for many now to understand the sheer immorality of imperialist subjugation and the insistence, in the words of *The Times*, that 'the brown, black and yellow races of the world' had to accept that 'inequality is inevitable . . . not due to inferior status but to facts of race'.[6] It is perhaps equally difficult to understand the moral importance millions placed upon challenging racial ideology and imperial rule. In May 1905 the Japanese navy laid waste to Russian forces. Russia's humiliation was felt around the world. All saw in it the defeat of a 'white' nation by a 'non-white' one. 'When everyone in Japan . . . came to believe in self-respect,' Mahatma Gandhi observed, 'the country became free', adding that now 'we, too, need to feel the spirit of self-respect'.[7]

But how, and on what moral basis, to challenge imperialism? Toussaint L'Ouverture's Haitian revolution had been fuelled by the moral claims of the French Revolution, the Rights of Man and the universalist philosophy of the Enlightenment. 'All progressive, rationalist and humanist ideas are implicit in it, and indeed came out of it,' wrote the historian and Marxist Eric Hobsbawm of the Enlightenment.[8] But it was not so simple. The Europe of the Enlightenment was also the Europe of imperial terror. If Europe was responsible for the enslavement of more than half the world, many wondered, what worth could there be in its political and moral ideas, which at best had failed to prevent that enslavement, at worst had provided its intellectual grounding? Did not those challenging European imperialism also need to challenge its ideas?

Faced with this conundrum, the answer from C.L.R. James was clear. 'We live in one world', he wrote in his 1969 essay 'Discovering Literature in Trinidad', 'and we have to find out what is taking place in the world. And I, a man of the Caribbean, have found that it is in the study of Western literature, Western philosophy and Western history that I have found out the things that I have found out, even about the underdeveloped countries.'[9] For James, the works of Sophocles and Shakespeare, of Dante and Descartes, of Melville and Marx, as much as of Tagore and Du Bois, Chinua Achebe and Langston Hughes, provided the peoples of Africa, Asia and the Americas with a means of breaking out of the particularities of their experiences and of entering a more universal form of discourse. At the same time the very fact of his anti-imperialism was a reflection of the immorality of Europe's treatment of non-European peoples. 'I denounce European colonialism,' James wrote, 'but I respect the learning and profound discoveries of Western civilisation.'[10] The problem for James lay not in the ideals of the Enlightenment but in their distortion, in the way in which they had been turned by Europeans into tribal values, for their benefit and for the enslavement of the rest of the world. James thought of himself not as crafting an alternative to Enlightenment values but as reclaiming them for all of humanity.

Of all the great twentieth-century anti-colonial radicals, few so combined a hatred for racism and imperialism with such an admiration of Western philosophy and culture. Most Third World radicals recognized with James, however, that the problem of racism and imperialism was not that it was a Western ideology, but that it was a system that often acted as an obstacle to the pursuit of the progressive ideals of the Enlightenment. Over time, though, opposition to European rule came increasingly to mean opposition to European ideas too. Ideas, many insisted, were a means of effecting power. European ideas were tainted because they were a means of effecting European power. The ideals that flowed out of the Enlightenment, however progressive they might seem, could not be wielded by those challenging European rule. They grew out of a particular culture, history and tradition; they spoke to a particular set of needs, desires and dispositions. Non-Europeans had to develop their own ideas, beliefs and values that grew out of their own distinct cultures, traditions, histories, psychological needs and dispositions. 'The conflict with Europe is waking all civilized Asia,' wrote the revered Indian poet Rabindranath Tagore. Asia is 'realizing herself consciously' and 'has understood – know thyself – that is the road to freedom. Imitating others is destruction.' He denounced the belief that the 'building up of a nation on the European pattern is the only type of civilization and the only goal of man'.[11]

Out of these claims came a host of separatist movements that set out to hew political, cultural and moral traditions distinct from those of Europeans. Among the most important was the 'Négritude' movement founded in the 1930s by Aimé Césaire, Léopold Sédar Senghor, later to be president of independent Senegal, and the French Guianan poet, politician and academic Léon-Gontran Damas. Césaire once wrote that Négritude was a means of answering the question that Senghor had asked of him when first they met: 'Who am I? Who are we? What are we in this white world?' Négritude was a literary and political movement that sought to answer this through the self-affirmation of black peoples, or the affirmation of the values of 'black culture'. As Césaire was to put it in his *Discours sur la Négritude*, 'Négritude, in my eyes, is not a philosophy' but 'a way of living within history'. With 'its deportation of populations, its transfer of people from one continent to another, its distant memories of old beliefs, its fragments of murdered cultures', the history of black people is the history of a community whose experience is 'unique'. How, Césaire asks, 'can we not believe that all this, which has its own coherence, constitutes a heritage?', a heritage of ideas, beliefs, values, dreams, hopes and aspirations distinct from those of the Europeans.[12] 'European reasoning', Senghor suggested, 'is discursive, by utilization; Negro-African reasoning is intuitive by participation.'[13] While this was always a controversial view, nevertheless Négritude, as the historian Stephen Howe observes, 'set the tone for much "Third World" and ethnic minority cultural nationalism that followed'.[14]

One figure stood at the crossroads, looking back towards the universalist ideals of L'Ouverture and James and forward to the separatist visions that were to dominate. Frantz Fanon was a psychiatrist, philosopher and revolutionary who wrote two works that became the Bible and the Qur'an of the anti-colonial movement – *Black Skin, White Masks* and *The Wretched of the Earth*.

Born in 1925 into a middle-class family in the French colony of Martinique, Fanon attended the most prestigious school on the island where his teachers included Aimé Césaire. After the fall of France in 1940, he escaped the island to join the Free French forces. But at the moment of victory, as Allied troops were poised to cross the Rhine into Germany, along with photojournalists, Fanon's regiment was 'bleached' of all non-white soldiers and Fanon and his fellow Caribbean soldiers were sent to Toulon on the Mediterranean coast instead. It was an experience deeply burnt into Fanon's consciousness. After returning to Martinique to help his friend and mentor Aimé Césaire run for the French National Assembly on a communist ticket, Fanon went back to France to study medicine and psychiatry.

Fanon's first book, *Black Skin, White Masks*, a reworking of a rejected doctoral thesis on 'The Disalienation of the Black', explored the psychological effects of racism and tried to explain the roots of what he saw as the feelings of dependency and inadequacy that black people experienced in a white world.

The colonized, he wrote, had to reject both the culture and the language of the colonizer: 'To speak . . . means above all to assume a culture, to support the weight of a civilization.'[15] It was an idea, indeed a sentence, that could have come straight from the pen of the great eighteenth-century German Romantic Johann Gottfried von Herder. In speaking French, Fanon insists, one is forced to accept the collective consciousness of the French, which identifies blackness with evil and sin. The black man (and Fanon's polemic primarily addresses men) attempts to escape the association of blackness with evil by donning a white mask, by thinking of himself as a universal subject in a society that advocates equality but which in reality treats those with black skins with contempt. He internalizes the cultural values of the colonizer, creating a self-perception divided between his cultural originality and the cultural code of the colonizer that he has been forced to appropriate and imitate. He necessarily becomes alienated from himself. Fanon has picked up here Marx's idea of individuals alienated by being confronted by the world they have helped to create. For Fanon, however, unlike for Marx, the world had been made alien not by distorted economic or social relationships, but by cultural and psychological dislocation.

The Wretched of the Earth was written in 1961, at the very end of Fanon's life, after he had been diagnosed with leukaemia and in the few months that he knew he had left. Taking the cue for the title from the first line of the '*Internationale*' ('Stand up, ye damned of the Earth'), Fanon sets out his argument about how to break the binary system in which black is bad and white is good. Europeans, Fanon wrote, 'are never done talking of Man, yet murder men everywhere they find them, at the corner of every one of their own streets, in all the corners of the globe'. The West 'saw itself as a spiritual adventure'. Yet it is 'in the name of the spirit of Europe that Europe has made her encroachments, that she has justified her crimes and legitimized the slavery in which she holds four-fifths of humanity'. The peoples of the Third World 'know with what sufferings humanity has paid for every one of their triumphs of the mind'. For peoples of the colonized world to find their humanity they must 'not imitate Europe', nor 'pay tribute to Europe by creating states, institutions and societies which draw their inspiration from her'.

Yet, for all his seeming disdain for European culture, for his all insistence that European ideas have helped enslave the non-European world, Fanon also accepted that 'All the elements of a solution to the great problems of humanity have, at different times, existed in European thought'. The problem was that 'Europeans have not carried out in practice the mission which fell to them'. The Third World will have to 'start a new history of Man', a new history that, while not forgetting 'Europe's crimes', will nevertheless 'have regard to the sometimes prodigious theses which Europe has put forward'.

In one sense, then, Fanon aligns himself with L'Ouverture and James. European thought contained within it 'all the elements of a solution to the great problems of humanity' but Europeans could not, or would not, combine those in thought and transform them into concrete reality. In another sense, though, he strides down a different course. Fanon is not simply ambiguous about European thought, but sees it as positively destructive of black culture and psychology.

Throughout his life, Fanon juggled with these two elements of his world-view. After his death, separatist groups, Third World movements, students of postcolonial studies all turned Fanon into an intellectual icon. But they did so largely by deprecating the universalist aspect of his thought in favour of the claim that the culture of the colonizer alienates the colonized from his own national culture. Senghor, Césaire and Fanon, and most Third World intellectuals drawn towards separatism, acknowledged their debt to European thinkers. Historians of 'Afrocentrism' such as Stephen Howe and Valentin Mudimbe point out that the real impetus for separatism came, paradoxically, not from the colonized but from the colonizer.[16] Or, rather, from Europeans who felt so guilty about colonization that they could perceive little in European thought that remained untainted. Jean-Paul Sartre wrote prefaces to Fanon's *Wretched of the Earth* and to Senghor's *Anthology of New Negro Poetry*. There is, he wrote in the former, 'nothing more consistent than a racist humanism since the European has only been able to become a man through creating slaves and monsters'.[17] Humanism, he wrote elsewhere, 'is the counterpart of racism: it is a practice of exclusion'.[18] Sartre's input transformed the public perception of thinkers such as Senghor and Fanon. It contributed greatly to the fame of their works, particularly of the *Anthology*, and propelled Négritude into the broader intellectual conversation. But it also transformed Négritude itself, 'stultified' it, creating, in Stephen Howe's words, 'the rhetoric of absolute Otherness'. Senghor, Mudimbe observed, 'had asked Sartre for a cloak to celebrate négritude; he was given a shroud'.[19]

3

In 1883 a German physicist made a field trip to the Arctic to study colour perception among the Inuit. He related in a letter the impact of meeting them:

> I often ask myself what advantages our 'good society' possesses over that of the 'savages'. The more I see of their customs the more I realise we have no right to look down on them . . . We have no right to blame them for their forms and superstitions which may seem ridiculous to us. We 'highly educated people' are much worse, relatively speaking . . . As a thinking person, for me the most important result of this trip lies in the strengthening of my point of view that the idea of a 'cultured' person is merely relative.[20]

That physicist was Franz Boas. He soon gave up Germany for America, and physics for anthropology. It is as an anthropologist that we now know him, and it is as an anthropologist that Boas transformed our vision of culture and of morality. He helped create both a new discipline, that of cultural anthropology, and a new concept of culture. In so doing he helped reshape moral thinking too.

At the heart of this new thinking were two fundamental ideas. The first was that culture, not biology, was the principal force that shaped human affairs; the second, that humanity comprised a multitude of cultures that could not be ranked on an evolutionary scale, but each of which had to be understood in its own terms. Boas' starting point, as it was of those who followed in his footsteps, was the desire to challenge racial science. He was passionately attached to egalitarian principles, but it was a very different idea of equality to that of the Enlightenment.

The revolutionary egalitarianism that arose out of the Enlightenment was positive and forward-looking. From Condorcet to Marx, such egalitarians had held that social progress could overcome artificial divisions and differences and reveal our essential commonality. For Marx in particular, it was not possible to talk of human flourishing without talking also of the social transformation necessary to create the conditions for such flourishing. Boas' egalitarianism arose, on the contrary, from a sense that progress was neither fully realizable nor necessarily welcome. His letter from the Arctic shows how much his egalitarianism was shaped by his disillusionment with the values of 'our' good society. For Boas no society was better, and none worse, than any other. What European or American intellectuals deemed the good life was simply one way among many of achieving social satisfaction, and not inherently the best way, especially for non-Europeans. Progress did not always improve a society. All too often it made different societies more alike, which was not always for the better. For Boas, human beings were equal not because social, cultural and economic differences could be overcome, and all humans aspire to a common civilization, but because diverse cultures were each as good as the others. There could be no such thing as a common civilization, only a common respect for a variety of different cultures.

Cultural relativism encouraged moral relativism, the belief that not just social practices but moral norms, too, vary from culture to culture. Such moral relativism has expressed itself in two ways. *Descriptive* moral relativism claims that, as a matter of empirical fact, there are widespread moral disagreements across different societies, and that these disagreements are more significant than any common moral views. *Metaethical* moral relativism insists that moral judgements can never have authority absolutely or universally but always only relative to particular traditions or societies or cultures. The standards of justification in the two societies may differ from one another and there is no rational basis for resolving these differences. Morality, as the anthropologist Ruth Benedict put it, 'is a convenient term for socially approved habits'.[21] And 'immorality', in the words of sociologist William Graham Sumner, 'never means anything but contrary to the mores of the time and place'.[22]

The moral challenge to universalism developed, then, both from within and without Europe, from anti-imperialists who saw liberation as meaning liberation from European ideals, and from European thinkers who began questioning those ideals.

4

In his *Histories*, Herodotus tells of an occasion when Darius, king of Persia, 'invited some Greeks who were present to a conference, and asked them how much money it would take for them to be prepared to eat the corpses of their fathers'. The Greeks replied that 'they would not do that for any amount of money'. Next, Darius 'summoned some members of the Indian tribe known as the Callatiae, who eat their parents, and asked them in the presence of the Greeks . . . how much money it would take for them to be willing to cremate their fathers' corpses'. The Indians 'cried out in horror and told him not to say such appalling things'. 'Each group', Herodotus suggests, 'regards its own [values] as being by far the best.' 'Custom', he concludes, 'is king of all.'[23]

Herodotus reminds us how deep are the historical roots of moral relativism. Not until the twentieth century, however, did belief in the relativity of moral norms become socially significant. Rousseau had observed that selfishness only has meaning in a society in which altruism is possible. The same could be said of moral relativism. Only a world that could contemplate the possibility of genuine universalism, and possessed the material resources to implement it, could also genuinely contemplate the possibility of moral relativism.

In the premodern world ethnocentrism was built into the social fabric. Christianity and Islam had, in different ways, burst through such ethnocentrism by insisting that what mattered was not the tribe to which you belonged, but the God that you acknowledged. The dignity of the individual derived not from his or her participation in a specific community, whether tribe or city state, but through having been created in the image of God. Mohism and Buddhism had gone further still, developing a form of universalism that did not require attachment to a particular God, but derived from the very fact of one's humanness. And yet the ability of any of these faiths or philosophies to overcome traditional tribalism or parochialism was limited by the economic backwardness of premodern communities. The preconditions for equality did not exist, hence the support traditionally of both Christianity and Islam for social hierarchy and slavery.

The economic conditions and social mechanisms created by modernity, and by capitalism, transformed the character both of universalism and of moral relativism. Since the material conditions now existed for the overcoming of social differences, the argument against equality and for the preservation of difference had to be moral and political. Moral relativism was no longer associated simply with an unreflective ethnocentrism, nor with restricted material circumstances. Rather, cultural and moral difference could only be embraced consciously as a good. Such an embrace of difference took both reactionary and liberal forms. There was, on the one side, conservative traditionalism for which universalist ideas were seen as destructive of the natural and time-honoured agencies necessary for the maintenance of social order. On the other side was a liberal pluralism that derived from revulsion at the horrors inflicted by European nations, at home and abroad, in the name of universalism.

Underneath both the progressive and the reactionary embrace of difference was disenchantment with Enlightenment rationalism and humanism. Ever since the French Revolution there had been a widespread belief that through the application of reason, human activities and organization could lead us to the good life. That belief had been enshrined in two different forms of the progressive ideal. One was the liberalism rooted in the works of John Locke and John Stuart Mill, the other the revolutionary currents that flowed out of the Radical Enlightenment and subsequently Marxism. Liberals and radicals both believed in the idea that humans could rationally transform society through the agency of their own efforts and that there were particular values, practices and institutions under which all humans best flourished. There were, of course, fierce disagreements about how society should be transformed and what those values, practices and institutions should be. Nevertheless, liberals and radicals held fast to universalist ideals and to the belief that progress could overcome social divisions. By the end of the nineteenth century many liberals had come to despair of any such transformation, and indeed to fear its consequences. The dissolution of old sources of authority had created intellectual turmoil – and the fear that intellectual turmoil could lead to social disorder. As the historian John Burrow observes, 'Anarchy – social anarchy as a fear, intellectual anarchy as a fact – is a word that constantly occurs' in intellectual debates from the 1850s on. As a result, Daniel Pick notes, pessimism 'began to colonise liberalism'.[24] By the end of the twentieth century such pessimism had colonized radicalism too.

From the emergence of new cultural movements and anti-imperialist struggles in Africa and Asia, to the creation of new labour organizations and the coming of mass democracy to Europe and America, the first decades of the twentieth century seemed to be a moment of radical hope. From Marxists to logical positivists, there were many who still saw themselves as upholding the traditions of the Enlightenment and for whom human reason could overcome any social or political obstacle. That sense of optimism and possibility has long since faded. Many of those movements for social change have disintegrated, and even the very idea of human mastery has come to be seen as suspect. The mastery of nature seems to have brought environmental havoc, global warming and the mass destruction of species. The attempt to master society has led to the death camps and the gulags, ethnic cleansing and tyrannical regimes. 'In a real sense', the ecologist Murray Bookchin has noted, 'we seem to be afraid of ourselves – of our uniquely human attributes. We seem to be suffering from a decline in human self-confidence and in our ability to create ethically meaningful lives that enrich humanity and the non-human world.'[25] Or, as the poet Roy Fuller put it in 'Translation':

I will stop expressing my belief in the rosy
Future of man, and accept the evidence
Of a couple of wretched wars and innumerable
    Abortive revolutions.

Anyone happy in this age and place
Is daft or corrupt. Better to abdicate
From a material and spiritual terrain
    Fit only for barbarians.

Toussaint L'Ouverture wrenched freedom from barbarism in the most improbable circumstances by wielding the moral force of universalist ideals as a weapon for social transformation. Two centuries on, the fading of the possibilities of social transformation has led many to condemn the weapon itself as barbaric.

CHAPTER SEVENTEEN

The unravelling of morality

1

In January 1872 a group of young intellectuals set up a conversation society in Cambridge, Massachusetts. The club lasted for less than a decade. But in those few years, the talk that wafted through the club like dandelion puffs in a breeze laid the seeds for much of modern American intellectual life. The conversation society was the Metaphysical Club, and its members were destined to be among the brightest stars in America's intellectual firmament: the psychologist William James, his brother the novelist Henry, the philosopher and mathematician Charles Sanders Peirce, and Oliver Wendell Holmes Jr, the future justice of the Supreme Court.

The club members had all come of age in the 1860s, a decade in which the intellectual and moral worlds of most Americans had been upended like a house in a Kansas tornado. Two events in particular, the cultural historian Louis Menand suggests, helped conjure up that tornado. The first was the publication in 1859 of Darwin's *On the Origin of Species*, the second the American Civil War, which broke out a year later. Darwin's theory swept away the idea of a supernatural intelligence governing the universe. The Civil War knocked down the foundations of much of the intellectual grounding of American politics, both North and South. Many saw the war as 'a failure of culture, a failure of ideas'. 'It took nearly half a century', Menand writes, 'for the United States to develop a culture to replace it, to find a set of ideas, and a way of thinking, that would help people cope with the conditions of modern life.' That new set of ideas had to make sense of a world 'shot through with contingency'.[1] It came to be labelled 'pragmatism', a term invented by Peirce and popularized by William James. The challenge for the pragmatists was to determine how, in a world in which there was no 'truth' or 'good' waiting to be discovered out there, it was possible to distinguish right from wrong, decide how to act and choose what to believe.

The 'contingency' of which Menand writes was not simply the product of the Civil War or of the publication of Darwin's masterpiece, nor was it merely an American phenomenon. Europe, too, had felt similar distress. On both sides of the Atlantic, the anxieties were driven by the twin crises of the age: that of faith and that of reason. Nietzsche had provided one response to the twin crises, contemptuously dispatching foundational notions of reason and truth, rejecting traditional ideas of right and wrong, excoriating the slave mentality of the herd, and embracing all that appeared heroic and life-affirming. From phenomenologists at the beginning of the twentieth century to postmodernists at the end, Nietzsche's 'philosophizing with a hammer' would continue to inspire particularly those within the Continental tradition. The distinctions between the 'Continental' and 'analytic' traditions are often overplayed. Nevertheless, much of the anglophone world strode down a different road, its response to the twin crises shaped much more by science, empiricism and analytical philosophy. A whole series of new approaches developed in America, Britain and Australia. Of these, pragmatism was perhaps the most important.

2

John Dewey was born in 1859, in the year of *On the Origin of Species*, on the eve of the American Civil War. He was too young to have been part of the Metaphysical Club. But he, along with Peirce and James, became the third member of the classical pragmatist triumvirate who most defined the school. More than any other thinker, it was Dewey who made pragmatism (or 'instrumentalism' as he called it) both respectable among professional philosophers and fashionable with the public.

Pragmatists often held divergent views. All, however, believed in a close relationship between the good, the true and the useful. A proposition was true if it worked or was useful in satisfying needs. They challenged the so-called 'correspondence theory of truth' that had held sway since before the time of Plato, the belief that something is true if it corresponds to, or agrees with, reality. According to Peirce, true opinions are those that inquirers will accept at the end of inquiry. They are views upon which we could not improve, irrespective of how much longer we continue to inquire or how much deeper we dig for the answers. For James and Dewey the truth is that which works. True statements are useful and useful statements are true.

Pragmatists looked upon ethics as they looked upon knowledge. Questions of right and wrong, like questions of true and false, could be resolved only empirically in terms of what worked within a particular social setting. The test of a value judgement was whether it resolved the conflict, satisfied the needs, eliminated the dangers that had raised the moral problem in the first place. It was Dewey who most developed this ethical tradition.

Dewey studied philosophy at Johns Hopkins University, where Charles Peirce had taught for a short time. He came to embrace pragmatism largely through his reading of *Principles of Psychology* by William James. Joining the newly founded University of Chicago in 1894, Dewey started developing educational theory, putting his new-found pragmatism into practice by setting up 'Laboratory schools', which still flourish, and which function under the motto 'Learning by doing'.

From educational theory Dewey moved to ethical theory. All earlier ethical theory, he complained, had sought to find a single, fixed ideal pattern of life or a single fixed law or duty as the ends of the moral quest. But such an end will be as elusive as the Holy Grail, as mythical as nirvana. There was for Dewey no such thing as *the* good, only particular goods, and these existed only if they happen to be particular solutions to particular problems with which a group of people is wrestling. Moral problems have a multitude of solutions, each specific to that problem and to the people who are seeking a solution. They are solved in the same way as scientific problems, by empirically gathering relevant facts and pragmatically working out how those facts might lead to a solution. Morality, in other words, was a form of social technology. What it was not about was the laying down of rules or laws or principles of conduct or the search for universal standards of behaviour. Instead of a single fixed end or ideal activity, we must, Dewey argued, make room for 'a plurality of changing, moving, individualized ends'.[2] Ends and goods vary from place to place, from time to time, from problem to problem. In one sense, this is my argument in this book. But Dewey, and the pragmatists, did not simply acknowledge the historical character of moral thought. In insisting that morality was merely a form of 'social technology', that morality, like truth, is simply that which works, and that moral answers could only be for specific, concrete, local questions, they appeared also to deny the possibility of universal moral principles and values.

For Dewey's critics, a key weakness of his approach was its failure to define what constituted intrinsically important values and what should be the ends to which we aspired. For Dewey that was its strength. He dismissed the traditional distinction between means and ends. The question that moral inquiries should answer is not, he insisted, 'How can I get to such and such end?', but rather 'What is the best solution to such and such problem, irrespective of the ends?' Means and ends, Dewey argued, were reciprocally determined. In real life, if not in the minds of moral philosophers, he claimed, people do not begin with an end, and then ask how to achieve it. Most people lack a proper vision of their ends until they also have a grasp of the course of action that will take them there. He rejected the idea that moral standards could be devised external to practice, or that any action or belief could possess intrinsic value regardless of context. Many people argue that torture, or slavery, is wrong in all circumstances. Dewey would respond that it may well be that torture or slavery would turn out to be morally wrong in all circumstances. But we cannot know that outside of those circumstances.

3

If pragmatism was one response to the problem of 'contingency', another was 'emotivism'. Pragmatists claimed that there could be no *a priori* answers to ethical questions. Context was everything. Emotivists questioned the possibility of even pragmatic solutions. Moral claims, they insisted, were nothing more than the expression of subjective desires.

The modern roots of emotivism can be traced to a book that came to be both one of the most famous ethical works of the twentieth century and one of the most troublesome: G.E. Moore's *Principia Ethica*. When it was published in 1903, John Maynard Keynes gushed that it was 'the beginning of a renaissance, the opening of a new heaven on a new earth'.[3] Mary Warnock suggests in her study of twentieth-century ethics that the *Principia Ethica* is 'the source from which the subsequent moral philosophy of the century has flowed, or at least as the most powerful influence upon this moral philosophy'.[4] Yet it is a work whose arguments are extraordinarily flimsy, highly dubious and have been all but shredded.

George Edward Moore (1873–1958) was, with Bertrand Russell, Ludwig Wittgenstein and Gottlob Frege, one of the founders of the analytic school in philosophy, which came to dominate the Anglo-American world. He was also, alongside Virginia Woolf, John Maynard Keynes, E.M. Forster and Lytton Strachey, an important member of the Bloomsbury Group, and while not as well known to the public, nevertheless wielded considerable influence through his social networks.

Moore wrote the *Principia Ethica*, so he tells us, in order to 'distinguish clearly two kinds of question, which moral philosophers have always professed to answer' but which 'they have almost always confused both with one another and with other questions'. The two questions are: 'What kind of things ought to exist for their own sake?' and 'What kind of actions ought we to perform?'

Moore's answer to the first question is that things that ought to exist for their own sake are things that are intrinsically good. It is, however, he insists, impossible to define what it is to be 'good'. Goodness is the name of a property that is simple and beyond analysis. We intuitively recognize that which is good, but we cannot analyse it in terms of anything more fundamental. Nor can any evidence be adduced to show that something is intrinsically good. All we can do is acknowledge it when we encounter it. 'If I am asked "what is good?"', Moore wrote, 'my answer is that good is good and that is the end of the matter.'[5]

Moore compares the concept of goodness to that of 'yellowness'. Yellow is, like good, simple and incapable of analysis, a property we understand by being directly acquainted with it, but which cannot be described or defined to anyone who has never seen that colour. The fact that 'yellow' is indefinable does not prevent us from being able to say what things have the property of being yellow. Similarly with goodness: the fact that it is indefinable does not mean that we cannot say what things possess the property of goodness.

To show that goodness cannot be equated with any non-moral property, Moore developed what came to be called the 'Open question argument'. If X is good, then the question 'Is it true that X is good?' is meaningless. But the question 'Is it true that X is good?' is not meaningless. It is, in Moore's words, an open question. Suppose X is pleasure, and that goodness can be defined as pleasure. The question 'Is pleasure good?' is not meaningless. It is an open question whether pleasure is good. Therefore, Moore concludes, X, whatever property it may be, cannot be equivalent to the good.

The trouble is that Moore's claim is less an argument than an assertion. Indeed, given that goodness is indefinable, it is difficult to know how one could construct an argument. Moore himself later acknowledged that 'I did not give any tenable explanation of what I meant by saying that "good" was not a natural property'.[6]

Moore's answer to the second question that he raised – 'What kind of actions ought we to perform?' – was more straightforward, to the point, indeed, of being trite. We ought to perform any action that 'will cause more good to exist in the Universe than any possible alternative'. 'Right', Moore wrote, is 'identical with "useful"' and so 'it follows that the end always will justify the means' and that 'no action which is not justified by its results can be right'.[7] Moore, in other words, was a utilitarian, but one who thought that goodness could not be measured, or even defined, but was simply recognized, and intuited.

4

The idea that moral truths were self-evident intuitions for which there could be no proof proved attractive and encouraged in Britain the creation of what came to be called the 'Cambridge Intuitionist school' (though Moore always denied that he was an 'intuitionist'). The trouble was that what was self-evident to one intuitionist was not necessarily self-evident to another. Moore had argued that one's duty was to produce as much good in the world as possible. Not so, responded fellow intuitionist W.D. Ross in his book *The Right and the Good*. 'Right', Ross suggested, was like 'good', a concept unanalysable but intuitively recognized. Certain kinds of actions, including keeping promises, telling the truth and repaying kindness, are right in themselves, whether or not they increase the amount of good in the world. These duties are 'self-evident' in the sense of being 'evident without any need of proof, or of evidence beyond itself'.[8] For Moore, not only were such duties not self-evident but they may not have been duties at all. If telling the truth creates more harm than good, then it is a duty to lie. Since no empirical fact or rational argument could settle this debate, as the conflicting claims were both deemed to be 'self-evident', so the very notion of moral truth began to disintegrate. If moral truths cannot be verified, many philosophers suggested, perhaps they are neither self-evident nor truths, but merely expressions of personal preference, of feelings and emotions. 'When we assert this or that has "value",' Bertrand Russell wrote, 'we are giving expression to our own emotions, not to a fact which would still be true if our personal feelings were different.'[9]

So arose 'emotivism', first sketched by A.J. Ayer in his groundbreaking 1936 book *Language, Truth and Logic*, which established him as the leading English representative of logical positivism. Ayer argued, like all logical positivists, that there are two types of statements that convey meaning. Empirical statements express matters of fact whose truths can be established through observation and verification. Analytical statements, such as mathematical truths, are necessarily true, though they cannot be verified empirically. Ethical propositions fall into neither category. They are literally meaningless because they convey no meaning. 'If I say to someone, "You acted wrongly in stealing that money",' Ayer wrote, 'I am not saying anything more than if I had simply said, "You stole that money". In adding that this action is wrong I am simply evincing my moral disapproval of it. It is as if I had said, "You stole that money" in a peculiar tone of horror, or written it with the addition of some special exclamation marks.'[10] The words 'right' and 'wrong' express not information but feelings. They also aim 'to arouse feelings, and so to stimulate action'.[11]

Moore was no emotivist, nor thought that values were simply subjective. Yet the argument he set running in the *Principia Ethica* led inexorably to Ayer's emotivism. The problem with this approach is the belief that the claim that 'murder is wrong' or that 'one should tell the truth' has no more force than the observation that 'I like ice cream' or 'I think the Black Keys are cool'. I might think it odd if someone hated ice cream, or preferred the music of Barry Manilow. But I recognize that these are simply personal preferences. In using terms such as 'ought' and 'good' I am, however, appealing to a standard that has greater authority, or at least that I want to have greater authority. For someone to think that it is right to murder people at will is qualitatively different from that individual thinking that Barry Manilow has a great voice. To suggest that slavery is a good would be more than simply 'odd'. The trouble with emotivism is that it finds it difficult – nay, impossible – to capture this distinction.

5

In the nineteenth century many physicists believed that the universe was filled with an invisible form of matter called ether, within which light and other forms of electromagnetic radiation travelled. A physicist who had suggested that ether was lighter than air would have been making a statement about the world that was wrong. He would have been equally wrong had he claimed that ether was heavier than air. Since ether does not exist, any statement about it is necessarily meaningless. Similarly, suggested the Australian philosopher J.L. Mackie, someone who claims that 'it is morally bad to steal' or 'charity is a moral good' is making statements about the world that are wrong. But so would someone claiming that there was nothing immoral about stealing or good about charity. Mackie was a pioneer, and most significant proponent, of 'error theory' and his 1977 book *Ethics: Inventing Right and Wrong* became important in the continuing unpicking of traditional notions of morality.

Emotivists had argued that there are no moral facts; in making moral claims we are simply expressing our feelings towards whatever we call 'good' or 'bad'. For Mackie moral claims were both more and less than expressions of feelings. Someone who says 'torture is wrong', or that 'same sex couples should be allowed to get married' is usually doing more than expressing feelings. They are making statements about the world. But, suggests Mackie, in making such statements they are in error, in the same way as that nineteenth-century physicist. There is no such thing as a moral fact, any more than there is such a thing as ether, and one cannot make moral statements that are either true or false, any more than one can make true or false statements about ether. Nevertheless, moral facts seem as real to many people today as ether did to nineteenth-century physicists. 'A belief in objective moral values', Mackie suggests, 'is built into ordinary moral thought and language, but holding this ingrained belief is false'.[12] Mackie has come to be seen as a paradigmatic moral 'nihilist', though he himself rejected that label, insisting that he was merely a moral 'sceptic'.

Mackie presents two main arguments against the existence of moral facts. The first is the so-called 'argument from relativity'. Moral claims are characterized by an enormous degree of variation and disagreement, disagreement that is often marked by an unusual degree of intractability. The best explanation for such variation and disagreement, Mackie argues, is not that there exists a realm of objective moral facts to which some cultures have better access than others, but that moral judgements solely 'reflect adherence to and participation in *different* ways of life'.[13] Whether moral claims really are as varied as Mackie suggests has been a matter of much debate.

The second argument against the objectivity of moral values is what Mackie calls 'the argument from queerness'. Objective values, Mackie suggests, would be radically different from anything in our experience. Plato's Forms are for Mackie an example of the queerness of objective values. If such queer things did exist, there would be no way of knowing them without a special, non-empirical mental mechanism, or intuition. This, Mackie suggests, is a 'lame answer' to the problem of how we can have access to objective values.

For values to be objective, Mackie argues, they must be features of the inanimate universe, an intrinsic part of the fabric of reality, either objects, like trees, or properties, like mass. But, he points out, values are not like this at all. For values to exist there must be a valuator – an agent – to impose a standard on what is otherwise an indifferent universe. Things and beliefs and practices are good only with respect to such agents and their goals. The question that neither Mackie nor the moral nihilists who followed him ever properly address is whether any such humanly imposed standard could be more than subjective. Moral claims may not be objective in the way that scientific claims are; but does that necessarily mean they cannot be right or wrong?

Human societies, Mackie observes, do not have fixed concepts of right and wrong, of good and bad; historically the meanings of moral concepts shift and bend and change as societies discover that old meanings are ill-fitted for new circumstances. They are free to do so, Mackie insists, only because values are subjective expressions of individual desire. It is true that notions of right and wrong are historically flexible. That, after all, is the story of this book. But the story of this book is also that moral changes do not happen on a whim; they are not arbitrary or random. Changes in notions of right and wrong do not merely follow their own course but are related to broader social, economic, political and intellectual shifts. At some historical moments that relationship is close, at others more distant, but never can that relationship be discarded. History does not, of course, unfold in some objective manner, nor follow a predetermined course to a given end. But neither is it simply 'one damn event after another'. There is a certain logic to historical change that derives from what has happened before, and the ability, capacity and needs of people to respond. Moral claims, in other words, are more than simply a matter of individual taste, attitude or preference. They are attempts to answer questions raised by historical developments, including problems posed in the history of moral thought itself. Historical shifts in the meanings of moral concepts do not necessarily reveal moral ideas to be merely subjective or arbitrary.

There is an even stronger sense in which moral claims are not merely subjective. Nihilists might see all moral judgements as mistaken, but most would nevertheless accept that it is better that people make certain kinds of mistaken moral judgements than others. From a nihilist point of view it is not wrong (any more than it is right) to believe that it is good to torture babies or that all Jews should be sent to death camps. Yet virtually all nihilists would also accept that it is better that people did not think that torturing babies was good, or that the Final Solution was morally acceptable. Even for a nihilist, then, it is *true* that some erroneous moral judgements are better than others. The question of truth, in other words, finds its way back into moral judgements, even nihilist ones.

Emotivists find it difficult to explain why making judgements about torture or the Final Solution is qualitatively different from making judgements about a particular style of music or flavour of ice cream. Nihilists, recognizing this difficulty, insist that, even though in reality moral judgements are no different from any other, we *perceive* them to be objective statements about the world. The key distinction between moral and other judgements is, for nihilists, psychological. This, however, is to miss the point. What makes moral judgements distinctive is not simply the way we perceive them but also their role in reality – not physical reality but social reality. To say that torture is wrong or truthfulness is good is not simply to give expression to a personal preference. It is also to define a social need. If everyone thinks that ice cream is bad or Barry Manilow good, then I might privately despair. But if everyone were to believe that truthfulness is bad and torture good, then there would be a tear in the very fabric of society.

The key distinction between moral claims and personal preferences is not psychological but *social*. A social need is not a fact, nor is it a scientifically objective claim. But it is undeniably more than merely subjective. The challenge is to define what that 'more' is.

6

A series of environmental catastrophes devastates the world. Blame falls upon scientists, leading to widespread anti-science riots. Labs are burnt down, physicists and biologists lynched, books and instruments destroyed. A Know-nothing political movement comes to power, abolishes the teaching of science and imprisons and executes scientists.

Eventually there is an attempt to resurrect science. The trouble is that all that remains of scientific knowledge are a few fragments. People debate the concept of relativity, the theory of evolution and the idea of dark matter. They learn by rote the surviving portions of the periodic table, and use expressions such as 'neutrino', 'mass' and 'specific gravity'. Nobody, however, understands the beliefs that led to those theories or expressions, and nobody understands that they don't understand them. The result is a kind of hollowed-out science. On the surface everyone has acquaintance with scientific terminology but no one possesses scientific knowledge.

So begins Alasdair MacIntyre's brilliant, bleak, frustrating and above all provocative 1981 book *After Virtue*. A work of unleavened academic philosophy, it became a most unlikely bestseller, and highly influential among historians, theologians and political theorists, not to mention policy makers. MacIntyre's 'disquieting suggestion' is that while no calamity of the sort he describes has befallen science, it is exactly what has happed to morality. True, no philosopher has been lynched, no seminar room torched, no riots erupted in response to the disastrous consequences of Kantianism or utilitarianism. Nevertheless, MacIntyre insists, moral thought is in the same state as science was in his fictive account, a state of 'grave disorder', and one in which the very disorder blinds us to the moral chaos that surrounds us. Moral thought has been hollowed out; everyone uses moral terms such as 'ought' and 'should', but no one truly understands them. We argue endlessly about the justice of wars, the morality of abortion, the nature of freedom, but we do not reach agreement; in fact, we cannot even agree about what would constitute a satisfactory resolution to these disagreements.

All over *After Virtue* are the fingerprints of the Cambridge philosopher Elizabeth Anscombe. In 1958 Anscombe, who has claim to be the most important British philosopher of the twentieth century, published a paper called 'Modern Moral Philosophy', which suggested that all contemporary moral theories were without foundation. From Kantianism to utilitarianism, all such theories use concepts such as 'morally ought' and 'morally right' but in a way that is devoid of meaning. In the ancient world the terms 'should' or 'ought' related to good and bad in the context of making things function better, whether ploughs or humans. The impact of monotheistic religion was to transform morality into a set of laws that had to be obeyed. Laws require a legislator and a police force. God was that legislator, the Church the enforcer. Modernity dethroned God and enfeebled the institutions of faith. New forms of morality, such as Kantianism and consequentialism, still viewed morality in terms of rules or laws, but no longer had any figure that could play the role of legislator. They lacked the proper foundations for the meaningful employment of their moral concepts. All these themes MacIntyre was to develop.

At the time Anscombe published her seminal paper, MacIntyre was a Marxist, though no longer in the Communist Party. By the time he wrote *After Virtue* he had been drawn to Aristotelian virtue ethics. Eventually he was, like Anscombe, led to Roman Catholicism. He is today one of the leading Thomist philosophers. Through all these twists and turns, a number of themes have remained constant. Whether as a Marxist or as a Catholic, MacIntyre has always expressed a loathing of liberal individualism, and an insistence on the social embeddedness of the individual. He has insisted, too, that morality can be understood only in its historical context. Yet he has been equally impassioned in his opposition to relativism, emotivism and nihilism. There has been, perhaps, no fiercer critic of the ideas sketched out in this chapter. MacIntyre's critique of modern moral philosophy is insightful. I have, indeed, drawn upon it in this book. The weaknesses of that critique are, however, equally revealing of how and why morality has unravelled.

Why is contemporary morality in such grave disorder? Because of the Enlightenment, MacIntyre argues. The Enlightenment rejected, indeed destroyed, the Aristotelian notion of a virtuous life that had shaped Western thought for nearly two millennia. It rejected, in particular, the notion of the *telos* – the insistence, not just in Aristotle but among all ancient thinkers and in the monotheistic religions, that human beings, like all objects in the cosmos, exist for a purpose, and that to be good was to act in a way that enabled them to fulfil that purpose. Enlightenment philosophers imagined humans not as creatures with definite functions that they might fulfil or neglect but as agents who possessed no true purpose apart from that created by their own will;

creatures governed, not by an external *telos* but solely by the dictates of their inner reason or desires. This shift, MacIntyre argues, was corrosive of the very idea of morality. By appealing to a *telos*, Aristotle and Aquinas had been able to distinguish between the way we actually are and the way we should be. Post-Enlightenment philosophers could no longer coherently do so. As a result they could find no moral anchor, no point of reference against which to adjudicate rival moral claims. And without such a point of reference, moral arguments become interminable and pointless. The end point in this journey comes with emotivism, which, for MacIntyre, is not simply a description of the theories produced by Ayer and his followers but of all post-Enlightenment moral theories. Even those moral philosophies, such as Kantianism, that appeal to a rational standard binding on all are deluding themselves because there is no possibility of such a standard, given the Enlightenment view of the sovereignty of the individual moral agent.

Having rejected the ancient concept of individuals as embedded in, and constituted by, specific communities, the post-Enlightenment world has come to see individual autonomy as the consummation of humankind's search for freedom. In fact, MacIntyre argues, such autonomy amounts to an emptiness, a moral vacuum. Because what MacIntyre calls the 'democratized self' has 'no necessary social content and no necessary social identity', so the self 'can assume any role or take any point of view, because it is in and for itself nothing'.[14] The crucial distinction between that which is 'good' and that which is 'believed to be good' becomes erased. There can now be no rational foundation to moral claims any more than there could be a rational foundation to scientific knowledge if there were no distinction between that which is 'true' and that which is 'believed to be true'. There is now also a new cleavage between facts and values. Facts having been wrenched away from values, nothing is left to temper the wildest flights of the moral imagination.

Ethics, MacIntyre argues, can only have meaning if there is a distinction between 'man-as-he-happens-to-be' and 'man-as-he-could-be'.[15] Morality is like a road map taking us from the former condition to the latter, teaching us how to overcome the weaknesses of our human nature and become what we are capable of becoming. If there no such distinction, there can be no road map, and hence no morality. What allowed the Ancients to distinguish between 'man-as-he-happens-to-be' and 'man-as-he-could-be' was their belief in *telos*. *Telos* was the bridge between the way we are and the way we should be. In the post-Enlightenment world, that bridge, and hence morality itself, crumbled.

7

It is true that modernity emerged partly through the overthrow of the Aristotelian conception of *telos*. Science expunged teleology from the natural world, 'disenchanting' it in the process. It is equally true that the liberal individualism deriving from Hobbes and the English social contract theorists viewed humans 'as though we had been shipwrecked on an uninhabited island with a group of other individuals, each of whom is a stranger to me and to all the others', every individual engaged not in common struggles to realize shared goals but in working out the 'rules which will safeguard each one maximally in such a situation'.[16] It is a view that has influenced a diverse set of moral thinkers from John Locke and David Hume to John Rawls and Robert Nozick.

Yet, the relationship between modernity and teleology is more complex than MacIntyre suggests, as was Enlightenment thinking about human nature. Hobbes' was not the only model of human nature. Rousseau, Hegel and Marx, all of whom while critical of the Enlightenment nevertheless also placed themselves under its wing, developed a distinct tradition, built in part through a critique of the Hobbesian individual. The critics of Hobbes pointed out that humans are not individuals who become social, but social beings whose individuality emerges through the bonds they create with others. Through this tradition there developed not simply a distinct concept of human nature but a distinct concept of history, too, and a new vision of humans as historical beings. This in turn led to a new concept of teleology. Teleological notions, expunged from nature, were introduced into the human world.

It is true that this new historical consciousness found voice in the Romantic challenge to the Enlightenment. Its most radical expression came, however, with those who married the Romantic vision of history to Enlightenment ideas of equality and freedom. Conservatives, such as Burke and Bradley, seized upon history as 'an idea of continuity', a means of resisting modernity, an instrument through which an individual could understand and accept his or her place in a long-crafted social order. Radicals viewed history as an idea not of continuity, but of change and transformation, as a means of negating all that which restricted freedom and reason.

There was an ambiguity in the radical vision of history. On the one hand it expressed the idea of humans as *made* by history, on the other of humans as *making* history. Agency was seen both as objective, embodied in impersonal historical forces, and as subjective, the product of human consciousness and activity. This ambiguity was perhaps greatest in Marx. In 'setting Hegel on his feet', Marx insisted that history was driven not by a mystical Spirit but by real material forces, and in particular by the conflicts that emerged from class antagonisms. This argument could be, and has been, read in two ways. Some have viewed class conflict and the 'iron laws of history' as propelling humanity through its various stages to the inevitable, and predestined, triumph of communism. Real, concrete human beings hardly play a role in this process, except as bearers of historical forces. Others have recognized that history has no meaning but as the product of human activity. History may reveal a pattern or even a logic, but it could never be inevitable or inexorable, and only human activity could bring historical change to fruition. 'Humans make history but not in circumstances of their choosing', as Marx himself put it, tying the two readings together.

How the idea of history was read, and not just by Marxists, depended upon which side of that equation – humans making history or the circumstances not of their choosing – seemed more compelling. While the possibilities of social transformation seemed real, and while revolutionary movements and liberation organizations possessed social significance, so the idea of humans making history seemed persuasive. As these movements and organizations disintegrated, and as the prospects of alternatives to capitalism receded, so the idea that we inhabit circumstances not of our choosing became more credible. Over time, not just the notion of humans making history but the very idea of historical progress itself came to be seen as suspect. Romantic communitarians, liberal empiricists and postmodern relativists – from very different philosophical starting points – all converged upon the point at which the human subject seemed to disappear, and agency, free will and progress all appeared as illusions.

Modernity did not destroy *telos* but transformed it. The distinction between 'man-as-he-happens-to-be' and 'man-as-he-could-be' came to be understood not in moral but in political terms. To be-as-one-could-be was also to make society-as-it-should-be. This was a step forward, not a step back. In the pre-modern world *telos* could be understood only in moral terms because there existed little possibility of willed social change. Modernity opened up new possibilities of social transformation, possibilities that refashioned the concept of *ought*. As people rejected the idea of society as a given, so *ought* became a political demand: how society ought to be was defined by the political possibilities of social change. Once those possibilities crumbled, so *ought* became dispossessed of meaning. Shorn of wider social significance, *ought* slowly became seen by many as a matter of individual desire. From pragmatism to emotivism, from relativism to nihilism, it is the breakdown of collective movements for social change that has been so corrosive of the idea of morality.

8

Humans, MacIntyre suggests, are 'story telling animals', and it is through telling stories that they discover themselves. 'I can only answer the question "What am I to do?"', he suggests, 'if I can answer the prior question "Of what story or stories do I find myself a part?"' That story links the past, the present and the future, not just of that individual but also of the community in which he or she lives, and in so doing gives a conception of his or her life as a unified whole. That is why 'The unity of a human is the unity of a narrative quest'.[17]

Through participation in a communal quest, MacIntyre argues, moral claims become more than merely subjective. The narrative quest consists not just in the goals that I set myself and the goods that I desire. It consists also in the goals and the goods of the community in which I am embedded. It is that social embeddedness that allows me to rise above my own desires and to understand those desires in broader, more objective terms.

MacIntyre's view of morality as emerging through collective endeavour is important, as is his insistence that through such collective endeavour morality rises above the subjective and the relative. His concept of the collective is, however, flawed. For MacIntyre, as it was for Burke and Bradley, a tradition is a collective bound primarily by its past, and one whose social relationships are enforced through authority. What is significant about a tradition, for MacIntyre, is that its history imposes a claim upon the present. 'What I am,' he insists, 'is in key part what I inherit.' I always exist as 'part of a history' and 'whether I like it or not, whether I recognize it or not', even if I reject the burden, I remain always 'one of the bearers of a tradition'.[18]

The problem with Enlightenment conceptions of morality, MacIntyre argues, is the insistence that the moral agent has 'to be able to stand back from any and every situation . . . and to pass judgement on it from a purely universal and abstract point of view'. But, MacIntyre insists, such a God's-eye view is impossible. Moral clarity comes not through detachment from society or tradition but through embeddedness in it. Not only can one not be detached from society or tradition, any more than one can be detached from one's body, but anyone who was so detached would possess no moral clarity because her moral sense would have nothing to ground it and so would float as free as her supposed detached self.

But if an individual cannot tear himself away from his social grounding, if he cannot rise above 'the family, the neighbourhood, the city, the tribe' and look upon them in a more objective fashion untainted by the relationships that have fashioned him, how can he be critical of the society, community or culture in which he is embedded? How can he challenge its ways of thinking and being? And how can there be any form of social or moral progress, or even change?

The problem faced by MacIntyre is the mirror image of that faced by a liberal individualist. The one seems incapable of acknowledging the social roots of moral agency, the other unable to explain how individual agency emerges out of social grounding. We can, however, while rejecting the idea of morality as being created by isolated individuals, also think of social embeddedness in a different way to MacIntyre, in terms not of tradition but of *transformation*. Movements for social transformation are defined less by a sense of a shared past (though most draw upon historical traditions) than by the ambition of a common future. They represent a social journey shaped not by the demands of the point of departure but by the hopes invested in the destination. With the coming of modernity, as the necessity of traditions gave way to the possibilities of collective change, so a new question was posed. People now asked themselves not simply 'What moral claims are rational given the social structure?', but also 'What social structures are rational?' What kind of society, what types of social institutions, what forms of social relations, will best allow moral lives to flourish?

In thinking neither of isolated individuals, nor of fixed traditions, but of social transformation, we also avoid the polarization between the God's-eye view and the worm's-eye view, between morality as abstract and universal and morality as concrete and contingent. Consider, for instance, slavery. There are no circumstances in which it is right for one human being to enslave another. Slavery is universally wrong. Yet the social conditions of the premodern world, the inability of such societies to raise their productive capacities, ensured that slavery remained woven into the social fabric. Not until the emergence of capitalism did the social and economic conditions for the abolition of slavery come into being. There were certainly arguments against slavery in the premodern world. Such opposition to slavery was rational from a God's-eye view, but not necessarily when viewed against the background of the societies in which the critics lived. Aristotle and Augustine were wrong in their support for slavery. And yet there was something rational in their arguments given the social conditions of their time.

Not till modernity could slavery be seen as wrong not just from a universal perspective but from the local perspective too. And not till modernity did opposition to slavery become rational from both a universal and a local perspective. The significance of modernity was that it made it possible to align that which was rational from the viewpoint of both the universal and the contingent by making possible social transformation. Here is the 'something more' that takes moral claims above subjective desires or local needs without at the same time making them objective in the way of a scientific truth.

CHAPTER EIGHTEEN

The search for ethical concrete

1

'Origin of man now solved,' Charles Darwin wrote in his notebook in 1838. 'He who understands baboon will do more for metaphysics than Locke.' He could have added, 'and for ethics too'. For it is in Darwin that scientific arguments about ethics today nearly all find their inspiration.

The scientific study of ethics has, over the past century, rested on two main props. The first has been the attempt to provide greater insight into human psychology, to understand better why humans might behave and respond in characteristic ways, and how it might be possible to change and shape such behaviours and responses for the better. The second has been the attempt to elucidate not just why people may act in good or bad ways, but also what constitute good and bad in the first place. From this second perspective, science can explain both why humans might behave charitably in certain circumstances or be cowardly in others, and also whether charity is a good or cowardice morally acceptable. As other sources of moral values have eroded, so the role of science in defining good and bad has become increasingly important.

The publication in 1859 of *On the Origin of Species* transformed the debate on human nature by suggesting in evolution by natural selection a mechanism by which to create without a Creator, to design without a designer. It also transformed the debate on morality.

There is, in fact, little about human nature or human morality in *The Origin of Species*, aside from a cryptic sentence at the end of the book. 'In the distant future . . .', Darwin wrote, 'Light will be thrown on the origin of man and his history.' It was, however, not 'in the distant future' but in 1871 that Darwin published *The Descent of Man*, in which he attempted to demonstrate how human mental qualities had been developed by nature in a gradual process. The germ of even the most complex ideas – reasoning, imagination, curiosity, aesthetic sense – was, Darwin argued, to be found within animals. Morality too.

'Of all the differences between man and the lower animals,' Darwin wrote, 'the moral sense or conscience is by far the most important.' Even so, non-human animals have the capacity for moral thinking, though that capacity is not as well developed as in humans. Morality is made possible by our 'social instincts' – our natural disposition to act for the benefit of others. 'Any animal whatever,' Darwin believed, 'endowed with well-marked social instincts . . . would inevitably acquire a social sense or conscience, as soon as its intellectual powers had become as well developed, or nearly as well developed, as in man.'[1] What characterized a moral action was its contribution to 'the general good', which could be understood only in the light of evolution: it was through the process of natural selection that the meaning of 'the general good' comes to be defined. Darwin adopts the arguments of eighteenth-century moral sense philosophers such as Shaftesbury, Butler and Hutcheson but updates them in the light of evolutionary theory.

Social instincts lead us to set aside our own natural interests and do what is for the good of the whole community. But how did social instincts evolve in the first place? Socially minded, altruistic individuals, who placed the interests of others before their own, were less likely to have survived and bred successfully. How does altruism spread in a population? Darwin himself was perplexed, observing, 'It is extremely doubtful whether the offspring of the more sympathetic and benevolent parents, or of those which were the most faithful to their comrades, would be reared in greater numbers than the children of selfish and treacherous parents of the same tribe.'[2] It was a conundrum that was not to be properly solved for a century.

2

Darwin was, at least, puzzled by the conundrum of evolved altruistic traits. Others rarely considered the question of how moral instincts may have evolved, simply assuming it as a fact. Perhaps the most influential of these was Herbert Spencer (1820–1903), a philosopher, biologist and sociologist who today is rarely read but who was, in the closing decades of the nineteenth century, the most celebrated intellectual of his age, the first, and possibly only, philosopher to sell over a million copies of his books during his lifetime.

In his early works on ethics, Spencer adopted a broadly utilitarian vision, but one in which the good was defined by God. Eventually, nature came to replace God, and the ends of moral life determined by evolution. It was a transformation fuelled as much by the intellectual crisis of his age as by Spencer's own loss of faith. 'Now that moral injunctions are losing the authority given by their supposed sacred origin,' he observed in his 1879 work *Data of Ethics*, 'the secularization of morals is becoming imperative.' There are, Spencer suggested, few things 'more disastrous than the decay and death of a regulative system no longer fit, before another and fitter regulative system has grown up to replace it'. Hence the 'pressing need' for 'the establishment of rules of conduct on a scientific basis'.[3]

When we talk of a 'good' knife or a 'bad' umbrella, Spencer observes, we refer not to intrinsic characters of knives or umbrellas, but rather to how 'well or ill [they are] adapted to achieve prescribed ends'. Human acts, too, are 'good or bad, according as they are well or ill adjusted to ends'. What are those ends? They are given by evolution. All organisms evolve to a certain end, which is 'self-preservation'. Evolution 'reaches its limit when individual life is the greatest, both in length and breadth'.[4] Spencer presents here a secularized, 'scientific', utilitarian version of the idea of *telos* developed by Aristotle and Aquinas, and whose loss was bemoaned by MacIntyre.

Morality, like all forms of conduct, has, Spencer insists, evolved. 'The conduct to which we apply the name good', he argued, 'is the relatively more evolved conduct; and that bad is the name we apply to conduct which is relatively less evolved'. The 'good' is any 'conduct furthering self-preservation', and 'bad' any 'conduct tending to self-destruction'. Self-preservation is not simply that of the individual but also of his or her offspring and of fellow human beings. Evolution creates ever-better 'adjustment of acts to ends'. The more evolved a people or a nation, the more their conduct produces the ends to which evolution strives. Spencer married a utilitarian idea of the good to an evolutionary story of how the good was attained, and in so doing sought to replace religion with science as the foundation of morality.

Spencer's teleological vision of evolution as a progressive journey, which owed more to Lamarck than to Darwin, did not survive long. Nor did his brand of evolutionary ethics. But his desire to find in science the moral certainties that had been lost with the decline of religion came to be influential. Those hostile to religion 'assume that the controlling agency furnished by it may safely be thrown aside, and the vacancy left unfilled by any other controlling agency', Spencer wrote in the preface to *Data of Ethics*. Believers, on the other hand, 'allege that in the absence of divine guidance it yields, no guidance can exist'. The consequence is a moral 'vacuum' for which one side 'wishes' and of which 'the other fears'.[5] This sense of a moral world caught in an abyss between a lost faith and a destructive nihilism was to return with greater force at the end of the twentieth century. With it would come a renewed desire to find in science the ethical concrete broken up with the death of God.

3

'Let us understand, once and for all, that the ethical progress of society depends, not on imitating the cosmic process, still less in running away from it but in combating it.' So insisted 'Darwin's bulldog' Thomas Huxley in his 1893 Romanes Lecture on 'Evolution and Ethics'. Huxley was among the fiercest and most eloquent defenders of Darwin's theory of evolution. He was also among the fiercest and most eloquent critics of evolutionary ethics. There was, Huxley insisted, no correlation between the moral and the natural. 'The thief and the murderer', he observed, 'follow nature just as much as the philanthropist.' The theory of evolution 'may teach us how the good and the evil tendencies of man may have come about' but 'it is incompetent' to explain 'why what we call the good is preferable to what we call evil'. Far from there being a correlation between the moral and the natural, there is, in fact, antagonism between the two. 'Social progress means a checking of the cosmic process at every step and the substitution for it of another, which may be called the ethical process.' 'In place of ruthless self-assertion', morality 'demands self-restraint'. Morality's 'influence is directed, not so much to the survival of the fittest, as to the fitting of as many as possible to survive'.[6]

Despite Huxley's eloquent warnings, evolutionary ethics flourished in the decades around the turn of the nineteenth century. Herbert Spencer had seen in every human being a balance between a 'selfish instinct' and a faculty of 'sympathy'. Darwin had stressed even more the importance to moral life of the evolved traits of benevolence and fellow feeling. Yet, as evolutionary ethics entered the popular domain, its proponents took their cue not from the idea of sympathy but from the metaphor that for many had come to define evolution: the survival of the fittest. Huxley himself had observed that a fundamental fallacy of evolutionary ethics was the belief that because 'animals and plants have advanced in perfection of organization by means of the struggle for existence' so humans 'as ethical beings must look to the same process to help them towards perfection'.[7] This, Huxley pointed out, was to confuse the idea of 'fitness' in the context of nature, with the notion of 'good' in a moral sense, when the two had very different, indeed often opposite, meanings. Nevertheless, in an age of cut-throat capitalism and imperialist expansion, and against a background of what Huxley called 'the fanatical individualism of our time', not only did evolutionary ethics flourish, but it came to be defined by the metaphor of the 'survival of the fittest' rather than by the idea of 'sympathy'.

Even when evolutionary ethicists turned their attention to the question of 'community' and 'fellow feeling', they did so primarily in the context of the struggle for survival. 'Community' in the late nineteenth century usually meant 'racial community' and 'fellow feeling' translated as 'racial sentiment'. It was an age in which even staunch liberals, such as Darwin and Huxley, took racial hierarchies as natural and racial struggle as a given. People saw in evolutionary theory the idea that the struggle for existence had created unequal races, that capitalist exploitation, colonial conquest and even genocide were simply the working out of the laws of natural selection, and that such conduct was necessary to improve the moral fibre of humankind.

4

It was not philosophical argument but moral revulsion that finally laid to waste evolutionary ethics. The experience of Nazism, the death camps and the Final Solution helped discredit not just racial ideas of difference, but biological notions of human similarities too. The very idea that human nature could, or should, be understood through the language of biology became taboo. The anthropologist Margaret Mead explained in her autobiography how she and her colleagues took a conscious decision not to explore the biological bases of human behaviour and await 'less troubled times'.[8] The idea that human behaviour was primarily a cultural artefact came to dominate postwar thinking.

Attitudes began to shift again in the 1970s. Along with bell-bottomed trousers and global recession came the return of human nature to scholarly debate. The publication of two books in the mid-1970s, neither of which were, paradoxically, primarily about humans, signalled the new mood. E.O. Wilson's *Sociobiology* and Richard Dawkins' *The Selfish Gene*, books whose very titles have helped sculpt the contemporary language of human nature, exposed the changing academic climate and reignited public debate.

There had been in the 1960s and '70s a revolution in evolutionary thinking. At its heart was the idea that Dawkins popularized as the 'selfish gene', the belief that natural selection works not upon the group, or even upon the individual, but upon the gene. Individuals die at the end of their lifetimes, a gene is potentially immortal. Genes are 'selfish' because their only function is to survive at the expense of their rivals. The body is simply a 'survival machine' built by genes to enable them to survive. Such claims led many, most notoriously the philosopher Mary Midgley, to read *The Selfish Gene* as an argument for *ethical* selfishness. 'Genes cannot be selfish or unselfish', she wrote in an infamous paper called 'Gene-juggling', 'any more than atoms can be jealous, elephants abstract or biscuits teleological'. Dawkins, she insisted, was 'an uncritical philosophic egoist' whose 'central point is that the emotional nature of man is exclusively self-interested'.The problem, as the writer Andrew Brown has observed, is that *The Selfish Gene* was 'a book about genes read as a book about people'.[9] It was a reading all too common to both sides of the debate.

The irony is that the revolution in evolutionary thought out of which the selfish gene theory emerged produced also a bundle of ideas to show how the selfish gene could create altruistic behaviour. The British biologist William Hamilton introduced the concept of 'kin selection', showing how it made evolutionary sense for an organism to sacrifice its interests to improve those of relatives that carry many of the same genes, if in doing so it increases the odds of those genes being transmitted to future generations. In human communities, though, individuals are often altruistic towards others to whom they are not related. To account for this, the American biologist Robert Trivers developed the notion of 'reciprocal altruism', showing how natural selection would favour altruism in those circumstances in which such altruism might be reciprocated – such as in human societies. The question that had so troubled Darwin – how natural selection could create the social instincts – had, seemingly, finally been resolved.[10]

It was not simply scientific but political developments, too, that helped transform the landscape of human nature. The relationship between the nature–nurture debate (to what degree are humans the products of their biology and to what degree of their environment?) and the political debate between left and right is a highly complex one. Many radicals, from the seventeenth century onwards, had used the idea of a common human nature and of natural law to promote social change. Many conservatives insisted on the importance of historical and cultural traditions as bulwarks against revolutionary change. Nevertheless, through the course of the twentieth century, the left came to be associated with cultural and social explanations of the human condition, while biological theories were regarded as the province of the right. As the traditional left crumbled in the 1970s and '80s, and Marxism fell into disrepute, so did the idea that human behaviour could be understood primarily in cultural terms. Biological and evolutionary explanations gained ground. The flowering of such explanations, in turn, cast further shadows over radical political and moral claims. 'The new sciences of human nature', the cognitive scientist Steven Pinker claimed in his book *The Blank Slate*, 'really do resonate with assumptions that historically were closer to the right than to the left.' They lend support to the ideas of philosophers such as Hobbes and Burke who recognized that humans are 'inherently limited in knowledge, wisdom and virtue, and all social arrangements must acknowledge those limits'.[11]

The revival of biological theories of human nature helped shape moral thinking in a number of ways. Moral philosophers, whether Aristotelian or Humean, whether conservative or radical, increasingly looked to the new sciences to provide evidential support for their particular vision of human nature. While philosophers looked to biology to substantiate their moral theories, biologists and psychologists wielded experimental data to shape the moral debate. The work of the American cognitive scientist Joshua Greene has become a major influence.

5

Imagine a runaway train. If it carries on down its present course it will kill five people. You cannot stop the train, but you can pull a switch and move the train onto another track, down which it will kill not five people but just one person. Should you pull the switch? This is the famous 'trolley' problem, a thought experiment first suggested by Philippa Foot in 1967,[12] and which since has become one of the most important tools in contemporary moral philosophy. (In Foot's original, the dilemma featured a runaway trolley, hence the common name of the problem.)

When faced with the question of whether or not to switch the runaway train, most people, unsurprisingly, say 'Yes'. Now imagine that you are standing on a bridge under which the runaway train will pass. You can stop the train – and the certain death of five people – by dropping a heavy weight in front of it. There is, standing next to you, an exceedingly fat man. Would it be moral for you to push him over the bridge and onto the track? Most people now say 'No', even though the moral dilemma is the same as before: should you kill one to save the five?

Or consider a dilemma first raised by Peter Singer forty years ago. You are driving along a country road when you hear a plea for help coming from some roadside bushes. You pull over, and see a man seriously injured, covered in blood and writhing in agony. He begs you to take him to a nearby hospital.

You want to help, but realize that if you take him the blood will ruin the leather upholstery of your car. So you leave him and drive off. Most people would consider that a monstrous act.

Now suppose you receive a letter that asks for a donation to help save the life of a girl in India. You decide you cannot afford to give to charity since you are saving up to buy a sofa and so you bin the letter. Few would deem that to be immoral.

Again, there seems to be no objective difference between these two cases. Yet to most people they appear unquestionably morally different. In both cases, Joshua Greene suggests, the difference lies not in the facts of the case but in the brains processing those facts. The perplexing, seemingly contradictory, ways that people approach many moral dilemmas reflect the manner in which human brains are wired. Our ancestors, Greene suggests, 'did not evolve in an environment in which total strangers on opposite sides of the world could save each others' lives by making relatively modest material sacrifices'. They evolved, rather, 'in an environment in which individuals standing face-to-face could save each others' lives, sometimes only through considerable personal sacrifice'. It makes sense, therefore, 'that we would have evolved altruistic instincts that direct us to help others in dire need, but mostly when the ones in need are presented in an "up-close-and-personal" way.'[13] We intuitively think it immoral not to help the driver but are less concerned about ignoring the girl in India. We also make a moral distinction between a case in which we personally kill someone and one in which the individual's death is the result of a more impersonal, mechanical action. We can, however, step back from the dilemma, and our intuitions, and take a more sober, reasoned view. If we do that, we realize that there is no moral distinction between the two cases in either of the scenarios.

For Greene, then, the intuitionists are right. We arrive at moral answers instinctively, intuitively. But not entirely instinctively, and not always. Human morality, Greene suggests, is a bit like a digital camera. It can work in both auto mode and in manual mode. In automatic, point-and-shoot mode, the camera can take pictures quickly and easily, but often goes awry in difficult conditions – in bright sunlight, for instance, or in scenes with high contrast. Auto mode, in other words, is fast but inflexible. In manual mode, the camera can be fine-tuned to take perfect photos in even the trickiest conditions. But such fine-tuning is fiddly and takes time. It also takes considerable experience. Manual mode is highly flexible, but it is slow and awkward to set up.

The same is true, Greene suggests, of moral thinking. Normally we rely on point-and-shoot moral answers. We respond quickly, instinctively, almost unthinkingly to moral problems. Our fast, instinctive point-and-shoot moral snapshot answers have developed against the background of our evolutionary history. In auto mode, our brains perceive it as moral to switch the train to a second track so that only one rather than five people are killed, and immoral to ignore the plight of an injured person to protect the leather in your car. But auto mode is not subtle or powerful enough to detect the moral link between the injured traveller and the poor child on the other side of the world, or between killing one to save the five by pulling a switch or by throwing a man off a bridge. We are, however, able to switch from auto to manual mode, to recalibrate our settings and to look at the dilemmas anew. When we do this, we see the moral links, and the moral answers, that auto mode fails to detect. Unlike in a camera, the two moral modes are often in conflict. We can reason our way to a moral answer, and still feel instinctively that it is the wrong answer.

Greene's argument is highly sophisticated. It is also highly contentious, and one for which, so far at least, there is no real evidence. There are other ways of understanding these different responses to moral dilemmas. When people distinguish between helping an injured man at the roadside and helping a girl in India, it may not be because they are using two different modes of moral thinking, one instinctive, the other reasoned. It may rather be that the kind of reasoning that yields useful moral answers is different from the kind of abstract reasoning championed by Singer and Greene. The roadside victim requires your help and only you can help; if you refuse to take him to hospital it would directly, and adversely, affect his wellbeing. The causes of poverty in India are myriad; the fact that you don't donate to a particular charity will not necessarily worsen that girl's situation, any more than your money will necessarily improve it. In any case, unlike in the case of the roadside victim, there are undoubtedly others who could also offer assistance. The two cases, in other words, are different in terms of what caused them, what may be necessary to improve wellbeing, and in the impact of one's actions. The two cases may be morally equivalent in an abstract sense. But in the reality of actually lived human lives, there is a moral gulf between them. In insisting that the two are moral equivalents, Singer and Greene ignore the context of moral reasoning. A similar argument could be made about the trolley dilemmas.

Strikingly, Greene, in perhaps the most contentious of his claims, suggests that the two modes of moral thinking correspond to different kinds of moral philosophies. In auto mode we construct moral answers akin to Kantianism. This is not so much because we are all evolved to be mini-Kants, but rather because Kantianism and, by implication, most other forms of ethical thinking are attempts to rationalize our instinctive moral responses. Not all moral theories are, however, like this. Utilitarianism, Greene suggests, is the product not of rationalization but of reason. It is what happens when we turn on manual mode moral thinking. Greene insists that one mode is not better than the other. Each is useful in different circumstances. Yet Greene clearly believes that utilitarianism is superior to Kantianism and other forms of moral philosophy. The distinction between auto and manual modes appears to be a means of validating the superiority of utilitarianism.[14]

6

The reinjection of Darwinian thinking into moral theory reignited the debate about facts and values. Some now argue that our brain architecture lends itself to particular moral philosophies. The analyst and ethicist William Casebeer claims, for instance, that 'the moral psychology required by virtue theory is the most neurobiologically plausible'. Indeed, 'neurobiological facts support a version of . . . moral realism', that 'norms are natural, and that they arise from and are justified by purely natural processes'. But, asks Joshua Greene, in an echo of both Hume and Huxley, 'How do we go from "This is how we think" to "This is how we ought to think"? . . . So long as people are capable of taking Kant's or Mill's advice, how does it follow from neuroscientific data – indeed how could it follow from such data – that people ought to ignore Kant's and Mill's recommendations in favour of Aristotle's? In other words, how does it follow from the proposition that Aristotelian moral thought is more natural than Kant's or Mill's that Aristotle's is better?'[15]

Greene's argument shows how, a century on from Spencer and the first generation of evolutionary ethicists, the understanding of the relationship between the natural and the moral has shifted. In the nineteenth century evolutionary ethicists claimed that that which was natural was moral. For Greene, our natural, instinctive responses can often blind us to the moral realities. These days, those who wish to collapse the distinction between fact and value look not to nature but to science to provide the standard for moral evaluation.

One of the most vocal proponents of the idea that science can answer all questions, including moral dilemmas, has been the American philosopher and neuroscientist Sam Harris. A leading so-called 'New Atheist', his early works, such as *The End of Faith* and *Letter to a Christian Nation*, were trenchant critiques of religion. In his more recent books he has attempted to use science to explain the human condition, tackling issues that were traditionally in the province of philosophy or religion, such as morality and free will.

In his bestselling 2010 book *The Moral Landscape*, Harris sets out to show, in the words of its subtitle, *How Science Can Determine Human Values*. What Hume failed to understand, he argues, is that science can bridge the gap between *ought* and *is* by turning moral claims into empirical facts. 'Questions about values', Harris observes, 'are really questions about the well-being of conscious creatures.' Values, therefore, 'translate into facts that can be scientifically understood: regarding positive and negative social emotions, the effects of specific laws on human relationships, the neurophysiology of happiness and suffering, etc.'. Science, and neuroscience in particular, do not simply explain why we might respond in particular ways to equality or to torture, as Greene suggests, but also whether equality is a good, and torture morally acceptable. Where there are disagreements over moral questions, science, Harris believes, will decide which view is right 'because the discrepant answers people give to them translate into differences in our brains, in the brains of others and in the world at large'.[16]

How does Harris establish that values are facts? There are, he says, certain kinds of lives that most would agree are bad, and certain kinds of lives that most would agree are good. Imagine a young widow whose seven-year-old daughter was 'raped and dismembered' in front of her by her own fourteen-year-old son 'goaded to this evil at the point of a machete by a press gang of drug-addled soldiers'. It was an act 'not entirely out of character with the other days of [a] life' that from the moment of birth has been 'a theatre of cruelty and violence'. Most people would accept that this woman was living what Harris calls 'a Bad Life'. Now imagine a woman who is 'married to the most loving, intelligent and charismatic person', who has a career that is 'intellectually stimulating and financially rewarding', who is able to devote herself 'to activities that bring [her] immense personal satisfaction' and who has 'just won a billion-dollar grant to benefit children in the developing world'. Not many people, I would imagine, would disagree with Harris that this woman is living 'a Good Life'.[17] Good circumstances give rise to good lives, bad circumstances to bad lives. It is objectively good to value a good life and objectively bad to value a bad life. Therefore, Harris suggests, there are objectively good values and objectively bad values; values are objective facts about the world.

To accept that murder and rape are bad is to accept that one is not a psychopath. But being able to distinguish between psychopaths and non-psychopaths is not the same as establishing the ontological status of non-psychopathic beliefs. Or, to put it another way, even most moral relativists abhor murder and rape. The insistence that because it seems obvious that rape and murder are bad, and that wealth and security are good, so there must be objective values, seems about as plausible as the argument that because there are gaps in the fossil record, so God must have created Adam and Eve.

Nor is it self-evident, as Harris suggests, that moral questions should relate solely to the 'well-being of conscious creatures'. Some philosophers insist that moral questions primarily relate to the wellbeing of humans, as autonomous moral agents, rather than to that of all conscious creatures. Others suggest that the wellbeing of ecosystems, or of the planet, should be taken into account. There may be rational arguments that can help distinguish between these claims, but there can be no empirical test that can do so. Nor, indeed, does Harris suggest any.

Let us grant that morality does relate solely to the wellbeing of conscious creatures. What scientific test can be used to define wellbeing? This, as we have already seen, has always been a problem for consequentialists. Harris accepts that 'wellbeing' is a fuzzy concept. But so, he points out, are many scientific categories. We cannot define with absolute accuracy what it means to be healthy but most people would know the objective difference between a healthy person and an unhealthy one. So it is with moral health. This, however, is to misunderstand the problem. The issue is not so much that wellbeing is a fuzzy category as that it can, in specific cases, be very well defined but in a number of different ways that are often conflicting in a manner that science cannot resolve.

Consider, for instance, the claim made by Harris that 'torture may be an ethical necessity in our war on terror'.[18] Since we are happy to accept 'collateral damage' in the 'war on terror', actions in which innocent noncombatants may be maimed or killed, why, he asks, should we cavil at torturing suspected terrorists? If the use of torture produces information, the good of which is greater than the badness of torturing another human being, then, Harris argues, we should not hesitate in putting people on the rack.

The question of whether torture works is a matter for debate. Many, for instance, have questioned claims that information obtained under torture was essential for the US Special Forces operation that tracked down and killed Osama bin Laden in 2011. The debate about torture runs much deeper, though, than the question of its utility. After all, only the most psychopathic would insist on torturing someone if such torture provides no result. The real moral debate begins when we accept that torture may be effective in certain cases. If we grant that torture can produce useful information, how should we respond? This is not a question that can be answered simply by enumerating the facts or by pulling out the scientific measuring tape and designing a scientific experiment. It is a question that demands answers to some of the most profound questions about the human condition. What does it mean to be human? How should one treat human beings? These are moral, not merely scientific or empirical, questions.

Harris takes an accountant's-eye view of torture. On one page of the ledger we note down the pain caused by torture, both to the individual and to the political system. On the other side we collate all the goods that come out of it. Do the goods add up to more than the bads? If so, it is time to get out the thumbscrews, and to do so in the name of 'science'. For opponents of torture, however, such totting up morality misses the essence of why torture is a bad. Torture is immoral not simply because it causes pain. Lots of acts cause unnecessary pain but are still accepted as moral. The difference, however, between torture and collateral damage in war is the difference between deliberately treating a human being as a piece of meat and unintentionally killing some people. The immorality of torture lies not simply in the pain that a torturer inflicts but in his blindness to the humanity of a human being. Every human being is both an object and a subject, both a biological being and a moral agent. In treating his victim as a slab of meat, the torturer is reducing him to a mere object. In so doing he hollows out the very substance of our moral lives.

Science cannot determine values because one cannot scientifically assess what is right and wrong without already having constructed a moral framework within which to evaluate the empirical data. Or, as Huxley put it, science 'may teach us how the good and the evil tendencies of man may have come about; but, in itself, it is incompetent to furnish any better reason why what we call good is preferable to what we call evil than we had before'.[19]

For Harris, as for many of the New Atheists, the desire to root morality in science derives from an aspiration to demonstrate the redundancy of religion to ethical thinking. The irony is that the classic argument against looking to God as the source of moral values – the Euthyphro dilemma – is equally applicable to the claim that science is, or should be, the arbiter of good and evil. In Plato's *Euthyphro*, Socrates asks the question: do the gods love the good because it is good, or is it good because it is loved by the gods? If the good is good simply because gods choose it, then the notion of the good becomes arbitrary. If, on the other hand, the gods choose the good because it is good, then the good is independent of the gods.

The same dilemma faces contemporary defenders of the claim that science defines moral values. Harris argues that wellbeing can be defined through data gained through fMRI scans, physiological observation, pharmacological measures, and other such techniques. Such studies may be able to tell us which brain states, neurotransmitters or hormones calibrate with particular real-world conditions. But whether those states, neurotransmitters or hormones are seen as indicators of wellbeing depends on whether we consider those real-life conditions as expressions of wellbeing. If wellbeing is defined simply by the existence of certain neural states, or by the presence of particular hormones or neurotransmitters, or because of certain evolutionary dispositions, then the notion of wellbeing is arbitrary. If such a definition is not to be arbitrary, then it can only be because the neural state, or the hormonal or neurotransmitter level, or the evolutionary disposition, correlates with a notion of wellbeing or of the good, which has been arrived at independently. The Euthyphro dilemma can no more be evaded by scientists claiming to have objective answers to questions of right and wrong than it can by theologists.

CHAPTER NINETEEN

Confucianism, communism and the clash of civilizations

1

It is the diary of a madman, written by someone suffering from 'a form of persecution complex', whose writing is 'most confused and incoherent'. The madman is convinced that all around him are cannibals. Eventually he begins studying Chinese history by reading the Confucian classics, only to find the words 'Eat People!' written between the lines. He is gripped by the fear that his brother, his doctor and his neighbours are all preparing to eat him. He begins to wonder whether he himself is a cannibal. 'It is possible', he writes, 'that I ate several pieces of my sister's flesh unwittingly, and now it is my turn.' He wonders how he could not be mad. 'How can a man like myself,' he asks himself, 'after four thousand years of man-caring history – even though I knew nothing about it at first – ever hope to face real men?' 'Perhaps', he desperately concludes, 'there are still children who have not eaten men? Save the children.'[1]

The Diary of a Madman, a short story written in 1918, was perhaps the most striking work of Lu Xun, China's greatest twentieth-century writer. Lu was a leading figure of the 'New Culture' movement that flourished in the early decades of the last century, decades in which China was ripped apart by cultural and social turmoil. For the writers and thinkers of the 'New Culture' the blame for all China's problems lay squarely with its old culture. Confucianism, Lu Xun suggests, had cannibalized Chinese society; but in a world in which everyone is a cannibal, those who try to tell the truth about cannibalism are deemed mad. That, in Lu's eyes, was the fate of China.

By the end of the nineteenth century China had become a semi-colony of the Western powers. The infamous Opium Wars – launched by Britain in 1840 after Beijing had tried to shut down its lucrative but illegal opium trade – destroyed Chinese control over its own territory. The treaties that ended the wars gave Western nations the right of extraterritoriality: each could run its own police force and court system, and enforce its own laws. Foreigners had the right to set up Christian missions without restrictions. Western navies could sail at will on any Chinese waterway.

British gunboats had not simply destroyed China's threadbare military defences. They had shattered, too, the nation's intellectual and philosophical self-assurance, its belief that its civilization was unmatched, its culture unrivalled, its history unbroken. Within half a century that history definitely was broken. The Qing Dynasty collapsed, bringing to an end three millennia of dynastic rule. In 1911 China became a republic.

The new republic was no stronger than the old dynasty had been. The fragile parliamentary democracy fragmented into rival regions ruled by warlords. There were two intellectual responses to the growing social chaos. The first was an attempt to rework the Confucian tradition; the second, the insistence that tradition itself was the problem. In the late nineteenth century, at a time when Western powers were carving up and humiliating the nation, many had found it difficult to make the case that China should take seriously Western ideas. By the early twentieth century so deep had that humiliation gone that even many traditionalists had come to accept that the West might provide a source not just of technology but also of ideas and moral codes. At the turn of the nineteenth century a host of Western philosophers, from Descartes to Marx, from Kant to James, were translated into Chinese for the first time. Later John Dewey and Bertrand Russell toured China giving lectures.

Philosophers such as Fung Yu Lan attempted to create a 'New Confucianism'. Fung, who had been a student of John Dewey's at Columbia University, tried to stitch together Confucian ideals and Western ideas. His aim, he suggested, was to modernize China while rejecting those philosophies, both Chinese and non-Chinese, that were not in keeping with the nation's traditions. He despised Daoism, which he labelled 'the philosophy of subtraction', because it was inward-looking and seeking unity with nature. He was equally critical of Mohism and most Western philosophies, which he described as 'philosophies of augmentation', being outward-looking and seeking to master nature. His New Confucianism, combining traditional Chinese thought with Western pragmatism, he saw as 'the middle way' between 'this-worldly' and 'other-worldly' philosophies.

Others embraced Western philosophy not to renovate tradition, but to shatter it. Fuel for anti-tradition sentiment was provided by the May Fourth Movement. It began as a protest of patriotic students outraged by Allied treachery at the Paris peace talks that ended the First World War. The Allies had refused to return to China the areas that had been colonized by the now-defeated Germans, handing them over to Japan instead. Fury at the Allies' betrayal soon turned into rage at China's own impotence, and at a historical tradition that had, it seemed, cannibalized its own people. Out of this rage emerged the New Cultural movement, a desire to build a new nation designed by 'Mr Democracy and Ms Science', as a popular slogan had it.

The liberal wing of anti-traditionalism was led by the philosopher Hu Shi who, like Fung, had been a student of John Dewey's and was fired by the desire to apply the 'scientific method' to every aspect of the human experience. Many of the liberal anti-traditionalists were drawn to the Kuomintang, or Nationalist Party, and to its leader, and first president of the republic, Sun Yat Sen. The radicals followed Chen Duxiu, a one-time government official who in 1921 helped found the main political alternative to the Nationalists: the Chinese Communist Party. He, like most of the founders of the Party, had little understanding or knowledge of Marxism, which was for him less an ideology than the promise of a radically new future. What shaped his beliefs, as it did that of so many Chinese modernizers in the early decades of the twentieth century, was a bastardized form of Darwinism. 'Evolution', Chen wrote, 'goes from feudalism to republicanism and from republicanism to communism. I have said that the republic has failed and that feudalism has been reborn, but I hope that soon the feudal forces will be wiped out again by democracy and the latter by socialism.'[2]

The Kuomintang came to power in 1928, under its new leader Chiang

Kai-shek. Chiang united the country after a decade of fragmentation, but he brought no respite from war. A ruthless dictator, he disposed of the opposition, and turned on his erstwhile supporters in the Communist Party. The Party was forced in 1934 to undertake the notorious Long March to the remote Shaanxi province, a 4,000-mile trek during which four in five of the 80,000 communists who began the journey died. Then, in 1937, Japan invaded China and for eight years waged a merciless war. After the surrender of Japan to the Allies in 1946, China was plunged into a new struggle, this time a civil war between the Kuomintang and the Communist Party, now led by Mao Zedong. Weakened by the war against Japan, robbed of popular support by their cruelty and corruption, the Nationalists proved no match for Mao's forces. Within three years Mao had all of China under his control and had forced Chiang to flee to Taiwan.

2

For more than two millennia, the identity of China, and the character of its social order, had been defined primarily in ethical terms, and given philosophical shape largely by Confucianism. When that tradition, and the social order and dynastic structure it sustained, broke in the twentieth century, inevitably there was chaos, a chaos made more turbulent by the distinctive role of ethics in Chinese society.

In Western Europe, Christianity had provided, for more than a millennium, a shared identity for peoples otherwise divided by language, nation or tribe, and a crucible within which all philosophical, political and moral discussion took place. The Church had been the continent's common voice and its moral guardian. Religion, certainly as it was understood in Europe, barely developed in China. The state, in the form of the imperial bureaucracy, had performed many of the roles and duties historically taken by the European Church, providing moral instruction, constructing a collective identity and creating a sense of shared values. Not only was the social role of the state different in China, so was its relationship to the ruling class. In Europe, different sections of the elite – nobles, clerics, merchants, the landed aristocracy, the urban bourgeoisie – had vied with each other for the reins of power, and had fought to control and constrain the authority of the state. Through these struggles the space was cleared for what we now know as civil society, a space that became central to the development of moral debate.

In China, the overwhelming power of the bureaucratic state stifled the growth of autonomous elite groups. The bureaucracy had faced little challenge from a landed aristocracy or an urban bourgeoisie, an established Church or an entrenched judiciary, dissident intellectuals or a politicized military. Only two institutions enjoyed true authority: the state and the family. Both were seen as being possessed of an almost spiritual quality, each acknowledged as a wellspring and guardian of moral values and righteous behaviour. The meritocratic character of the bureaucracy – an elite created through examination rather than accident of birth, an innovation not introduced in Europe until the Napoleonic era – combined with its social power had held in check the ambitions of other sections of the elite. At the same time, it had constrained the space for the development of civil society. There was little room for political and moral debate independently of the state.

In Europe, the erosion of the authority of the Church from the middle of the second millennium had transformed the debate about ethics. The hauling up of the traditional moral anchor had left many fearing that moral norms would simply float free, without compass or chart. Others saw it as a form of liberation. As the role of the Church in setting boundaries diminished, so there opened up new secular public spaces for moral thinking and debate. In China ethical prescriptions had always been broadly secular. Confucianism had been little concerned with God or the soul, with sin or salvation, providing instead pragmatic rules for behaviour in this world, rules that stressed virtue, decorum, filial piety and social discipline. The collapse of the dynastic structure, and the disillusionment with the Confucian tradition that came with it, wrenched free the traditional moral anchor, just as the erosion of Church authority had in Europe. But whereas in Europe social and intellectual tools had already been fashioned, and new public spaces created, for thinking anew about morality, in China the collapse of the Qing Dynasty left neither alternative systems of values nor the intellectual and cultural means through which to develop them. This was one reason for the scramble to embrace

Western philosophies at the turn of the nineteenth century. But because such ideas had not already been incubated within the Chinese intellectual tradition, they inevitably carried little social weight.

The four decades of chaos and social fragmentation that followed the creation of the republic in 1911 was not unusual in Chinese history. There had often been much longer periods of social turbulence between dynasties. Previously, however, Confucianism had always provided a framework within which each new dynasty could subsequently establish its own identity and order. Even on those occasions on which foreign dynasties imposed themselves upon the Chinese people (as happened with the Yuan, who were Mongols, and the Manchu Qing), those dynasties came to absorb the Confucian vision and ruled in time according to traditional norms. The tumult of the first half of the twentieth century was different. What had collapsed was not simply a particular dynasty, but the whole dynastic system. With it collapsed, too, the very basis on which had been built, for two millennia, China's social and moral order.

Nothing seemed more to express the rupture in China's history than the 1949 revolution and the coming to power of the Chinese Communist Party. As economic historian Roy Bin Wong observed of Mao's communists, 'the affirmation of their identity has rested as much on an opposition to their own "feudal" past and the "bourgeois" West as it has on any positive set of goals and values'.[3]

In Mao's China, Confucius was condemned as the 'faithful running-dog of the slave-owning aristocracy' whose 'reactionary ideology has been in continuous use by successive reactionary ruling classes'.[4] Yet, for all the anti-Confucian propaganda, there were, Wong suggests, lines of continuity between the Qing Dynasty and the communist period. What Mao created was a modern version of the bureaucratic state, 'a new status hierarchy to replace the old Confucian hierarchy of literati and officials. Being a party member became the principal means to achieve status and power.'[5]

The bureaucratic state had emerged early in Chinese imperial history as an efficient instrument for enforcing rule. But what had been an ideal mechanism for realizing order in a premodern world became increasingly an impediment with the development of modernity. In the premodern world, the structure of the community, the role of the individual in it and the rules of morality that defined right and wrong behaviours were all bound together either by divine law, as in Europe, or through tradition, as in China. Ethics and politics were inextricably linked because social structures were taken to be immovable. In modern societies they are inextricably linked for the opposite reason: because social structures are fiercely contested. Without such contestation – without, that is, autonomous groups struggling over different visions of society and of the good – it was difficult in nineteenth- and twentieth-century China either to create the mechanisms for social change or for the governing elite to establish political legitimacy. That which gave strength to the early Chinese Empire proved corrosive of the late imperial dynasties.

This became even more true of the post-1949 communist regime. For the Qing Dynasty, its identity and authority had been rooted in its embrace of tradition. Mao's China was built on the embrace of modernity and the rejection of tradition. It was built also on the suppression of civil society, the exclusion of the masses from the political process, and the containment of any notion of political debate or challenge. The only mechanism through which to effect political change or social transformation was top-down, often violent, mass mobilization, as in the Great Leap Forward and the Cultural Revolution. The Great Leap Forward was the catastrophic attempt in the late 1950s to turn China instantly from an agricultural to an industrial nation through forced collectivization, vast investment in steel production, and the use of coercion and terror that some estimate to have killed up to 2 million people. The result was a huge drop in both agricultural and industrial production, and a mass famine during which any number from 18 million to 42 million are said to have died. The Cultural Revolution, launched by Mao in 1966 after his return to power following the debacle of the Great Leap Forward, was supposedly to remove bourgeois and traditional elements from Chinese society, crush 'the old ideas, culture, customs, and habits of the exploiting classes', prevent the return of capitalism and cleanse the Party of revisionist thought. It led to a mass purge of government officials, the formation of the Red Guards, a paramilitary youth movement eventually several million strong, widespread arrests and imprisonment, and the destruction of countless ancient buildings, artefacts, books and paintings. Foreign scholars put the death toll at between 300,000 and 3 million, though a working conference of the Communist

Party's Central Committee in 1978 suggested that 20 million had died and 100 million had been persecuted in the decade-long Revolution.

What connects post-1949 China to pre-1911 China is not so much that Mao had reinvented the bureaucratic state. It is rather that in both imperial and Maoist China, the suppression of civil society, and the exclusion of the masses from the political sphere, left a chasm where moral and political debate should have been. Ideas of good and bad, and of human flourishing, could only be defined from above and had to be imposed from the top, often with extraordinary violence, and always with disastrous consequences.

3

The spectacular opening ceremony of the 2008 Beijing Olympic Games boasted 3,000 performers in flowing Zhou-era robes, waving bamboo slips of texts and chanting quotations from the *Analects*: 'Friends have come from afar, how happy we are' and 'All men are brothers within the four seas'. 'Confucius', the narrator told us, 'provided wise advice on how to achieve order and harmony in society.'

The choreography of the opening ceremony consummated before a global audience a courtship that had been more than three decades in the making. Even during the Mao era, Martin Jacques observes, Confucian values and ways of thinking 'although officially disavowed' nevertheless 'continued to be very influential, albeit in a subterranean form, remaining in some measure the common sense of the people'.[6] In fact, as Roy Bin Wong suggests, Confucianism was more than simply the 'common sense of the people'. Whatever the state may have officially proclaimed, unofficially it relied upon Confucian notions of hierarchy and authority to hold together a social order, particularly one that was rent by Maoist mass mobilizations. What had been a surreptitious nod towards Confucian ideology in Maoist China became, after Mao, a warm embrace, as China opened itself up to competition and the market, and hence also potentially to greater social dislocation and disorder. The quicker has been the pace of economic reform over the past three decades, the greater has been the desire of the Chinese government to proclaim its commitment to Confucianism. Over the past decade, Beijing has established more than four hundred 'Confucian Institutes' across the world to promote Chinese culture. In 2011 the government even erected a statue of Kongzi in Tiananmen Square, symbolically next to that of Mao. 'In a moment of wishful thinking', the political philosopher Daniel A. Bell, who teaches at Beijing's Tsinghua University, mused, 'I once speculated that the Chinese Communist Party might rename itself the Chinese Confucian Party in the next decade or two . . . My prediction, it seems, has been vindicated by events – sooner than anticipated.'[7]

Alongside the government's new-found admiration for Kongzi, there has emerged a new cadre of Confucian academics. Many work independently of the state, and many have found themselves at times in conflict with the state. Nevertheless, the academic renovation of Confucianism and the state's embrace of Kongzi have become closely intertwined.

Perhaps the most important of the new generation of Confucian philosophers is Jiang Qing. Born in 1953, Jiang was initially drawn to Marxism. As an undergraduate student, he wrote a thesis called *Return to Marx* criticizing the Chinese Communist Party for having abandoned the humanitarian essence of Marx's early works. It became an underground sensation, and brought him to the notice of the authorities, who did not take too kindly to the criticism. Eventually Jiang found his way, via existentialism and Buddhism, to Confucianism. Both existentialism and Buddhism, he argued, provided moral guidance for the individual but had little to say about the morality of the collective or about national politics. Only Confucianism was able to address such wider issues. In 2001 Jiang quit his academic post and established a Confucian seminary in the remote mountains of Guizhou in southern China.

The starting point for Jiang's renewal of Confucianism is a critique of New Confucianism, the ideological renovation upon which philosophers such as Fung Yu Lan and Mou Zongsan had embarked in the early twentieth century. The New Confucianists, Jiang claims, had become bedazzled by 'Mr Democracy and Ms Science'. Neither the scientific outlook nor the beliefs of liberal democracy, he claims, are compatible with Confucianism or with Chinese culture. An addiction to democracy and science has, in Jiang's eyes, led New Confucianists to abandon Kong's original principles, becoming instead, like Buddhists, obsessed with individual moral development. The fixation on self-cultivation has undermined the family and the community, and led to the abandonment of ritual, and created a blind spot about history and tradition.

Democracy, for Jiang, is 'flawed as an ideal'. Placing too much importance on the will of the people has, in the West, led to 'extreme secularization, contractualism, utilitarianism, selfishness, commercialism, capitalization, vulgarization, hedonism . . . and lack of morality'. 'The political problem of today's world', Jiang insists, is not a lack of democracy but that 'democracy itself presents a serious problem'.[8] The trouble with Western-style democracy is that it rests upon a single source of legitimacy – popular will. Since humans are by nature irrational and selfish, popular will often descends into immorality. Civil legitimacy alone is insufficient to build a moral social order. Nor can such an order be built on the Western concept of 'equality'. Since people are by nature unequal, differing in virtue, intelligence, ability and knowledge, so the idea of equal rights, irrespective of an individual's moral standing, makes little sense.

A Confucian system, Jiang insists, must be based on the traditional concept that 'The sovereign rules through the heaven, the earth, and the people'. Popular will must always be balanced by sagely wisdom. Historically, governance in China rested on three sources: 'the legitimacy of heaven (a sacred, transcendent sense of natural morality), the legitimacy of earth (wisdom from history and culture) and the legitimacy of the human (political obedience through popular will)'.[9] To recreate such a system in the modern world, Jiang suggests the establishment of a 'tricameral legislature'. This would comprise 'a House of Exemplary Persons that represents sacred legitimacy; a House of the Nation that represents historical and cultural legitimacy; and a House of the People that represents popular legitimacy'. Members of the House of Exemplary Persons would be 'nominated by scholars and examined on their knowledge of Confucian classics'. The House of the Nation would comprise 'descendants of great sages and rulers, along with representatives of China's major religions'; it would be led by a 'direct descendant of Confucius'. Members of the House of the People would be 'elected either by popular vote or as heads of occupational groups'.[10]

There might seem something quite bizarre about Jiang's proposals. Why, after all, should a 'direct descendant of Confucius' have a privileged political role? And why, in the twenty-first century, should 'knowledge of Confucian classics' be the sole criterion for being thought of as politically exemplary? Jiang has, nevertheless, become perhaps the most influential contemporary philosopher in China and has gained considerable support both from within the Chinese Communist Party and from Western intellectuals who themselves have become tired of democracy. Jiang and Bell wrote a joint op-ed in the *New York Times* in 2012 setting out the case for such a political structure, showing how seriously these proposals are now taken in certain quarters.[11] It is not out of the question that some version of Jiang's tricameral proposal may be realized.

At the heart of Jiang's ethics is what the political philosopher Christopher Ford calls 'meritoligarchic' thinking, by which he means 'the conviction by some members of a cultural and intellectual elite that they are ideally suited to rule benevolently over ignorant and uneducated masses who should not be trusted with the ability to choose and change their rulers'. Such ideas tend 'to pop up whenever a ruling elite faces pressure to give more political power to the masses', as, for instance, in the debates in Britain and America in the nineteenth century over the extension of the franchise.[12] In the ancient world there was something progressive about the meritoligarchic idea, because it stood in opposition to rule by bloodline. In the modern world, it is regressive because it stands in opposition not to aristocracy but to democracy.

4

'With the rise of China', Martin Jacques has written, 'Western universalism will cease to be universal – and its values and outlook will become steadily less influential. The emergence of China as a global power in effect relativizes everything.'[13] The transformation of China into an economic superpower raises important and challenging questions about how we perceive the world. Our understanding of history and culture will unquestionably change. The Era of the Warring States may come to be seen to be as significant as the

Peloponnesian War, or 1911, the end of the dynastic era, as important a date as 1789, and the fall of the French monarchy. Kongzi, Mo Tzu and Zhu Xi may become as well known as Plato, Aristotle and Aquinas. Lu Xun could be regarded as fine a writer as James Joyce.

But what of our understanding of morality? To what extent will the rise of China and the decline of Europe and America transform the way we understand moral values? Will universalism be seen merely as a form of Western particularism? Will 'everything be relativized'?

The story of this book is the story of how the centre of gravity of moral thinking has historically shifted. In the ancient world, Greece, Israel, Persia, India and China were all sources of civilization and of distinctive moral philosophies. The concepts that developed at each source were shaped by the particularities of the local culture and social needs; there were, nevertheless, also common themes that spanned continents, from the idea of virtue to the Golden Rule. The rise of monotheism, and in particular of Christianity, transformed the discussion of ethics in Europe, establishing the idea of rule-based morality, guided and anchored by a divine intelligence, and developing ideas of universalism. The emergence of Islam at the end of the first millennium CE, and its expansion through the beginning of the second, created a new centre of intellectual gravity. Drawing upon the heritage of Greece, Persia and India, as well as the Judaic and Christian traditions, the Islamic Empire came to be a bridge both between the ancient world and early modernity and between East and West. The only empire that in its day could challenge the philosophical and technological supremacy of the Islamic Empire was China, where the arrival of Buddhism from India triggered a renaissance in Confucian thinking. What we can see in this history is not moral progress, in the sense that we can witness scientific or technological progress, but the maturing, development and deepening of moral philosophy.

In the first two millennia, the millennia either side of the birth of Christ, the development of moral thought ranged across the world. In the second millennium, however, it became increasingly focused upon the West. There have certainly been major moral thinkers from outside Europe and America in the second millennium, some of whom have been discussed in this book, from Zhu Xi to Ibn Rushd, from Anton Wilhelm Amo to Sarvepalli Radhakrishnan, from Frantz Fanon to Fung Yu Lan. Nevertheless, the key thinkers, ideas and movements came primarily from the West, which is why the second half of this book does not hop across the globe as the first half does.

In part, Western influence on moral development reflected the economic and political power of the West. Not only was Europe (and later America) at the heart of philosophical, cultural and scientific progress, but colonialism, imperialism and globalization spread these ideas worldwide and forced all other intellectual traditions to be understood against the background of Western thought. As the great student of Indian philosophy Wilhelm Halbfass writes, Europe 'brought about the historical situation within which India and Europe came to face each other . . . to speak and listen to one another'. As a result, 'even in their rejection of, or their self-affirmation against, European ideas and orientations, modern Indian thinkers are not free from such ideas. Explicit or implicit reference to the West, and membership in a Westernized world, is an irreversible premise of modern Indian thought.'[14]

For some contemporary thinkers it is *only* because of Western power that Western ideas have lodged in the global imagination. Over the past three decades, postcolonial theory has made the link between the physical subjugation of the Third World through colonialism and the intellectual subordination of non-Western ideas, history and values. Just as Western politicians and generals annex foreign lands, postcolonial theorists argue, so Western intellectuals impose their knowledge upon the rest of the world. Western thought, the historian Robert Young believes, 'articulates a philosophical structure which uncannily simulates the project of nineteenth-century imperialism'. Western knowledge 'mimics . . . the geographic and economic absorption of the non-European world by the West'.[15]

It is, however, implausible to imagine the ascendency of Western philosophy as the result of nothing more than naked power. Ideas themselves possess power. Darwin's theory of evolution, Locke's concept of liberty, Kant's categorical imperative, Marx's critique of capitalism – such ideas caught the global imagination not simply because they could hitch a ride on the back of empire but also because they provided a persuasive explanation about how the natural world might work, or because they addressed urgent social or political needs. Consider the concept of universalism. This was not the product of Western imperialism. Its origins lie in the ancient world, elements to be found in Stoicism, Buddhism and Mohism. Greek notions of universalism and cosmopolitanism became filtered through Christianity and Islam before becoming secularized in the Enlightenment. What made Enlightenment universalism different was not simply the intellectual content (though the concept became transformed through the seventeenth and eighteenth centuries) but also the social context. In the ancient world universalism could be nothing more than a dream or a desire because social constraints precluded the possibility of realizing it. Modernity brought with it the possibility of breaking such constraints.

The intellectual, economic, social and political revolutions that swept through Europe from the seventeenth century onwards laid the foundations for the soaring power of a handful of European nations. They made possible a new kind of empire with unprecedented global reach. They created also the intellectual and social mechanisms for challenging that power and that empire, conjuring up new kinds of collectives, new forms of collective action, and new moral and political ideals, such as those of liberty, equality, democracy and rights. Or, to put it another way, what made Enlightenment ideas truly universal was that they became weapons in the hands of those who fought Western imperialism, as Toussaint L'Ouverture and many others recognized. The ideals of liberty, equality, democracy and rights are not specific to the West. They were applicable to Haitians, to Indians and to South Africans. They are, today, applicable to the Chinese.

It is true that philosophers such as Jiang Qing and many of his supporters in the West suggest that China's specific history and culture require that it tread its own path to modernity. The Chinese, Martin Jacques insists, 'live in and through their history, however distant it may be, to a degree which is quite different from other societies'.[16] China is not a nation state but a 'civilization state'. The distinctiveness of Chinese culture and history, Jacques argues, has afforded it a distinctive set of ideals and it cannot be expected either to adopt 'Western values' or to follow the 'Western path' to modernity.

These are not new arguments. They ironically echo ones heard in Europe two centuries ago as Romantics and conservatives railed against the revolutionary aims of Enlightenment *philosophes*. The German Romantic philosopher Johann Gottfried von Herder insisted that what made each people or nation unique was its culture: the language, literature, history and modes of living that expressed the unchanging spirit of a people. The values, beliefs and histories of different peoples were incommensurate, each culture authentic in its own terms, each adapted to its local environment. 'Let us follow our own path,' Herder beseeched, 'let men speak of our nation, our literature, our language: they are ours, they are ourselves, let that be enough.'[17]

Herder was no conservative. Critical he may have been of many Enlightenment beliefs, but at the heart of Herder's philosophy remained a deep-seated belief in equality and in universal human capacities. Not so for the conservatives, such as Edmund Burke or Joseph de Maistre, who used arguments about cultural authenticity and difference to make a case against democracy and equality, to defend tradition and hierarchy, and to demonize the racial Other.

It is, in other words, not the specialness of Chinese civilization that leads Jiang and Jacques to suggest that it should reject universalist ideas, or that such ideas are merely European. Rather, the idea that a particular culture or civilization is special has historically been used to challenge universalist claims, including in Europe.

Romantic ideas of cultural distinctiveness have recently been recycled through the 'clash of civilizations' thesis. First coined by the historian Bernard Lewis, the idea was popularized in the 1990s by the American political scientist Samuel Huntington. The conflicts that had convulsed Europe over the past centuries, Huntington wrote, from the wars of religion between Protestants and Catholics to the Cold War, were all 'conflicts within Western civilization'. The 'battle lines of the future', on the other hand, would be *between* civilizations. Such struggles would be 'far more fundamental' than any war unleashed by 'differences among political ideologies and political regimes'. The 'people of different civilizations have different views on the relations between God and man, the individual and the group, the citizen and the state, parents and children, husband and wife, as well as differing views of the relative importance of rights and responsibilities, liberty and authority, equality and hierarchy'. Huntington identified a number of distinct civilizations, including Confucian, Japanese, Buddhist, Hindu, Orthodox, Latin

American and African. The primary struggle would, he thought, be between the Christian West and the Islamic East.[18] It is, indeed, as part of the 'war on terror' that the thesis has primarily been deployed over the past decade. But, as the arguments of Jiang and Jacques show, it may soon become a key theme in discussions about China.

Civilizations, however, are not self-enclosed entities. They are 'civilizations' precisely because they are porous, fluid, open to wider influences. There are no historically transcendent civilizational values. What today we describe as 'Western' values would leave Aquinas and Dante bewildered, and even more so Augustine and Plato. On the other hand, Aquinas and Dante would have understood the Islamic values of Ibn Sina or Ibn Rushd. They would probably have understood the values of Kongzi better than they would those of Bentham or Mill, Nietzsche or Sartre, Dewey or Moore. It is equally questionable whether Kong would recognize his philosophy in the Neo-Confucianism of Zhu Xi, the New Confucianism of Fung Yu Lan, or even the return to 'authentic' Confucian thought of Jiang Qing. In any case, Chinese moral philosophy is not synonymous with Confucianism. Certainly, Confucianism has dominated the public sphere and has been indispensable in securing social order. But there have been many other philosophies that have also shaped Chinese culture – Mohism, Daoism and Buddhism to name but three. Equally, there are a number of Western conservative, communitarian, even radical traditions that accept, in part or in whole, Jiang's critique of democracy, his excoriation of rampant individualism, his desire to restore the ethical importance of the community.

The real conflict is not between the ideas of Europe and those of China. It is between those philosophies, some of which have developed in Europe, some in China, that view human flourishing in more universalist terms, and those, again that are present in both European and Chinese traditions, that understand it in a narrower, more parochial way.

One of the key problems in contemporary discussions of the 'war on terror' has been the view, held by both jihadis and by many in the West, that what we are witnessing is a global struggle between the West and Islam, a clash of civilizations between two monolithic blocs. The consequence has been, on both sides, a demonization of the Other. We should be wary of a similar polarization in the discussions about the relationship between China and the West. The rise of China as a world power will inevitably unsettle the debate about morality. But it will not simply set up a clash of civilizations between the ideals of China and those of the West – unless we choose to frame it so.

CHAPTER TWENTY

The Fall of Man

1

> We shall not cease from exploration
> And the end of all our exploring
> Will be to arrive where we started
> And know the place for the first time.

T.S. Eliot's oft-quoted lines from *Little Gidding* seem an apt epigram with which to end an exploration of the history of moral thought. This book has not simply told the story of the quest for the moral compass. It has also tried to use that story to comprehend what morality is, and how it fits into our lives. And in so doing it has, perhaps paradoxically, questioned implicitly the very idea of the compass as a metaphor for moral exploration.

Ethics, as Alasdair MacIntyre has observed, can have meaning only if we are able to draw a distinction between 'man-as-he-happens-to-be' and 'man-as-he-could-be'.[1] Morality is like a map guiding us from the former condition to the latter. It is, however, a most unusual kind of map. Most maps help you locate the starting point of the journey and the destination, and pinpoint the routes that could take you from the one to the other. Not so morality. On the moral map the starting point, the destination and the route are all created during the journey itself. 'Man-as-he-happens-to-be' is not a given. The understanding of what it is to be human, of human nature, has changed over time. And it has changed as the vision of 'man-as-he-could-be' has also transformed. The significant turning points in the history of morality are key moments of social change. They are also moments that express decisive shifts in the story of how we have come to understand what it is to be human.

In the ancient world fate was seen as a social reality and there was no evading it. Whether in the *Iliad* or the *Vedas*, human life was defined by the inevitability of death, the universality of sorrow and suffering, the tragedy of being answerable for one's actions and yet imprisoned by fate. Morality, especially for the Greeks, helped impose order upon an unpredictable world, and carved out dignity and honour within it.

From the sixth century BCE, as the heroic world gave way to more settled, productive and innovative societies, whether in Greece, India or China, so the idea of human dignity acquired new meaning. For Socrates and Buddha, Kongzi and Mo Tzu, the starting point of moral discussion was the idea of humans as rational beings; all, to a greater or lesser degree, looked to reason as a means of finding answers in a world constrained by fate, an argument taken furthest in the ancient world by Aristotle.

Monotheism transformed the vision of human nature and the character of moral thinking. All three monotheistic faiths developed during times of great social dislocation, each fashioned in such circumstances a distinct kind of moral anchor. There was a new reason to be moral: because God, all-seeing, all-knowing, loving yet wrathful, requires it of you. Monotheism made humans both greater and lesser than they had been before. They had been created by God in His image. Yet they were now seen as weak, corrupt, flawed and broken; reason had become subservient to faith.

The emergence of the modern world, from about the sixteenth century onwards, brought major changes that transformed the language of morality. The idea that morality should be invested in God became less plausible. Traditional communities disintegrated. Social structures were no longer given but became debated politically and challenged physically. The concept of individual autonomy became far more important. These changes were all intimately linked. The dissolution of traditional communities unleashed new political and moral conflicts. Those conflicts were an expression of the new sense of agency, of the new belief in the possibility of humanly willed social change. The growing belief that humans could, on their own account, transform society and establish standards of right and wrong helped encourage disbelief in God. The political challenge to the old social order helped further disintegrate traditional communities. The emergence of autonomy was not, as critics such as MacIntyre claim, merely an expression of individual desire. It was a manifestation, too, of the collective desire for political and social change, and of the possibility, for the first time in history, of such change.

2

'Man's final conquest has proved to be the abolition of Man.' So wrote the Christian philosopher C.S. Lewis in a book that is now largely forgotten but was once highly influential (the US magazine *National Review* placed it in the top ten of the '100 Best Non-Fiction Books of the 20th Century'[2]). Published in 1943, *The Abolition of Man* excoriates modernity for imagining that humans can create their own values. 'There never has been, and never will be,' Lewis insisted, 'a radically new judgement of value in the history of the world . . . The human mind has no more power of inventing a new value than of imagining a new primary colour, or, indeed, of creating a new sun and a new sky for it to move into.'[3] To deny that there were objective values in a transcendental sense was to deny civilized life itself.

Common to all ancient religions and philosophies was, Lewis claimed, 'the doctrine of objective value, the belief that certain attitudes are really true, and others are really false'. It is a belief to be found in 'Platonic, Aristotelian, Stoic, Christian and Oriental [philosophies] alike'. All believed in a 'reality beyond all predicates', which Lewis, bizarrely, calls the 'Tao', though others 'may call [it] Natural Law'. The Tao is 'the sole source of all value judgements. If it is rejected, all value is rejected.' In the modern world morality has been replaced by ideology. All ideologies 'consist of the fragments of the Tao itself, arbitrarily wrenched from their context in the whole, and then swollen to madness in their isolation'. The 'rebellion of the new ideologies against the Tao' is, Lewis suggests, 'a rebellion of the branches against the tree'. Were the rebels to succeed, 'they would find that they had destroyed themselves'.[4] The echo of Anscombe and Bradley, Dostoevsky and MacIntyre, is unmistakable.

The insistence that 'there never has been, and never will be, a radically new judgement of value in the history of the world' flies, of course, in the face of the history of moral thought. That history is the story of the crafting of new norms, and of the remaking of old ones. Nor is the question of whether morality is objective or subjective merely a modern conundrum. It is a question that has always troubled, and divided, moral thinkers. Some ancient traditions, from pantheistic Hinduism to monotheistic Christianity, and thinkers from Plato to al-Ghazali, saw moral rules as transcendentally fixed. Other traditions took a more relativistic view. Ironically, Daoism, which Lewis takes to be the model of objective moral thinking, was possibly the most relativistic of all. Many thinkers, Kongzi, Buddha and Aristotle among them, adopted an ambiguous stance, marrying elements of both.

If the claim that humans have never created new moral concepts is unsustainable, equally so is the insistence that without God (or some kind of transcendent realm), it is not possible to establish a proper ethical framework. It is not simply from the standpoint of twenty-first-century atheism that one can question this claim. For more than two millennia, Chinese society rested upon a strong ethical framework created by Confucianism, a philosophy that denied the need for God. Buddhism, too, has been able to establish a strong moral code without leaning upon a deity. Lewis may discuss 'Oriental philosophies' and celebrate the Tao. Yet only from the blinkered perspective of Western monotheism could one suggest that without God there could be no morality.

Nor does faith in God relieve believers of the necessity to think for themselves about what is right and wrong. In the past, Europeans burnt thousands of witches and enslaved millions of people, claiming that God had sanctified such practices. Today few believe this. It is not that God has changed His mind but that humans have. As societies transform so do moral values; that is the story of this book. Jews and Christians interpret the Bible differently today than they did a millennium, or two millennia, ago. To 'interpret the Bible differently' means to bring to their reading of the Bible a different moral framework. Even today, some Christians, reading passages in Leviticus and in Paul's Epistles, think that the Bible justifies the execution of gays. Others, reading the same words differently, insist that practising homosexuals are committing no sin at all. Each reads the Bible in a way that allows them to fit it into their own moral universe, a universe that necessarily exists independently of the Bible, and allows every believer to interpret their Holy Book.

The same is true of Muslims. Jihadi literalists, 'bridge builders' such as Tariq Ramadan and liberals such as Irshad Manji, all read the same Qur'an. Each brings to their reading already formed moral views about women's rights, homosexuality, abortion, apostasy, just war, free speech, criminal punishments, and much else. Each finds in the Qur'an values that justify that particular moral framework.

Belief in God, in other words, does not obviate the need for every believer to make up their own minds about what is right and what is wrong, independently of the Holy Books. There is no getting away from the Euthyphro dilemma.

3

What modernity brought was not the destruction of morality, as C.S. Lewis imagines, but rather a distinctive way of thinking about it. As new possibilities of social transformation were opened up, as people rejected the idea of society as a given, so *ought* became a political, as much as a moral, demand. People asked themselves not simply 'What moral claims are rational given the social structure?', but also 'What social structures are rational?' What kind of society, what types of social institutions, what forms of social relations, will best allow human beings to flourish?

The capacity to ask and to answer such questions has been nourished by two kinds of development. The first has been the creation of new forms of social conversation. Political and moral debate moved out from the confines of a small elite and became central to the very functioning of societies. From the printing press to the mass media, from political parties to social networking, a range of mechanisms has helped transform the constituency that is able to engage in such debates and the kinds of debate in which it can engage. At the same time, new tools have been fashioned, from the democratic process to revolutionary movements, from labour strikes to national liberation struggles, to enable people to act upon those social conversations to remake social conditions, to try to lever the world from the way it was to the way it should be.

These two developments helped take moral claims beyond the subjective and the relative. The new kinds of social conversations flourished not just within societies but between societies too. They became more universal, detached from specific social structures. At the same time, the mechanisms of social transformation enhanced the universalist possibilities inherent in the new social conversations. Social change had meaning beyond the boundaries of a particular community or society. The idea of democracy had universal significance. The reverberations of the French Revolution were felt throughout Europe and, indeed, well beyond Europe. A protest movement in Tunisia helped provoke the 'Arab Spring' throughout North Africa and the Middle East.

Questions of morality do not have objective answers in the way that scientific questions do, but neither are they merely expressions of subjective desire or taste. To say that torture is wrong or truthfulness is good is qualitatively different from saying that light travels at 299,792,458 metres per second or that DNA is a double helix. It is also qualitatively different from saying that ice cream is good or Barry Manilow execrable. As I suggested when discussing emotivism and nihilism, if everyone thinks that ice cream is bad or Barry Manilow good, I might privately despair. But if everyone were to believe that truthfulness is bad and torture good, that would damage all our lives in a fundamental way. There would be a tear in the very fabric of society. Moral questions may not have objective answers but they do have rational ones, answers rooted in a rationality that emerges out of social need. To bring reason to bear upon social relations, to define a rational answer to a moral question, requires social engagement and collective action. It is the breakdown over the past century of such engagement and such action that has proved so devastating for moral thinking.

The real problem, in other words, is not the 'Abolition of Man' but what we might call, using the language of C.S. Lewis, the 'Fall of Man'. The death of God only made sense against the background of a new kind of faith: faith in humans being capable of acting rationally and morally without guidance from beyond. It was that faith that drove Enlightenment humanism and the optimism of the eighteenth and nineteenth centuries. By the end of the nineteenth century that faith, too, had begun to be eaten away. The history of the twentieth century – two world wars, the Depression and the Holocaust, Auschwitz and the gulags, climate change and ethnic cleansing – helped further gnaw away at Enlightenment hope. We no longer believe, as Canadian scholar and politician Michael Ignatieff has observed, that 'material progress entails or enables moral progress'. We eat well, we drink well, we live well, Ignatieff observed, 'but we do not have good dreams'.[5]

The history of the twentieth century, the anthropologist Rob Foley observes, has transformed our vision of humanity, leading to 'a loss of confidence in the extent to which humans could be said to be on a pedestal above the swamp of animal brutishness':

> The camps of Dachau and Belsen, the millions killed in religious wars, the extent of poverty, famine and disease, and the almost boundless capacity of humans to do damage to each other at national and personal levels have, in the twentieth century, rather dented human self-esteem.

The Victorians believed that humans were closer to angels than to apes. During the course of the twentieth century, however, Foley notes, 'apes have become more angelic' while humans have become 'more apish'. 'Where it was originally thought that humans were the advanced and progressive form of life and other animals the more primitive,' Foley concludes, 'now it may be argued that the animal within us is our noble side, and humanity or civilization the blacker side – a complete reversal of the original Victorian image.'[6]

The quest for a moral compass has been a historical journey not simply to find answers to questions of right and wrong, good and bad, but also to understand what it is to be human, what humans should be, and the relationship between the two. The 'Fall of Man', the loss of faith in the human capacity to act rationally and morally, and collectively to transform the world, has narrowed the conception of what humans could be, confined our notion of what we are and eroded the link between the two. The result is a polarization of the moral debate between those who insist that morality is nothing more than individual preference and those who desperately search for some external agent or realm in which to fix the objectivity of values, whether that be God or science, nature or the transcendent. The real problem with contemporary morality, the reason it appears fractious and fractured, is, paradoxically, not moral but social.

4

'Man should not ask what the meaning of his life is,' Viktor Frankl wrote, 'but rather must recognize that it is he who is asked.' Published in 1946, three years after *The Abolition of Man*, Frankl's *Man's Search for Meaning* presents a strikingly different vision of the human condition, and of morality. Frankl had spent three years incarcerated in German concentration camps, including six months in Auschwitz. *Man's Search for Meaning* is a meditation on that experience, a reflection on the ability of human beings to survive even the most degrading and tormenting of circumstances.

'This is a profoundly religious book', suggests Rabbi Harold Kushner in the foreword to the second edition. In one sense it is. 'We have come to know Man as he really is,' wrote Frankl at the very end of his book. 'After all, man is that being who invented the gas chambers of Auschwitz; however, he is also that being who entered those gas chambers upright, with the Lord's Prayer or the *Shema Yisrael* on his lips.' It is, however, a strikingly different kind of faith to that of Lewis. Frankl's book is a hymn not to a transcendent deity but to the human spirit. Humans, he suggests, find themselves only through creating meaning in the world. But meaning is not something to be discovered. It is something that humans, and only humans, create. They do so by acting upon the world. 'Man is ultimately self-determining,' Frankl wrote. 'Man does not simply exist but always decides what his existence will be.'[7]

Frankl was reflecting on individuals, and their capacity to survive even the darkest of horrors. His understanding of humans as creators of value and as makers of meaning applies equally to humans as a collective. It is only through others that we find our individuality, and it is only through others that we come to appreciate the meaning of values and the value of meaning.

'Man-as-he-happens-to-be' embodies an understanding not simply of what it is to be human, but also of the tools we possess to transform ourselves. The understanding of what it is to be human only makes sense in light of our conception of the kind of beings we want to be and of the kind of world in which we want to live. It is in the relationship between 'man-as-he-happens-to-be' and 'man-as-he-could-be' that we come to discover the why and the how of morality.

It is comforting to imagine that notions of right and wrong, good and bad, come predefined by some external authority, that there already exists a moral map, and that our job is merely to work out how to navigate it, to find our way to the given moral north. It is comforting because such a belief protects us from the responsibility, even terror, of truly having to make moral choices; choice becomes reduced to accepting or rejecting that which is already decided. Once we required such comfort because human societies were not sufficiently developed for us to imagine how we could create our own moral maps. Today we require such comfort because we have lost faith in our ability to be moral cartographers, leading many to recoil at the very thought of humans as moral map makers.

The human condition is, however, that of possessing no moral safety net. No God, no scientific law, nor yet any amount of ethical concrete, can protect us from the dangers of falling off the moral tightrope that we are condemned to walk as human beings. It can be a highly disconcerting prospect. Or it can be a highly exhilarating one. The choice is ours.

Notes

Chapter One

1 *Iliad*, 1: 1–6
2 *Iliad*, 1: 503–27; 3: 379–81; 4: 39–41
3 *Iliad*, 3: 360–440
4 Blakemore, *Mind Machine*, pp. 269–71
5 *Iliad*, 1: 199–221
6 *Iliad*, 19: 71–109
7 Olson, *World on Paper*, p. 238
8 Gottlieb, *Dream of Reason*, p. 3
9 Cicero, *Tusculan Disputations*, V.IV.10–11
10 Waterfield, *First Philosophers*, pp. 17–18 T29; 6, T22; 125, F10
11 Ondaatje, *The English Patient*, p. 126
12 *First Philosophers*, p. 14 T15
13 Sansone, *Ancient Greek Civilization*, p. 113

Chapter Two

1 Gottlieb, *Dream of Reason*, p. 150
2 Cicero, *Tusculan Disputations*, V.IV.10–11
3 Plato, *Cratyus*, 386c in *Complete Works*

4 Plato, *Euthyphro*, 5a in *Complete Works*
5 Gottlieb, *Dream of Reason*, p.151
6 *Dream of Reason*, p.176
7 Plato, *Republic*, 336b, 336b, 338c, 336b, 338c, 344b,c in *Complete Works*; all other quotes from *The Republic* are from this edition.
8 *Republic*, 435b,c
9 *Republic*, 431d
10 *Republic*, 563d,e, 579e
11 *Republic*, 589e
12 *Republic*, 515c
13 *Republic*, 517a

Chapter Three

1 Aristotle, *Ethics*, I.i.1094a1–3
2 *Ethics*, I.i.1094a 18–24
3 *Ethics*, I.iv.1095a 20
4 *Ethics*, I.v.1095b 35–1096a 2
5 Plato, *Gorgias*, 474b, 475c
6 *Ethics*, I.iv.1096a 1, I.vi.1096a 23–9
7 *Ethics*, II.ii.1104a 11–25
8 Russell, *History of Western Philosophy*, p. 168
9 *Ethics*, II.vi.1106a 28–33
10 *Ethics*, II.ix.1109a 27–9
11 *Ethics*, IV.ii.1122b 27; *Politics*, VI1.ix.1328b 36–8
12 *Politics*, 1.ii.1253a 19; 1.ii.1253a 23; V1.i.1337a 27–30; *Ethics*, I.ii.1094b 6–10
13 *Ethics*, X.ix.1180a 5; X.ix.1180b 29
14 *Ethics*, II.i.1103b 4
15 *Politics*, III.vi.1279a 17–20; III.vii. 1279a 32–35; III.vii.1279b 6–7
16 *Politics*, IV.xi.1295b 7–8; IV.xi.1295b 40
17 *Politics*, II.ii.1261b6

18 Russell, *History of Western Philosophy*, p. 102
19 Long and Sedley, *Hellenistic Philosophers*, vol. 1, p.155
20 Marcus Aurelius, *Meditations*, VII, 28
21 Long and Sedley, *Hellenistic Philosophers*, vol. 1, p.114
22 Russell, *History of Western Philosophy*, pp. 231–2
23 Long and Sedley, *Hellenistic Philosophers*, vol. 1, p. 389
24 Epictetus, *Enchiridion*, VIII
25 Murray, *Stoic Philosophy*, p. 47
26 Plutarch, 'On Stoic Self-Contradiction', in *Complete Works*, vol. 3 [http://ebooks.adelaide.edu.au/p/plutarch/essays/complete.html#chapter5]; Seneca, 'On Providence', in *Dialogues and Essays*, p.11
27 Plutarch, *Plutarch's Lives*, vol. 8, p. 407
28 Marx, 'The Eighteenth Brumaire of Louis Bonaparte' [http://www.marxists.org/archive/marx/works/1852/18th-brumaire/ch01.htm]
29 Epictetus, *Discourses*, bk 1, ch. 9

Chapter Four

1 Exodus 3:2, 3, 5, 6; all quotations from the Authorized King James Version of the Bible
2 Exodus 3:7, 10, 13
3 Genesis 12: 1–3
4 Exodus, 19:5, 21:5
5 Heschel, *The Prophets*, p. 5
6 Deuteronomy 7:2–5
7 Isaiah 55:8, 9
8 Leviticus 20:10; 18:22; 26:7; 26: 21–2; 19:18; 19:34
9 The Biblical scholar Richard Baukham takes a different view in his book *Jesus and the Eyewitnesses*
10 Matthew 5:21–2, 27–8, 38–9, 43–4
11 Matthew 6:2, 21, 24; 7:12
12 Eagleton, *Reason, Faith and Revolution*, p. 19

13 Lewis, *Mere Christianity*, pp. 51, 52
14 Ephesians 2:8
15 Acts 9:3–4
16 Hebrews 9:12–14
17 Colossians 1:24; Romans 1, 26, 24
18 Catechism of the Catholic Church, 403 [http://www.vatican.va/archive/ENG0015/_P1C.HTM]
19 Plotinus, *Enneads*, I.2.3
20 Augustine, *Confessions*, VIII: 29
21 *Confessions*, II: 4
22 McGrath, *Christian Theology*, p. 366
23 Augustine, *De Bono Coniugali*, 1: 27
24 Rees, *Letters of Pelagius and his Followers*, pp. 53–4
25 Long, *Christian Ethics*, p.1
26 Freeman, *Closing of the Western Mind*, p. 322; MacMullen, *Christianising the Roman Empire*, p. 32
27 Rist, *Augustine*, p. 213; Augustine, *City of God*, XIX:15
28 Augustine, *City of God*, XIX: 6
29 Rist, *Augustine*, p. 232
30 MacCulloch, *History of Christianity*, p. 297; Matthew 19:24; Salzman, *Making of a Christian Aristocracy*, p. 208

Chapter Five

1 Buitenen, *Mahabharata*; Narayan, *Ramayana*
2 Vidyalankar, *Holy Vedas*
3 Olivelle, *Upanisads*
4 Thapar, *From Lineage to State*, p.134
5 Jaspers, *Way to Wisdom*, p. 98
6 Rahula, *What the Buddha Taught*; Lopez, *Buddhist Scriptures*
7 Buddha, *Dīgha Nikāya; Majjhima Nikāya*
8 Conze, *Buddhism*, p. 7

Chapter Six

1 Fung, *Short History of Chinese Philosophy*, pp. 7, 12
2 Wu, *Fundamentals of Chinese Philosophy*, p. 11
3 Confucius, *Analects*, 15:24
4 *Analects*, 8:2
5 *Analects*, 12:11
6 *Analects*, 12:1, 17:23
7 *Short History of Chinese Philosophy*, p. 147
8 Mo Tzu, *Basic Writings* §III
9 *Short History of Chinese Philosophy*, p. 56
10 *Analects*, 7:1
11 Mo Tzu, *Basic Writings* §I
12 *Basic Writings* §I; Fung, *Short History of Chinese Philosophy*, p. 59
13 Fraser, 'Mohism'
14 Liu, 'Yesterday's Stray Dog Becomes Today's Guard Dog', in *No Enemies, No Hatred*, p. 194
15 Harré, *One Thousand Years of Philosophy*, p. 92
16 Billington, *Understanding Eastern Philosophy*, p. 72
17 *Understanding Eastern Philosophy*, p. 132
18 *Short History of Chinese Philosophy*, p. 301

Chapter Seven

1 Ling, *Muhammad*, p. 43
2 Qur'an, sura 96
3 Aslan, *No God but God*, p. 34
4 Holland, *In the Shadow of the Sword*
5 Qur'an, sura 104
6 Guillaume, *Life of Muhammad*, p. 464
7 Aslan, *No God but God*, p. 114

Chapter Eight

1 Ibn Tufail, *Hayy Ibn Yaqzan*, #16, #21
2 *Hayy Ibn Yaqzan*, #42
3 *Hayy Ibn Yaqzan*, #109, #110
4 Ibn Rushd, *On the Harmony of Religion and Philosophy*, p. 50
5 Most of the poems and quotes are taken from Nicholson, *Literary History of the Arabs*, pp. 316–22
6 Lapidus, 'State and Religion in Islamic Societies', pp. 3–27
7 Watt, *Faith and Practice of Al-Ghazali*, p. 59
8 Fakhry, *History of Islamic Philosophy*, p. 219
9 *History of Islamic Philosophy*, p.193
10 Zarruq, Istrabadi and Hanson, *The Principles of Sufism*

Chapter Nine

1 Bettenson and Maunder, *Documents of the Christian Church*, p. 6
2 Aquinas, *Summa Theologica*, I.II.2.8
3 *Summa Theologia*, I.II.94.2
4 *Summa Theologica*, II.II.23.28
5 *Summa Theologica*, I.II.62.1; I.II.63.2
6 *Summa Theologica*, I.II.91.4
7 *Divine Comedy*, *Inferno*, III: 1–9
8 Dante, *Divine Comedy*, *Inferno*, XXXIV, 53–4; XXXIV: 55–6
9 Auerbach, *Dante*, p. 88
10 *Divine Comedy*, *Purgatorio*, XVI: 67–72
11 *Divine Comedy*, *Purgatorio*, XVI: 103–5
12 *Divine Comedy*, *Purgatorio*, XVI: 106–11; 127–9

Chapter Ten

1 Cassirer, Kristeller and Randall, *The Renaissance Philosophy of Man*, p. 224
2 Janin, *University in Medieval Life*, p. 152
3 http://bookofconcord.org/heidelberg.php
4 Morrison, *Martin Luther*, p. 105
5 Luther, *Essential Martin Luther*, p. 161
6 Brecht, *Martin Luther*, vol. 1, p. 460
7 MacCulloch, *History of Christianity*, p. 614
8 Tarnas, *Passion of the Western Mind*, p. 239
9 Purkiss, *English Civil War*, p. 511
10 Lund, *Documents from the History of Lutheranism*, p. 44

Chapter Eleven

1 *Antigone*, 210–14, in Sophocles, *Three Theban Plays*
2 *Antigone*, 943, 962
3 Aristotle, *Politics*, VIII.i.1337a 27–30
4 Aquinas, *Summa Theologica*, I.II.91.4
5 Rorty, *Truth and Progress*, p. 113
6 Hobbes, *Leviathan*, ch. 13
7 *Leviathan*, ch. 14
8 *Leviathan*, ch. 13
9 Israel, *Radical Enlightenment*, p. 159
10 *Radical Enlightenment*, p. 172
11 Gay, *Enlightenment*, vol. 2, pp. 43–4
12 Kant, 'What is Enlightenment?'
13 *Radical Enlightenment*, p. vi
14 *Enlightenment*, vol. 2, p. 162
15 *Enlightenment*, vol. 2, p. 5, 3
16 Israel, *Enlightenment Contested*, pp. 551–2

Chapter Twelve

1 Hume, *Treatise of Human Nature*, III.I.II
2 Hume, 'A Kind of History of My Life', p. 348
3 *Treatise of Human Nature*, I.III.XIV
4 Russell, *History of Western Philosophy*, pp. 610-11
5 Norton (ed.), *Cambridge Companion to Hume*, p. 5
6 Hume, *Treatise of Human Nature*, II.III.III
7 *Treatise of Human Nature*, III.I.II
8 *Treatise of Human Nature*, III.II.I (italics in original)
9 Aristotle, *Politics*, 1.ii. 1253a 19; 1.ii.1253a 23
10 Mandeville, *Fable of the Bees*, p. xv
11 MacIntyre, *Short History of Ethics*, p. 157
12 Pagden, *The Enlightenment*, p. 58
13 Kant, *Critique of Pure Reason*, p. 92
14 Kant, *Groundwork of the Metaphysics of Morals*, p. 27
15 *Groundwork of the Metaphysics of Morals*, p. 26
16 *Groundwork of the Metaphysics of Morals*, p. 433
17 Bentham, *Introduction to the Principles of Morals and Legislation*, p. 1
18 Bentham, *Rationale of Reward*, p. 206
19 Scruton, *Short History of Modern Philosophy*, p. 222
20 The illustration and figures come from Kenny, *New History of Western Philosophy*, vol. 4, p. 369
21 *Short History of Modern Philosophy*, p. 225
22 Kenny, *New History of Western Philosophy*, vol. 4, p. 5
23 Mill, *Autobiography*, p. 150; *Utilitarianism*, pp. 258, 260
24 Payne, *Utilitarianism as Secondary Ethic*, p. 14

Chapter Thirteen

1 Hegel, 'Lectures on the Philosophy of History', §21
2 Marx and Engels, *Collected Works*, vol. 16, p. 474
3 *BusinessWeek*, 25 May 1998

4 Hegel, *Phenomenology of Spirit*, pp. 104–10
5 Rousseau, *Emile*, bk. IV
6 Rousseau, *First and Second Discourses*, p. 144
7 Lovejoy, 'The Supposed Primitivism of Rousseau's Discourse on Inequality', pp. 165–86
8 Israel, *Democratic Enlightenment*, p. 639
9 Rousseau, *Social Contract*, 3.4.8, 2.3.1
10 Bradley, *Ethical Studies*, p. 157
11 *Ethical Studies*, p. 157
12 O'Gorman, *Edmund Burke*, p. 53
13 Bradley, *Ethical Studies*, p. 167
14 Scruton, *Short History of Modern Philosophy*, p. 208
15 Marx and Engels, *Collected Works*, vol. 42, p. 1
16 Tucker, *Philosophy and Myth in Karl Marx*, p. 12
17 Trotsky, *Their Morals and Ours*, pp. 20–21
18 Eagleton, *On Evil*, pp.13–14
19 Marx, *Capital*, 1.III.7.I [http://www.marxists.org/archive/marx/works/1867-c1/ch07.htm]
20 Marx, *Economic and Philosophical Manuscripts of 1844* [http://www.marxists.org/archive/marx/works/1844/manuscripts/labour.htm]
21 Marx, *The German Ideology* [http://www.marxists.org/archive/marx/works/1845/german-ideology/ch03abs.htm]
22 Engels, *Condition of the Working Class in England* [http://www.marxists.org/archive/marx/works/1845/condition-working-class/ch04.htm]
23 *Capital*, 1.VII.25.IV [http://www.marxists.org/archive/marx/works/1867-c1/ch25.htm]
24 *Economic and Philosophical Manuscripts of 1844* [http://www.marxists.org/archive/marx/works/1844/manuscripts/labour.htm]
25 MacIntyre, *After Virtue*, p. 261
26 Marx, 'Theses on Feuerbach' §11 [http://marxists.anu.edu.au/archive/marx/works/1845/theses/index.htm]

Chapter Fourteen

1 Darrow, *Attorney for the Damned*, p. 70

2 David Gibson, 'Is Anders Breivik a "Christian Terrorist"?', Huffington Post (26 July 2011) [http://www.huffingtonpost.com/2011/07/26/anders-breivik-christian-terrorist_n_910379.html]; Jerry Newcombe, 'Norwegian Murderer not "Christian," but one of Nietzsche's "Blond Beasts of Prey"' [http://www.truthinaction.org/index.php/2011/07/norwegian-murderer-not-christian/]; 'Anders Breivik, post-modern Crusader' [http://theoptimisticconservative.wordpress.com/2011/07/25/anders-breivik-post-modern-crusader]; Chuck Colson, 'The Columbine Tapes' [http://www.breakpoint.org/commentaries/4758-the-columbine-tapes]

3 Nietzsche, *The Gay Science*, 3.108

4 Nietzsche, *Thus Spoke Zarathustra*, 2: Of Self Overcoming

5 Nietzsche, *Twilight of the Idols*, IV.2

6 *Twilight of the Idols*, IX.5

7 *The Gay Science*, 1.4

8 See, for instance, Burrow, *Crisis of Reason*

9 Nietzsche, *Beyond Good and Evil*, 1.1, 1.6, 1.5; *The Gay Science*, 3.265; *Genealogy of Morals*, III.12

10 *The Gay Science*, §373, §123

11 *Beyond Good and Evil*, I.4

12 Nietzsche, *Thus Spoke Zarathustra*, Prologue, §3

13 Nietzsche, *The Antichrist*, §2

14 Dostoevsky, *Crime and Punishment*, pp. 280, 279

15 *Thus Spoke Zarathustra*, Of Old and New Law-tables: 3.12.10; *Beyond Good and Evil*, 9.258

16 Lukács, *Destruction of Reason*, p. 340

17 Leiter, 'Nietzsche's Moral and Political Philosophy'

18 Nietzsche, *Ecce Homo*, Preface, §4

19 Pick, *Faces of Degeneration*, p. 60

20 See Malik, *The Meaning of Race*, esp. chs. 3 & 4

21 *Faces of Degeneration*, p. 20

22 *Ecce Homo*, 'Birth of Tragedy', §4; Knox, *The Races of Men*, pp. 268–9

23 Scruton, *Short History of Western Philosophy*, p. 187
24 Wolin, *Seduction of Unreason*, p. 58

Chapter Fifteen

1 Genesis 22: 1–3
2 Kierkegaard, *Journals and Papers*, 1 August 1835, I A 75
3 Kierkegaard, *Fear and Trembling/Repetition*, pp. 10–14
4 *Fear and Trembling/Repetition*, p. 55
5 Lévy, *Le Siècle de Sartre*
6 Sartre, 'Sartre on the Nobel Prize'
7 Sartre, *Existentialism and Humanism*, p. 27
8 *Existentialism and Humanism*, p. 28
9 Sartre, *Being and Nothingness*, p. 25
10 *Existentialism and Humanism*, p. 34
11 Kierkegaard, *The Concept of Anxiety*, p. 61
12 Camus, *Myth of Sysiphus*, pp. 28, 51
13 Marx, 'The eighteenth Brumaire of Louis Napoleon' [http://www.marxists.org/archive/marx/works/1852/18th-brumaire/ch01.htm]
14 Sartre, *Critique of Dialectical Reason*, p. 331
15 *Being and Nothingness*, p. 25

Chapter Sixteen

1 Césaire, *Toussaint Louverture*, p. 24
2 Blackburn, 'The French Revolution and New World Slavery', p. 89
3 Malik, *Meaning of Race*, p. 115
4 Roosevelt, *Winning of the West*, vol. 3, p. 28
5 Mishra, *From the Ruins of Empire*, Prologue
6 *The Times*, 12 September 1910
7 *From the Ruins of Empire*, Prologue
8 Hobsbawm, *Age of Revolution*, p. 35

9 James, 'Discovering Literature in Trinidad', *Spheres of Existence*, p. 238
10 James, 'The Making of the Caribbean People', *Spheres of Existence*, p. 179
11 *From the Ruins of Empire*, ch. 5
12 Césaire, *Discours sur le colonialism*, p. 82
13 Senghor, *African Socialism*, p. 74
14 Howe, *Afrocentrism*, p. 24
15 Fanon, *Black Skin, White Masks*, pp. 17–18
16 Howe, *Afrocentrism*; Mudimbe, *Invention of Africa*
17 Sartre, 'Preface', in Fanon, *Wretched of the Earth*, p. 22
18 Sartre, *Critique of Dialectical Reason*, vol. 1, *Theory of Practical Ensembles*, p. 752
19 *Invention of Africa*, p. 85
20 Stocking, *Race, Culture and Evolution*, p. 148
21 Benedict, 'Anthropology and the Abnormal', p. 73
22 Lukes, *Moral Relativism*, p. 25
23 Herodotus, *Histories*, 3.38
24 Burrow, *Evolution and Society*, p. 93; Pick, *Faces of Degeneration*, p. 57
25 Bookchin, *Re-Enchanting Humanity*, p. 1

Chapter Seventeen

1 Menand, *Metaphysical Club*, p. x, p. 439
2 Dewey, *Reconstruction in Philosophy and Essays*, p. 173
3 MacIntyre, *After Virtue*, p. 14
4 Warnock, *Ethics Since 1900*, pp. 1–2
5 Moore, *Principia Ethica*, I.6
6 Kenny, *New History of Western Philosophy*, vol, 4, p. 243
7 *Principia Ethica*, V.89
8 Ross, *Right and the Good*, p. 29
9 Russell, *On Ethics*, p. 138
10 Ayer, *Language, Truth and Logic*, p. 142
11 *Language, Truth and Logic*, p.143
12 Mackie, *Ethics: Inventing Right and Wrong*, p. 49
13 *Ethics: Inventing Right and Wrong*, p. 36

14 *After Virtue*, p. 32
15 *After Virtue*, p. 52
16 *After Virtue*, p. 250
17 *After Virtue*, pp. 201, 203
18 *After Virtue*, p. 221

Chapter Eighteen

1 Darwin, *Descent of Man*, pp. 71–2
2 *Descent of Man*, p.163
3 Spencer, *Data of Ethics*, Preface
4 *Data of Ethics*, III.8
5 *Data of Ethics*, Preface
6 Paradis and Williams, *Evolution and Ethics*, pp. 141, 138, 139–40
7 *Evolution and Ethics*, p. 138
8 Mead, *Blackberry Winter*, p. 222
9 Midgley, 'Gene-juggling'; Brown, *Darwin Wars*, p. 30
10 Hamilton, 'The evolution of altruistic behaviour' & 'The Genetical Basis of Social Behaviour (Parts 1 & 2)' in Hamilton, *Narrow Roads of Gene Land*; Trivers, 'The evolution of reciprocal altruism'
11 Pinker, *Blank Slate*, pp. 283, 287
12 Foot, 'The Problem of Abortion and the Doctrine of the Double Effect in Virtues and Vices'
13 Greene, 'From neural "is" to moral "ought"'
14 Greene, 'The Secret Joke of Kant's Soul'
15 Casebeer, 'Moral cognition and its neural constituents'; Greene, 'From neural "is" to moral "ought"'
16 Harris, *Moral Landscape*, pp.1–2, 4
17 *Moral Landscape*, p.15
18 Harris, 'In defense of torture'; *End of Faith*, pp. 192–9
19 *Evolution and Ethics*, p. 138

Chapter Nineteen

1 Lu Xun, *The Real Story of Ah-Q and Other Tales of China*, pp. 21–31
2 Brière, *Fifty Years of Chinese Philosophy*, p. 24
3 Wong, *China Transformed*, p.196
4 *Peking Review*, vol. 17, 6, 8 February 1974, pp. 7–12 [http://www.massline.org/PekingReview/PR1974/PR1974-06g.htm]
5 *China Transformed*, p.195
6 Jacques, *When China Rules the World*, ch. 7, loc. 4204
7 Bell, 'A Visit to a Confucian Academy'
8 Jiang, *A Confucian Constitutional Order*, p. 36
9 Jiang and Bell, 'A Confucian Constitution for China'
10 'A Confucian Constitution for China'
11 'A Confucian Constitution for China'
12 Ford, 'A State of Moral Confucian'
13 *When China Rules the World*, ch. 11, loc. 9200
14 Halbfass, *India and Europe*, p. 369
15 Young, *White Mythologies*, p. 3
16 *When China Rules the World*, ch. 7, loc. 4125
17 Berlin, *Vico and Herder*, p. 182
18 Huntington, 'The Clash of Civilizations'

Chapter Twenty

1 MacIntyre, *After Virtue*, p. 52
2 http://old.nationalreview.com/100best/100_books.html
3 Lewis, *Abolition of Man*, p. 43–4
4 *Abolition of Man*, pp. 18, 17, 43, 44
5 Ignatieff, 'Ascent of Man'
6 Foley, *Humans Before Humanity*, p. 39
7 Frankl, *Man's Search for Meaning*, pp. 133, 131

Bibliography

Aeschylus, *The Oresteian Trilogy* (Penguin, 1959)

Al-Ghazali, A.H.M., *The Incoherence of the Philosophers* (University of Chicago Press, 2002)

Al-Khalili, J., *Pathfinders: The Golden Age of Arabic Science* (Allen Lane, 2010)

Arendt, H., *Men in Dark Times* (Harcourt Brace, 1955)

Aristotle, *The Metaphysics* (Penguin, 1998)

Aristotle, *The Nicomachean Ethics* (Penguin, 1955)

Aristotle, *The Politics* (Penguin, 2000)

Arkush, D., and Lee, L.O. (eds.), *Land without Ghosts: Chinese Impressions of America from the Mid-Nineteenth Century to the Present* (University of California Press, 1993)

Aquinas, T., *Summa Contra Gentiles*, 5 vols. (University of Notre Dame Press, 1975)

Aquinas, T., *Summa Theologica*, 5 vols. (Hayes Barton, 2007)

Aslan, R., *No God but God: The Origins, Evolution and Future of Islam* (Heinemann, 2006)

Auerbach, E., *Dante: The Poet of the Secular World* (New York Review of Books, 2007)

Augustine, *Confessions* (Oxford University Press, 1991)

Augustine, *De Bono Coniugali, De Sancta Virginitate* (Clarendon Press, 2001)

Augustine, *The City of God Against the Pagans* (Cambridge University Press, 1998)

Ayer, A.J., *Language, Truth and Logic* (Pelican, 1971)

Baukham, R., *Jesus and the Eyewitnesses: The Gospels as Eyewitness Testimony* (William B. Eerdmans, 2008)

Bell, D.A., 'A Visit to a Confucian Academy', *Dissent*, 22 September 2008

Benedict, R., 'Anthropology and the Abnormal', *Journal of General Psychology*, 101 (1934)

Bentham, J., *Introduction to the Principles of Morals and Legislation* (Dover, 2009)

Bentham, J., *The Rationale of Reward* (Robert Heward, 1830)

Berlin, I., *Vico and Herder: Two Studies in the History of Ideas* (Hogarth Press, 1976)

Bettenson, H., and Maunder, C. (eds.), *Documents of the Christian Church* (Oxford University Press, 2011)

Billington, R., *Understanding Eastern Philosophy* (Routledge, 1997)

Blackburn, R., 'The French Revolution and New World Slavery' in Osborne (ed.), *Socialism and the Limits of Liberalism*

Blakemore, C., *The Mind Machine* (BBC Books, 1988)

Bookchin, M., *Re-Enchanting Humanity: A Defence of the Human Spirit Against Anti-Humanism, Misanthropy, Mysticism and Primitivism* (Cassell, 1995)

Bradley, F.H., *Ethical Studies* (Cambridge University Press, 2012)

Bradley, K.R., 'Seneca and Slavery', *Classica et Medievalia* 37 (1986)

Brecht, M., *Martin Luther*, 3 vols. (Augsburg Fortress, 1985–93)

Brenkert, G.C., *Marx's Ethics of Freedom* (Routledge & Kegan Paul, 1983)

Brière, O., *Fifty Years of Chinese Philosophy 1898–1950* (Allen & Unwin, 1956)

Brown, A., *The Darwin Wars: How Stupid Genes Became Selfish Gods* (Simon & Schuster, 1999)

Buddha, *Dīgha Nikāya: The Long Discourses of the Buddha* (Wisdom Publications, 1987)

Buddha, *Majjhima Nikāya: The Middle Length Discourses of the Buddha* (Wisdom Publications, 1995)

Buitenen, J.A.B. van, (ed), *The Mahabharata* (University of Chicago Press, 1980)

Burke, E., *Collected Works* (Rivington, 1815–27)

Burrow, J.W., *The Crisis of Reason: European Thought, 1848–1914* (Yale University Press, 2000)

Burrow, J.W., *Evolution and Society: A Study in Victorian Social Theory* (Cambridge University Press, 1966)

Camus, A., *The Myth of Sisyphus* (Vintage, 1991)

Casebeer, W.D. 'Moral cognition and its neural constituents', *Nature Reviews Neuroscience* 4 (2003)

Cassirer, E., Kristeller, P.O. and Randall, J.H., eds., *The Renaissance Philosophy of Man* (University of Chicago Press, 1948)

Césaire, A., *Discours sur le colonialism* (Présence Africaine, 2004)

Césaire, A., *Toussaint Louverture: La Révolution française et le problème colonial* (Présence Africaine, 1961)

Chan, W.T., *A Source Book in Chinese Philosophy* (Princeton University Press, 1963)

Cicero, *The Tusculan Disputations: Also Treatises on the Nature of Gods and on the Commonwealth* (Harper & Brothers, 1877) [http://www.gutenberg.org/files/14988/14988-h/14988-h.htm]

Cohen, P.A., *Discovering History in China: American Historical Writing on the Recent Chinese Past* (Columbia University Press, 1984)

Confucius, *The Analects* (Oxford University Press, 1993)

Conze, E., *Buddhism: A Short History* (Oneworld, 1993)

Dante, A., *The Divine Comedy* (Oxford University Press, 1981)

Darrow, C., *Attorney for the Damned: Clarence Darrow in the Courtroom* (University of Chicago Press, 2012)

Darwin, C., *The Descent of Man: And Selection in Relation to Sex* (Princeton University Press, 1981)

Dawkins, R., *The Selfish Gene* (Oxford University Press, 1976)

Descartes, R., *The Philosophical Works of Descartes*, 2 vols. (Cambridge University Press, 1931)

Dewey, J., *Reconstruction in Philosophy; The Middle Works 1899–1924*, vol. 12: *Reconstruction in Philosophy and Essays 1920* (Southern Illinois University Press, 1982)

Diogenes, L., *The Lives of Eminent Philosophers* (Loeb Classical Library, 1925) [http://en.wikisource.org/wiki/Lives_of_the_Eminent_Philosophers]

Dostoevsky, F., *Crime and Punishment* (Penguin, 2003)

Eagleton, T., *Reason, Faith and Revolution: Reflections on the God Debate* (Yale University Press, 2009)

Eagleton, T., *On Evil* (Yale University Press, 2010)

Engels, F., *The Condition of the Working Class in England* (Oxford World Classics, 2009)

Epictetus, *Enchiridion* (Prometheus Books, 1995)

Epictetus, *Discourses* [http://classics.mit.edu/Epictetus/discourses.1.one.html]

Fakhry, M., *A History of Islamic Philosophy* (Columbia University Press, 2004)

Fakhry, M., *Averroes: His Life, Works and Influence* (Oneworld, 2001)

Fanon, F., *Black Skin, White Masks* (Grove Press, 1994)

Fanon, F., *The Wretched of the Earth* (Penguin, 2001)

Farber, P.L., *The Temptations of Evolutionary Ethics* (University of California Press, 1994)

Foley, R., *Humans Before Humanity* (Blackwell, 1997)

Ford, C., 'A State of Moral Confucian', *New Paradigms Forum*, 13 July 2012 [http://www.newparadigmsforum.com/NPFtestsite/?p=1360]

Foot, P., 'The Problem of Abortion and the Doctrine of the Double Effect in Virtues and Vices', *Oxford Review* 5 (1967)

Frankl, V.E., *Man's Search for Meaning* (Rider, 2004)

Fraser, C., 'Mohism', in Zalta (ed.), *The Stanford Encyclopedia of Philosophy* [http://plato.stanford.edu/archives/fall2012/entries/mohism/]

Freeman, C., *The Closing of the Western Mind: The Rise of Faith and the Fall of Reason* (Pimlico, 2003)

Fung Yu Lan, *A Short History of Chinese Philosophy: A Systematic Account of Chinese Philosophy from its Origins to the Present Day* (Free Press, 1976)

Gay, P., *The Enlightenment: An Interpretation*, 2 vols. (Norton, 1996)

Gottlieb, A., *The Dream of Reason: A History of Philosophy from the Greeks to the Renaissance* (Penguin, 2000)

Greene, J.D., 'From neural "is" to moral "ought": what are the moral implications of neuroscientific moral psychology?', *Nature Reviews Neuroscience* 4 (2003)

Greene, J.D., 'The Secret Joke of Kant's Soul', in Sinnott-Armstrong (ed.), *Moral Psychology, vol 3: The Neuroscience of Morality*

Guillaume, A., *Life of Muhammad: A Translation of Ibn Ishaq's Sirat Rasul Allah* (Oxford University Press, 1979)

Halbfass, W., *India and Europe: An Essay in Understanding* (State University of New York Press, 1988)

Hamilton, W.D., *Narrow Roads of Gene Land, vol. 1: Evolution of Social Behaviour* (W.H. Freeman, 1996)

Harré, R., *One Thousand Years of Philosophy: From Ramanuja to Wittgenstein* (Blackwell, 2000)

Harris, S., *The Moral Landscape: How Science Can Determine Human Values* (Free Press, 2010)

Harris, S., *The End of Faith: Religion, Terror and the Future of Reason* (Free Press, 2005)

Harris, S., 'In defense of torture', Huffington Post, 17 October 2005 [http://www.huffingtonpost.com/sam-harris/in-defense-of-torture_b_8993.html]

Hebermann, C.G., Pace, E.A., Pallen, C.B., Shahan, T.J., and Wynne, J.J., (eds.), *Catholic Encyclopaedia* (Robert Appleton & Co, 1907–12) [http://www.catholiconline.org/encyclopedia/]

Hegel, G.W.F., *Lectures on the Philosophy of History* [http://www.marxists.org/reference/archive/hegel/works/hi/hiconten.htm]

Hegel, G.W.F., *Phenomenology of Spirit* (Oxford University Press, 1979)

Herodotus, *The Histories* (Oxford University Press, 1998)

Hertz, J.R. (ed.), *The Pentateuch and Haftorahs: Hebrew Text English Translation and Commentary* (The Soncino Press, 1960)

Heschel, A.J., *The Prophets* (Harper & Row, 1969)

Hobbes, T., *Leviathan* (Penguin 1981)

Hobsbawm, E.J., *The Age of Revolution 1789–1848* (Spectre, 1973)

Holland, T., *In the Shadow of the Sword* (Little, Brown, 2012)

Homer, *The Iliad* (Penguin, 1987)

Howe, S., *Afrocentrism: Mythical Pasts and Imagined Homes* (Verso, 1998)

Hume, D., *A Treatise of Human Nature* (Penguin, 1969)

Hume, D., *An Enquiry Concerning the Principles of Morals* (Oxford University Press, 1998)

Hume, D., 'A Kind of History of My Life', in Norton (ed.), *The Cambridge Companion to Hume*

Huntington, S.P., 'The Clash of Civilizations', *Foreign Affairs* 72 (1993)

Ibn Rushd, *On the Harmony of Religion and Philosophy* (Gibb Memorial Trust, 2007)

Ibn Tufail, *The Improvement of Human Reason* (Dodo Press, n.d.)

Ignatieff, M., 'Ascent of Man', *Prospect* (October 1999)

Israel, J.I., *Radical Enlightenment: Philosophy and the Making of Modernity, 1650–1750* (Oxford University Press, 2001)

Israel, J.I., *Enlightenment Contested: Philosophy, Modernity and the Emancipation of Man 1670–1752* (Oxford University Press, 2006)

Israel, J.I., *Democratic Enlightenment: Philosophy, Revolution and Human Rights 1750–1790* (Oxford University Press, 2011)

Jacques, M., *When China Rules the World: The End of the Western World and the Birth of a New Global Order* (Penguin, 2012)

James, C.L.R., *The Black Jacobins: Toussaint L'Ouverture and the San Domingo Revolution* (Secker & Warburg, 1938)

James, C.L.R., *Spheres of Existence: Selected Writings* (Allison & Busby, 1980)

James, W., *Pragmatism: A New Name for Some Old Ways of Thinking: A Series of Lectures* (Arc Minor, 2008)

Janin, H., *The University in Medieval Life, 1179–1499* (McFarland, 2008)

Jaspers, K., *The Way to Wisdom: An Introduction to Philosophy* (Yale University Press, 2003)

Jiang, Q., *A Confucian Constitutional Order: How China's Ancient Past Can Shape Its Political Future* (Princeton University Press, 2012)

Jiang, Q., and Bell, D. A., 'A Confucian Constitution for China', *New York Times*, 10 July 2012

Kant, I., *Groundwork of the Metaphysics of Morals* (Routledge, 2002)

Kant, I., *Critique of Pure Reason* (Macmillan, 1929)

Kant, I., 'What is Enlightenment?' [http://www.columbia.edu/acis/ets/CCREAD/etscc/kant.html]

Kenny, A., *A New History of Western Philosophy*, 4 vols. (Oxford University Press, 2004–7)

Kierkegaard, S., *The Concept of Anxiety* (Princeton University Press, 1981)

Kierkegaard, S., *Either/Or: A Fragment of Life* (Penguin, 1992)

Kierkegaard, S., *Fear and Trembling/Repetition* (Kierkegaard's Writings, vol. VI) (Princeton University Press, 1983)

Kierkegaard, S., *Journals and Papers* (Indiana University Press, 1976) 1 August 1835

Knox, R., *The Races of Men: A Philosophical Enquiry into the Influence of Race over the Destinies of Men* (Henry Renshaw, 1850)

Lapidus, I.M., 'State and Religion in Islamic Societies', *Past and Present*, 151 (1996)

Leiter, B., 'Nietzsche's Moral and Political Philosophy', in Zalta (ed.), *The Stanford Encyclopedia of Philosophy* [http://plato.stanford.edu/archives/sum2011/entries/nietzsche-moral-political/].

Lévy, B-H., *Le Siècle de Sartre* (Grasset, 2000)

Lewis, C.S., *The Problem of Pain* (Harper Collins, 1996)

Lewis, C.S., *The Abolition of Man* (Lits, 2010)

Lewis, C.S., *Mere Christianity* (William Collins, 2012)

Ling, M., *Muhammad: His Life Based on the Earliest Sources* (Islamic Texts Society, 1983)

Liu Xiaobo, *No Enemies, No Hatred: Selected Essays and Poems* (Belknap Press, 2012)

Long, A.A., and Sedley, D.N., *The Hellenistic Philosophers*, vol. 1: *Translations of the Principal Sources with Philosophical Commentary* (Cambridge University Press, 1987)

Long, D.S., *Christian Ethics: A Very Short Introduction* (Oxford University Press, 2010)

Lopez, D., *Buddhist Scriptures* (Penguin, 2004)

Lovejoy, O.J., 'The Supposed Primitivism of Rousseau's Discourse on Inequality', *Modern Philology*, 21 (1923)

Lukács, G., *The Destruction of Reason* (Merlin Press, 1980)

Lukes, S., *Moral Relativism* (Profile, 2008)

Lund, E., *Documents from the History of Lutheranism, 1517–1750* (Fortress Press, 2002)

Luther, M., *The Essential Martin Luther* (Wilder Publications, 2008)

Lu Xun, *The Real Story of Ah-Q and Other Tales of China: The Complete Fiction of Lu Xun* (Penguin, 2009)

MacCulloch, D., *A History of Christianity: The First Three Thousand Years* (Allen Lane, 2009)

MacIntyre, A., *After Virtue: A Study in Moral Theory* (Duckworth, 1981)

MacIntyre, A., *A Short History of Ethics* (Routledge, 2002)

Mackie, J.L., *Ethics: Inventing Right and Wrong* (Penguin, 1990)

MacMullen, R., *Christianising the Roman Empire: AD 100–400* (Yale University Press, 1984)

Malik, K., *The Meaning of Race: Race, History and Culture in Western Society* (Macmillan, 1996)

Mandeville, B., *The Fable of the Bees and Other Writings* (Hackett, 1997)

Marcus Aurelius, *The Meditations of Marcus Aurelius, The Harvard Classics*, vol. 2, part 3 (P.F. Collier & Son, 1909–14) [http://www.bartleby.com/2/3/]

Marx, K., and Engels, F., *Collected Works* (Progress Publishers/Lawrence & Wishart, 1975–2005)

McGrath, A., *Christian Theology: An Introduction* (Blackwell, 2007)

Mead, M., *Blackberry Winter* (Kodansha International, 1995)

Menand, L., *The Metaphysical Club: A Study of Ideas in America* (Farrar, Straus & Giroux, 2001)

Midgley, M., 'Gene-juggling' *Philosophy*, 54 (1979)

Mill, J.S., *Autobiography and Literary Essays* (Taylor & Francis, 1981)

Mill, J.S., *Utilitarianism* (Collins, 1962)

Mishra, P., *From the Ruins of Empire: The Revolt Against the West and the Remaking of Asia* (Allen Lane, 2012)

Mo Tzu, *Basic Writings of Mo Tzu, Hsün Tzu and Han Fei Tzu* (Columbia University Press, 1967)

Moore, G.E., *Principia Ethica* (Cambridge University Press, 1993)

Morrison, J.A., *Martin Luther: The Great Reformer* (Christian Liberty Press, 2003)

Mudimbe, V., *The Invention of Africa: Gnosis, Philosophy and the Order of Knowledge* (African Systems of Thought) (James Currey, 1990)

Murray, G., *The Stoic Philosophy* (G.P. Puttnam, 1915)

Narayan, R.K., *The Ramayana: A Shortened Modern Prose Version Of The Indian Epic* (Penguin, 2006)

Nasr, S.H., *Islamic Spirituality*, 2 vols. (Crossroads, 1991–7)

Nicholson, R.A., *A Literary History of the Arabs* (Routledge, 1962)

Nietzsche, F., *Thus Spoke Zarathustra* (Penguin, 1974)

Nietzsche, F., *Beyond Good and Evil* (Penguin, 2003)

Nietzsche, F., *The Gay Science: With a Prelude in German Rhymes and An Appendix of Songs* (Cambridge University Press, 2001)

Nietzsche, F., *Twilight of the Idols* (Oxford University Press, 2008)

Nietzsche, F., *The Antichrist* (Soho Books, 2010)

Nietzsche, F., *Ecce Homo: How To Become What You Are* (Oxford University Press, 2009)

Nietzsche, F., *On the Genealogy of Morals: A Polemic* (Oxford University Press, 2008)

Norton, D.F. (ed.), *The Cambridge Companion to Hume* (Cambridge University Press, 1993)

O'Gorman, F., *Edmund Burke: His Political Philosophy*, 2 vols. (Routledge, 2004)

Olivelle, P. *Upanisads* (Oxford World's Classics, 2008)

Olson, D.R., *The World on Paper: The Conceptual and Cognitive Implications of Writing and Reading* (Cambridge University Press, 1996)

Ondaatje, M., *The English Patient* (Bloomsbury, 2004)

Osborne, P. (ed.), *Socialism and the Limits of Liberalism* (Verso, 1991)

Overton, R., *An Arrow Against Every Tyrant* [http://www.constitution.org/lev/eng_lev_05.htm]

Pagden, A., *The Enlightenment: And Why it Still Matters* (Oxford University Press, 2013)

Paradis, J., and Williams, G.C., *Evolution and Ethics: T.H. Huxley's Evolution and Ethics With New Essays on Its Victorian and Sociobiological Context* (Princeton University Press, 1989)

Payne, S.R., *Utilitarianism as Secondary Ethic* (Yale Divinity School, 2006) [http://www.sethpayne.com/wp-content/uploads/2009/01/bentham.pdf]

Pick, D., *Faces of Degeneration: A European Disorder c. 1848–1918* (Cambridge University Press, 1989)

Pinker, S., *The Blank Slate: The Modern Denial of Human Nature* (Allen Lane, 2002)

Plato, *Complete Works* (Hackett, 1996)

Plotinus, *The Enneads* (Penguin, 1991)

Plutarch, *The Complete Works of Plutarch*, vol. 3: *Essays and Miscellanies* (Crowell, 1909)

Plutarch, *Plutarch's Lives*, vol. 7: *Sertorius and Eumenes, Phocion and Cato the Younger* (Harvard University Press, 1959)

Purkiss, D., *The English Civil War: A People's History* (Harper Collins, 2006)

Rahula, W., *What the Buddha Taught* (Grove Press, 1974)

Rainey, L.D., *Confucius and Confucianism: The Essentials* (Wiley Blackwell, 2010)

Rees, B.R., *The Letters of Pelagius and his Followers* (The Boydell Press, 1991)

Rist, J.M., *Augustine: Ancient Thought Baptized* (Cambridge University Press, 1994)

Roosevelt, T., *The Winning of the West*, 4 vols. (Kessinger, 2004)

Rorty, R., *Truth and Progress: Philosophical Papers*, vol. 3 (Cambridge University Press, 1998)

Ross, W.D., *The Right and the Good* (Oxford University Press, 1930)

Rousseau, J.J., *The First and Second Discourses* (St Martin's Press, 1964)

Rousseau, J.J., *The Social Contract and Other Later Political Writings* (Cambridge University Press, 1997)

Rousseau, J.J., *Emile, Or, On Education* [ebook: http://www.gutenberg.org/ebooks/5427]

Russell, B., *The History of Western Philosophy* (Routledge, 2004)

Russell, B., *On Ethics: Selections from the Writings of Bertrand Russell* (Routledge, 1999)

Salzman, M.R., *The Making of a Christian Aristocracy: Social and Religious Change in the Western Roman Empire* (Harvard University Press, 2004)

Sanders, E.P., *Paul* (Oxford University Press, 1991)

Sansone, D., *Ancient Greek Civilization* (Blackwell, 2004)

Sartre, J-P., *Critique of Dialectical Reason*, vol. 1: *Theory of Practical Ensembles* (New Left Books, 1976)

Sartre, J-P., *Being and Nothingness: An Essay on Phenomenological Ontology* (Routledge, 2003)

Sartre, J-P., *Existentialism and Humanism* (Methuen, 1948)

Sartre, J-P., 'Sartre on the Nobel Prize', *New York Review of Books*, 17 December 1964 [http://www.nybooks.com/articles/archives/1964/dec/17/sartre-on-the-nobel-prize/]

Sartre, J-P., 'Preface', in Fanon, *The Wretched of the Earth*

Schopenhauer, A., *The World as Will and Representation* (Dover, 1969)

Scruton, R., *A Short History of Modern Philosophy* (Routledge, 1984)

Seneca, L.A., *Dialogues and Essays* (Oxford University Press, 2007)

Senghor, L.S., *On African Socialism* (Pall Mall, 1964)

Sharif, M.M., *A History of Muslim Philosophy* (Harrassowitz, 1966)

Sheikh, S.M., *Islamic Philosophy* (Octagon Press, 1982)

Sinnott-Armstrong, W. (ed.), *Moral Psychology*, vol. 3: *The Neuroscience of Morality: Emotion, Disease, and Development* (MIT Press, 2007)

Sophocles, *The Three Theban Plays* (Penguin, 1984)

Spencer, H., *Data of Ethics* (Ulan Press, 2012)

Stevenson, C.L., *Ethics and Language* (Yale University Press, 1950)

Stocking, G.W. Jr., *Race, Culture and Evolution: Essays in the History of Anthropology* (Chicago University Press, 1968)

Tarnas, R., *The Passion of the Western Mind: Understanding the Ideas That Have Shaped Our World View* (Pimlico, 1996)

Thapar, R., *From Lineage to State* (OUP, 1984)

Trivers, R.L., 'The evolution of reciprocal altruism', *Quarterly Review of Biology*, 46 (1971), p. 35–57

Trotsky, L., *Their Morals and Ours: Marxist versus liberal views on morality* (Pathfinder, 1973)

Tucker, R.C., *Philosophy and Myth in Karl Marx* (Cambridge University Press, 1971)

Vidyalankar, P., *The Holy Vedas* (Clarion Books, 2004)

Warnock, M., *Ethics since 1900* (Oxford University Press, 1978)

Waterfield, R. (ed.), *The First Philosophers: The Presocratics and the Sophists* (Oxford University Press, 2000)

Watt, W.M., *The Faith and Practice of Al-Ghazali* (Oneworld, 2000)

Wolin, R., *The Seduction of Unreason: The Intellectual Romance with Fascism from Nietzsche to Postmodernism* (Princeton University Press, 2004)

Wong, R.B., *China Transformed: Historical Change and the Limits of European Experience* (Cornell University Press, 2000)

Wu, L., *Fundamentals of Chinese Philosophy* (University Press of America, 1986)

Young, R., *White Mythologies: Writing History and the West* (Routledge, 1990)

Zalta, E.N. (ed.), *The Stanford Encyclopedia of Philosophy* (Fall 2012 edn) [http://plato.stanford.edu/]

Zarruq, A., Istrabadi, Z., and Hanson, H.Y., *The Principles of Sufism* (Amal Press, 2008)

Acknowledgements

A book such as this draws inevitably upon the wisdom and erudition of more people than I can mention. I am particularly indebted to Rushanna Ahmed, Toby Andrew, Russell Blackford, Billy Carvaka, Austin Dacey, Frederik Giertsen, John Gillott, Anthony Grayling, Tom Holland, Michael Ignatieff, Jonathan Israel, Nasreen Khan, Susan Neiman, Patrick O'Donnell, Elizabeth Oldfield, Jonathan Rée, Mona Siddiqui, Nick Spencer, Ray Tallis, Laurie Taylor and Linda Woodhead. They have pored over the manuscript, spotted errors, questioned interpretations, discussed, debated, disagreed and been unstintingly generous with their time, knowledge and resources. My thanks to them all.

Index